The All New
Diabetic Cookbook

Kitty E. Maynard, R.N.

Lucian Maynard, R.N.

Theodore G. Duncan, M.D.

RUTLEDGE HILL PRESS®

Nashville, Tennessee

Published in Nashville, Tennessee, by Rutledge Hill Press®, 211 Seventh Avenue North, Nashville, Tennessee 37219.

Distributed in Canada by H. B. Fenn & Company, Ltd., 34 Nixon Road, Bolton, Ontario L7E 1W2.

Distributed in Australia by The Five Mile Press Pty., Ltd., 22 Summit Road, Noble Park, Victoria 3174.

Distributed in New Zealand by Tandem Press, 2 Rugby Road, Birkenhead, Auckland 10.

Distributed in the United Kingdom by Verulam Publishing, Ltd., 152a Park Street Lane, Park Street, St. Albans, Hertfordshire AL2 2AU.

The exchange lists are the basis of a meal planning system designed by a committee of the American Diabetes Association and The American Dietetic Association. While designed primarily for people with diabetes and others who must follow special diets, the exchange lists are based on principles of good nutrition that apply to everyone. © American Diabetes Association, The American Dietetic Association.

Nutritional analyses: Dolores McKenna, Jamie Pope

Typography by Compass Communications

Design by Bateman Design

Library of Congress Cataloging-in-Publication Data

Maynard, Kitty, 1955–
    The all-new diabetic cookbook / Kitty E. Maynard, Lucian Maynard, Theodore G. Duncan.
        p.   cm.
    ISBN 1-55853-675-2 (pbk.)
    1. Diabetes—Diet therapy—Recipes.   I. Maynard, Lucian, 1952–   .   II. Duncan, Theodore G.   III. Title.
    RC662.M379   1998
    641.5'6314—dc21   98-37923
                                                                                                          CIP

Printed in the United States of America

1 2 3 4 5 6 7 8 9-02 01 00 99 98

Contents

ACKNOWLEDGMENTS *6*

INTRODUCTION *7*

STRAIGHT TALK ABOUT DIET AND DIABETES *9*

PRACTICAL TIPS FOR LIVING WITH DIABETES *23*

A GUIDE TO MEAL PLANNING *33*

METRIC CONVERSION *53*

BEVERAGES *55*

APPETIZERS AND SNACKS *75*

SOUPS *93*

SALADS *117*

BREADS *137*

ENTREES
Beef *161*
Poultry *171*
Seafood *189*
Pasta, Potatoes, Rice, Grains *209*

VEGETABLES *229*

SALSAS, SAUCES, DRESSINGS, AND SPREADS *249*

KIDS' MEALS *267*

DESSERTS *277*

GENERAL INDEX *294*

RECIPES INDEX *296*

Acknowledgments

WE ARE PLEASED TO ACKNOWLEDGE the following individuals and organizations for providing photographs for the color inserts: National Livestock and Meat Board (Oriental Beef Kabobs); National Cattlemen's Beef Association (Spicy-Tangy Beef Soup); National Fisheries Institute (Spicy Crab Soup, Tuna Chowder, Cajun Shrimp, and Oyster Soup); Tom Bagley/Styling by Gail Greco (Couscous Vegetable and Feta Cheese Salad, Black Jack Muffins); Florida Department of Agriculture and Consumer Services, Bureau of Seafood and Aquaculture (Satellite Beach Salad, Ybor City Fillets, Wakulla Grilled Grouper, Santa Rosa Shrimp); Red Star® Yeast & Products (Baked Potato Bread, Cheesy Broccoli/Cauliflower Bread, Whole Wheat Carrot Bread, Zucchini Bread, Pepper Sweet Corn Bread); Wisconsin Beef Council (Stir-Fry Beef and Spinach with Noodles), Florida Department of Natural Resources, Bureau of Seafood Marketing (Rock Shrimp and Oyster Maque Choux); Hershey Foods Corporation (Mostaccioi al Forno, Manicotti with Eggplant-Tomato Relish, Manicotti with Ratatouille Sauce, Savory Jumbo Shells); U.S. Apple Association (Lemon Pepper Chicken, Shrimp with Oriental Ginger Apple Barbecue Sauce, Ham with Mustard Garlic Apple-cue Sauce); Kitchens of Sara Lee (Light and Easy Poundcake).

We would like to extend a special thanks to Delores A. McKenna, B.S., and Jamie Pope, M.S., R.D., for their work on the nutritional analysis and Jamie Lynch, M.S., R.D., C.D.E., L.D.N., for her work on the meal plans.

Introduction

EVERY TIME WE START A NEW BOOK, we sit down and discuss what will make it better than before. The decision was easy this time because of the recent developments of nutritious foods. The medical community has modified the ADA's (American Diabetes Association) diabetic diet of the past to a regular diet with no added concentrated sugar. Everyone can enjoy healthy living by eating a low-sugar, low-salt, and low-fat diet that can be remarkably high in taste. What was once considered a diabetic diet is now recommended healthy eating. Fresh fruits can take the place of artificial sweeteners and fresh vegetables enhance the flavors of recipes.

New features of this edition include meatless recipes for vegetarians as well as recipes for children. These new recipes posed challenges for us. Our daughter is a vegetarian, so we relied on her assistance for the vegetarian recipes. We searched grocery stores and specialty food stores for products that were tasty and easy to prepare. Through this learning process we have developed recipes that are tasty and healthy.

The other new section is for children. It is very difficult for a family when a child is diagnosed with diabetes, and the most challenging part is the diet control. We wanted to concentrate on fun recipes, fun things to eat when friends are over. Thanks to the parents, kids are being brought up on less sugar and more vegetables, so they don't feel deprived when restricted from sweets. We have two teenage boys who consider a midnight snack to be steamed vegetables with Italian seasoning. And believe it or not, their friends find this snack to be a treat when they spend the night. We hope that this trend is permanent.

Our family, like many of yours, has all of the diet restrictions and health problems that pose great barriers when preparing meals, but overcoming those barriers is now much simpler. The food industry has helped restricted-diet cooking by providing an abundance of fresh vegetables year round, improved frozen food selections, and new, healthy products that stimulate creativity in cooking.

Our goal is for you to have fun with these recipes, spice up your life, and enjoy healthy eating. This book allows everyone—your family and friends—to enjoy eating healthy without compromising taste.

—Kitty and Lucian Maynard

Straight Talk About Diet and Diabetes

Theodore Duncan, M.D.

AS A DOCTOR WHO HAS TREATED people with diabetes for more than thirty years, I know that dietary concerns are uppermost in people's minds and meal planning is one of a patient's biggest challenges. The first question most diabetics ask when newly diagnosed is, "Doc, what can I eat?" But there's more to successful diabetes management than just food selection.

Both diet and exercise are essential to good health. The eating and exercise patterns of various populations over the past few decades show that decreased exercise combined with an abundance of foods—especially foods rich in saturated fats and cholesterol—increase the incidence of diabetes and heart disease. Fortunately, the reverse is also true. In World War II, for instance, increased activity and the reduced availability of food decreased the number of new cases of diabetes by 40 percent in both Germany and England. Ironically, the rate remained low during the war and did not rise again until the Marshall Plan, instituted after the war, provided ample food for Germany and other European countries. While humanitarian in its intent, the abundant supply of food was followed by a stunning increase in new cases of diabetes. Similarly, before 1945, diabetes was essentially nonexistent among Eskimos and Native Americans, but as these populations adopted the typical American eating and activity patterns, the incidence of diabetes increased markedly. Today diabetes is the seventh leading cause of death.

There is no doubt that chronic diseases are related to what we eat and how active we are. Since learning that obesity and diets high in saturated fats and cholesterol are risk factors for heart disease, many Americans have been eating fewer eggs, high-fat dairy products (such as whole milk, cheese, ice cream, butter, and whipped cream), and fatty meats, choosing instead fish, the white meat of chicken and turkey, and low-fat dairy products. Combining these diets with increased exercise has resulted in a decrease in new cases of heart disease.

Disease rarely concerns those who are young; unfortunately, no one can afford to postpone healthful dietary and activity habits until middle age. Medical research indicates that the early signs of coronary disease can be found in the majority of Americans between the ages of eighteen and twenty-five. By instituting a healthier diet earlier in life, the risk of many health problems can be reduced.

How Diet Affects Diabetes

Diabetes is a chronic, systemic disease involving metabolism disorders and high blood sugar caused by defects in insulin secretion, insulin action, or both. Chronic hyperglycemia, or high blood sugar leads to long-term damage, dysfunction, and failure of the eyes, kidneys, nerves, heart, and blood vessels.

There are two well-recognized types of diabetes: type 1 and type 2. Of the more than sixteen million Americans who have diabetes 50 percent are undiagnosed and 90 percent (most of whom are obese) have type 2 diabetes.

Type 1 diabetes usually occurs before puberty. The onset is abrupt, and the person is usually undernourished. An elevated blood sugar usually causes the person to urinate frequently, be very thirsty, and have a ravenous appetite. Insulin therapy brings the blood sugar under control, and the symptoms disappear. Because blood sugar fluctuates widely in response to small changes in the insulin dosage, exercise, and stress, control of type 1 diabetes is sometimes difficult. The best starting point for treatment is to follow the American Diabetes Association diet and eat three meals and prescribed snacks at regular intervals to help control the disease and prevent low blood sugar. Insulin is the most frequently used medication to control this type of diabetes.

Type 2 diabetes commonly develops after the age of thirty-five. The onset is usually gradual and is commonly found in obese persons who have diabetes in their family history. Often, these persons have few or no symptoms and may have elevated sugars without knowing it for years before symptoms begin. With treatment blood-sugar values are reduced. Often the diabetes can be controlled by diet and exercise alone or, if not, by the use of oral medication to lower the blood sugar. It is estimated that 80 percent of people with type 2 diabetes would require no medication if they reduced their weight and followed an effective exercise program. Unfortunately not many are able to achieve this goal.

Designing a Diabetic Diet

At first glance the so-called "diabetic diet" may appear rather complex, especially if you just learned that you have diabetes and have never needed to plan your meals in the past. On closer examination however, the diet becomes understandable and simple to follow.

Like any other nutritionally balanced diet, the diabetic meal plan fulfills certain criteria. The goals for the diet include:

- appropriate calories for maintaining growth and ideal weight

- to achieve as near-normal blood glucose levels as possible

- to delay or prevent food related risk factors, including coronary artery disease, high blood pressure, kidney disease, and hypoglycemia related to food and exercise problems

- to obtain optimal blood lipid levels

Total daily caloric needs are estimated by a physician or dietitian to provide sufficient calories for energy and for tissue building. The necessary proportions of fat, carbohydrate, protein, and essential vitamins and minerals are also calculated. Those receiving insulin therapy usually need help in planning the appropriate timing of meals and snacks to prevent low blood-sugar reactions.

About 50 percent of those with diabetes have hypertension—chronic high blood pressure. Restricting sodium in the diet can help lower blood pressure to near-normal values, which usually range from a systolic blood pressure value below 135 and a diastolic value below 85. Keeping the blood pressure within this range will help prevent or slow the progression of abnormal changes in the eyes, kidneys, and heart and will markedly reduce the risk of stroke. Sometimes diet changes alone can make this happen. In other cases blood-pressure-lowering medications are needed. If you have hypertension, your doctor or dietitian may recommend that you cut the sodium in your diet to approximately two grams daily. This means eliminating salt from cooking and adding no salt to food during meals.

Practical Tips for Eliminating Salt from the Diet.

- Do not use additional salt at the table.

- Avoid processed foods.

- Read labels on canned foods for salt (sodium) content.

- Check for added salt.

- Do not eat foods preserved in salt or brine, for example:

corned beef	canned salmon	bacon
anchovies	frankfurters	ham
lunch meat	scrapple	sausage

- When dining out ask that your food be prepared without salt. Some restaurants may offer limited-salt-selections on their menus.

Substitute herbs and spices for salt and give your foods new and exciting flavors. For example, use rosemary, mint, or garlic instead of salt when serving lamb. Mustard, bay leaf, bell pepper, and green pepper enhance the flavor of beef. Baste fish with lemon juice and pepper as you broil or bake it.

Cholesterol and Fats

Diabetes is associated with a marked increase in coronary artery disease in both men and women. The major causes of this disease are high cholesterol, hypertension, obesity, and smoking. Over time, a diet high in fats or cholesterol can cause a buildup in the walls of your arteries that can slow or block the flow of blood in your heart. A blockage, or occlusion, causes a "heart attack," or myocardial infarction.

Cholesterol is a waxy substance that is manufactured in the body and also is present in food of animal origin. There is no cholesterol in plant foods such as vegetables, fruits, cereals, grains, and nuts.

Saturated fats, usually solid at room temperature, are found in foods of animal origin such as pork, lamb, beef, ham, and dairy products—butter, whole milk, cream, and cheese. Saturated fat is also present in some vegetable oils such as cocoa butter, coconut oil, palm oil, and hydrogenated vegetable oils.

Polyunsaturated fats are most abundant in vegetable cooking oils. These fats, which tend to *lower* the blood cholesterol level, include: corn, sesame, cottonseed, and safflower oil.

Monounsaturated fats help prevent heart disease, so they are safe to include in your diet. They include peanut, canola, and olive oils as well as avocados, almonds, pecans, and cashews.

Your doctor will order a blood test or "lipid profile" to learn your cholesterol levels. The total cholesterol in your blood is subdivided into separate components. The low density lipoprotein (LDL) cholesterol, referred to as the "bad cholesterol," carries most of the cholesterol in the blood: an excessive amount can lead to cholesterol buildup in the arteries. The high density lipoprotein (HDL) cholesterol, the "good cholesterol," facilitates the removal of cholesterol from the blood. A total blood-cholesterol level under 200 or lower is desirable. A person with an elevated cholesterol value greater than 240 has twice the risk of heart disease compared with a person whose cholesterol is 200. The HDL becomes more beneficial as its value rises. Values less than 35 increase the risk of heart disease.

Triglycerides are also part of the lipid profile. Some experts say that high levels of triglycerides increase the risk of heart disease, but others question this opinion. High levels of triglycerides are frequently associated with low levels of HDL.

To review: All fats are made up of saturated and unsaturated fatty acids; saturated fats, which come from animal products elevate cholesterol levels. Monounsaturated fats lower the LDL, the bad cholesterol, without lowering the HDL, the good cholesterol. Limit your fat intake to less than 30 percent of your total calories each day, and when you need to use oil in cooking or salad dressings, choose a monounsaturated type like peanut, canola, or olive oil.

Calculating Your Ideal Weight and Caloric Intake

An appropriate diet is as essential to the successful treatment of diabetes as insulin, oral medications, and exercise. You must plan your diet so that you eat the recommended portions of fat, carbohydrate, protein, and other nutrients essential for maintaining your ideal weight and good health. First and foremost, consider food as a source of energy needed by your body for physical and mental activity and for maintaining tissue and structures. If you eat more calories than needed for these activities, your body will store them as fat, and you will gain weight. If you don't eat enough, you may lose weight and become malnourished. The total number of calories each person needs varies with age, build, gender, and activity. There are many methods for determining the ideal weight and the number of calories required to maintain good function. The following method is easy to calculate.

An adult woman with a medium frame is allotted 100 pounds for the first five feet in height and an additional five pounds for each inch over five feet. An adult male with a medium frame is allotted 106 pounds for the first five feet and six pounds for each additional inch. If the person has a small frame, subtract 10 percent and if the frame is large add an additional 10 percent. For example, a 5 foot 4 inch woman with a medium frame has an ideal weight of 120 pounds [100 + 20 (5 pounds x 4 inches)]. A 6 foot man with a large frame has an ideal weight of 196 pounds [106 + 72 (6 pounds x 12 inches) = 178 pounds x 10 percent (18 pounds) = 196 pounds].

To determine the number of daily calories needed to maintain the ideal body weight, first multiply the ideal weight by ten then adjust for the activity level. For example, if the ideal body weight is 130 pounds, the basal number of calories needed every twenty-four hours is 1,300 calories. Add 20 percent for a sedentary lifestyle, 33 percent for light physical activity, 50 percent for moderate physical activity, or 75 percent for heavy activity.

Obesity is a particularly vexing and perplexing problem. If this is an issue you are facing, realize that a weight reduction program is only successful if you make a real "I will" rather than an "I'll try" commitment. Your weight-loss diet should be designed to allow you to lose one to two pounds per week in a slow and deliberate manner until you reach your desired weight. This process may take months or years. Once the goal is finally achieved, a more moderate diet can be instituted to maintain the desired weight.

Dietary Guidelines for Americans, 1995, published by the U.S. Department of Agriculture and the U.S. Department of Health and Human Services, reports, "many people are not sure how much they should lose. Weight losses of only 5–10 percent of body weight may improve many of the problems associated with overweight, such as high blood pressure and diabetes. Even a smaller loss can make a difference."

Getting the Most Benefits

In 1995 the American Diabetes Association and the American Dietetic Association revised their exchange lists for meal planning to provide an effective guide for selecting meals and snacks. The lists sort foods into three major groups—the carbohydrate group, the meat and meat substitute group, and the fat group. The carbohydrate group includes starch, fruit, milk-skim, low fat, and whole—vegetables, and other carbohydrates. The meat and meat-substitute group includes very lean, lean, medium-fat, and high-fat meats. The final group, the fat group, includes monounsaturated fats, polyunsaturated fats, and saturated fats.

The exchange lists also define "free foods"—food substances that contain fewer than twenty calories or fewer than five grams of carbohydrate per serving. They also outline the exchanges for choices at the most popular fast-food restaurants. For example, six chicken nuggets contain one carbohydrate, two medium-fat meats, and one fat serving. Foods containing excessive salt are also noted on the lists.

Each food in any one group contains the same number of calories as the other foods in that specific list. For example, one fruit exchange, one unpeeled small apple, ¾ cups blueberries, or ½ large grapefruit contains fifteen grams of carbohydrate and totals sixty calories. Each item can be used interchangeably as a dessert or a snack.

The amount of food to be selected from the exchange lists for each meal varies according to the total daily caloric requirement. The number of calories required each day and the proportions that are appropriate for meals and snacks should be carefully explained by a dietitian or diabetes nurse-educator.

The revised exchange lists group all carbohydrate-containing foods in one category, an arrangement that permits an easy method of carbohydrate counting. Carbohydrate is the major nutrient affecting the after-eating (postprandial) blood-sugar elevation; most carbohydrate is converted into glucose within two hours after eating. Only about half of the protein and even less of the fat we eat is eventually changed to glucose. Some dietitians use carbohydrate counting to estimate the number of units of insulin needed before meals or snacks to keep the blood sugar well regulated. Carbohydrate counting and other facts about carbohydrates are discussed below.

How to Count Your Carbohydrates

Foods with the most carbohydrates are:

- fruits and vegetables
- grain products such as bread, pasta, rice, oats, cereals, cookies, and crackers
- beans, peas, and lentils
- dairy products, particularly milk and yogurt
- sugar and sugar-sweetened foods

Between 55 percent and 60 percent of the calories consumed in a day should come from carbohydrates. If you are following a diet plan that specifies two thousand calories per day, up to twelve hundred calories should come from carbohydrate. Dietary carbohydrate is measured in grams. Since the body can derive four calories from one gram of carbohydrate, eating twelve hundred calories of carbohydrates means consuming three hundred grams of carbohydrates a day. If we distribute three hundred grams over four meals (breakfast, lunch, dinner, evening snack), each meal would contain approximately seventy-five grams of carbohydrates.

The partial Food Exchange Lists for Meal Planning shown here (complete list on page 35) provide one of the easiest methods for counting carbohydrates. Each list assigns an average carbohydrate value for all the exchanges in that particular food group:

- Starch List — fifteen grams carbohydrate per exchange
- Fruit List — fifteen grams carbohydrate per exchange
- Milk List — twelve grams carbohydrate per exchange
- Vegetable List — five grams carbohydrate per exchange
- Meat List* — 0 grams carbohydrate per exchange
- Fat List — 0 grams carbohydrate per exchange

*Foods in the Meat List contain more protein than foods in other groups. The body can convert some of this protein to carbohydrate, approximately twelve grams of carbohydrate for a three-ounce serving.

Exchange values are averages. If the carbohydrate content of a day's intake is estimated using exchanges, there may be a fairly large difference between that estimate and the actual value. For a more accurate, though more time consuming, carbohydrate count add the specific carbohydrate value for each food in a meal. The amount of carbohydrate per serving of a particular food is listed on nutrition labels and in reference books.

Using the information on nutrition labels to count carbohydrates became easier when the U.S. Food and Drug Administration and the USDA established new regulations that became effective in 1994. The regulations require a label of nutrition facts to be printed on most food packages. The label must list the calories, grams of fat, cholesterol, carbohydrates, protein, sodium, and other pertinent dietary components of that food. (The nutrition analyses accompanying the recipes in this book supply the same information found on the new food labels.) Serving sizes have been standardized to reflect the amounts of the food most people actually eat. A sample of the new Nutrition Facts label for a serving of canned turkey chili with beans is shown here.

Nutrition Facts
Canned Turkey Chili with Beans
Serving Size 1 cup (245 g)
Servings Per Container About 2

Amount per Serving

Calories 210	From Fat 25

	% Daily Value*
Total Fat 3 g	4 %
Saturated Fat 1 g	4 %
Cholesterol 40 mg	13 %
Sodium 990 mg	41 %
Total Carbohydrates 26 g	9 %
Dietary Fiber 5 g	21 %
Sugars 5 g	
Protein 21 g	

Vitamin A 40 %	Vitamin C 35 %
Calcium 8 %	Iron 20 %

*Percent Daily Values are based on a 2,000 calorie diet.

The total-carbohydrate value from this label can be used directly. The most precise measure of carbohydrate however is calculated by subtracting the dietary fiber figure from the total carbohydrate figure because dietary fiber is not digested. If you count carbohydrates using exchanges, dividing the carbohydrate value in the label by fifteen will give you the number of exchanges per serving of this food.

Whether you count individual grams of carbohydrates or use exchanges, you will need to become familiar with typical serving sizes. Exchange lists provide serving sizes by individual items (one waffle or one kiwi), by cups, tablespoons, teaspoons, or ounces. Nutrition labels also list values based on these measured servings, so it will be helpful to have good measuring cups and spoons and a small food scale when you begin counting carbohydrates. After a while you'll be able to estimate the specified serving size of most familiar foods without measuring. But this will take practice.

A discussion of carbohydrate counting would not be complete without mentioning the impact different carbohydrates have on your blood sugar. Some carbohydrates are digested and absorbed relatively slowly and will not raise your blood sugar as fast or as high as others. Based on this effect, researchers have ranked certain, mostly carbohydrate-containing, foods into what they call a "glycemic index." The higher the glycemic index, the greater impact the food will have on your blood sugar. For example, 15 grams of carbohydrate from a white potato have a higher index value and will raise your blood sugar higher than an equal amount of carbohydrate from a sweet potato. Cornflakes can raise your blood sugar higher and faster than a comparable serving of table sugar.

The glycemic index of a food will not *precisely* predict how your blood sugar will be affected. Absorption of carbohydrates can be slowed down or speeded up by other components of a meal including:

• the amount of fat and protein in the meal
• the amount and type of fiber in the meal
• how fast and in what order foods are eaten
• whether foods are eaten raw or cooked

When combined with other tools such as carbohydrate counting, consulting the Food Guide Pyramid (page 17), and using the exchange lists, the glycemic index of foods can be a useful tool in managing your blood sugar.

The new food-labeling regulations also place stricter definitions on terms used to describe the level of a nutrient in a food. Some of the core terms include:

Free—No amount or one of no physiological consequence based on serving size
Calorie-free-5 calories or less per serving
Sodium-free—5 milligrams or less per serving
Fat-free—0.5 gram of fat or less per serving
Cholesterol-free—2 milligrams cholesterol or less per serving
Sugar-free—0.5 gram sugar or less per serving
Low-calorie—40 calories or less per serving
Low-sodium—140 milligrams or less per serving
Very low-sodium—35 milligrams or less per serving
Low-fat—3 grams of fat or less per serving
Low-saturated fat—1 gram saturated fat or less per serving
Low-cholesterol—20 milligrams cholesterol or less and less than 2 grams or less of saturated fat per serving
Reduced—Nutritionally altered product containing 25 percent less of a nutrient or 25 percent fewer calories than a reference food
Less—25 percent less of a nutrient or 25 percent fewer calories than a reference food
Light—This term can mean two things:
First, that a product contains 33 percent fewer calories or 50 percent of the fat in a reference food. If 50 percent or more of the calories come from fat, reduction must be 50 percent of the fat
Second, that the sodium content of a low-calorie, low-fat food has been reduced by 50 percent. It may also be used to describe properties such as texture and color as in "light and fluffy" or "light brown sugar"
High—20 percent or more of the Daily Value for a nutrient
Good Source—10 to 19 percent of the daily value for a nutrient

Diet Is Important to Health for Everyone

The *Dietary Guidelines for Americans* booklet, first published in 1980 by the USDA and the U.S. Department of Health and Human Services and revised in 1990 and 1995, reflects the government's commitment to promote the health of its people through good nutrition. The guidelines are useful for those with diabetes as well as for the general public. They recommend a diet low in fat, saturated fat, and cholesterol, and high in fruits, vegetables, and grain products. Sugar, salt, and alcohol are to be used in moderation. The guidelines recommend balancing the food you eat with physical activity to maintain or improve your weight.

The Food Guide Pyramid was introduced by the USDA to graphically illustrate these dietary guidelines.

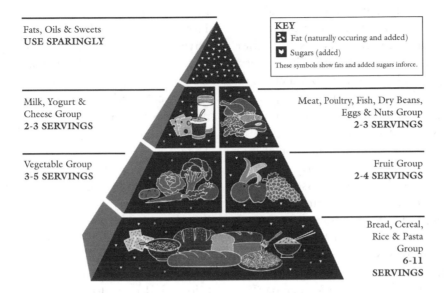

Fats, Oils & Sweets
USE SPARINGLY

KEY
Fat (naturally occuring and added)
Sugars (added)
These symbols show fats and added sugars inforce.

Milk, Yogurt &
Cheese Group
2-3 SERVINGS

Meat, Poultry, Fish, Dry Beans,
Eggs & Nuts Group
2-3 SERVINGS

Vegetable Group
3-5 SERVINGS

Fruit Group
2-4 SERVINGS

Bread, Cereal,
Rice & Pasta
Group
**6-11
SERVINGS**

It places at the top those foods that should be used sparingly: fats, oils, and sweets, which provide calories but few nutrients. The second level contains foods derived mostly from animal sources: the milk, yogurt, and cheese group, and the meat, poultry, fish, dry beans, eggs, and nuts group. Two to three servings a day are recommended from each of these groups.

As the pyramid broadens toward the base, the recommended serving sizes increase. The third level consists of the vegetable group, with three to five servings recommended daily and the fruit group with two to four servings recommended daily. The base of the pyramid represents the foundation of a healthful diet—recommending six to eleven daily servings of bread, cereal, rice, and pasta, emphasizing whole-grain products. Using the Food Guide Pyramid as an outline, you can easily follow the recommendations described in the *Dietary Guidelines for Americans.*

Special Dietary Components

Fiber
The high-fiber/high-carbohydrate diet has generated a good deal of interest in recent years.

Research has shown that a diet high in soluble fiber can help reduce the need for insulin or oral hypoglycemics, and some people with type 2 diabetes can eliminate diabetes medications altogether through a program containing a high-fiber diet, exercise, and weight loss if needed.

Fiber is not digested, but it absorbs water and encourages the passage of other foods through the digestive tract. It is found primarily in plant-based foods such as fruits, vegetable, cereals, grains, and beans. There are two types of fiber. The water-soluble fiber found in beans, oats, and fruits may help to decrease blood cholesterol and control blood-sugar values. Water-insoluble fiber, found mostly in the bran of various grains, provides bulk and, according to some studies, can decrease the risk of colon cancer. Because of fiber's bulkiness, it also helps curb the appetite, enabling people on weight-loss diets to lose excess weight. Research is ongoing, as the effect of high fiber foods on other nutrients in the diet is not yet clear.

If you increase your fiber intake, do so gradually to allow your body to adjust. Since some health benefits associated with a high-fiber diet may come from other components in the foods, not merely the fiber, it is best to obtain fiber from foods rather than from supplements. The current recommendations are to consume between twenty to fifty grams of fiber per day. The new Nutrition Facts food labels list the amount of fiber in a standard serving of that particular food.

Alcohol

There are many questions about alcoholic beverages in the diabetic diet, but the primary problem is calories-empty calories with little nutritional value. Hard liquor (whisky, bourbon, rye, gin, brandy, rum) contains about 80 calories per ounce. One glass of beer has 80 to 150 calories, and a 3½-ounce glass of dry wine has 80 calories. If you are on a weight-loss diet, consider the contribution of these empty calories and consume alcohol sparingly.

Some research suggests that moderate drinking is linked to lower risk for coronary heart disease in some individuals. However, higher levels of alcohol can raise the risk for other chronic diseases and accidents. Alcoholic beverages have been used throughout human history to enhance the enjoyment of meals, and generally they may be included in the diabetic diet. However, it would be prudent for a person with diabetes to drink sparingly. The *Dietary Guidelines* advise that if you drink alcoholic beverages, do so in moderation with meals and when consumption does not put you or others at risk.

Sugars

Sweeteners come in many names and forms, and some are acceptable under certain conditions. As yet there are no established guidelines for their uses. The decision to use these products must be made on an individual basis.

There are two categories of sweeteners: caloric and noncaloric. All caloric sweeteners provide 4 calories per gram, or approximately 120 calories per ounce of weight. But there is a difference in their sweetness.

Sucrose

Table sugar, as sucrose is commonly known, is a combination of glucose and fructose that is extracted from sugar beets and cane. Light, dark, brown, and raw sugars are all sucrose, and each conveys the same number of calories when eaten. Invert sugar, commonly used by candy manufacturers and commercial bakers is made by processing sucrose so that it breaks down into "free" glucose and fructose. If ingested, glucose causes a rapid increase in blood sugar and should be avoided.

Research has shown that sucrose does not increase blood sugar faster or higher than a number of other carbohydrate-containing foods such as potatoes and bread. Based on these studies, the American Diabetes Association states that consumption of a modest amount of sucrose is acceptable, depending on the how well your blood sugar is managed.

Fructose

Many persons do not realize that fructose is similar to sucrose in its caloric content. It is a very sweet form of sugar, about twice as sweet as table sugar, that occurs naturally in honey, fruit, and other plant-derived foods. As a sweetener, it is often more popular than saccharin or other sugar substitutes because it has a consistency more like that of ordinary table sugar. However, the caloric difference between fructose and table sugar is insignificant, regardless of how it is prepared. It is also a good deal more expensive than table sugar.

Fructose may be safely used by people whose diabetes is under good control. It causes a less immediate rise in blood sugar than does sucrose, although it ultimately will elevate blood sugar because the liver can convert it to glucose. In some persons fructose may cause flatulence and diarrhea, and its long-term effects are still unclear. Until more is known about fructose, it is reasonable to use it in moderate amounts, provided the calories are considered and it is not used as an exclusive substitute for sugar.

Honey and Syrups

Honey has been suggested as a better sweetener since it occurs naturally and contains additional nutrients. It consists of a large amount of glucose and can cause a rapid, high elevation in blood sugar when used in excess.

Corn syrups are produced by breaking down cornstarch into a mixture of maltose, glucose, and other sugar molecules. The amount of these sugars in corn syrup varies widely, and many syrups contain more glucose than can usually be tolerated by people with diabetes.

Since the American Diabetes Association recommends consuming only a modest amount of sugar, it is wise to be aware of sugar's many names. Dextrose, glucose, sucrose, corn syrup, corn syrup solids, sorghum, sugar cane syrup, brown sugar, honey, maple syrup, and molasses all are sugars and need to be considered when designing a diet.

Artificial Sweeteners

Calorie-free sugar substitutes, or artificial sweeteners, do not raise blood glucose levels because they do not contain any carbohydrates. Artificial sweeteners include saccharine and aspartame (Equal® or Nutrasweet®).

Saccharine

Saccharine is three hundred to five hundred times sweeter than sucrose and contains no calories. The Food and Drug Administration imposed a partial ban of saccharine in 1977 because research showed that it caused cancer in laboratory animals. The public objected so strongly that Congress imposed a moratorium on the ban, and now all products containing saccharine are required to display a warning label. Saccharine is still used in some sugar-free sodas and low-calorie jellies, jams, toppings, and syrups. There are also saccharine tabletop sugar substitutes called Featherweight®, Sprinkle Sweet®, and Sweet 'n Low®.

Aspartame

Aspartame is two hundred times sweeter

than table sugar, so only small amounts are required. It is a low-calorie sweetener made from two amino acids-aspartic acid and phenylananine. It has been approved for use in drink mixes, cold cereal, gelatins, puddings, dairy products, sugarless gum, and as a table sweetener. Since it breaks down at higher temperatures, however, it is not often used in baked goods. It has no aftertaste or known serious side effects, and since it is metabolized as a protein, it does not affect the blood-sugar level.

Sugar Alcohols

Four sugar alcohols are currently available in the United States: mannitol, sorbitol, xylitol, and maltitol. You can recognize a sugar alcohol listed on a food label by looking for the suffix -ol. Sugar alcohols are distinct from artificial sweeteners such as Equal® or Sweet 'n Low® because they supply as much, if not more, caloric energy than regular table sugar. In comparison, artificial sweeteners provide virtually no caloric energy.

In the past sugar alcohols were recommended for people with diabetes because the body either absorbs these sugars more slowly or converts them to glucose more slowly, so they do not cause as sharp a rise in blood sugar as table sugar does. However, sugar alcohols may cause bloating and diarrhea when more than 30 grams, the amount in ten to fifteen hard candies, are consumed per day. These possible side effects, along with their additional calories, make them a less desirable choice for managing diabetes than their sucrose counterparts. If you are looking for a sugar substitute, consider an artificial sweetener instead of a sugar alcohol, since artificial sweeteners contribute virtually no carbohydrates to foods and most have fewer or no calories.

Mannitol

Mannitol has only 70 percent of the relative sweetness of sugar. Because it is less sweet than sucrose, more needs to be used. Since it contains virtually the same amount of calories as regular sugar, it may cause the food product to be higher in calories than if regular sugar were used. Mannitol causes bloating and diarrhea when consumed in significant amounts.

Sorbitol

Sorbitol has only 50 percent of the relative sweetness of sugar. Because it is only half as sweet as sugar, twice the amount (with twice as many calories) must be used to get the same sweetness. It also has a tendency to cause diarrhea. It is often used as an ingredient in sugar-free gums and candies.

Xylitol

Xylitol has the same relative sweetness as sugar. This benefit, as well as its reported reputation for preventing dental caries, is far outweighed by studies that link it to tumor formation in animals. For this reason, the United States has voluntarily curtailed its use in food products. Before the curtailment, xylitol was a popular ingredient in chewing gums.

Maltitol

Maltitol has 75 percent of the relative sweetness of sugar. It is not widely used because its manufacture from maltose is expensive.

Get Your Team Involved

Get your diabetes management team-your diabetes nurse-educator, dietitian, physician, and others-involved! All will work together to provide you with essential information to guide you through a good diabetes-management program. Participate in a diabetes education program, and join a support group. Cruise the Web and find a chat group. A good start is the Diabetes Education and Research Center's Website (www.libertynet.org/~diabetes).

Practical Tips for Living with Diabetes

Theodore Duncan, M.D.

LEARNING THAT YOU, A FRIEND, OR loved one has been diagnosed as having diabetes can be quite devastating. But consider the advice shared by the famous physician Sir William Osler, professor of medicine at Johns Hopkins University who said, "If you wish to live to a ripe old age, get a chronic disease and care for it." There is wisdom in these words because diabetes is a life-long disease. And although complications occur and you lifespan can be shortened, if you pay attention to good management and treatment you will definitely decrease diabetes-related problems, extend your life expectancy, and improve your quality of life.

You may have no symptoms. Or you may experience symptoms of urinary frequency, thirst, fatigue, increased hunger, and weight loss. Your diabetes may be diagnosed during a routine physical examination when blood sugar test results exceed the normal values of 126 milligrams fasting or 200 milligrams after eating on two occasions.

Diabetes affects the young and old of either sex. More than sixteen million people have the disease in the United States, but only 50 percent are aware of their condition. About 6 percent of the country's population is affected, and the rate of new cases increases each year. Some ethnic groups throughout our nation show a higher incidence of diabetes than others. One Native American tribe shows a rate of 12 percent, and another reports a rate of 50 percent of those older than fifty.

People often ask, "Why did I develop diabetes at this point in my life? Why not five or ten years ago?" Although most people with diabetes may have a preset genetic pattern that increases their likelihood of developing the disease, certain factors can act as "the straw that breaks the camel's back," producing the classic symptoms linked to high blood sugar. These "straws" include: obesity, pregnancy, and stress caused by accident, surgery, infection, death of a loved one, loss of a job, or other factors.

In diabetes, insulin, the hormone that facilitates the normal blood-sugar metabolism, is either absent or ineffectively used in the peripheral cells of the body. In type 1 diabetes no insulin is produced, thus insulin injections are required. The disease usually occurs before age thirty. Type 2 diabetes, which generally occurs later in life, accounts for 90 percent of the diabetic population in the United States, and the majority of these individuals are obese. Onset is more gradual than in type 1, and elevated blood sugar may occur several years before signs of poor control appear. Diet is the backbone of the therapy for treating this type of diabetes, and if followed faithfully and incorporated with an exercise program, medication may be unnecessary. Some people need to take antidiabetic medications and/or insulin to achieve and maintain good blood-sugar control.

Each person's program must be customized, because many influences can affect the disease. Adjustments in diet, insulin, and oral drugs may be necessary to achieve maximum control.

Charles H. Best, M.D., a co-discoverer of insulin, urged those with diabetes to recognize their responsibility in managing their treatment, not only through good personal hygiene but also in being aware of the need to change or modify their medication to maintain good blood-sugar control and thus minimize complications. "A well educated individual can cope with the day-to-day management of diabetes and has a degree of security that allows normal, productive life, with diabetes regulated to the status of 'minor nuisance' in the background," said Dr. Best. "Ignorance perpetrates insecurity and fear. All knowledge helps you take care of some of the duties of the physician for treatment."

The diagnoses of diabetes requires you to acquire new knowledge, skills, and attitudes to successfully manage the disease and to enjoy optimal health. These changes work best when they involve your family and other support systems. It is essential for you and your family to realize that it is both feasible and desirable to control dia-

betes rather than having diabetes control you. Knowledge is the key.

Find the best possible health care. Look for a physician who has experience in diabetes treatment—an endocrinologist or diabetologist. Your health-care team should also include a dietitian, a certified diabetes nurse-educator, an ophthalmologist, a podiatrist, a dentist and other specialists who have experience in treating those with diabetes.

Enroll in diabetes education classes; the rewards you gain through education will help you establish better control, reduce complications, and gain a security that only comes to a well-educated patient.

An important study was initiated in 1985 at twenty-nine medical centers in the United States to determine whether lowering the blood glucose prevents or slows the progression of long-term complications in people with diabetes? The researchers chose a group of younger, insulin-dependent type 1 patients for the study and carefully worked to maintain their blood sugars at near-normal values. The scientists evaluated the eyes, kidneys, and the nervous system—all known areas that can be affected and cause complications in people with diabetes. The final results showed a 76 percent reduction in eye complications, a 54 percent reduction in kidney problems, and a 60 percent reduction in neuropathy complications. While it might not be feasible for all persons with diabetes to follow the strict regimen and careful use of insulin that these study participants followed, it was still obvious that lowering the blood sugar definitely resulted in fewer complications. For this reason and many others it makes good sense to control your diabetes as closely as you can by:

- taking your diabetes medication—pills or insulin—as prescribed
- testing your blood sugar on a regular basis
- getting regular checkups from your physician
- having your eyes and feet examined yearly or as needed
- following a physical fitness program
- maintaining your weight and eating the prescribed diet
- maintaining a glycosylated hemoglobin (HbA$_{1c}$) level at or below 7

Exercise Is Essential

Unfortunately, persons with diabetes often neglect one of the cornerstones of the treatment for diabetes. The "couch potato" who fails to exercise has a shortened life expectancy and elevated cholesterol values; he or she usually has poor control of the diabetes and is often obese. Exercise can reverse these conditions, improve fitness, and actually improve psychological well-being. It helps in weight reduction by decreasing body fats and increasing muscle tissue. When you exercise you expand your physical capacity and gain more self-confidence due to your improved self-image. All these factors help improve the quality of your life.

Exercise takes three basic forms: muscle strengthening, aerobic, and flexion. Weight lifting increases and strengthens the muscle tissue and improves the bone density, making a fracture less likely. Aerobic exercises improve the lung and heart efficiency and help improve exercise capacity. Stretching exercises help maintain flexibility. A regular exercise program will help lower the blood lipids, triglycerides and cholesterol while increasing the "good" cholesterol (HDL) and protecting against heart disease. Exercise improves and returns many of the body functions to normal. It lowers the blood sugar and makes the body's peripheral cells more sensitive to insulin thus improving the blood-sugar control.

If your have diabetes, physical activity must be made an integral part of your life. Don't avoid it!

Before you begin an exercise program, discuss it with your physician. Make certain that no medical contraindications exist. Once approved, start slowly and work progressively to build toward an energetic program. Start with five minutes of exercises each day and gradually build to thirty to sixty minutes of continuous exercise at least three times weekly. Incorporate exercise into your daily living as well. Park the car a half-mile from work and walk the rest of the way. Use stairs not elevators. Use the malls in inclement weather to provide uninterrupted opportunities for your regular walks. Take a walk at your lunch break. Use a push lawn mower rather than the riding kind.

Keep in mind the fact that family members of obese individuals and those with diabetes are at greater risk for diabetes themselves. Urge your spouse and children to join you in exercising. By following an active weight-reduction and exercise program family members may delay or prevent the onset of diabetes in their own bodies.

While exercise provides great benefits, be aware that if you are being treated with insulin you are at more risk of hypoglycemia when you exercise if certain precautions are not taken. Additional snacks such as dried fruit, an orange, Gatorade, or a bagel may be required before, during, and after exercise. These can include dried fruit, an orange, Gatorade or a bagel to maintain good blood sugar control during the activity. Since exercise does lower the blood sugar, your physician may recommend a decrease in your insulin dosage prior to strenuous exercise. Blood-sugar testing before and after physical activity provides guidelines for the amount of insulin you require.

Get your doctor's approval for your exercise program then make a commitment to stick with it. Make it enjoyable, and you will be well rewarded with fewer complications and a better quality of life.

Blood-Sugar Monitoring

Twenty years ago, before the era of blood sugar testing at home, the study was done in the doctor's office monthly or several times a year. Today self blood-sugar testing is a tool that allows you to judge the amount of insulin or oral medications needed for the control of your diabetes. Being able to monitor your own situation and adjust your therapy accordingly gives you a feeling of independence. By monitoring yourself, you can learn the direct effect of exercise, insulin, diet, oral agents, and stress on your blood-sugar values. When you are ill, under stress, or experiencing poor control, self blood-sugar testing may be needed three or four times a day to guide you in adjusting your therapy. Conversely, when control is good, you'll possibly need fewer blood-sugar tests each day. When you have monitored your blood sugar for some time, you will learn just how much insulin is required for different situations. This improved control of your diabetes will result in fewer complications and, of course, fewer diabetes-related hospitalizations. Women whose pregnancies are complicated by diabetes often can keep their blood-sugar values almost within normal limits during the entire pregnancy and decrease complications in both mother and child by consistently using self-monitoring. Similarly, complications in those who are confined to bed because of stroke or other debilitating conditions can be reduced when family members or visiting nurses use simple monitoring procedures to obtain blood-sugar values.

The test requires a drop of blood that is obtained by a finger stick. For most people, anticipating the finger puncture is more stressful than the actual stick itself. A variety of lancets are available to obtain the droplet of blood. One of the most popular types uses a spring-loaded device that ejects the needle just the right depth into the skin to produce the tiny amount of blood needed for testing. After the drop of blood is placed on a strip or meter, the blood-sugar value usually is available in less than a minute. To gain the maximum benefits from testing your blood sugar keep a daily record with testing times before breakfast, lunch, supper, and the nighttime snack. Some people also test their blood sugar after meals to determine the effectiveness of their therapy on the after-eating (postprandial) period. These daily blood sugars, listed clearly in a record book, provide a "snapshot" of blood-sugar concentration at any given moment. A single reading may give little information, but if recorded in a logbook and reviewed periodically, patterns of high or low sugars become apparent, enabling you and your physician to make the appropriate changes in your therapy. If your blood sugar is high, therapy is usually increased. Low blood sugars indicate a need to lower the dose of insulin or oral medications you take.

Many types of blood sugar monitors

are available. Consult your doctor or diabetes nurse-educator about the best one for you. The cost of the meter and corresponding strips is frequently paid by health insurance and medicare.

To assess blood sugar values over a longer period of time, we have been using the glycosylated hemoglobin and the fructosamine tests.

Glycosylated Hemoglobin (HbA$_{1c}$) Test

Unlike the blood-sugar tests that determine the blood sugar level at that particular moment, the glycosylated hemoglobin test, a laboratory blood test helps you and your doctor know your average blood sugar during the past two to four months and give a greater amount of control.

Glycosylated hemoglobin is formed when glucose and other sugars attach to hemoglobin in the red blood cell. The upper limit of the normal range for non-diabetics is 6.5 percent. An elevated blood-sugar reading indicates that the amount of sugar incorporated into the hemoglobin has increased. Elevated values usually signal poor control over the disease and an increased chance of future complications unless the values return to the normal range.

Fructosamine Test

While the glycosylated hemoglobin test assesses average blood-sugar level during the past two to four months, the fructosamine test indicates the status of blood-sugar control during the past two to three weeks. Since the test can show changes occurring in less than a month, it can be used for evaluating recent changes in diabetes treatment such as starting new medication. When daily blood sugars have been neglected and no information concerning control is available, a once-a-week fructosamine home test gives essential information that will help guide therapy. (A once-a-week test should not be substituted for daily monitoring of blood sugars). Home fructosamine testing can offer new information not supplied by the blood-sugar or the glycosylated hemoglobin test.

The following chart shows fructosamine levels and glycosylated hemoglobin levels as related to different average blood-glucose values.

Average blood glucose (mg/dl)	Home fructosamine level (pmol/liter)	HbA$_{1c}$ level (%)
330		13
300	475	12
270		11
240	400	10
210		9
180	325	8
150		7
120	250	6
90		5
60	175	4

Diabetes Self-Management, May/June 1998, p 25.

Hypoglycemia

Hypoglycemia, or low blood sugar, is caused by excessive use of blood-sugar-lowering medication (usually insulin), a delayed meal, a forgotten snack, or increased exercise that uses additional glucose calories for energy. Preventing hypoglycemia is important, because it can be hazardous. Low blood sugar usually occurs before meals, after a period of fasting in the early morning, or during or after exercise. This condition can cause a multitude of symptoms including frontal headaches, nervousness, tremors, sweating, confusion, forgetfulness, or just not feeling right. In severe cases unconsciousness occurs.

If the symptoms clear after eating, hypoglycemia should be suspected even though tests do not show a low blood-sugar value. You may not recognize hypoglycemia when it occurs because there may be no obvious symptoms-at least none you recognize yourself. You may be totally unable to detect any changes or problems while a friend or spouse will diagnose the low sugar immediately and provide food to treat this dangerous and unpleasant event. Usually after eating, the symptoms clear, and normal thinking ability resumes. That is when you should ask, "What caused this low sugar?"

If you take insulin or oral medication to control your diabetes you can have low sugar reactions or shock due to decreased food intake (either because of delaying a meal or decreasing the day's total calories) or increased exercise without the proper adjustment in calories and insulin or taking too much insulin. Such episodes are preventable if you anticipate the day's activities and adjust your diet and insulin accordingly.

Remember, the symptoms of hypoglycemia may vary from time to time and show no characteristic pattern. No two people are alike. Fortunately, impending episodes of hypoglycemia usually give ample warning and can be prevented by drinking orange juice or regular soda or eating candy or other carbohydrate food. For this reason you must at all times keep candy, glucose tablets, or other substances containing sugar available to treat low blood-sugar reactions in case of emergency. Carry these foods with you at all times, especially when driving. And alert your family members and co-workers to the situation but make sure they understand that if you become unconscious or unresponsive, no one should attempt to give you anything by mouth. Instead, glucagon, a hormone that raises the blood sugar, may be injected, and within fifteen to twenty minutes your blood sugar should return to normal limits. When awakened, you should drink orange juice or eat a sandwich to prevent further hypoglycemia attacks.

Prevention is essential. Try to follow a regular daily routine eating meals and between-meal snacks on schedule to help protect yourself against low-blood sugar. When you plan some extra exercise add additional calories to your diet to supplement those that will be used.

If your low blood sugar is not caused by a change in diet or exercise, the most likely cause is excessive insulin. In that case, decrease your insulin and contact your physician to help make adjustments in your dietary and medication regimen.

Dining Out

Educational material repeatedly emphasizes that good diabetes control can only be achieved by properly managing insulin, diet, and exercise. Food must be considered, first and foremost, as a source of calories that provides your body with energy needed for physical and mental activity and for maintaining your body structure. Staying at your ideal weight depends upon a delicate balance between caloric intake and caloric use. If you have an average life expectancy you will ingest some seventy-six thousand meals during your lifetime. By the age of twenty, you will have already ingested more than twenty-four tons of food! If the balance between your caloric intake and use shifts only a little bit in the wrong direction or if you eat too much carbohydrate or cholesterol, you will encounter, far more than others who do not have diabetes, the problems of obesity, malnutrition, and hyperlipidemia (high cholesterol). Your education in diabetes management will stress daily food requirements, meal planning, and changes in diet to cope with special situations. Once you are secure in this knowledge, there is no reason you cannot "go out on the town," celebrate, and have a good meal-but in moderation.

When you eat out, try to conform to your regular diet plan and eat at your regular mealtimes. Plan ahead in case there is a delay or other schedule change. For example, if dinner is scheduled for 8:00 P.M. instead of your normal 6:00 P.M. eat a small sandwich at the normal mealtime and select a smaller serving at the restaurant. You may feel more comfortable if you call the restaurant before leaving home to discuss the menu to ensure that your meal will not be delayed. If your order is delayed longer than anticipated, snack on a few crackers. These precautions are usually necessary only for persons using insulin; those who use oral medication or diet alone need not be as worried about the change in mealtime.

Choosing the correct foods at most restaurants is not difficult. Frequently restaurants offer special low cholesterol or low-fat entrees or smaller "lite" portions. In general, select oil or soft margarine rather than butter, and order fish, a chicken or turkey breast that is poached, baked, or broiled but not fried. Do not eat the skin. Request that sauces and dressings for salads and vegetables be served on the side so you can choose the correct amount. Your starch exchange could include baked or boiled potatoes or steamed rice, and for the vegetable select those that are prepared raw, stewed, steamed, or boiled. Enjoy fresh fruit, angel food cake, or low-fat frozen yogurt as a dessert.

While full-menu restaurants don't have to be off limits, be aware that fast food can be hazardous to your health. Avoid French fries, cheeseburgers, hot-dogs and other high-fat foods, including very high calorie milkshakes. Fortunately, many fast-food chains now offer healthier choices: salad bars, grilled rather than fried chicken, baked potatoes, or chili, for example.

Alcohol and Alcoholic Beverages

Some doctors and health-care providers advise individuals with diabetes not to use alcohol in any form fearing that good control may be less easily maintained once alcohol is consumed. Others believe that one or two drinks a day does not affect the blood-sugar values to any great extent if good control exists. They suggest that all patients with diabetes should be able to observe special festive occasions—to toast the bride and groom, for example—and to celebrate in moderation. Alcohol should be consumed only with a meal because in the fasting state it may decrease the blood sugar values too low. To ensure stability, test your blood sugar before and after drinking since its effect may last many hours after you have had the last drink. Remember, too, that when your mental acuity is decreased due to alcohol, you may not recognize the symptoms of hypoglycemia.

Also be aware that alcohol has many calories with nonnutritional value. A dry white wine has fewer calories than a sweet wine. Be smart. Put less liquor in your mixed drink, use no-calorie mixers, choose lite beer, and opt for 80 proof instead of 100 proof alcohol.

The following list of alcoholic beverages shows their corresponding caloric content:

4 oz dry wine	80 calories
4 oz sweet wine	105 calories
4 oz champagne	100 calories
12 oz beer, regular	150 calories
12 oz beer, lite	100 calories
2 oz dessert wine	70 calories
2 oz 80 proof distilled liquor	134 calories
2 oz 90 proof distilled liquor	150 calories
2 oz 100 proof distilled liquor	166 calories

Mixers also add to the caloric count:

8 oz bitter lemon	128 calories
6 oz cola	78 calories
8 oz ginger ale	80 calories
club soda	no calories

There is a great variety of beverage options. Enjoy, but use alcohol wisely.

Traveling with Diabetes

We all need an occasional vacation whether it is hiking in the Swiss Alps or just relaxing by the swimming pool. Such changes can be good; they relieve the stresses of normal living. But changes do require planning and modifications in therapy for those with diabetes. Here are some tips to help you maintain your diabetes management routine as you travel.

Get required immunizations early. Get a letter from your physician stating your diagnosis, medications, drug sensitivities, allergies, and any equipment you will be carrying, including syringes, blood-glucose monitoring equipment, and possibly an insulin infusion system (a "pump"). Carry extra prescriptions for your medications in case you misplace or run out of pills or insulin. Wear a medical identification bracelet indicating that you have diabetes. Having these items available can help get you through customs and airport security checkpoints and will provide the necessary information for your medical care to pharmacists or physicians in the new location. This kind of preparation can eliminate a lot of hassle should problems arise.

Make a checklist of the diabetic supplies you must take including insulin, syringes, swabs, blood-sugar testing equipment, identification bracelet, extra snack food, emergency supplies, and medications to relieve common maladies associated with travel—vomiting and diarrhea. Keep these things in a small utility bag or medical kit and keep it with you at all times. Do not include it in your checked luggage that must be transported in the plane's cargo hold.

When you are planing an extended plane trip, think about the effect of time changes on your routine. Flying east from New York to London will shorten your day by six hours; conversely, flying west from New York to Honolulu extends the day. Eastern flights cause more concern for patients using insulin therapy. Usually, if you are taking a small dose of insulin, for example less than twenty units, you need not change the dosage. Some insulins inherently have an effective blood-sugar-lowering length of action for a specific period of time; for instance, NPH can be effective for about twenty-four hours. If six hours is "taken" from your day because you are traveling east, your physician may advise you to decrease the insulin dosage you take the morning of the day you travel. If you also take insulin before supper or at bedtime, that dose can usually be decreased or eliminated. When you start the new day on the plane, take your normal morning insulin dosage at breakfast time, and when you reach your destination proceed in your new time zone as you did at home.

Planning a trip westward usually poses no problem. Your current dosage of insulin is probably sufficient to "cover" the extended period of time without difficulty, but always check with your physician to be safe. When you settle in to your destination adjust your diet and/or insulin to compen-sate for your changes in activity. Remember that increased activity may warrant a decrease in the insulin dosage or an increase in calories. Conversely, decreased activity, such as reading a book while lying on the beach, requires less insulin or a decrease in food to maintain good control. Whenever possible, establish a regular eating pattern—three meals on time—and continue your prescribed between-meal snacks to help prevent low blood sugar. Always carry hard candy, wrapped crackers, or other nourishment to eat in case of low blood sugar or in the event a meal is delayed.

Handling Sick Days

People with diabetes, like everyone else, have their fair share of minor illnesses, including nausea, vomiting, diarrhea, upper respiratory infections, sunburn, menstrual cramps, etc. You need to be able to cope with minor metabolic stresses while maintaining relatively good control of your diabetes.

The common cold, sore throat, and similar illnesses usually raise blood-sugar levels and increase the insulin requirement slightly. When minor aches and pains or headaches occur, over-the-counter remedies usually are sufficient to help control the symptoms. If you have a fever, go to bed and keep warm. If necessary, substitute soft foods and liquids for your normal diabetic diet, but remember to maintain your meal schedule.

When you are ill, you might not feel like testing your blood sugar as faithfully as usual-resist this temptation! Illness indicates potential danger, and as much information as possible must be available to you and your physician so that appropriate oral blood-sugar medication, insulin, fluids and diet changes may be instituted as needed. Before you call your physician, be prepared to tell him or her your current diabetes medication and dosage in addition to your blood-sugar values and other symptoms.

Never skip your insulin! Sometimes people mistakenly believe because they are eating less due to illness they need no insulin. This incorrect assumption can lead to elevated blood-sugar values and possibly to diabetic coma. Continue to test your blood sugar. If it becomes more elevated, additional insulin or oral agents may be necessary. If your blood sugar is too low or if you are having low-blood-sugar symptoms, the dosage of your diabetes medication must be decreased. Low blood sugar is always a potential threat when you are consuming fewer calories. Persistent vomiting with near-normal blood sugar can indicate potential hypoglycemia. Try to maintain adequate fluid and caloric intake by sipping a small amount of soup on an hourly basis, supplemented by fruit juices or regular colas.

Using an External Insulin Pump

Most people with type 1 diabetes take insulin by injection once or twice a day; others need four daily injections. Their lives are structured to incorporate three meals and snacks eaten at specific times-a schedule that is usually not too flexible. Some people live within these parameters. For those who have trouble coping with such a rigid schedule, the external insulin pump offers a greater flexibility in lifestyle. Basically, the pump provides an alternative to injections for delivering insulin. The insulin is delivered through a fine tube usually inserted into the subcutaneous tissue of the abdominal wall. The pumping mechanism, not much larger than a pager, may be clipped to a belt or a pocket and can be removed temporarily for swimming and bathing.

The pump delivers two types of doses, the basal dose and the bolus dose. The basal dose of insulin, needed to maintain blood sugar control in the fasting state, is injected at a constant rate, one microdrop every few seconds. Prior to eating a meal, the user programs the pump to give a bolus dose, a specific number of additional units of insulin, to control the blood sugar for that one meal.

By using the pump more than thirty-five thousand people with diabetes enjoy the greater flexibility in meal planning and exercise schedules, possible prevention of long-term complications, enhanced feeling of well being, and improved blood-sugar control.

Before embarking on this program, you must have a good knowledge of diabetes and be faithfully testing your blood sugar at regular and frequent intervals. You must be willing to learn new technology and feel comfortable with and confident about regulating and adjusting the dosages.

Studies confirm that good blood-sugar control is the most important factor in delaying or preventing the complications of type 1 or type 2 diabetes. If you are highly motivated to keep your blood sugar under maximum control to prevent complications and if you desire a more flexible lifestyle, consider the external insulin pump. Ask a member of your diabetes care team for more information concerning the pump. Talk to someone who is using it, and contact the manufacturer for additional details.

A Guide to Meal Planning

THE GOALS OF SUCCESSFUL MEAL planning are to control your weight, blood-sugar levels, blood-fat levels, and to reduce the need for additional diabetes medications. A good meal plan will also improve and maintain your overall health, allowing you to enjoy your favorite activities and feel your best throughout your lifetime.

Just as there is not one exercise program that works for all people, there is not one diet prescription that works for everyone with diabetes. Everyone does not have the same activities, and therefore must take in the appropriate amount of calories. A calorie diet sheet may be simple to follow at first, but it lacks flexibility. Its inability to meet your particular needs along with its failure to address lifestyle changes will make it a poor choice over the long term, and diabetes is a condition requiring your long-term attention. Only a dietitian, or other healthcare provider trained in nutrition, can provide you with a thorough nutritional assessment and design individualized treatment goals. Since your lifestyle and personal factors change over time, as do your symptoms and complications, your individualized diet should be evaluated periodically (at least once a year) and adjusted accordingly. Meeting regularly with your dietitian is essential to maintaining a meal plan that best fits your changing lifestyle.

A good understanding of dietary basics, including what to eat, when to eat, how much to eat, and how to balance your diabetes medications with your meals and activity level, will help you find many pleasurable ways of combining foods to make healthy meals. Recipes such as the ones provided in this book can start you on your way to achieving your dietary goals.

Working with the Exchange System

Good health depends on eating a variety of foods that contain the right amounts of calories, carbohydrates, proteins, fats, vitamins, minerals, fiber, and water. Exchange Lists for Meal Planning take into consideration these components. The Lists were developed in 1950 by the American Diabetes Association and the American Dietetic Association, and were revised in 1995 to reflect new food products and eating patterns. Once you and your dietitian have a meal plan worked out, you may begin to refer to the exchange lists provided here to make your selections. Your dietitian will instruct you on how many calories you should eat depending on your size, age, and activity level. He or she will also tell you how many grams of carbohydrate, protein, fat, and fiber you should consume in a day.

The exchange lists group similar foods together. Any food on a list can be "exchanged" or traded for any other food on the same list. Thus, if your diet counselor recommends two starch exchanges for your morning meal, you can refer to the Starch List and select, for instance, half a cup of bran cereal and a slice of whole wheat bread to meet that goal.

There are three main groups of lists—the carbohydrate group, the meat and meat substitute group (protein), and the fat group. Starch, fruit, milk, and vegetables fall under the carbohydrate group.

Foods in the carbohydrate group supply most of the carbohydrate you will eat in a day. Each serving provides between twelve and fifteen grams of carbohydrate. Carbohydrate foods can supply a fair amount of protein and some fat depending on the type of product.

Foods in the meat and meat substitutes group supply most of your protein, approximately seven grams for a 1-ounce serving of meat or cheese. Meat, fish, and poultry supply little carbohydrate, but the meat

substitutes (beans, peas, and lentils) contain a fair amount. Meats can supply a significant amount of fat, depending on your selection. This group is divided into four sections: very lean, lean, medium fat, and high-fat.

Foods in the fat group supply mostly fat, usually five grams per exchange. Nuts and seeds, however, contain small amounts of protein. All fats are high in calories and should be eaten in moderation, especially if you are following a weight-reduction plan.

When considering the nutrients of foods, remember to consult the Nutrition Facts food label (page 15). This will give you the most accurate breakdown of nutrients in a serving of a particular food. Numbers on the food label can be compared to information in the exchange list. For example, if a label lists twenty-two grams of carbohydrate per serving, you can divide those grams by fifteen to arrive at the number of carbohydrate exchanges supplied by that food, in this case 22/15 or 1.5 exchanges. Your diet counselor will help make these comparisons.

Each recipe in this book is accompanied by a nutritional analysis similar to the information found on the Nutrition Facts food label. The exchanges for one serving of that recipe are also listed. These tools can help you use the recipes in this book according to the guidelines set for you by your dietitian.

Exchange Lists for Meal Planning

Fat List

Fats are divided into three groups, based on the main type of fat they contain: monounsaturated, polyunsaturated, and saturated. Small amounts of monounsaturated and polyunsaturated fats in the foods we eat are linked with good health benefits. Saturated fats are linked with heart disease and cancer. In general, one fat exchange is:

- 1 teaspoon of regular margarine or vegetable oil
- 1 tablespoon of regular salad dressings

Monounsaturated Fats List
One fat exchange equals:
5 grams fat and
45 calories

Avocado, medium	1/8 (1 oz)
Oil (canola, olive, peanut)	1 tsp
Olives: ripe (black)	8 large
green, stuffed*	10 large
Nuts	
almonds, cashews	6 nuts
mixed (50% peanuts)	6 nuts
peanuts	10 nuts
pecans	4 halves
Peanut butter, smooth or crunchy	2 tsp
Sesame seeds	1 Tbsp
Tahini paste	2 tsp

Polyunsaturated Fats List
One fat exchange equals:
5 grams fat and
45 calories

Margarine: stick, tub, or squeeze ....1 tsp
   lower-fat (30% to 50% vegetable oil) ....1 Tbsp
Mayonnaise: regular..1 tsp
   reduced-fat..1 Tbsp
Nuts, walnuts, English ....4 halves
Oil (corn, safflower, soybean)..1 tsp
Salad dressing: regular*...1 Tbsp
   reduced-fat..2 Tbsp
Miracle Whip® Salad Dressing: regular..2 tsp
   reduced-fat..1 Tbsp
Seeds: pumpkin, sunflower ....1 Tbsp

* = 400 mg or more sodium per exchange.

Saturated Fats List*
One fat exchange equals:
5 grams of fat and
45 calories

Bacon, cooked..1 slice (20 slices/lb)
Bacon, grease ....1 tsp
Butter: stick ....1 tsp
   whipped..2 tsp
   reduced-fat..1 Tbsp
Chitterlings, boiled ....2 Tbsp (1/2 oz)
Coconut, sweetened, shredded ....2 Tbsp
Cream, half and half..2 Tbsp
Cream cheese: regular ....1 Tbsp (1/2 oz)
   reduced-fat..2 Tbsp (1 oz)
Fatback or salt pork, see below†
Shortening or lard..1 tsp
Sour cream: regular ....2 Tbsp
   reduced-fat..3 Tbsp

†Use a piece 1 in. x 1 in. x ¼ in. if you plan to eat the fatback cooked with vegetables.
Use a piece 2 in. x 1 in. x ½ in. when eating only the vegetables with the fatback removed.
*Saturated fats can raise blood cholesterol levels.

Fast Foods[†]

Food	Serving Size	Exchange Per Serving
Burritos with beef*	2	4 carbs, 2 med-fat meats, 2 fats
Chicken nuggets*	6	1 carbs, 2 med-fat meats, 1 fat
Chicken breast and wing, breaded and fried*	1 each	1 carb, 4 med-fat meats, 2 fats
Fish sandwich/tartar sauce*	1	3 carbs, 1 med-fat meat, 3 fats
French fries, thin*	20-25	2 carbs, 2 fats
Hamburger, regular	1	2 carbs, 2 med-fat meats
Hamburger, large*	1	2 carbs, 3 med-fat meats, 1 fat
Hot dog with bun*	1	1 carb, 1 high-fat meat, 1 fat
Individual pan pizza*	1	5 carbs, 3 med-fat meats, 3 fats
Soft-serve cone*	1 medium	2 carbs, 1 fat
Submarine sandwich*	1 sub (6 in)	3 carbs, 1 veg, 2 med-fat meats, 1 fat
Taco, hard shell*	1 (6 oz)	2 carbs, 2 med-fat meats, 2 fats
Taco, soft shell*	1 (3 oz)	1 carb, 1 med-fat meat, 1 fat

* = 400 mg or more of sodium per exchange.
†Ask at your fast-food restaurant for nutrition information about your favorite fast foods.

Free Foods List

A *free food* is any food or drink that contains less than 20 calories or less than 5 grams of carbohydrate per serving. Foods with a serving size listed should be limited to three servings per day. Be sure to spread them out throughout the day. If you eat all three servings at one time, it could affect you blood glucose level. Foods listed without a serving size can be eaten as often as you like.

Fat-free or Reduced-fat Foods

Cream cheese, fat-free	1 Tbsp
Creamers, nondairy, liquid	1 Tbsp
Creamers, nondairy, powdered	2 tsp
Mayonnaise, fat-free	1 Tbsp
Mayonnaise, reduced-fat	1 tsp
Margarine, fat-free	4 Tbsp
Margarine, reduced-fat	1 tsp
Miracle Whip®, nonfat	1 Tbsp
Miracle Whip®, reduced-fat	1 tsp
Nonstick cooking spray	
Salad dressing, fat-free	1 Tbsp
Salad dressing, fat-free Italian	2 Tbsp
Salsa	¼ cup
Sour cream, fat-free, reduced-fat	1 Tbsp
Whipped topping, regular or light	2 Tbsp

Sugar-free or Low-sugar Foods

Candy, hard, sugar-free...1 candy
Gelatin dessert, sugar-free
Gelatin, unflavored
Gum, sugar-free
Jam or jelly, low-sugar or light...2 tsp
Sugar substitutes†
Syrup, sugar-free ....2 Tbsp

†Sugar substitutes, alternatives, or replacements that are approved by the Food and Drug Administration (FDA) are safe to use. Common brand names include:

Equal® (aspartame)	Sweet-10® (saccharin)
Sprinkle Sweet® (saccharin)	Sugar Twin® (saccharin)
Sweet One® (acesulfame K)	Sweet 'n Low® (saccharin)

Drinks

Bouillon, broth, consommé*
Bouillon or broth, low-sodium
Carbonated or mineral water
Club soda
Cocoa powder, unsweetened...1 Tbsp
Coffee
Diet soft drinks, sugar-free
Drink mixes, sugar-free
Tea
Tonic water, sugar-free

Condiments

Catsup...1 Tbsp
Horseradish
Lemon juice
Lime juice
Mustard
Pickles, dill* ....1½ large
Soy sauce, regular or light*
Taco sauce ....1 Tbsp
Vinegar

Seasonings

Be careful with seasonings that contain sodium or are salts, such as garlic or celery salt, and lemon pepper.

Flavoring extracts	Spices
Garlic	Tabasco® or hot pepper sauce
Herbs, fresh or dried	Wine, used in cooking
Pimiento	Worcestershire sauce

* = 400 mg or more of sodium per exchange.

Fruit List

Fresh, frozen, canned, and dried fruits and fruit juices are on this list. In general, one fruit exchange is:

 1 small to medium fresh fruit
 ½ cup of canned or fresh fruit or fruit juice
 ¼ cup of dried fruit

One fruit exchange equals
15 grams carbohydrate and
60 calories
(The weight includes skin, core, seeds, and rind)

Fruit

Apple, unpeeled, small ....1 (4 oz)	Kiwi ....1 (3½ oz)
Applesauce, unsweetened.......................½ cup	Mandarin oranges, canned ....¾ cup
Apples, dried...4 rings	Mango, small................½ fruit (5½ oz) or ½ cup
Apricots, fresh ....4 whole (5½ oz)	Nectarine, small......................................1 (5 oz)
Apricots, dried ....8 halves	Orange, small ....1 (6 1/2 oz)
Apricots, canned ....½ cup	Papaya....................½ fruit (8 oz) or 1 cup cubes
Banana, small...1 (4 oz)	Peach, medium, fresh ....1 (6 oz)
Blackberries ....¾ cup	Peaches, canned ....½ cup
Blueberries...¾ cup	Pear, large, fresh ....½ (4 oz)
Cantaloupe, small ....⅓ melon (11 oz)	Pears, canned...½ cup
or 1 cup cubes	Pineapple, fresh ....¾ cup
Cherries, sweet, fresh ....12 (3 oz)	Pineapple, canned ....½ cup
Cherries, sweet, canned ....½ cup	Plums, small...2 (5 oz)
Dates 3	Plums, canned ....½ cup
Figs, fresh ....1½ large	Prunes, dried 3
or 2 medium (3½ oz)	Raisins..2 Tbsp
Figs, dried ....1½ cup	Raspberries ....1 cup
Fruit cocktail..½ cup	Strawberries ....1¼ cup whole berries
Grapefruit, large......................................½ (11 oz)	Tangerines, small ....2 (8 oz)
Grapefruit sections, canned ....¾ cup	Watermelon ....1 slice (13½ oz)
Grapes, small ....17 (3 oz)	or 1¼ cup cubes
Honeydew melon ....1 slice (10 oz)	
or 1 cup cubes	

Fruit Juice

Apple juice/cider ....½ cup	Grapefruit juice ....½ cup
Cranberry juice cocktail ....⅓ cup	Orange juice ....½ cup
Cranberry juice cocktail, reduced calorie ....1 cup	Pineapple juice ....½ cup
Fruit juice blends, 100% juice......................⅓ cup	Prune juice ....⅓ cup
Grape juice ....⅓ cup	

Meat and Meat Substitutes List

Meat and meat substitutes that contain both protein and fat are on this list. In general, one meat exchange is:
- 1 oz meat, fish, poultry, or cheese
- ½ cup beans, peas, and lentils

Based on the amount of fat they contain, meats are divided into very lean, lean, medium-fat, and high-fat lists. This is done so you can see which ones contain the least amount of fat. One ounce (one exchange) of each of these includes:

	Carbohydrate (grams)	Protein (grams)	Fat (grams)	Calories
Very lean	0	7	0-1	35
Lean	0	7	3	55
Medium-fat	0	7	5	75
High-fat	0	7	8	100

Very Lean Meat and Substitutes List
One exchange equals:
0 grams carbohydrate
7 grams protein
0-1 grams fat and
35 calories

• One very lean meat exchange is equal to any one of the following items:

Poultry: Chicken or turkey (white meat, no skin)
   Cornish hen (no skin) ....1 oz
Fish: Fresh or frozen cod, flounder, haddock, halibut,
   trout, or tuna (fresh or canned in water) ....1 oz
Shellfish: Clams, crab, lobster, scallops, shrimp,
   imitation shellfish ....1 oz
Game: Duck or pheasant (no skin), venison,
   buffalo, ostrich ....1 oz
Cheese with 1 gram or less fat per ounce:
   Nonfat or low-fat cottage cheese ....¼ cup
   Fat-free cheese ....1 oz
Other: Processed sandwich meats with 1 gram or less fat per ounce,
   such as deli thin, shaved meats, chipped beef*, turkey ham..........................1 oz
   Egg whites...2
   Egg substitutes, plain...¼ cup
   Hot dogs with 1 gram or less fat per ounce*...1 oz

Kidney (high in cholesterol) ....1 oz
Sausage with 1 gram or less fat per ounce ....1 oz

•Count as one very lean meat and one starch exchange.
Beans, peas, lentils (cooked) ....½ cup

* = 400 mg or more sodium per exchange.

Lean Meat and Substitutes List
One exchange equals:
0 grams carbohydrate
7 grams protein
3 grams fat and
55 calories

•One lean meat exchange is equal to any one of the following items:

Beef: USDA Select Choice grades of lean beef trimmed of fat,
    such as round, sirloin, and flank steak; tenderloin; roast
    (rib, chuck, rump); steak (T-bone, porterhouse, cubed),
    ground round ....1 oz
Pork: Lean pork, such as fresh ham; canned, cured, or boiled
    ham; Canadian bacon*; Tenderloin, center loin chop ....1 oz
Lamb: Roast, chop, leg..1 oz
Veal: Lean chop, roast...1 oz
Poultry: Chicken, turkey (dark meat, no skin), chicken (white meat,
    with skin), domestic duck or goose (well-drained of fat, no skin) ....1 oz
Fish:
    Herring (uncreamed or smoked)..1 oz
    Oysters ....6 medium
    Salmon (fresh or canned), catfish...1 oz
    Sardines (canned) ....2 medium
    Tuna (canned in oil, drained) ....1 oz
Game: Goose (no skin), rabbit ....1 oz
Cheese:
    4.5%-fat cottage cheese ....¼ cup
    Grated Parmesan ....2 Tbsp
    Cheeses with 3 grams or less fat per ounce ....1 oz
Other:
    Hot dogs with 3 grams or less fat per ounce* ....1½ oz
    Processed sandwich meat with 3 grams or less
        fat per ounce, such as turkey, pastrami, or kielbasa.................................1 oz
Liver, heart (high in cholesterol) ....1 oz

* = 400 mg or more sodium per exchange

Medium-Fat Meat and Substitutes List
One exchange equals:
0 grams carbohydrate
7 grams protein
5 grams fat and
75 calories

• One medium-fat meat exchange is equal to any one of the following items.

Beef: Most beef products fall into this category
(ground beef, meatloaf, corned beef, short ribs,
prime grades of meat trimmed of fat, such as prime rib) ....1 oz
Pork: Top loin, chop, Boston butt, cutlet...1 oz
Lamb: Rib roast, ground ....1 oz
Veal: Cutlet (ground or cubed, unbreaded)..1 oz
Poultry: Chicken (dark meat, with skin), ground turkey, or
ground chicken, fried chicken (with skin) ....1 oz
Fish: Any fried fish product ....1 oz
Cheese: With 5 grams or less fat per ounce
Feta...1 oz
Mozzarella ....1 oz
Ricotta...¼ cup (2 oz)
Other:
Egg (high in cholesterol, limit to 3 per week)...1
Sausage with 5 grams or less fat per ounce..1 oz
Soy milk ....1 cup
Tempeh ....¼ cup
Tofu ....4 oz or ½ cup

High-Fat Meat and Substitutes List
One exchange equals
0 grams carbohydrate
7 grams protein
8 grams fat and
100 calories

Remember these items are high in saturated fat, cholesterol, and calories and may raise blood cholesterol levels if eaten on a regular basis.

• One high-fat meat exchange is equal to any one of the following items:

Pork: Spareribs, ground pork, pork sausage ....1 oz
Cheese: All regular cheeses, such as American*,
Cheddar, Monterey Jack, Swiss ....1 oz

Other: Processed sandwich meats with 8 grams or less fat per ounce,
 such as bologna, pimento loaf, salami...1 oz
Sausage: Bratwurst, Italian, knockwurst,
 Polish, smoked ....1 oz
Hot dog (turkey or chicken)*...1 (10/lb)
Bacon: 3 slices (20 slices/lb)

• Count as one high-fat meat plus one fat exchange.
 Hot dog (beef, pork, or combination)* 1 (10/lb)

•Count as one high-fat meat plus two fat exchanges.
 Peanut butter (contains unsaturated fat) ....2 Tbsp

* = 400 mg or more sodium per exchange.

Milk List

Different types of milk and milk products are on this list. Cheeses are on the Meat list
and cream and other dairy fats are on the Fat list. Based on the amount of fat they contain, milks are divided into skim/very low-fat milk, low-fat milk, and whole milk. One
choice of these includes:

	Carbohydrate (grams)	Protein (grams)	Fat (grams)	Calories
Skim/very low-fat	12	8	0-3	90
Low-fat	12	8	5	120
Whole	12	8	8	150

One milk exchange equals
12 grams carbohydrate and
8 grams protein

Skim and Very Low-fat Milk
(0-3 grams fat per serving)

Skim milk...1 cup
½% milk...1 cup
1% milk..1 cup
Nonfat or low-fat buttermilk ....1 cup
Evaporated skim milk ....½ cup
Plain nonfat yogurt ....¾ cup
Nonfat or low-fat fruit-flavored yogurt sweetened
 with aspartame or with a nonnutritive sweetener ....1 cup

Low-fat
(5 grams fat per serving)

2% milk...1 cup
Plain low-fat yogurt..¾ cup
Sweet acidophilus milk..1 cup

Whole Milk
(8 grams fat per serving)

Whole milk...1 cup
Evaporated whole milk ....½ cup
Goat's milk...1 cup
Kefir...1 cup

Starch List

Cereals, grains, pasta, breads, crackers, snacks, starchy vegetables, and cooked beans, peas, and lentils are starches. In general, one starch is:

- ½ cup of cereal, grain, pasta, or starchy vegetable
- 1 ounce of a bread product, such as one slice of bread
- ¾ to one ounce of most snack foods (some snack foods may also have added fat).

One starch exchange equals
15 grams carbohydrate
3 grams protein
0-1 gram fat and
80 calories

Bread

Bagel ....1/2 (1 oz)
Bread, reduced-calorie ....2 slices (1½ oz)
Bread, white, whole-wheat,
pumpernickel, rye ....1 slice (1 oz)
Bread sticks, crisp,
4 in long x ½ in...............................2 (⅔ oz)
English muffin ....½
Hot dog or hamburger bun ....½ (1 oz)
Pita, 6 in across ....½
Raisin bread, unfrosted ....1 slice (1 oz)

Roll, plain, small 1 (1oz)
Tortilla, corn, 6 in across....................................1
Tortilla, flour, 7-8 in across...............................1
Waffle, 4½ in square, reduced-fat.....................1

Cereals and Grains

Bran cereals..½ cup
Bulgur...½ cup
Cereals..½ cup
Cereals, unsweetened, ready-to-eat..........¾ cup
Cornmeal (dry)...3 Tbsp

Couscous ....⅓ cup
Flour (dry) ....3 Tbsp
Granola, low-fat................................¼ cup
Grape-Nuts® ....¼ cup
Grits ....½ cup
Kasha..½ cup
Millet..¼ cup
Muesli...¼ cup
Oats ....½ cup
Pasta...½ cup
Puffed cereal ....1½ cups
Rice milk ....½ cup
Rice, white or brown ....⅓ cup
Shredded Wheat®................................½ cup
Sugar-frosted cereal ....½ cup
Wheat germ ....3 Tbsp

Starchy Vegetables

Baked beans ....⅓ cup
Corn ....½ cup
Corn on cob, medium ....1 (5 oz)
Mixed vegetables with corn, peas,
or pasta...1 cup
Peas, green...½ cup
Plantain...½ cup
Potato, baked or boiled ....1 small (3 oz)
Squash, winter (acorn, butternut) ....1 cup
Yam, sweet potato, plain..................½ cup

Crackers and Snacks

Animal crackers 8
Graham crackers ....2½ in square
Matzoh ....¾ oz
Melba toast...4 slices
Oyster crackers 24
Popcorn (popped, no fat added
or low-fat microwave ....3 cups

Pretzels ....¾ oz
Rice cakes, 4 in across......................2
Saltine-type crackers 6
Snack chips, fat-free
(tortilla, potato) ....15-20 (¾ oz)
Whole-wheat crackers,
no fat added ....2-5 (¾ oz)

Beans, Peas, and Lentils

(Count as one starch exchange, plus one very
lean meat exchange)
Beans and peas (garbanzo, pinto,
kidney, white, split, black-eyed).................½ cup
Lima beans ....⅔ cup
Lentils..½ cup
*Miso...3 Tbsp

*400 mg or more sodium per exchange

Starchy Foods Prepared With Fat

(Count as one starch exchange, plus one fat
exchange)

Biscuit, 2½ in across.........................1
Chow mein noodles ....½ cup
Corn bread, 2 in cube.......................1 (2 oz)
Crackers, round butter type 6
Croutons ....1 cup
French-fried potatoes ....16-25 (3 oz)
Granola ....¼ cup
Muffin, small ....1 (1 1/2 oz)
Pancake, 4 in across 2
Popcorn, microwave ....3 cups
Sandwich crackers, cheese or
peanut butter filling 3
Stuffing, bread (prepared) ....⅓ cup
Taco shell, 6 in across 2
Waffle, 4½ in square........................1
Whole-wheat crackers, fat added.........4-6 (1 oz)

Starches often swell in cooking, so a small amount of uncooked starch will become a much larger amount of cooked food. The following table shows some of the changes.

Food (Starch)	Uncooked	Cooked
Oatmeal	3 Tbsp	½ cup
Cream of Wheat	2 Tbsp	½ cup
Grits	3 Tbsp	½ cup
Rice	2 Tbsp	⅓ cup
Spaghetti	¼ cup	½ cup
Noodles	⅓ cup	½ cup
Macaroni	¼ cup	½ cup
Dried Beans	¼ cup	½ cup
Dried Peas	¼ cup	½ cup
Lentils	3 Tbsp	½ cup

Other Carbohydrates List

You can substitute four choices from this list for a starch, fruit, or milk choice on your meal plan. Some choices will also count as one or more fat choices.

One exchange equals
15 grams carbohydrate
1 starch, 1 fruit, or 1 milk

Food	Serving Size	Exchanges Per Serving
Angel food cake, unfrosted	1/12th cake	2 carbohydrates
Brownie, small, unfrosted	2 in square	1 carbohydrate, 1 fat
Cake, unfrosted	2 in square	1 carbohydrate, 1 fat
Cake, frosted	2 in square	2 carbohydrate, 1 fat
Cookie, fat-free	2 small	1 carbohydrate
Cookie or sandwich cookie with creme filling	2 small	1 carbohydrate, 1 fat
Cranberry sauce, jellied	¼ cup	1½ carbohydrates
Cupcake, frosted	1 small	2 carbohydrates, 1 fat
Doughnut, plain cake	1 medium (1½ oz)	1½ carbohydrates, 2 fats
Doughnut, glazed	3¾ in across (2 oz)	2 carbohydrates, 2 fats
Fruit juice bars, frozen, 100% juice	1 bar (3 oz)	1 carbohydrate
Fruit snacks, chewy (pureed fruit concentrate)	1 roll (¾ oz)	1 carbohydrate
Fruit spreads, 100% fruit	1 Tbsp	1 carbohydrate
Gelatin, regular	½ cup	1 carbohydrate
Gingersnaps	3	1 carbohydrate
Granola bar	1 bar	1 carbohydrate, 1 fat
Granola bar, fat-free	1 bar	2 carbohydrates
Honey	1 Tbsp	1 carbohydrate

Hummus	1/3 cup	1 carbohydrate, 1 fat
Ice cream	1/2 cup	1 carbohydrate, 2 fats
Ice cream, light	1/2 cup	1 carbohydrate, 1 fat
Ice cream, fat-free, no sugar added	1/2 cup	1 carbohydrate
Jam or jelly, regular	1 Tbsp	1 carbohydrate
Milk, chocolate, whole	1 cup	2 carbohydrates, 1 fat
Pie, fruit, 2 crusts	1/6 pie	3 carbohydrates, 2 fats
Pie, pumpkin or custard	1/8 pie	1 carbohydrate, 2 fats
Potato chips	12-18 (1 oz)	1 carbohydrate, 2 fats
Pudding, regular (made with low-fat milk)	1/2 cup	2 carbohydrates
Pudding, sugar-free (made with low-fat milk)	1/2 cup	1 carbohydrate
Salad dressing, fat-free*	1/4 cup	1 carbohydrate
Sherbet, sorbet	1/2 cup	2 carbohydrates
Spaghetti or pasta sauce, canned*	1/2 cup	1 carbohydrate, 1 fat
Sugar	1 Tbsp	1/2 carbohydrate
Sweet roll or Danish	1 (2 1/2 oz)	2 1/2 carbohydrate, 2 fats
Syrup, light	2 Tbsp	1 carbohydrate
Syrup, regular	1/4 cup	4 carbohydrates
Tortilla chips	6-12 (1oz)	1 carbohydrate, 2 fats
Vanilla wafers	5	1 carbohydrate, 1 fat
Yogurt, frozen, low-fat, fat-free	1/3 cup	1 carbohydrate, 0-1 fat
Yogurt, frozen, fat-free, no sugar added	1/2 cup	1 carbohydrate
Yogurt, low-fat with fruit	1 cup	3 carbohydrates, 0-1 fat

* = 400 mg or more of sodium per exchange.

Vegetable List

Vegetables that contain small amounts of carbohydrates and calories are on this list. Vegetables contain important nutrients. Try to eat at least 2 or 3 vegetable choices each day. In general, one vegetable exchange is:

   1/2 cup of cooked vegetables or vegetable juice
   1 cup of raw vegetables

If you eat 1 to 2 vegetable choices at a meal or snack, you do not have to count the calories or carbohydrates because they contain small amounts of these nutrients.

One vegetable exchange equals
5 grams carbohydrate
2 grams protein
0 grams fat and
25 calories

Artichoke
Artichoke hearts
Asparagus
Beans (green, wax, Italian)
Bean sprouts
Cabbage
Carrots
Cauliflower
Celery
Cucumber
Eggplant
Green onions or scallions
Greens (collard, kale,
mustard, turnip)

Kohlrabi
Leeks
Mixed vegetables
    (without corn, peas, or pasta)
Mushrooms
Okra
Onions
Pea pods
Peppers (all varieties)
Radishes
Salad greens (endive,
    escarole, lettuce,
    romaine, spinach)

Sauerkraut*
Spinach
Summer squash
Tomato
Tomatoes, canned
Tomato sauce*
Tomato/vegetable juice*
Turnips
Water chestnuts
Watercress
Zucchini

* = 400 mg or more sodium per exchange

Combination Foods List

Many of the foods we eat are mixed together in various combinations. these combination foods do not fit into any one exchange list. Often it is hard to tell what is in a casserole dish or prepared food item. This is a list of exchanges for some typical combination foods. This list will help you fit these foods into your meal plan. Ask your dietitian for information about any other combination foods you would like to eat.

Food	Serving Size	Exchanges Per Serving
Entrees		
Tuna noodle casserole, lasagna, spaghetti with meatballs, chili with beans, macaroni and cheese*	1 cup (8 oz)	2 carbs, 2 med-fat meats
Chow mein (without noodles or rice)*	2 cups (16 oz)	1 carbs, 2 lean meats
Pizza, cheese, thin crust*	¼ of 10 in (5 oz)	2 carbs, 2 med-fat meats, 1 fat
Pizza, meat topping, thin crust*	¼ of 10 in (5 oz)	2 carbs, 2 med-fat meats, 2 fats
Pot pie*	1 (7 oz)	2 carbs, 1 med-fat meat, 4 fats

Frozen entrees

Salisbury streak with gravy,
    mashed potato* ....1 (11 oz) ....2 carbs, 3 med-fat meats, 3-4 fats
Turkey with gravy, mashed potato,
    dressing* ....1 (11 oz).......................2 carbs, 2 med-fat meats, 2 fats
Entree with less than
300 calories*..1 (8 oz) ....2 carbs, 3 lean meats

Soups

Bean*..1 cup (8 oz) ....1 carb, 1 very lean meat
Cream (made with water)*..............................1 cup ....1 carb, 1 fat
Split pea (made with water)* ....½ cup (4 oz)..1 carbohydrate
Tomato (made with water)*............................1 cup ....1 carbohydrate
Vegetable beef, chicken noodle, or
other broth-type ....1 cup ....1 carbohydrate

* = 400 mg or more sodium per exchange.

1,500 Calorie Meal Plan

	Calories	Carbohydrate (gm)	Fat (gm)
Breakfast			
(exchanges: 1 fat, 1 fruit, 1 meat, and 2 starch)			
1–2-ounce bagel	160	30.0	2.0
1½ tablespoon low-fat cream cheese	45	0.0	5.0
¾ cup blueberries	60	15.0	0.0
1 cup skim milk or fat-free, artificially sweetened yogurt	100	15.0	0.0
Total	365	60.0	7.0
Lunch			
(exchanges: 2¼ fat, 3¼ meat, 1/4 Milk, 2¼ starch, and 1½ vegetable)			
3 ounces Turkey with mustard	105	0.0	3.0
2 slices regular sandwich bread	160	30.0	2.0
1 cup Herbed Tomato Soup	154	17.3	6.6
1 cup lettuce salad (free)	0	0.0	0.0
1 tablespoon reduced-fat dressing	45	0.0	5.0
Total	464	47.3	16.6
Snack			
(exchange: ½ fat, and 2 starch)			
5 vanilla wafers	80	15.0	3.0
Supper			
(exchanges: 2 fat, ⅓ fruit, 3 meat, ⅓ milk, 3 starch, and 1 vegetable)			
1 piece Baked Fried Chicken	142	6.3	2.5
3-inch square Summer Squash Casserole	64	9.5	1.1
½ cup mashed potatoes with 1 teaspoon fat-free margarine	125	15.0	5.0
½ cup Cranberry and Pineapple Sherbet	50	9.4	0.1
1 one-ounce roll	80	15.0	1.0
1 teaspoon fat-free margarine	45	0.0	5.0
Total	506	55.2	14.7
Snack			
(exchanges: ½ milk and ⅓ starch)			
1 package fat-free, sugarless hot chocolate mixed with water	60	10.0	1.0
19 oyster-style crackers	36	5.0	2.0
Total	96	15.0	3.0
Daily Total	**1,511**	**192.5**	**44.3**

24% calories from fat   **54% calories from carbohydrate**

2,000 Calorie Meal Plan

	Calories	Carbohydrate (gm)	Fat (gm)
Breakfast			
(exchanges: 1 fat, 1 fruit, 1 meat, and 2½ starch)			
½ cup oatmeal	80	15.0	0.0
½-inch slice Banana Bread	141	21.0	5.0
1 teaspoon margarine	45	0.0	5.0
2 tablespoons raisins	60	15.0	0.0
1 cup fat-free milk	90	12.0	0.0
¼ cup low-fat cottage cheese	55	2.0	5.0
Total	471	65.0	15.0
Lunch			
(exchanges: 2½ fat, 1 fruit, 1½ meat, 3½ starch, and 1 vegetable)			
3-inch slice Vegetable Lasagna II	260	33.2	6.6
½-inch slice Herb Bread	124	21.3	2.4
2 cup salad	25	5.0	0.0
1 tablspoon reduced-fat dressing	45	0.0	5.0
¼ cantaloupe	60	15.0	0.0
Total	514	74.5	14.0
Snack			
(exchange: 2 starch)			
6 cups low-fat popcorn	80	15.0	3.0
Supper			
(exchanges: 3 fat, 1¾ fruit, 3 meat, 3 starch, and 1 vegetable)			
4 ounces Cheese & Sesame Chicken	183	7.8	5.0
⅔ cup rice with 2 teaspoons margarine	250	30.0	10.0
1 cup Roasted Vegetables	74	13.1	2.5
¾ cup Winter Fruit Medley	124	21.5	2.4
Total	631	72.4	19.9
Snack			
(exchanges: 1 milk and 1 starch)			
8 ounces fat-free yogurt	100	15.0	0.0
3 tablespoons Grape Nuts®	80	15.0	0.0
Total	180	15.0	3.0
Daily Total	**2,001**	**271.9**	**53.9**

24% calories from fat   **54% calories from carbohydrate**

2,500 Calorie Meal Plan

	Calories	Carbohydrate (gm)	Fat (gm)
Breakfast			
(exchanges: 1 fat, 1 fruit, 2 meat, and 4 starch)			
½ cup egg substitute	80	15.0	0.0
with 1 teaspoon margarine	45	0.0	5.0
2 two-ounce english muffins	60	15.0	0.0
1¼ cup strawberries	55	2.0	5.0
Total	471	65.0	15.0
Lunch			
(exchanges: 4 fat, 4 meat, 4½ starch, and 2 vegetables)			
4-ounce tuna with 1 teaspoon mayonnaise	185	0.0	5.0
2 half-inch slices Whole Wheat Bread	230	39.2	5.4
1 cup Fresh Broccoli & Cauliflower Salad	141	12.4	9.5
1.5 ounces pretzels	160	30.0	2.0
Total	716	81.6	21.9
Snack			
(exchange: 2 starch)			
2 ounces tortilla chips	180	30.0	2.0
4 tablespoons Mexican Salsa	free	free	free
Total	180	30.0	2.0
Supper			
(exchanges: 4½ fat, ½ fruit, 3 meat, 3 starch, and 3 vegetables)			
4 ounce Baked Beef Tenderloin			
with vegetables	277	8.3	11.6
1 cup French Green Beans Almondine	96	11	5.2
1 medium baked potato	160	30	0
2 tablespoons low-fat margarine	90	0	10
⅔ cup Old-Fashioned Apple Crunch	195	17.4	8.5
Total	818	66.7	35.3
Snack			
(exchanges: 1 milk and 1 starch)			
2 ounce fat-free cheese	70	4.0	0.0
12 low-fat crackers	160	30.0	0.0
1 small apple	60	15.0	0.0
Total	290	49.0	0.0
Daily Total	**2,459**	**302.3**	**66.2**

24% calories from fat   **54% calories from carbohydrate**

Metric Conversions

These are approximate conversions. Never mix metric and customary measures in one recipe. All spoon measurements used throughout this book are level, unless otherwise specified.

British Measurement: The British standard tablespoon holds 17.7 ml, the American standard measuring spoon holds 14.2 ml. The British standard $1/2$ pint (275 ml) equals 10 fl oz (a British standard cup). The American and Canadian standard $1/2$ pint equals 8 fl oz (an American and Canadian standard cup). The British fl oz is 1.04 times the American fluid ounce.

Oven temperatures

275°F	140°C
300	150
325	170
350	180
375	190
400	200
425	220
450	230
475	240

General Conversion Table

When You Know	Multiply	To Find
ounces (oz)	28	grams (gm)
pounds (lb)	0.45	kilograms (kg)
teaspoons (tsp)	5	mililiters (ml)
tablespoons (Tbsp)	15	mililiters (ml)
fluid ounces (fl oz)	30	mililiters (ml)
cups (c	0.24	liters (l)
pints (pt)	0.47	liters (l)
quarts (qt)	0.95	liters (l)

Weight Measurement Conversion

U.S. Ounces (to nearest equivalent)	U.S. Pounds (to nearest equivalent)	Metric (to nearest equivalent)
0.035 oz		1 gm
1 oz		28.35 gm
1$3/4$ oz		50 gm
2 oz	$1/8$ lb	57 gm
3$1/2$ oz		100 gm
4 oz	$1/4$ lb	113 gm
6 oz	$3/8$ lb	170 gm
8 oz	$1/2$ lb	227 gm
8$3/4$ oz		250 gm = $1/4$ kg
10 oz	$5/8$ lb	284 gm
12 oz	$3/4$ lb	340 gm
14 oz	$7/8$ lb	397 gm
16 oz	1 lb	454 gm
17$1/2$ oz	1$1/8$ lb	500 gm = $1/2$ kg
26$1/4$ oz	1$5/8$ lb	750 gm = $3/4$ kg
35 oz	2$1/4$ lb	1,000 gm = 1 kg

Liquid Measurement Conversion

U.S. Measure	Fl Ounces	Metric
$1/4$ tsp		1.25 ml
1 tsp		5 ml
2 tsp		1 cl
1 Tbsp	$1/2$ oz	15 ml
2 Tbsp	1 oz	30 ml
3 Tbsp	1$1/2$ oz	45 ml
$1/4$ c = 4 Tbsp	2 oz	59 ml
$1/3$ c	2$2/3$ oz	79 ml
$3/8$ c	3 oz	88 ml
6 Tbsp + 2 tsp	3$1/3$ oz	100 ml = 1 dl
$1/2$ c	4 oz	118 ml
$5/8$ c	5 oz	148 ml
$2/3$ c	5$1/3$ oz	158 ml
$3/4$ c	6 oz	177 ml
$7/8$ c	7 oz	207 ml
1 c	8 oz	237 ml
2 c = 1 pt	16 oz	474 ml
4 c = 1 qt	32 oz	948 ml
1 qt + 3 Tbsp	33$1/2$ oz	1 l
2 qt = $1/2$ gal	64 oz	1.89 l
2 qt + 6 Tbsp	67 oz	2 l
3 qt = $3/4$ gal	96 oz	2.84 l
3 qt + 9 Tbsp	100$1/2$ oz	3 l
4 qt = 1 gal	128 oz	3.79 l

Beverages

Creamed Iced Tea

6 Servings

6	tea bags	28	ounces sugar-free cream soda
3	cups boiling water		Fruit for garnish

Steep the tea bags in boiling water for 3 to 5 minutes. Pour the tea into a large pitcher. When ready to serve add the cream soda. Serve in 8-ounce glasses over ice and garnish with fruit.

Exchange Values Per Serving
1 Serving = 1 Cup
Free

1 Calorie
(0% from Fat)
0 gm Total Fat
0 gm Saturated Fat
0 mg Cholesterol
26 mg Sodium
0.5 gm Carbohydrates
0 gm Dietary Fiber
0 gm Protein
47 mg Potassium

Spiced Russian Tea

18 Servings

2	quarts water		Juice of 2 oranges
1	cinnamon stick, broken in half		Juice of 1 lemon
10	whole cloves	¼	cup cranapple juice
6	tea bags	4	packets artificial sweetener

Bring the water to a boil in a pan with the cinnamon stick and cloves. Add the tea bags and reduce the heat to a simmer. Brew until a deep golden color, about 5 minutes. Strain the tea. Pour into a 4-quart container and add the juices and artificial sweetener. Serve warm or over ice.

Exchange Values Per Serving
1 Serving = 1 Cup
Free

8 Calories
(3% from Fat)
0 gm Total Fat
0 gm Saturated Fat
0 mg Cholesterol
4 mg Sodium
2.0 gm Carbohydrates
0.1 gm Dietary Fiber
0.1 gm Protein
55 mg Potassium

Hot Spiced Tea

32 Servings

2   packages (.3 ounce each) sugar-free strawberry gelatin
½   gallon boiling water
6   cinnamon sticks
12   cloves
1   pint water
1   quart weak tea
1   cup pure lemon juice
1   quart water
     Artificial sweetener to taste (about 8 packets)
1   can (46 ounces) unsweetened pineapple juice

Dissolve the gelatin in boiling water in a pan. In a separate pan, simmer the cinnamon sticks and cloves in 1 pint of water for 30 minutes. Combine all of the ingredients. Add more water or juice if desired. Serve warm but do not boil.

Hot Spiced Coffee

4 Servings

3   cups hot, strong coffee
1   cinnamon stick
3   whole cloves
½   teaspoon ground allspice
1   tablespoon grated orange peel
     Artificial sweetener to taste
     Orange wedges for garnish

Pour the coffee into a pitcher and stir in the cinnamon stick, cloves, allspice, and orange peel. Let stand for 2 hours. Pour the coffee through a sieve to remove the cloves and cinnamon sticks. Pour into tall glasses filled with ice and add artificial sweetener to taste. Garnish with an orange wedge.

Fall Apple Coffee

8 Servings

1   quart unsweetened apple juice
1   quart hot, strong coffee
6   oranges, sliced wafer thin
2   3-inch cinnamon sticks
    Pinch of ground allspice

Pinch of grated nutmeg
Pinch of ground cloves
Brown sugar substitute to equal ⅓ cup brown sugar

Place all of the ingredients except the brown sugar substitute in a large saucepan and bring to a boil over medium heat. Reduce heat and simmer for 10 minutes. Remove from the heat and add the brown sugar substitute. Stir well and pour into a pitcher. Serve in 8-ounce mugs.

Exchange Values Per Serving
1 Serving = 1 Cup
1½ Fruit

103 Calories
(1% from Fat)
0.1 gm Total Fat
0 gm Saturated Fat
0 mg Cholesterol
15 mg Sodium
25.2 gm Carbohydrates
2.0 gm Dietary Fiber
0.9 gm Protein
353 mg Potassium

Instant Breakfast Drink

32 Servings

2   cups orange-flavored, sugar-free instant breakfast drink
1   cup unsweetened instant tea mix

1   teaspoon ground cloves
1   teaspoon cinnamon

Combine all of the ingredients in a bowl and mix well. Store in an airtight container. To serve, put 2 rounded tablespoons of mix in a mug, fill with boiling water, and stir well.

Exchange Values Per Serving
1 Serving = 2 Tablespoons
Free

9 Calories
(2% from Fat)
0 gm Total Fat
0 gm Saturated Fat
0 mg Cholesterol
7 mg Sodium
1.6 gm Carbohydrates
0.1 gm Dietary Fiber
0 gm Protein
73 mg Potassium

Breakfast Tomato Juice

1 Serving

1   can (6 ounces) low-sodium tomato juice

½   teaspoon lemon juice

Dash of low-sodium Worcestershire sauce

Dash of salt

1   packet artificial sweetener

Combine all of the ingredients in a glass. Stir to blend.

Exchange Values Per Serving

1 Serving = ¾ Cup
1¼ Vegetable

35 Calories
(2% from Fat)
0.1 gm Total Fat
0 gm Saturated Fat
0 mg Cholesterol
29 mg Sodium
8.6 gm Carbohydrates
1.4 gm Dietary Fiber
1.3 gm Protein
388 mg Potassium

Tart and Bubbly Wake-Up Drink

2 Servings

⅔   cup unsweetened pineapple juice

3   cranberry-raspberry ice cubes (see **Fruit Cubes and Fizz, page 65**)

½   cup sugar-free lemon-lime soda

Combine all of the ingredients in a pitcher and serve in 2 chilled wine glasses.

In place of pineapple juice, you can substitute orange juice or apple juice. Sugar-free, red-colored soda also adds a twist to this drink.

Exchange Values Per Serving

1 Serving = ⅔ Cup
1 Fruit

57 Calories
(2% from Fat)
0.1 gm Total Fat
0 gm Saturated Fat
0 mg Cholesterol
10 mg Sodium
14.1 gm Carbohydrates
1.5 gm Dietary Fiber
0.5 gm Protein
147 mg Potassium

Fruity Good-Morning Drink

3 Servings

1 banana	1¼ cups hulled strawberries
1 cup fat-free plain yogurt	½ teaspoon vanilla extract
1½ cups unsweetened orange juice, chilled	1 packet artificial sweetener
	3 fresh mint sprigs

Blend all of the ingredients except the mint in a blender. Pour into three 5-ounce glasses. Garnish with fresh mint.

Exchange Values Per Serving
1 Serving = ⅔ Cup
1⅔ Fruit
½ Milk

158 Calories
(4% from Fat)
0.8 gm Total Fat
0 gm Saturated Fat
1 mg Cholesterol
60 mg Sodium
32.8 gm Carbohydrates
2.6 gm Dietary Fiber
6.0 gm Protein
694 mg Potassium

Orange Monster Drink

16 Servings

2 quarts fresh unsweetened orange juice	20 whole cloves
3 3-inch cinnamon sticks	3 tablespoons grated orange peel
	8 packets artificial sweetener

Place all of the ingredients except the sweetener in a large saucepan. Bring to a boil, reduce the heat, and simmer for 5 minutes. Strain the mixture through a colander into a large pitcher and add the sweetener.

Exchange Values Per Serving
1 Serving = ½ Cup
1 Fruit

59 Calories
(4% from Fat)
0.3 gm Total Fat
0 gm Saturated Fat
0 mg Cholesterol
1 mg Sodium
13.8 gm Carbohydrates
0.4 gm Dietary Fiber
0.9 gm Protein
252 mg Potassium

An Apricot Drink

6 Servings

**Exchange Values Per
Serving**
  1 Serving = 1¼ Cup
  1 Fruit
  1 Milk

160 Calories
  (1% from Fat)
  0.3 gm Total Fat
  0.2 gm Saturated Fat
  3.1 mg Cholesterol
  138 mg Sodium
  30.1 gm Carbohydrates
  0.9 gm Dietary Fiber
  10.1 gm Protein
  430 mg Potassium

3   cups chopped fresh apricots, skins removed (or drained canned apricots)

4   tablespoons unsweetened pure-fruit apricot preserves

4   cups fat-free plain yogurt
    Fat-free milk, as needed to make drink smooth

Place the apricots and preserves in a blender and blend until puréed, about 2 minutes. Add the yogurt and pulse again to blend. Add just enough milk to achieve a creamy consistency. Refrigerate for 1 hour before serving.

Mint Tea

8 Servings

**Exchange Values Per
Serving**
  1 Serving = 1 Cup
  Free

14 Calories
  (5% from Fat)
  0.1 gm Total Fat
  0 gm Saturated Fat
  0 mg Cholesterol
  5 mg Sodium
  3.5 Carbohydrates
  0.2 gm Dietary Fiber
  0.1 gm Protein
  91 mg Potassium

2   cups chopped mint
2   lemons
1   quart water
6   packets artificial sweetener

1   quart unsweetened tea
6   fresh cherries
    Mint sprigs for garnish

Place the mint in a large stew pot. Peel the lemons and shred the rind. Sprinkle over the mint. Place the water in a separate pot and add the juice of both lemons. Bring to a boil and remove from the heat immediately. Pour over the mint and lemon rinds. Cover the stew pot and let mixture stand until cool. When cool use a potato masher to press the mint, squeezing more mint-flavor into the juice. Strain. Add the sweetener, and refrigerate. Add to unsweetened tea in equal parts as needed. Serve with a fresh cherry and a sprig of mint.

Southern Mint Juleps

10 Servings

4	or 5 sprigs fresh mint	10	packets artificial sweetener
2	cups cold water	1½	quarts sugar-free ginger ale
¾	cup lemon juice (fresh, if possible)		Lemon slices for garnish

Rinse the mint leaves and discard the stems. Place the water and lemon juice in a medium-size pitcher and mix. Stir in the mint leaves and the artificial sweetener. Let stand for 30 minutes. Fill a large pitcher with ice cubes, and strain the liquid over the ice. Add the ginger ale and float lemon slices on the top of the drinks.

Exchange Values Per Serving
1 Serving = 1 Cup
Free

9 Calories
(0% from Fat)
0 gm Total Fat
0 gm Saturated Fat
0 mg Cholesterol
23 mg Sodium
2.8 gm Carbohydrates
0.1 gm Dietary Fiber
0.1 gm Protein
30 mg Potassium

Blackberry Buzz

8 Servings

1	cup lemonade, artificially sweetened and made from a concentrate	1	cup club soda
		1	quart sugar-free ginger ale
2	cups canned or frozen blackberries, with juice		Artificial sweetener to taste

Combine all of the ingredients except the ginger ale in a blender and blend for 20 seconds or until smooth. Put some ice cubes in frosted mugs, and add 4 ounces of the blender mixture until they are half filled. Fill the mugs with ginger ale, stir, and serve. Artificial sweetener may be needed.

Exchange Values Per Serving
1 Serving = ⅔ Cup
½ Fruit

27 Calories
(5% from Fat)
0.2 gm Total Fat
0 gm Saturated Fat
0 mg Cholesterol
26 mg Sodium
6.7 gm Carbohydrates
1.9 gm Dietary Fiber
0.4 gm Protein
56 mg Potassium

Cantaloupe Refresher

6 Servings

Exchange Values Per Serving
1 Serving = ⅔ Cup
1 Fruit

79 Calories
(3% from Fat)
0.3 gm Total Fat
0.1 gm Saturated Fat
0 mg Cholesterol
16 mg Sodium
18.3 gm Carbohydrates
0.6 gm Dietary Fiber
1.8 gm Protein
339 mg Potassium

1 medium cantaloupe, diced	2 packets artificial sweetener
3 tablespoons lime juice	½ cup fat-free vanilla frozen yogurt
2½ cups unsweetened orange juice	

Place all of the ingredients except the yogurt in a blender and blend until smooth. Add the yogurt and purée.

A Peach of a Punch

14 Servings

Exchange Values Per Serving
1 Serving = 5 ounces (with Fruit)
1¼ Fruit

76 Calories
(1% from Fat)
0.1 gm Total Fat
0 gm Saturated Fat
0 mg Cholesterol
10 mg Sodium
18.8 gm Carbohydrates
0.1 gm Dietary Fiber
0.4 gm Protein
198 mg Potassium

1 can (46 ounces) unsweetened pure peach nectar	1 teaspoon ground nutmeg
4 peaches, cored, peeled, and pureed	2 tablespoons lime juice, fresh if possible
2 cups unsweetened orange juice	¼ cup brown sugar substitute
3 2-inch cinnamon sticks, crumbled	Grated orange peel for garnish
6 whole cloves	

Combine the peach nectar, pureed peaches, and orange juice in a large saucepan. Bring to a boil, reduce the heat, and simmer. Add the spices and stir. Add the lime juice and stir. Remove from the heat and add the brown sugar substitute. Stir until well blended and dissolved. Place a strainer over a prewarmed punch bowl and strain the punch. Ladle into 5-ounce punch cups and sprinkle each with a bit of grated orange peel.

Brunch Punch

40 Servings

1½ cups unsweetened orange juice
1½ cups lemonade, artificially sweetened
1½ cups limeade
1½ cups tangerine juice, or 3 tangerines squeezed to make 1½ cups juice

1 can (46 ounces) unsweetened pineapple juice
2 quarts chilled sugar-free ginger ale

Place all of the ingredients except the ginger ale in a large pitcher and blend well. Chill 2 hours. When ready to serve, pour in a punch bowl and add the ginger ale.

Exchange Values Per Serving
1 Serving = ½ Cup
½ Fruit

29 Calories
(1% from Fat)
0 gm Total Fat
0 gm Saturated Fat
0 mg Cholesterol
9 mg Sodium
7.2 gm Carbohydrates
0.1 gm Dietary Fiber
0.2 gm Protein
82 mg Potassium

Citrus Punch

16 Servings

6 small tea bags
4 cups boiling water
8 packets artificial sweetener
1 can (6 ounces) unsweetened frozen concentrated orange juice, undiluted

1 can (6 ounces) frozen concentrate for lemonade, undiluted
10 cups cold water

Steep the tea bags in boiling water for about 5 minutes. Do not continue to boil. Discard the tea bags and add the remaining ingredients. Serve over ice.

Exchange Values Per Serving
1 Serving = 1 Cup
½ Fruit

39 Calories
(1% from Fat)
0 gm Total Fat
0 gm Saturated Fat
0 mg Cholesterol
7 mg Sodium
9.7 gm Carbohydrates
0.1 gm Dietary Fiber
0.3 gm Protein
101 mg Potassium

Cranberry Fizz Punch

18 Servings

Exchange Values Per Serving
1 Serving = 1 Cup
1 Fruit

66 Calories
(1% from Fat)
0.1 gm Total Fat
0 gm Saturated Fat
0 mg Cholesterol
12 mg Sodium
16.4 gm Carbohydrates
0.2 gm Dietary Fiber
0.4 gm Protein
146 mg Potassium

1   can (6 ounces) frozen concentrate for lemonade
1   can (6 ounces) unsweetened frozen concentrated orange juice
1   quart low-calorie cranberry juice
1   can (46 ounces) unsweetened pineapple juice
1   quart sugar-free ginger ale, chilled

Reconstitute the lemonade and orange juice according to the package directions. Pour into a large container. Add the cranberry and pineapple juices. Chill. Add the ginger ale just before serving.

Tea Punch

40 Servings

Exchange Values Per Serving
1 Serving = ½ Cup
¼ Fruit

15 Calories
(3% from Fat)
0.1 gm Total Fat
0 gm Saturated Fat
0 mg Cholesterol
8 mg Sodium
3.8 gm Carbohydrates
0.1 gm Dietary Fiber
0.2 gm Protein
78 mg Potassium

6   cups extra-strong tea
3   cups unsweetened orange juice
2   cups unsweetened grapefruit juice
½   cup lime juice
½   cup lemon juice
7   cups sugar-free ginger ale
    Mint sprigs and wafer-thin lemon slices for garnish
    Artificial sweetener to taste

Combine the tea and the juices in a punch bowl and stir well. Refrigerate until ready to serve. Just before serving, add sugar-free ginger ale and some ice cubes and stir. Garnish by floating mint sprigs and lemon slices in the punch.

Fruit Cubes and Fizz

2 Servings

¼ cup lemon juice
2½ cups strawberries, halved

12 ounces sugar-free red-colored or lemon-lime soda

Pour lemon juice into a small narrow bowl; dip each strawberry into the juice. Place on a cookie sheet so that the fruit is not touching. Place in the freezer and allow to freeze solid. (When frozen these pieces can be transferred to a freezer bag and kept until needed.) Place desired number of strawberries in a glass and fill with soda. This drink tastes great and looks pretty.

Exchange Values Per Serving
  1 Serving = 1 Cup
  1 Fruit

64 Calories
  (8% from Fat)
  0.7 gm Total Fat
  0 gm Saturated Fat
  0 mg Cholesterol
  31 mg Sodium
  15.9 gm Carbohydrates
  4.4 gm Dietary Fiber
  1.3 gm Protein
  350 mg Potassium

Fruity Punch

50 Servings

1 package (.3 ounces) sugar-free cherry gelatin
1 quart boiling water
3 quarts cool water

1 can (46 ounces) unsweetened pineapple juice
1 quart sugar-free lemon-lime soda
Lemon and lime slices for garnish

Dissolve the gelatin in the boiling water. Add the cool water and pineapple juice. Chill in the refrigerator. When ready to serve, pour into a punch bowl and add the sugar-free soda. Stir well. Garnish with sliced lemons and limes. This punch is beautiful for weddings and at Christmas.

Exchange Values Per Serving
  1 Serving = ⅔ Cup
  1/4 Fruit

19 Calories
  (0% from Fat)
  0 gm Total Fat
  0 gm Saturated Fat
  0 mg Cholesterol
  8 mg Sodium
  3.3 gm Carbohydrates
  0.1 gm Dietary Fiber
  1.5 gm Protein
  67 mg Potassium

Fruity Slush

24 Servings

Exchange Values Per Serving
1 Serving = 1 Cup
2 Fruit

122 Calories
(1% from Fat)
0.2 gm Total Fat
0.1 gm Saturated Fat
0 mg Cholesterol
16 mg Sodium
30.3 gm Carbohydrates
1.0 gm Dietary Fiber
1.2 gm Protein
370 mg Potassium

6   cups water
6   packets artificial sweetener
1   can (46 ounces) unsweetened pineapple juice
2   cans (12 ounces) unsweetened frozen concentrated orange juice, undiluted
1   can (12 ounces) frozen concentrate for lemonade, undiluted
5   bananas
    Mint sprigs and colorful straws for garnish
4   cans (12 ounces) sugar-free lemon-lime soda

Bring the water to a boil, cool for 10 minutes, and then stir in the artificial sweetener. Add the remaining ingredients except the lemon-lime soda and pour into five 1-quart freezer containers or several ice cube trays. Freeze. When ready to serve, fill glasses with 3 ounces of lemon-lime flavored soft drink, 5 ounces of the mixture, and several ice cubes. Serve with a sprig of mint and a colorful straw.

Lime-Raspberry Refresher

8 Servings

Exchange Values Per Serving
1 Serving = ⅔ Cup
¼ Fruit

14 Calories
(7% from Fat)
0.1 gm Total Fat
0 gm Saturated Fat
0 mg Cholesterol
29 mg Sodium
3.8 gm Carbohydrates
1.2 gm Dietary Fiber
0.3 gm Protein
50 mg Potassium

1   cup crushed unsweetened raspberries, frozen or fresh
⅓   cup lime juice (about 4 fresh limes, squeezed)
1½   quarts sugar-free ginger ale
    Artificial sweetener to taste

In a food processor, process the raspberries and lime juice. Carefully stir in the ginger ale and serve over crushed ice. Sweeten to taste.

Oriental Beef Kabobs (page 89)

Spicy-Tangy Beef Soup (page 108)

Spicy Crab Soup (page 111), Tuna Chowder (page 114), Cajun Shrimp and Oyster Soup (page 112)

Couscous Vegetable and Feta Cheese Salad (page 123)

Orange Frosty

3 Servings

1   can (6 ounces) unsweetened frozen concentrated orange juice, undiluted
2¼ cups fat-free milk

1   teaspoon vanilla extract
2   packets artificial sweetener
½   cup crushed ice

Combine all of the ingredients in a food processor and blend until smooth. Serve immediately.

Exchange Values Per Serving
1 Serving = 1¼ Cup
¾ Fruit
1½ Milk

162 Calories
(2% from Fat)
0.5 gm Total Fat
0.2 gm Saturated Fat
3.3 mg Cholesterol
97 mg Sodium
31.7 gm Carbohydrates
1.5 gm Dietary Fiber
7.6 gm Protein
687 mg Potassium

Frosty Strawberry Delight

4 Servings

2½ cups fresh ripe strawberries
1   container (8 ounces) fat-free vanilla frozen yogurt
1   cup fat-free milk
½   cup sugar-free red-colored soda, cherry or strawberry flavored

2   packets artificial sweetener
Strawberries and mint leaves for garnish

In a blender or food processor mix the strawberries, yogurt, and milk. Slowly stir in the soda and serve. Garnish with a whole strawberry and mint leaf.

Exchange Values Per Serving
1 Serving = 1 Cup
½ Fruit
¼ Milk
1¼ Starch

138 Calories
(3% from Fat)
0.5 gm Total Fat
0.1 gm Saturated Fat
1.1 mg Cholesterol
88 mg Sodium
28.2 gm Carbohydrates
2.1 gm Dietary Fiber
5.8 gm Protein
257 mg Potassium

A Fruit Shake

4 Servings

Exchange Values Per Serving
1 Serving = ⅔ Cup
1 Fruit
½ Milk

82 Calories
(2% from Fat)
0.2 gm Total Fat
0 gm Saturated Fat
0 mg Cholesterol
42 mg Sodium
18.3 gm Carbohydrates
1.3 gm Dietary Fiber
3.4 gm Protein
335 mg Potassium

1	cup fat-free vanilla yogurt	4	packets artificial sweetener
½	cup sliced fresh strawberries	1½	cup crushed ice
½	cup diced fresh papaya		Cantaloupe slices for garnish
½	cup diced cantaloupe		

Place the yogurt, strawberries, papaya, cantaloupe, and sweetener in a food processor or blender. Process until smooth. Add the crushed ice and blend thoroughly. Pour into frosted glasses and garnish with cantaloupe slices.

Strawberry Grog

12 Servings

Exchange Values Per Serving
1 Serving = 1 Cup
Free

46 Calories
(0% from Fat)
0 gm Total Fat
0 gm Saturated Fat
0 mg Cholesterol
50 mg Sodium
0.2 gm Carbohydrates
0 gm Dietary Fiber
11.5 gm Protein
257 mg Potassium

2	packages (.3 ounce each) sugar-free strawberry gelatin	1	bottle (2 liters) sugar-free lemon-lime or club soda

Carefully pour the gelatin into the soda and cap immediately. Place this mixture in the refrigerator overnight. Serve over crushed ice.

Strawberry Parfait Drink

6 Servings

1	pint fresh, or 2 cups frozen, strawberries, cleaned and chopped	1	cup crushed ice
½	cup evaporated fat-free milk	2	packets artificial sweetener
½	cup fat-free vanilla yogurt	6	whole strawberries for garnish

Combine all of the ingredients except the garnish in a blender. Blend at high speed until smooth. Serve in punch cups or in tulip champagne glasses with a strawberry on the side of the glass.

Exchange Values Per Serving
   1 Serving = ¾ Cup
   ½ Fruit
   ½ Milk

58 Calories
   (2% from Fat)
   0 gm Total Fat
   0 gm Saturated Fat
   0.8 mg Cholesterol
   39 mg Sodium
   12.2 gm Carbohydrates
   1.5 gm Dietary Fiber
   2.8 gm Protein
   214 mg Potassium

A Carrot Cocktail

6 Servings

3	cups unsweetened pineapple juice	½	teaspoon lemon juice
2	large carrots, cut into very small pieces	¼	cup fat-free plain yogurt
		1½	cups crushed ice

Place the pineapple juice and carrots in a food processor or blender and liquefy. Add the remaining ingredients and blend again until liquefied. Serve immediately.

Exchange Values Per Serving
   1 Serving = ⅔ Cup
   1 Fruit
   ½ Vegetable

81 Calories
   (1% from Fat)
   0.1 gm Total Fat
   0 gm Saturated Fat
   0.2 mg Cholesterol
   19 mg Sodium
   19.1 gm Carbohydrates
   1.0 gm Dietary Fiber
   1.3 gm Protein
   272 mg Potassium

Hearty Tomato Saucy Drink

6 Servings

Exchange Values Per Serving
1 Serving = ½ Cup
¾ Vegetable

20 Calories
(0% from Fat)
0 gm Total Fat
0 gm Saturated Fat
0 mg Cholesterol
34 mg Sodium
4.8 gm Carbohydrates
0.5 gm Dietary Fiber
0.5 gm Protein
20 mg Potassium

10   ounces stewed tomatoes, fresh or canned
 2   tablespoons lemon juice
 2   tablespoons lime juice
 1   teaspoon low-sodium Worcestershire sauce
 4   drops hot sauce
 1   cup cold water
      Lime slices for garnish

Place the stewed tomatoes, juices, and seasonings in a blender and blend for 30 seconds on medium speed. Add the cold water, stir, and pour into glasses filled with crushed ice. Garnish each with a slice of lime.

Tomato Frappe

6 Servings

Exchange Values Per Serving
1 Serving = ⅔ Cup
1¼ Vegetable

35 Calories
(3% from Fat)
0.1 gm Total Fat
0 gm Saturated Fat
0 mg Cholesterol
39 mg Sodium
8.8 gm Carbohydrates
1.6 gm Dietary Fiber
1.5 gm Protein
419 mg Potassium

 1   tablespoon fat-free margarine
 3   tablespoons finely chopped onion
 1   tablespoon lemon juice
      Generous dash of low-sodium Worcestershire sauce
      Generous dash of hot sauce
4½   cups low-sodium tomato juice
      Lemon wedges and straws for garnish

Melt the margarine in a skillet and sauté the onion until tender and translucent. Place the sautéed onion, lemon juice, Worcestershire sauce, hot sauce, and tomato juice in a blender. Blend for 1 minute or until smooth. Pour into a metal baking pan and freeze. Half an hour before needed, take the tomato mix out of the freezer. Allow to thaw just enough to break into chunks. Place in a food processor and blend until smooth. Don't let it melt. Serve in sherbet glasses with a lemon wedge and straws.

Spiced Low-fat Buttermilk

4 Servings

16 ounces low-fat buttermilk
½ teaspoon rum flavoring
    Dash of grated nutmeg

Dash of cinnamon
Cinnamon sticks

Stir together all of the ingredients except the cinnamon sticks in a bowl and chill covered. Serve in small glass punch cups and place a stick of cinnamon in each cup.

Exchange Values Per Serving
1 Serving = ½ Cup
½ Fat
½ Milk

31 Calories
(4% from Fat)
0.1 gm Total Fat
0 gm Saturated Fat
0 mg Cholesterol
27 mg Sodium
6.3 gm Carbohydrates
3.3 gm Dietary Fiber
2.1 gm Protein
210 mg Potassium

Warmed Wintry Milk

4 Servings

3 cups fat-free milk
2 packets artificial sweetener

½ teaspoon almond extract
1 teaspoon rum flavoring

In a small saucepan warm the milk to scald only. Remove from the heat and add the sweetener and flavorings. Stir to blend well. Serve immediately in warmed mugs or pour into a thermos for travel in cold weather.

Exchange Values Per Serving
1 Serving = ⅔ Cup
1 Milk

71 Calories
(5% from Fat)
0.4 gm Total Fat
0.2 gm Saturated Fat
3.3 mg Cholesterol
95 mg Sodium
9.4 gm Carbohydrates
0 gm Dietary Fiber
6.3 gm Protein
305 mg Potassium

Holiday Eggless Eggnog

5 Servings

Exchange Values Per Serving
1 Serving = 1 Cup
¼ Fat
¼ Milk
1½ Starch

146 Calories
(0% from Fat)
0.1 gm Total Fat
0.1 gm Saturated Fat
1 mg Cholesterol
137 mg Sodium
26.9 gm Carbohydrates
0 gm Dietary Fiber
6.7 gm Protein
115 mg Potassium

1 quart fat-free, sugar-free frozen yogurt, melted	Fat-free non-dairy whipped topping, frozen
⅔ cup evaporated fat-free milk	½ teaspoon freshly grated nutmeg
¼ cup dark spiced rum	

In a pitcher whisk together the yogurt, milk, and rum. Cover and chill for 30 minutes. Pour into individual cups and top with whipped topping and sprinkle with nutmeg.

Christmas Wassail

20 Servings

Exchange Values Per Serving
1 Serving = ½ Cup
1 Fruit

60 Calories
(1% from Fat)
0.1 gm Total Fat
0 gm Saturated Fat
0 mg Cholesterol
6 mg Sodium
14.7 gm Carbohydrates
0.2 gm Dietary Fiber
0.2 gm Protein
115 mg Potassium

4 cups unsweetened apple juice	2 whole cloves
3 cups unsweetened pineapple juice	4 packets artificial sweetener
2 cups cranberry juice cocktail	Lemon slices
¼ teaspoon grated nutmeg	Apple slices
1 cinnamon stick, broken in half	Orange slices

Combine the apple juice, pineapple juice, cranberry juice, nutmeg, cinnamon stick, and cloves in a saucepan over medium heat. Simmer for 10 minutes; do not boil. Pour into a punch bowl and add the sweetener, lemon slices, apple slices, and orange slices to the top. Stir and serve.

Chocolate Café Borgia

12 Servings

12   packets (1 ounce each) instant, sugar-free hot cocoa mix
12   cups of freshly perked coffee

Fat-free, non-dairy whipped topping
Grated orange peel for garnish

In a large mug combine 1 packet of the cocoa mix with 1 cup of hot coffee. Stir well. Garnish each serving with 2 tablespoons whipped topping and sprinkle with grated orange peel.

Exchange Values Per Serving
1 Serving = 1 Cup
1½ Starch

113 Calories
(4% from Fat)
0.5 gm Total Fat
0.2 gm Saturated Fat
1 mg Cholesterol
322 mg Sodium
22.9 gm Carbohydrates
1.5 gm Dietary Fiber
5.1 gm Protein
129 mg Potassium

Chocolate Coffee Milkshake

2 Servings

1   cup cold fat-free milk
3   ice cubes, crushed
1   cup vanilla frozen yogurt
1   teaspoon instant coffee powder
1   teaspoon sugar-free fat-free instant cocoa mix

Artificial sweetener to taste
Fat-free non-dairy whipped topping

Place all of the ingredients (except whipped topping), in a blender and blend until creamy. Serve in a fluted glass topped with whipped topping.

Exchange Values Per Serving
1 Serving = 1 Cup
½ Milk
1½ Starch

163 Calories
(2% from Fat)
0.3 gm Total Fat
0.2 gm Saturated Fat
2 mg Cholesterol
165 mg Sodium
31.2 gm Carbohydrates
0.2 gm Dietary Fiber
8.8 gm Protein
235 mg Potassium

Appetizers and Snacks

Colonial Orange-Spiced Walnuts

24 Servings

1 package (.3 ounce) orange sugar-free gelatin	½ tablespoon grated orange peel
2 cups boiling water	¼ teaspoon ground ginger
1½ cups walnut halves	⅛ teaspoon ground cloves
	Pinch of grated nutmeg

In a heavy skillet combine the gelatin and boiling water. Add the remaining ingredients and return to a boil. Stir until most of the liquid is evaporated. Drain on a paper towel. Spread on a baking sheet to cool.

Exchange Values Per Serving
1 Serving = 1 Tablespoon
1 Fat

49 Calories
(75% from Fat)
4.4 gm Total Fat
0.3 gm Saturated Fat
0 mg Cholesterol
1 mg Sodium
1.0 gm Carbohydrates
0.4 gm Dietary Fiber
2.2 gm Protein
49 mg Potassium

Garlic and Parmesan Pecans

32 Servings

2 tablespoons low-fat margarine	½ teaspoon low-sodium Worcestershire sauce
½ teaspoon garlic powder	2 cups pecan halves and large pieces
½ teaspoon Dijon mustard	⅓ cup grated Parmesan cheese
½ teaspoon brown mustard	

Heat the margarine in a medium skillet until melted. Stir in the garlic powder, mustards, and Worcestershire sauce. Add the pecans and coat with the mixture. Continue to cook over low heat for 3 to 5 minutes to roast lightly. Remove from the heat and drain. Place in a plastic bag and sprinkle with cheese, tossing lightly. Spread on a baking sheet to dry.

Exchange Values Per Serving
1 Serving = 1 Tablespoon
1 Fat

52 Calories
(81% from Fat)
4.9 gm Total Fat
0.4 gm Saturated Fat
0 mg Cholesterol
17 mg Sodium
1.7 gm Carbohydrates
0.5 gm Dietary Fiber
0.9 gm Protein
33 mg Potassium

Stuffed Apricots

16 Servings

Exchange Values Per
Serving
  1 Serving = 1 Stuffed
  Apricot
  Free

14 Calories
  (8% from Fat)
  0.1 gm Total Fat
  0 gm Saturated Fat
  0 mg Cholesterol
  21 mg Sodium
  2.6 gm Carbohydrates
  0.4 gm Dietary Fiber
  0.8 gm Protein
  59 mg Potassium

¼	cup fat-free cream cheese	1	teaspoon apricot pure-fruit jam
¼	teaspoon grated orange peel	½	teaspoon vanilla extract
1	teaspoon unsweetened orange juice	16	medium-sized dried apricot halves

In a small bowl, combine cream cheese, orange peel, orange juice, apricot jam, and vanilla extract. Blend well. Place 1 level teaspoon of cheese mixture on each of the 16 apricot halves. Use as a garnish for chicken.

Cheese and Pears

12 Servings

Exchange Values Per
Serving
  1 Serving = 4 Pear
    Wedges
  ½ Fat
  1 Fruit
  ½ Meat

111 Calories
  (40% from Fat)
  5.2 gm Total Fat
  3.1 gm Saturated Fat
  16 mg Cholesterol
  122 mg Sodium
  13.5 gm Carbohydrates
  2.0 gm Dietary Fiber
  4.0 gm Protein
  128 mg Potassium

6	large pears	½	cup fat-free cottage cheese
8	ounces Neufchâtel cheese, softened	¼	cup crumbled low-fat blue cheese

Wash pears and pat dry; cut out center of each pear with an apple corer. Combine remaining ingredients, mixing well. Fill pears with cheese mixture; cover and chill thoroughly.

To serve, cut each pear into 8 wedges to make 48 appetizers or snacks.

Cheddar-Dijon Dip

10 Servings

2   cups shredded low-fat Cheddar
    cheese
2   tablespoons low-fat margarine
1   tablespoon Dijon mustard

8   ounces fat-free plain yogurt
½   cup chopped pecans
2   tablespoons chopped parsley

Process the cheese, margarine, and mustard in a blender or food processor with a metal blade until smooth. Add the yogurt and blend until smooth. Spoon the mixture into a bowl and gently stir in the pecans and parsley. Refrigerate for 1 to 2 hours. Serve as a dip with vegetables or crackers.

Exchange Values Per Serving
   1 Serving = 3
   Tablespoons
   1 Fat
   1 Meat

117 Calories
   (54% from Fat)
   7.3 gm Total Fat
   1.5 gm Saturated Fat
   8 mg Cholesterol
   105 mg Sodium
   3.9 gm Carbohydrates
   0.5 gm Dietary Fiber
   9.8 gm Protein
   158 mg Potassium

Dilly Dip

16 Servings

6   ounces fat-free plain yogurt
⅓   cup fat-free mayonnaise
1   tablespoon instant minced onion

1   teaspoon celery salt
1   tablespoon parsley flakes
1   tablespoon dried dill weed

Combine all of the ingredients in a small bowl, and mix well. Cover and refrigerate for several hours to blend the flavors. Serve with raw vegetables.

Exchange Values Per Serving
   1 Serving = 1
   Tablespoon
   Free

11 Calories
   (2% from Fat)
   0 gm Total Fat
   0 gm Saturated Fat
   0 mg Cholesterol
   171 mg Sodium
   1.8 gm Carbohydrates
   0.1 gm Dietary Fiber
   0.7 gm Protein
   38 mg Potassium

Exchange Values Per Serving
1 Serving = 1 Tablespoon
¼ Fat

17 Calories
(55% from Fat)
1.2 gm Total Fat
0.2 gm Saturated Fat
0 mg Cholesterol
23 mg Sodium
1.8 gm Carbohydrates
0.9 gm Dietary Fiber
0.3 gm Protein
79 mg Potassium

Guacamole Dip

24 Servings

2 large avocados, pitted and peeled	⅓ cup chopped green chilies
2 tablespoons fat-free plain yogurt	Hot sauce to taste
⅛ teaspoon garlic powder	½ small onion, chopped
1 teaspoon lemon or lime juice	1 small tomato, chopped

Mash the avocado in a food processor. Add the yogurt, garlic powder, lemon or lime juice, green chilies, hot sauce, onion, and tomato. Purée in the processor until smooth.

This dip is best if refrigerated for 2 days to allow the flavors to blend.

Exchange Values Per Serving
1 Serving = 1 Tablespoon
¼ Starch

19 Calories
(8% from Fat)
0.2 gm Total Fat
0 gm Saturated Fat
0 mg Cholesterol
107 mg Sodium
3.6 gm Carbohydrates
1.2 gm Dietary Fiber
1.1 gm Protein
68 mg Potassium

Texas Bean Dip

40 Servings

1 can (15½ ounces) black beans, drained	½ cup mild picante sauce
1 can (15½ ounces) red beans, drained	½ teaspoon ground cumin
1 teaspoon canola oil	½ teaspoon chili powder
2 garlic cloves, minced	1 tablespoon diced jalapeño pepper
½ cup chopped onion	¼ cup low-fat Monterey Jack cheese
½ cup diced tomato	1 tablespoon lime juice, fresh or frozen
	Low-fat tortillas

Place beans in a bowl; partially mash until chunky.

Heat oil in a frying pan. Add onion and garlic; sauté for 4 minutes over medium heat. Add beans, tomato, picante sauce, cumin, chili powder, and pepper. Cook for 5 minutes or until thick, stirring constantly. Remove from heat and add cheese and lime juice. Stir until well blended and cheese has melted. Serve warm with low-fat tortillas.

Hotty Totty Onion Dip

48 Servings

| 1 | can (10½ ounces) reduced-fat cream of onion soup | 8 | ounces fat-free plain yogurt |
| | | 1 | cup low-sodium salsa |

Combine all of the ingredients in a medium saucepan. Cover and cook slowly until heated through. Serve warm with vegetables.

Exchange Values Per Serving
  1 Serving = 1 Tablespoon
  Free

10 Calories
  (29% from Fat)
  0.3 gm Total Fat
  0.1 gm Saturated Fat
  1 mg Cholesterol
  74 mg Sodium
  1.4 gm Carbohydrates
  0.1 gm Dietary Fiber
  0.4 gm Protein
  12 mg Potassium

Munchy Crunchy Vegetable Dip

56 Servings

1½	cups fat-free plain yogurt	½	cup finely chopped broccoli
1	cup fat-free mayonnaise	1	package low-sodium dry vegetable soup mix
1	can (8 ounces) sliced water chestnuts, drained	1	teaspoon low-sodium Worcestershire sauce
½	cup finely chopped carrots		

Combine all the ingredients in a medium bowl and mix well. Cover and refrigerate for several hours to allow the flavors to blend. Serve with choice of vegetables.

Exchange Values Per Serving
  1 Serving = 1 Tablespoon
  ¼ Fat

15 Calories
  (18% from Fat)
  0.3 gm Total Fat
  0 gm Saturated Fat
  0 mg Cholesterol
  77 mg Sodium
  2.7 gm Carbohydrates
  0.3 gm Dietary Fiber
  0.5 gm Protein
  25 mg Potassium

Blue Cheese Avocado Dip

8 Servings

Exchange Values Per
Serving
1 Serving = 1
Tablespoon
1½ Fat
½ Milk
¼ Starch

145 Calories
(44% from Fat)
7.1 gm Total Fat
1.6 gm Saturated Fat
1 mg Cholesterol
89 mg Sodium
16.2 gm Carbohydrates
4.1 gm Dietary Fiber
5.0 gm Protein
594 mg Potassium

2 tablespoons chopped onion
2 avocados, peeled and pitted
1½ teaspoons fresh lemon juice
1½ cups fat-free sour cream

¼ cup low-fat blue cheese, crumbled
Salt-free seasoning
Fat-free tortilla chips or crackers

Purée onion, avocados, and lemon juice in food processor. Blend with sour cream, cheese, and herbs. Chill 1 hour. After chilling, adjust seasoning to taste if necessary. Serve with chips or crackers.

Spinach Vegetable Dip

56 Servings

Exchange Values Per
Serving
1 Serving = 1
Tablespoon
Free

8 Calories
(2% from Fat)
0 gm Total Fat
0 gm Saturated Fat
0 mg Cholesterol
59 mg Sodium
1.4 gm Carbohydrates
0.2 gm Dietary Fiber
0.4 gm Protein
17 mg Potassium

8 ounces fat-free plain yogurt
1 cup fat-free mayonnaise
¾ package low-sodium leek soup mix
1 package (10 ounces) frozen chopped spinach, thawed and well drained

½ cup chopped parsley
½ cup chopped green onions
1 teaspoon dried dill weed
1 teaspoon Italian salad dressing mix
Raw vegetables

In a food processor combine all of the ingredients and mix well. Place in an airtight container and refrigerate. Just before serving, place in a bowl and surround with raw vegetables.

Herb Dip with Asparagus

6 Servings

8 ounces fat-free cream cheese	⅛ teaspoon dried tarragon
⅓ cup fat-free sour cream	⅛ teaspoon dried basil
3 green onions, chopped	⅛ teaspoon dried marjoram
2 tablespoons capers, drained	Salt-free seasoning
2 tablespoons finely chopped fresh parsley	1 teaspoon lemon pepper seasoning
1 tablespoon Dijon mustard	1 pound thin asparagus, blanched

Combine all ingredients except asparagus in a bowl and blend until smooth, using just enough sour cream to achieve a soft consistency. Cover and chill. Serve with blanched asparagus for dipping.

Exchange Values Per Serving
1 Serving = 1 Tablespoon
¾ Meat
¼ Vegetable

74 Calories
(14% from Fat)
1.2 gm Total Fat
0.4 gm Saturated Fat
3 mg Cholesterol
453 mg Sodium
6.8 gm Carbohydrates
1.0 gm Dietary Fiber
8.6 gm Protein
390 mg Potassium

Shrimp Dip

6 Servings

8 ounces fat-free cream cheese	⅓ cup finely chopped green onions
½ cup fat-free mayonnaise	⅛ teaspoon garlic powder
1 can (4½ ounces) tiny cocktail shrimp, drained and rinsed	

Mix cream cheese and mayonnaise in a bowl until well blended. Stir in remaining ingredients. Chill for 1 hour before serving. Great to place in the middle of a vegetable platter. Makes 2 cups.

Exchange Values Per Serving
1 Serving = ⅓ Cup
1½ Meat

76 Calories
(12% from Fat)
0.9 gm Total Fat
0.4 gm Saturated Fat
40 mg Cholesterol
383 mg Sodium
5.3 gm Carbohydrates
0.1 gm Dietary Fiber
10.4 gm Protein
122 mg Potassium

Crab Pie Appetizer

32 Servings

Exchange Values Per Serving
1 Serving = 1 Phyllo Cup
¼ Fat
¼ Meat
¾ Starch
¼ Vegetable

78 Calories
(20% from Fat)
1.7 gm Total Fat
0.3 gm Saturated Fat
1 mg Cholesterol
188 mg Sodium
11.7 gm Carbohydrates
0.4 gm Dietary Fiber
3.5 gm Protein
48 mg Potassium

2   teaspoons unbleached flour
⅛   teaspoon dried thyme, crushed
⅛   teaspoon pepper
1   carton egg substitute
¼   cup chopped red bell pepper
1   can (13½ ounces) artichoke hearts, drained and chopped
6   ounces crabmeat substitute, diced

Nonstick cooking spray
32   phyllo pastry sheets, cut into squares
3   tablespoons low-fat grated Parmesan cheese
2   tablespoons freeze-dried chives
1   tablespoon low-fat margarine.

Combine flour, thyme, pepper, and egg substitute in a bowl. Add peppers, artichokes, and crabmeat substitute. Stir well.

Preheat the oven to 350°. Coat muffin tins with nonstick cooking spray. Gently press phyllo squares into each muffin cup allowing the ends to overlap the top. Spoon the crabmeat mixture evenly into the phyllo cups. Sprinkle with cheese and chives. Brush the edges of the phyllo with margarine.

Bake for 20 minutes or until the filling is set and edges of the phyllo are golden brown.

Your Own Crispy Crackers

19 Servings

Exchange Values Per Serving
1 Serving = 5 Crackers
1¾ Fat
1¼ Starch

172 Calories
(45% from Fat)
8.6 gm Total Fat
0.9 gm Saturated Fat
0 mg Cholesterol
2 mg Sodium
20.2 gm Carbohydrates
1.7 gm Dietary Fiber
3.9 gm Protein
130 mg Potassium

2   cups rolled oats, quick-cooking or regular
1½   cups all-purpose flour
⅓   cup finely ground pecans
1½   tablespoons brown sugar
½   teaspoon salt substitute
⅔   cup water
½   cup safflower oil
Nonstick cooking spray
6   tablespoons sesame seeds

Crush the oats in a food processor. Combine the crushed oats, flour, pecans, brown sugar, and salt substitute in a large bowl. Mix until well blended. Add the water and oil, and blend thoroughly.

Preheat oven to 325°. Divide dough into 3 balls. Place each ball on a 16 x 12-inch baking sheet that has been coated with nonstick cooking spray. Roll the dough all the way to the edges; this will be very thin. Sprinkle the dough lightly with sesame seeds.

With a pastry or pizza wheel, cut the dough into 2-inch squares or diamonds. Bake for 30 to 35 minutes or until golden brown. Remove carefully with a spatula. Store in an airtight container for up to a month. These may also be frozen.

Shrimp and Cheese Spread

24 Servings

¼ cup fat-free cottage cheese
¼ cup fat-free plain yogurt
2 tablespoons low-sodium tomato juice
½ teaspoon lemon juice
1 tablespoon minced parsley

1 cup ground or finely minced shrimp
¼ teaspoon paprika
   Hot sauce to taste
   Fat-free crackers or celery

Whip together the cottage cheese and yogurt in a bowl until creamy. Blend in the remaining ingredients and refrigerate. Serve with fat-free crackers or celery.

Exchange Values Per Serving
1 Serving = 1 Tablespoon
¼ Meat

10 Calories
(11% from Fat)
0.1 gm Total Fat
0.3 gm Saturated Fat
9 mg Cholesterol
28 mg Sodium
0.4 gm Carbohydrates
0 gm Dietary Fiber
1.7 gm Protein
23 mg Potassium

Chicken Spread

8 Servings

2 pounds chicken breasts, skinned
1 small onion, cut into pieces
1 carrot, cut into pieces
   Salt-free seasoning to taste
8 ounces Neufchâtel cheese, softened
1 tablespoon fat-free mayonnaise
1 tablespoon grated onion
1 tablespoon sweet pickle juice
½ cup finely chopped celery

   Dash of curry powder
¼ teaspoon pepper
½ teaspoon chopped pimiento
   Dash of hot sauce
   Dash of garlic powder
   Nonstick cooking spray
   Leaf lettuce
   Vegetables for garnish

Place chicken in unsalted water in a large pot. Add onion, carrot, and salt-free seasoning to taste. Cover and cook until tender. Chop chicken into fine pieces. Save 2 tablespoons of broth for later use.

Combine Neufchâtel cheese and mayonnaise in a bowl, beating until smooth; add onion, pickle juice, celery, curry, pepper, pimiento, hot sauce, and garlic powder and mix well.

Stir in chicken and reserved chicken broth. Lightly coat four ½-inch molds or one 2-cup mold with cooking spray; press in chicken mixture. Chill.

Unmold on lettuce-lined serving plate; garnish with colorful vegetables such as radishes, carrots, red peppers, and green peppers.

Exchange Values Per Serving
1 Serving = ¼ Cup
1 Fat
3½ Meat
½ Vegetable

204 Calories
(43% from Fat)
9.6 gm Total Fat
5.0 gm Saturated Fat
78 mg Cholesterol
202 mg Sodium
3.9 gm Carbohydrates
0.6 gm Dietary Fiber
24.5 gm Protein
349 mg Potassium

Vegetable Spread

2 Servings

Exchange Values Per Serving
1 Serving = 1 Tablespoon
2½ Meat
½ Starch
¼ Vegetable

103 Calories
(7% from Fat)
0.9 gm Total Fat
0.5 gm Saturated Fat
11 mg Cholesterol
253 mg Sodium
6.7 gm Carbohydrates
0.7 gm Dietary Fiber
17.3 gm Protein
233 mg Potassium

2 tablespoons chopped celery	2 tablespoons chopped radish
2 tablespoons chopped red bell pepper	1 cup fat-free ricotta cheese
2 tablespoons chopped green onions	¼ teaspoon dried dill weed
2 tablespoons chopped carrot	Fresh pepper to taste

In a food processor finely dice the chopped vegetables. Discard any large chunks. In a small bowl mix cheese, dill, and pepper until well blended. Add cheese mixture to vegetables. Cover and refrigerate until ready to serve.

Artichoke Spread

20 Servings

Exchange Values Per Serving
1 Serving = 1 Tablespoon
¼ Meat
¼ Vegetable

26 Calories
(30% from Fat)
0.8 gm Total Fat
0.5 gm Saturated Fat
2 mg Cholesterol
176 mg Sodium
2.6 gm Carbohydrates
0.2 gm Dietary Fiber
1.6 gm Protein
51 mg Potassium

⅔ cup grated Parmesan cheese	1 can (13½ ounces) artichoke hearts, chopped
⅔ cup fat-free mayonnaise	1 teaspoon salt-free seasoning
1 can (4½ ounces) green chilies, diced	Fat-free crackers

Preheat the oven to 350°. Mix all of the ingredients (except the crackers) in a large bowl. Pour into a casserole dish. Bake for 20 minutes (or microwave on high for 3 minutes). Serve with thin, fat-free crackers.

Zucchini Cheese Spread

16 Servings

4   ounces low-fat Cheddar cheese
1   small zucchini, grated
¾   cup fat-free mayonnaise
½   cup toasted walnuts, chopped
1   teaspoon fresh lemon juice

1   tablespoon fresh chopped oregano
6   drops hot sauce
    Fat-free crackers
    Celery ribs

In a bowl combine all ingredients (except crackers and celery) and refrigerate for 1 hour or overnight. Serve with crackers and celery ribs.

Exchange Values Per Serving
1 Serving = 1 Ounce
1 Fat
¼ Meat

63 Calories
(58% from Fat)
4.2 gm Total Fat
0.9 gm Saturated Fat
5 mg Cholesterol
141 mg Sodium
3.9 gm Carbohydrates
0.3 gm Dietary Fiber
3.0 gm Protein
39 mg Potassium

Marinated Vegetables

10 Servings

1   pound asparagus
1   pound broccoli
1   pound cauliflower
1   pound baby carrots
12 medium mushrooms
2   cucumbers

3   tomatoes
¼   cup virgin olive oil
1   teaspoon minced garlic
½   cup low-sodium dill pickle juice
4   tablespoons dried dill weed
¼   teaspoon white pepper

Steam the asparagus, broccoli, cauliflower, and carrots. Cool and in a large bowl combine with the mushrooms, cucumbers, and tomatoes. In a separate bowl combine the oil, garlic, pickle juice, dill, and pepper. Pour over the vegetables and chill overnight. Arrange on plates for a beautiful luncheon start.

Exchange Values Per Serving
1 Serving = ½ Cup
1 Fat
2¾ Vegetable

122 Calories
(43% from Fat)
6.5 gm Total Fat
0.9 gm Saturated Fat
0 mg Cholesterol
48 mg Sodium
13.9 gm Carbohydrates
4.8 gm Dietary Fiber
5.0 gm Protein
784 mg Potassium

Italian Carrot Antipasto

6 Servings

Exchange Values Per Serving
1 Serving = ¼ Cup
1½ Fat
2 Vegetable

137 Calories
(50% from Fat)
7.5 gm Total Fat
1.0 gm Saturated Fat
0 mg Cholesterol
45 mg Sodium
9.9 gm Carbohydrates
2.8 gm Dietary Fiber
1.9 gm Protein
429 mg Potassium

1	pound tender young carrots	1 teaspoon celery seed
¾	cup dry white wine	1 teaspoon sugar
¾	cup white wine vinegar	Pinch of pepper
4	cups water	1 head of lettuce, chopped
3	tablespoons virgin olive oil	1 teaspoon chopped basil
2	garlic cloves, minced	1 teaspoon Dijon mustard
	Small bunch fresh parsley	

Wash and scrape the carrots; cut them into strips. Combine the carrots, wine, vinegar, water, oil, garlic, parsley, celery seed, sugar, and pepper in an enamel saucepan. Bring to a boil over moderate heat and cook for about 10 minutes. Remove from the heat and allow to cool.

Remove the carrots and boil the marinade until reduced to about 2 cups. Toss the carrots in a large bowl with the chopped lettuce. Pour the marinade over carrots and lettuce and sprinkle with basil. Toss with the mustard and chill.

Cherry Tomato Appetizers

10 Servings

Exchange Values Per Serving
1 Serving = 2 Tomatoes
1 Fat
½ Vegetable

78 Calories
(58% from Fat)
5.5 gm Total Fat
1.1 gm Saturated Fat
0 mg Cholesterol
8 mg Sodium
7.5 gm Carbohydrates
3.7 gm Dietary Fiber
1.4 gm Protein
539 mg Potassium

20	cherry tomatoes	6 drops hot sauce
2	medium avocados, peeled	1 tablespoon fat-free sour cream
1	tablespoon lemon juice	¼ teaspoon salt substitute
1	tablespoon minced onion	

Slice tops off cherry tomatoes. Working carefully, use a small spoon to remove pulp and seeds. Turn tomatoes over on paper towels and drain for 20 minutes. Mash avocados in a mixing bowl. You should have about 1 cup of purée. Mix in remaining ingredients. Fill tomatoes with mixture.

Stuffed Tomatoes

12 Servings

24 cherry tomatoes
¼ cup fat-free cottage cheese
½ medium cucumber, shredded and
    drained
½ cup tuna in water, drained
2 tablespoons finely chopped kosher
    dill pickles
    Dash of pepper

Using a small spoon, remove the inside of the cherry tomatoes and reserve in a bowl. Add the cottage cheese, cucumber, tuna, pickles, and pepper to the bowl. Mix and stuff the reserved cherry tomatoes.

Exchange Values Per Serving
  1 Serving = 2 Tomatoes
  ½ Meat
  ½ Vegetable

23 Calories
  (8% from Fat)
  0.2 gm Total Fat
  0 gm Saturated Fat
  3 mg Cholesterol
  71 mg Sodium
  2.2 gm Carbohydrates
  0.6 gm Dietary Fiber
  3.4 gm Protein
  121 mg Potassium

Stuffed Dill Mushrooms

18 Servings

24 large mushrooms
3 green onions
3 tablespoons low-fat margarine
⅛ teaspoon white pepper
¾ ounce grated Parmesan cheese
2 tablespoons fresh, chopped dill
    weed
6 ounces fat-free cottage cheese
    Nonstick cooking spray

Remove and reserve the stems from 18 of the mushrooms. Cut the remaining mushrooms in quarters and place in a food processor (with a metal blade). Process for 25 quick pulses. Set aside. Finely chop the onions, and set aside.

In a large skillet sauté the chopped mushrooms in melted margarine until done, about 4 minutes. Add the onions and cook for 30 seconds to wilt. Season with pepper and reserve.

Place the Parmesan cheese and dill in a food processor (with a metal blade). Process until fine. Add the cottage cheese and process until smooth. Add the mushroom and green onion mixture and pulse 5 times. Cover and chill until firm, about 30 minutes.

Preheat oven to 400°. Fill each mushroom cap with the mushroom and cheese mixture and place on a sprayed baking sheet. Bake for about 4 minutes, until slightly bubbly, then reduce the temperature to 300° and bake for 4 to 5 minutes more. The mushrooms should be firm. Serve immediately.

Exchange Values Per Serving
  1 Serving = 1
  Mushroom
  ¼ Fat
  ¼ Meat
  ⅛ Vegetable

31 Calories
  (40% from Fat)
  1.5 gm Total Fat
  0.4 gm Saturated Fat
  1 mg Cholesterol
  65 mg Sodium
  2.4 gm Carbohydrates
  0.5 gm Dietary Fiber
  2.5 gm Protein
  159 mg Potassium

Stuffed Mushroom Caps

12 Servings

Exchange Values Per Serving
1 Serving = 2 Mushrooms
¾ Vegetable

24 Calories
(25% from Fat)
0.8 gm Total Fat
0.1 gm Saturated Fat
0 mg Cholesterol
14 mg Sodium
3.5 gm Carbohydrates
0.9 gm Dietary Fiber
1.7 gm Protein
317 mg Potassium

24 large mushrooms, washed and dried
1 tablespoon low-fat margarine
1 green onion, finely sliced
1 ounce fat-free cottage cheese
1 tablespoon chopped fresh parsley
2 teaspoons lemon juice
½ tablespoon salt substitute
1 small tomato, peeled, seeded, and finely chopped
Nonstick cooking spray

Remove and finely chop mushroom stems. Melt margarine over medium heat in a pan and sauté chopped stems and onion until most of the liquid is reduced. Set aside to cool.

Preheat oven to 375°. In a mixing bowl, beat cottage cheese, parsley, lemon juice, and salt substitute until well mixed. Gently stir in the tomato and chopped mushroom mixture. Stuff each mushroom cap with mixture and place on a baking sheet that has been coated with cooking spray. Bake for 10 minutes.

Pasta Bites

12 Servings

Exchange Values Per Serving
1 Serving = 4 Pasta Bites
¼ Meat
1¾ Starch

141 Calories
(6% from Fat)
1.0 gm Total Fat
0.2 gm Saturated Fat
1 mg Cholesterol
67 mg Sodium
26.4 gm Carbohydrates
0.8 gm Dietary Fiber
5.8 gm Protein
34 mg Potassium

48 medium-sized pasta shells, uncooked
½ cup firmly packed fresh spinach
½ cup firmly packed fresh basil
2 tablespoons grated Parmesan cheese
¼ teaspoon white pepper
1 garlic clove, minced
⅓ cup fat-free cream cheese
1 2-ounce jar diced pimiento, drained

Cook pasta according to package directions, omitting salt; let cool.

In a food processor combine spinach, basil, Parmesan, white pepper, and garlic. Process until smooth. Set aside.

Place a small amount of cream cheese in each macaroni shell. Top with spinach mixture and diced pimento.

Holiday Chopped Liver

4 Servings

1 chicken or duck liver	1 small onion, chopped and sautéed
3 tablespoons low-sodium soy sauce	1 tablespoon low-fat margarine
1 teaspoon low-sodium Worcestershire sauce	

Simmer the liver in the soy and Worcestershire sauces in a skillet until pink. Transfer to a food processor with the onion and pulse. Add the margarine and pulse. Chill. This mixture will stiffen as it chills.

Exchange Values Per Serving

1 Serving = 1 Tablespoon
¼ Fat
¼ Meat
¼ Vegetable

41 Calories
(42% from Fat)
1.9 gm Total Fat
0.4 gm Saturated Fat
57 mg Cholesterol
489 mg Sodium
3.1 gm Carbohydrates
0.4 gm Dietary Fiber
2.9 gm Protein
81 mg Potassium

Oriental Beef Kabobs

8 Servings

10 ounces boneless beef sirloin steak	½ teaspoon Oriental roasted sesame oil
2 tablespoons low-sodium hoisin sauce	3 green onions with tops, cut into 2-inch pieces
1 tablespoon dry sherry	
1 teaspoon brown sugar	

Cut the steak into ¼-inch thick strips. Combine the hoisin sauce, sherry, brown sugar, and sesame oil in a bowl. Alternately weave beef strips and green onions on eight 6-inch bamboo skewers.

To microwave, arrange in spokelike fashion on a rack in a microwave-safe baking dish. Brush with the sauce. Cover with waxed paper and microwave at medium or 50 percent power for 3 minutes. Turn the kabobs over and around to bring the inside to the outside. Brush with the remaining sauce and continue cooking, covered, at medium for 2 to 3 minutes.

To grill, place skewers over medium coals on grill. Brush with sauce. Cover and cook until done, 15 to 20 minutes, brushing kabobs with sauce and turning kabobs every five minutes.

Exchange Values Per Serving

1 Serving = 1 Kabob
½ Fat
1 Meat

83 Calories
(51% from Fat)
4.7 gm Total Fat
1.8 gm Saturated Fat
26 mg Cholesterol
169 mg Sodium
1.3 gm Carbohydrates
0.1 gm Dietary Fiber
8.2 gm Protein
121 mg Potassium

Beef Fajitas with Pico de Gallo

4 Servings

Exchange Values Per Serving

1 Serving = 2 Tortillas filled with ⅓ cup Pico de Gallo
1½ Fat
4⅓ Meat
3⅔ Starch
½ Vegetable

539 Calories

(25% from Fat)
14.8 gm Total Fat
3.8 gm Saturated Fat
76.6 mg Cholesterol
632 mg Sodium
59.7 gm Carbohydrate
4.1 gm Dietary Fiber
39.8 gm Protein
618 mg Potassium

1	pound boneless beef top round or top sirloin steak, cut ¾ inch thick
2	tablespoons fresh lime juice
2	teaspoons virgin olive oil
2	large garlic cloves, minced
8	small flour tortillas

1	cup seeded chopped tomato
½	cup diced zucchini
¼	cup chopped fresh cilantro
¼	cup prepared picante sauce or salsa
1	tablespoon fresh lime juice

Place beef or steak in a plastic bag. Add lime juice, olive oil, and garlic turning to coat. Close bag securely and marinate in refrigerator 20 to 30 minutes, turning once. Wrap tortillas securely in heavy duty aluminum foil and set aside.

To prepare Pico de Gallo combine in a mixing bowl tomato, zucchini, cilantro, picante sauce, and lime juice. Mix well.

Remove steak from marinade and place it on a grill over medium, ash-covered coals. Grill steak, uncovered, 8 to 9 minutes (10 to 12 minutes for top sirloin steak) for medium rare to medium doneness, turning occasionally. During last 5 minutes, place tortilla packet on outer edge of grill, turning occasionally. Trim fat from steak; carve crosswise into very thin slices. Serve beef in tortillas with Pico de Gallo.

Herb Meatballs

6 Servings

½ pound extra-lean ground beef
½ cup breadcrumbs
½ cup cooked wild rice
½ cup egg substitute
1 small onion, finely chopped
1 teaspoon low-sodium Worcestershire sauce

½ teaspoon dried thyme
1 tablespoon dried parsley flakes
1 teaspoon pepper
1 can (10¾ ounces) reduced-fat cream of celery soup
1 soup can (10¾ ounces) evaporated fat-free milk

Preheat oven to 350°.

Combine the ground beef, breadcrumbs, wild rice, egg substitute, onion, Worcestershire sauce, thyme, parsley, and pepper in a mixing bowl. Add ¼ cup of the soup to the mixture and form into meatballs. Arrange meatballs on a shallow baking sheet and bake until browned. Combine the remaining soup and evaporated milk in a medium saucepan to make a sauce. Add the meatballs and cook for 15 minutes over medium heat.

Exchange Values Per Serving
1 Serving = 3 Meatballs
½ Fat
1¾ Meat
½ Milk
1 Starch

240 Calories
(31% from Fat)
8.1 gm Total Fat
3.0 gm Saturated Fat
37 mg Cholesterol
593 mg Sodium
21.9 gm Carbohydrates
1.2 gm Dietary Fiber
19.0 gm Protein
451 mg Potassium

Christmas Night Miniature Meatballs

10 Servings

2 tablespoons low-sodium soy sauce
¼ cup water
½ garlic clove, minced

½ teaspoon grated nutmeg
1 pound extra-lean ground turkey
Nonstick cooking spray

Combine the soy sauce, water, minced garlic, and nutmeg in a large bowl and stir. Add the ground turkey and mix lightly but thoroughly.

Preheat the oven to 350°. Form into meatballs 1 inch in diameter. Arrange meatballs in a lightly sprayed baking dish. Bake uncovered for 15 minutes. Place on a heated tray or in a chafing dish and serve with toothpicks.

Exchange Values Per Serving
1 Serving = 2 Meatballs
¼ Fat
1 Meat

61 Calories
(53% from Fat)
3.6 gm Total Fat
1.1 gm Saturated Fat
33 mg Cholesterol
151 mg Sodium
0.7 gm Carbohydrates
0.1 gm Dietary Fiber
6.4 gm Protein
77 mg Potassium

Piney Cheese Balls

8 Servings

Exchange Values Per Serving
1 Serving = 1 Tablespoon
3½ Fat
¼ Fruit
¾ Meat

266 Calories
(74% from Fat)
22.3 gm Total Fat
9.0 gm Saturated Fat
43 mg Cholesterol
234 mg Sodium
8.1 gm Carbohydrates
1.3 gm Dietary Fiber
9.6 gm Protein
204 mg Potassium

16 ounces Neufchâtel cheese
1   can (8 ounces) crushed pineapple in pineapple juice, drained
2   tablespoons chopped sweet onion
1   tablespoon low-sodium Worcestershire sauce
1   tablespoon salt-free seasoning
1   cup chopped unsalted walnuts

Mix together all of the ingredients (except the walnuts) in a bowl. Divide and shape into 2 balls. Chill for 30 minutes. Roll cheese balls in the walnuts. This appetizer is best if made a day or two ahead.

Soups

Herbed Tomato Soup

8 Servings

¼ cup low-fat margarine, divided
2 tablespoons virgin olive oil
1 large onion, thinly sliced
4 sprigs fresh thyme, or 1 teaspoon dried
4 large basil leaves, chopped, or 1 teaspoon dried
  Salt-free seasoning, to taste
2 cans (14½ ounces each) low-sodium peeled whole tomatoes with liquid

3 tablespoons tomato paste
⅓ cup all-purpose flour
4 cups low-sodium chicken broth, divided
1 teaspoon sugar
1 cup evaporated fat-free milk
  Croutons for garnish

Exchange Values Per Serving
  1 Serving = 1 Cup
  1¼ Fat
  ¼ Meat
  ¼ Milk
  ¼ Starch
  1½ Vegetable

154 Calories
  (39% from Fat)
  6.6 gm Total Fat
  1.0 gm Saturated Fat
  1.2 mg Cholesterol
  337 mg Sodium
  17.3 gm Carbohydrates
  1.9 gm Dietary Fiber
  5.6 gm Protein
  205 mg Potassium

Melt ¼ cup of margarine in a large saucepan over medium heat and add olive oil. Add onion, thyme, basil, salt-free seasoning. Cook, stirring occasionally, until the onion is wilted. Add tomatoes and tomato paste and stir to blend. Simmer 10 minutes.

Place flour in a small mixing bowl, and add 5 tablespoons of broth, stirring to blend. Combine flour mixture with tomato mixture. Add remaining broth and simmer 30 minutes, stirring frequently to prevent scorching. Purée soup in food processor; return to heat and add sugar and evaporated milk. Simmer, stirring occasionally, 5 minutes. Serve hot or cold; garnish with croutons.

Roasted Red Pepper Soup

6 Servings

3   large red bell peppers, peeled,
    seeded, and roasted
2   cans (14½ ounces each) low-
    sodium stewed tomatoes, drained

2   garlic cloves, minced
3   tablespoons virgin olive oil
3   cups low-sodium chicken broth
    Pepper to taste

Purée peppers and tomatoes in a food processor. Gently heat garlic in olive oil—do not brown. Stir in pepper purée and chicken broth and bring to a boil. Season with pepper. Serve hot or cold.

This is a bright red soup that looks pretty when served in white bowls.

Exchange Values Per Serving
1 Serving = 1 Cup
1¼ Fat
¼ Meat
2 Vegetable

105 Calories
(57% from Fat)
6.9 gm Total Fat
0.9 gm Saturated Fat
0 mg Cholesterol
198 mg Sodium
9.1 gm Carbohydrates
2.1 gm Dietary Fiber
2.5 gm Protein
159 mg Potassium

Spinach Florentine Soup

6 Servings

½   pound ground turkey
½   cup chopped onion
2   cans (14½ ounces each) low-
    sodium chicken broth
3½ cups water
1½ cups uncooked fine noodles

1   package (10 ounces) frozen
    chopped spinach
½   cup shredded, low-fat Cheddar
    cheese
1   tablespoon low-sodium soy sauce

In large saucepan brown turkey and cook onion until tender, stirring to separate meat. Pour off and discard any excess fat. Add remaining ingredients. Bring to a boil and reduce heat. Simmer for 10 minutes or until noodles are tender, stirring occasionally.

Exchange Values Per Serving
1 Serving = 1 Cup
¼ Fat
1¾ Meat
½ Starch
½ Vegetable

149 Calories
(32% from Fat)
5.1 gm Total Fat
1.5 gm Saturated Fat
41.2 mg Cholesterol
262 mg Sodium
9.5 gm Carbohydrates
1.5 gm Dietary Fiber
15.1 gm Protein
155 mg Potassium

Quick French Onion Soup

6 Servings

4   cans (14½ ounces each) low-sodium beef broth
5   cups water
½   cup low-sodium tomato juice

2   cups fresh onion rings
6   small unsalted melba toast rounds
    Grated Parmesan cheese

In a large saucepan bring the beef broth to a boil and reduce heat. Add the tomato juice and onions. Cover and simmer gently for 25 to 30 minutes. Serve in warmed bowls. Top each with a melba toast round. Sprinkle Parmesan cheese over soup.

Exchange Values Per Serving
1 Serving = 1 Cup
1 Meat
¼ Starch
1 Vegetable

93 Calories
(17% from Fat)
1.2 gm Total Fat
1.0 gm Saturated Fat
3.9 mg Cholesterol
317 mg Sodium
9.5 gm Carbohydrates
1.4 gm Dietary Fiber
10.1 gm Protein
405 mg Potassium

Cucumber Avocado Bisque

6 Servings

1   medium cucumber, peeled and seeded
½   medium avocado, peeled and pitted
3   green onions, chopped
1   cup low-sodium chicken broth

1   cup fat-free sour cream
2   tablespoons fresh lemon juice
    Paprika or chopped fresh parsley for garnish

Blend all ingredients (except garnish) in food processor for 10 to 15 seconds. Cover and chill. Serve in chilled mugs or soup bowls; garnish with paprika or chopped fresh parsley.

Exchange Values Per Serving
1 Serving = ½ Cup
½ Fat
½ Milk
¼ Starch
¼ Vegetable

83 Calories
(28% from Fat)
2.6 gm Total Fat
0.4 gm Saturated Fat
0 mg Cholesterol
47 mg Sodium
11.1 gm Carbohydrates
1.2 gm Dietary Fiber
3.8 gm Protein
277 mg Potassium

Creamy Cucumber Soup

4 Servings

Exchange Values Per Serving
1 Serving = 1 Cup
⅓ Meat
¼ Milk
½ Starch
1 Vegetable

90 Calories
(4% from Fat)
0.4 gm Total Fat
0.1 gm Saturated Fat
1.0 mg Cholesterol
79 mg Sodium
15.5 gm Carbohydrates
1.7 gm Dietary Fiber
6.3 gm Protein
529 mg Potassium

2   medium cucumbers, peeled and sliced (about 3 cups)
1   cup water
¼   cup onion slices
¼   teaspoon salt substitute
⅛   teaspoon pepper
¼   cup all-purpose flour
2   cups low-sodium chicken broth
¼   teaspoon ground cloves
¼   teaspoon paprika
1   cup fat-free plain yogurt
1   tablespoon finely chopped dill weed

Combine the cucumber slices with water, onion, salt substitute, and pepper in a 2-quart saucepan. Cook over medium heat until the cucumbers are very soft, approximately 30 minutes. Put through a strainer or blend in a food processor until smooth. Set aside.

Combine the flour with ½ of the chicken broth in the same saucepan. Stir until smooth and gradually add the remaining chicken broth and blend well. Add the cucumber purée, cloves, and paprika. Stir over medium heat until the mixture begins to simmer. Reduce the heat and simmer for an additional 2 minutes. Do not boil. Remove from the heat and refrigerate.

Before serving, stir in the yogurt and dill. Serve very cold in chilled bowls. This soup is very refreshing!

Carrot and Ginger Soup

8 Servings

Exchange Values Per Serving
1 Serving = ¾ Cup
½ Fat
2½ Vegetable

98 Calories
(27% from Fat)
3.0 gm Total Fat
0.5 gm Saturated Fat
0.3 mg Cholesterol
239 mg Sodium
15.7 gm Carbohydrates
3.5 gm Dietary Fiber
2.7 gm Protein
539 mg Potassium

¼   cup low-sodium chicken broth
1   pound peeled, sliced carrots
1   can (14½ ounces) low-sodium peeled whole tomatoes
2   large onions, chopped
1   garlic clove, minced
½   cup orange juice, unsweetened
2   tablespoons chopped parsley
2   teaspoons salt-free seasoning
    Pepper to taste
1   teaspoon ginger
½   cup fat-free milk
¼   cup low-fat margarine

Place the chicken broth, carrots, tomatoes, onions, garlic, orange juice, parsley, salt-free seasoning, pepper, and ginger in a large stockpot. Cover with water and cook until tender. Remove from the pot when tender and purée in a food processor. Return to the pot and add the fat-free milk and margarine. Stir and simmer for approximately 10 more minutes. This can be served in a cleaned out pumpkin and heated in a warm oven for about 5 minutes.

Cream of Carrot Soup

6 Servings

½ cup chopped fresh cilantro or
   parsley, or 2 tablespoons dried
1 pound carrots, finely chopped
2 medium onions, finely chopped
2 ribs celery, finely chopped
3 tablespoons low-fat margarine
1 tablespoon all-purpose flour

4 cups low-sodium chicken broth
¾ cup egg substitute
½ cup evaporated fat-free milk
¼ teaspoon freshly ground black
   pepper
Fresh cilantro or parsley for
garnish

Sauté cilantro and vegetables in margarine in a pan until tender, about 10 to 15 minutes. Add flour and blend. Stir in chicken broth, cover, and cook over medium heat until carrots are soft, about 15 to 20 minutes. Strain cooked vegetables and return broth to pan. In food processor purée vegetable mixture, 2 cups at a time, until smooth. Add purée to broth, stirring until smooth. Process egg substitute and evaporated milk until blended. With processor running, gradually add 1 cup of hot soup. Stir egg yolk mixture gradually into remaining soup. Stir in pepper and simmer until slightly thickened and hot; do not boil. Just before serving, sprinkle with chopped cilantro or parsley.

Exchange Values Per Serving
1 Serving = ¾ Cup
½ Fat
¾ Meat
¼ Milk
2 Vegetable

133 Calories
(28% from Fat)
4.2 gm Total Fat
0.8 gm Saturated Fat
1.1 mg Cholesterol
201 mg Sodium
16.0 gm Carbohydrates
3.5 gm Dietary Fiber
8.4 gm Protein
557 mg Potassium

Cream of Broccoli Soup

6 Servings

2 tablespoons low-sodium chicken
   broth
2 tablespoons all-purpose flour
½ teaspoon salt substitute
   Pepper to taste

1½ cups low-sodium chicken broth
2 cups fat-free milk
¼ cup nonfat dry milk
10 broccoli spears, cooked

In a saucepan, place 2 tablespoons of chicken broth and slowly add flour stirring with a whisk. Warm over medium heat. Add salt substitute and pepper and blend. Gradually add the 1½ cups chicken broth, stirring over medium heat until the mixture thickens. Add the milk and stir until smooth.

Place the nonfat dry milk and 5 broccoli spears into a blender, blend until smooth, and then add to the cooked mixture. Chop the remaining broccoli and add to the soup. Simmer for 5 minutes and serve.

Exchange Values Per Serving
1 Serving = ¾ Cup
½ Milk
½ Vegetable

62 Calories
(3% from Fat)
0.2 gm Total Fat
0.1 gm Saturated Fat
2.0 mg Cholesterol
82 mg Sodium
9.1 gm Carbohydrates
0.9 gm Dietary Fiber
5.4 gm Protein
370 mg Potassium

Mushroom Soup

10 Servings

Exchange Values Per Serving
1 Serving = 6 Ounces
2 Fat
½ Meat
½ Milk
1½ Vegetable

222 Calories
(39% from Fat)
9.9 gm Total Fat
1.2 gm Saturated Fat
2.0 mg Cholesterol
234 mg Sodium
21.3 gm Carbohydrates
3.5 gm Dietary Fiber
13.6 gm Protein
803 mg Potassium

4 medium onions, minced
2 garlic cloves, minced
¼ cup low-fat margarine
2 pounds fresh mushrooms, coarsely chopped
2 cups evaporated fat-free milk
2 tablespoons nonfat dry milk

2 cups low-sodium beef broth
1 tablespoon low-sodium Worcestershire sauce
1 cup grated Parmesan cheese
1 cup sliced almonds, toasted
Chopped fresh parsley

Sauté onion and garlic in margarine in a Dutch oven over medium heat until onion is tender. Add mushrooms, and cook over low heat 10 minutes, or until tender. Mix evaporated and dry milk, making sure powder is dissolved. Add milk and broth gradually. Add Worcestershire sauce. Continue to cook until thoroughly heated. Do not boil. Sprinkle servings with cheese, almonds, and parsley.

Creamy Squash Soup

6 Servings

Exchange Values Per Serving
1 Serving = 1 Cup
¼ Fat
¼ Meat
½ Starch
1 Vegetable

66 Calories
(16% from Fat)
1.2 gm Total Fat
0.3 gm Saturated Fat
0.3 mg Cholesterol
71 mg Sodium
11.7 gm Carbohydrates
2.4 gm Dietary Fiber
3.2 gm Protein
383 mg Potassium

1 tablespoon low-fat margarine
3 cups diced butternut squash
2 cups thinly sliced carrots
¾ cup chopped onion
2 cans (14½ ounces each) low-sodium chicken broth

¼ teaspoon ground white pepper
¼ teaspoon grated nutmeg
¼ teaspoon cinnamon
¼ cup fat-free milk
1 tablespoon nonfat dry milk

Melt margarine in a large saucepan over medium heat. Add squash, carrots and onion. Cover and cook for 8 minutes. Stir occasionally. Add broth and bring to a boil. Reduce heat and cover; simmer 25 minutes or until the vegetables are very tender.

Purée mixture in batches in a food processor or blender. Return to the saucepan. Add pepper, nutmeg and cinnamon. Bring to a simmer. Mix in both milks until well blended. Add to squash mixture and stir just to blend slightly.

Satellite Beach Salad (page 130)

Black Jack Muffins (page 151)

FACING PAGE: *Baked Potato Bread (page 138), Cheesy Broccoli/Cauliflower Bread (page 138), Whole Wheat Carrot Bread (page 139), Zucchini Bread (page 141), Pepper Sweet Corn Bread (page 159)*

Stir-Fry Beef and Spinach with Noodles (page 166)

Savory Zucchini Soup

8 Servings

1¼	teaspoons Italian seasoning	1½	cups low-sodium chicken broth
1½	cups chopped onions	2½	cups fat-free milk
1½	cups chopped celery	¼	teaspoon white pepper
1½	tablespoons low-fat margarine	2	chicken bouillon cubes
1½	cups grated unpeeled zucchini		

Sauté the seasonings, onions, and celery in margarine in a skillet until transparent. Add the zucchini and chicken broth. Simmer for 10 minutes.

Just before serving, add the fat-free milk, pepper, and bouillon cubes. Heat to serving temperature, but do not boil.

Exchange Values Per Serving
1 Serving = ¾ Cup
¼ Fat
¼ Milk
½ Vegetable

60 Calories
(20% from Fat)
1.3 gm Total Fat
0.3 gm Saturated Fat
1.4 mg Cholesterol
98 mg Sodium
8.4 gm Carbohydrates
1.3 gm Dietary Fiber
3.8 gm Protein
304 mg Potassium

Cauliflower Soup

6 Servings

2	tablespoons chopped onion	½	head cauliflower, cooked and puréed
4	tablespoons low-fat margarine	½	package turkey sausage, cooked, drained, and crumbled
½	cup evaporated fat-free milk		
¼	cup egg substitute		
2	tablespoons low-fat Cheddar cheese		

Sauté onion in margarine in a skillet. Add evaporated milk and heat gently; do not boil. Whip egg substitute into the milk mixture. Stir in cheese and cauliflower purée. Continue stirring to blend flavors. This soup is excellent with sausage.

Exchange Values Per Serving
1 Serving = ¾ Cup
1¾ Fat
1¼ Meat
¼ Milk
½ Vegetable

169 Calories
(62% from Fat)
11.0 gm Total Fat
2.9 gm Saturated Fat
31.5 mg Cholesterol
352 mg Sodium
5.0 gm Carbohydrates
1.2 gm Dietary Fiber
11.1 gm Protein
179 mg Potassium

Hearty Potato Soup

8 Servings

Exchange Values Per Serving
1 Serving = ¾ Cup
¼ Fat
¼ Milk
1 Starch
¾ Vegetable

110 Calories
(8% from Fat)
1.0 gm Total Fat
0.3 gm Saturated Fat
1.4 mg Cholesterol
104 mg Sodium
21.1 gm Carbohydrates
2.3 gm Dietary Fiber
4.8 gm Protein
635 mg Potassium

1 medium onion, chopped	¼ cup diced celery
⅓ cup chopped green bell pepper	4 small potatoes, pared and diced
1 garlic clove, minced	Pinch of grated nutmeg
1 tablespoon low-fat margarine	1½ teaspoons curry powder
½ cup low-sodium chicken broth	2½ cups fat-free milk
2 carrots, diced	Pinch of salt and pepper

Sauté the onion, green pepper, and garlic in margarine in a saucepan for 3 to 4 minutes. Add the remaining ingredients and stir. Add salt and pepper to taste. Simmer for 35 to 45 minutes or until the potatoes are tender. Pour into a blender and purée. Pour back into the saucepan and warm thoroughly.

Potato and Leek Soup

6 Servings

Exchange Values Per Serving
1 Serving = ¾ Cup
½ Fat
¼ Meat
¼ Milk
1½ Starch
2¼ Vegetable

202 Calories
(14% from Fat)
3.3 gm Total Fat
0.6 gm Saturated Fat
0.7 mg Cholesterol
125 mg Sodium
37.8 gm Carbohydrates
3.8 gm Dietary Fiber
6.8 gm Protein
921 mg Potassium

4 leeks	5 medium potatoes, peeled and thinly sliced
1 medium onion	1 cup fat-free milk
1 bunch green onions	Fresh chives
3 tablespoons low-fat margarine	
4 cups low-sodium chicken broth	

Chop the leeks, onion, and green onions, and sauté in the margarine in a skillet until slightly brown. Add the chicken broth and potatoes, and cook until soft. Purée in a blender. Add the fat-free milk and reheat, but do not boil. Serve with chopped fresh chives as a garnish.

Fall Harvest Chowder

8 Servings

1 large potato, peeled and cubed	1 tablespoon low-fat margarine
3 tablespoons low-fat margarine	½ cup broccoli florets
¼ cup all-purpose flour	½ cup cauliflower florets
4 cups low-sodium chicken broth	2 cups fat-free milk
1 large onion, minced	1 garlic clove, minced
2 ribs celery, minced	Pepper to taste
1 large carrot, finely chopped	

Place the potato in cold water and bring to a boil. Cool and reserve. Melt the margarine in a saucepan over medium heat, and add the flour slowly to make a roux.

Bring the chicken broth to a boil in a stockpot and thicken with the roux. Bring back to a boil, and reduce the heat to a simmer.

Sauté the onion, celery, and carrots in remaining margarine in a pan for 10 minutes, stirring constantly. Add the vegetables for the last 5 minutes of cooking. Strain the chicken broth into this mixture and add the potato cubes. Bring to a boil and simmer until the vegetables are done. Add the fat-free milk and seasonings, and gently return to just boiling. Serve at once.

Exchange Values Per Serving
1 Serving = ¾ Cup
½ Fat
¼ Meat
¼ Milk
½ Starch
½ Vegetable

107 Calories
(25% from Fat)
3.1 gm Total Fat
0.6 gm Saturated Fat
1.1 mg Cholesterol
118 mg Sodium
15.4 gm Carbohydrates
1.7 gm Dietary Fiber
4.8 gm Protein
399 mg Potassium

Hearty Vegetable Soup

6 Servings

1 can (14½ ounces) low-sodium beef broth	1 can (8 ounces) diced tomatoes
1 can (14½ ounces) low-sodium vegetable soup	½ cup small macaroni, uncooked
3½ cups water	1 medium onion, sliced
2 cups cabbage, cut in long thin shreds	2 tablespoons grated Parmesan cheese
½ pound fat-free frankfurters, sliced	1 medium garlic clove, minced
	½ teaspoon caraway seed

In a large saucepan combine all ingredients. Bring to boil; reduce heat. Simmer for 30 minutes or until thoroughly heated, stirring occasionally. Kids love this soup!

Exchange Values Per Serving
1 Serving = ¾ Cup
¼ Fat
¾ Meat
1¼ Starch
1 Vegetable

161 Calories
(13% from Fat)
2.4 gm Total Fat
0.7 gm Saturated Fat
12.6 mg Cholesterol
803 mg Sodium
24.9 gm Carbohydrates
2.2 gm Dietary Fiber
10.4 gm Protein
320 mg Potassium

Fall Harvest Soup

6 Servings

Exchange Values Per Serving
1 Serving = 1 Cup
½ Fruit
¼ Meat
¼ Milk
1 Starch

103 Calories
(4% from Fat)
0.6 gm Total Fat
0.2 gm Saturated Fat
0.7 mg Cholesterol
67 mg Sodium
22.1 gm Carbohydrates
3.1 gm Dietary Fiber
5.0 gm Protein
803 mg Potassium

1 2-pound butternut squash, peeled and cubed
4 cups low-sodium chicken broth
2 cooking apples, peeled and quartered

2 tablespoons lemon juice
   Pepper to taste
¼ teaspoon grated nutmeg
   Salt-free seasoning, to taste
1 cup fat-free milk

Cook the squash in a saucepan in chicken broth over medium-low heat until tender, about 10 minutes; do not boil. Add the apples and cook until soft. Purée the squash and apples in a food processor. Add to the broth the squash and apples, and the lemon juice and seasonings to taste. Stir in the milk. Heat thoroughly, but do not boil.

Swiss Cheese Vegetable Bisque

8 Servings

Exchange Values Per Serving
1 Serving = ¾ Cup
½ Fat
1½ Meat
¼ Milk
1 Vegetable

147 Calories
(25% from Fat)
4.2 gm Total Fat
1.4 gm Saturated Fat
11.2 mg Cholesterol
210 mg Sodium
13.1 gm Carbohydrates
2.6 gm Dietary Fiber
14.8 gm Protein
443 mg Potassium

3 tablespoons low-fat margarine
3 tablespoons all-purpose flour
4 cups low-sodium chicken broth
1 pound fresh broccoli, coarsely chopped
2 carrots, chopped
1 rib celery, chopped
1 small onion, chopped

1 garlic clove, minced
¼ teaspoon dried thyme
⅛ teaspoon pepper
1 cup evaporated fat-free milk
¼ cup egg substitute
8 ounces shredded low-fat Swiss cheese

In a large, heavy saucepan melt margarine. Add flour gradually, and cook several minutes, stirring constantly. Remove from heat and gradually blend in broth; bring mixture to a boil while stirring. Add broccoli, carrots, celery, onion, garlic, thyme, and pepper. Cover and simmer until vegetables are tender, about 8 minutes. Blend milk and egg into soup. Sprinkle 1 ounce of cheese on top of each serving.

Vegetable Soup

8 Servings

3½ cups boiling water
4 cups whole, skinless tomatoes
2 chicken bouillon cubes
2 beef bouillon cubes
1 large onion, chopped
2 medium carrots, chopped
2 stalks celery, chopped
2 potatoes, skinned and diced

1 clove garlic, minced
1 teaspoon pepper
1 whole turnip, chopped
1 cup canned green beans
1 cup frozen cauliflower
½ teaspoon rubbed sage
1 tablespoon low-sodium soy sauce

Combine all of the ingredients in a large pot. Bring to a boil, stirring to dissolve the bouillon. Cover and simmer gently for 1½ hours. Stir occasionally.

Exchange Values Per Serving
1 Serving = 1 Cup
½ Starch
2 Vegetable

101 Calories
(1% from Fat)
0.1 gm Total Fat
0 gm Saturated Fat
0 mg Cholesterol
425 mg Sodium
20.4 gm Carbohydrates
3.8 gm Dietary Fiber
3.1 gm Protein
344 mg Potassium

Vegetable and Pasta Soup

8 Servings

1 cup chopped onion
¾ cup sliced carrots
¾ cup sliced celery
1 garlic clove, minced
6½ cups low-sodium vegetable broth
6 cups water
1 can (28 ounces) whole tomatoes in water

1 can (6-ounces) tomato paste
2 teaspoons salt-free seasoning
3 cups chopped green cabbage
1 cup fresh or canned green beans
2 cups cooked tubular vegetable pasta

Place all of the ingredients (except the pasta) in a large stew pot. Bring to a boil and then reduce to a simmer. Simmer for 1 to 1½ hours, or until vegetables are tender. Add the pasta to the soup. Warm throughout and serve.

Exchange Values Per Serving
1 Serving = 1½ Cups
1½ Starch
2½ Vegetable

172 Calories
(2% from Fat)
0.5 gm Total Fat
0.1 gm Saturated Fat
0 mg Cholesterol
334 mg Sodium
35.3 gm Carbohydrates
4.5 gm Dietary Fiber
6.3 gm Protein
717 mg Potassium

Cold Weather Soup

6 Servings

6 cups water	2 medium ribs celery, chopped
4 cans (14½ ounces each) low-sodium chicken broth	1 medium onion, chopped
2 medium carrots, pared and diced	1 small white turnip, chopped
1 large potato, pared and diced	⅛ teaspoon grated nutmeg
1 cup cabbage, shredded	⅛ teaspoon pepper
	¼ cup dry white wine

Bring the water and broth to a boil in a 3-quart stockpot. Add the carrots, potato, cabbage, celery, onion, turnip, nutmeg, and pepper. Bring to a boil, lower the temperature to simmer, and add the wine. Simmer, until the vegetables are tender, about 25 minutes.

Mexican Corn Soup

8 Servings

4 cups frozen corn kernels	½ teaspoon cinnamon
1 cup low-sodium chicken broth	3 tablespoons chopped mild green chilies
¼ cup low-fat margarine	
2½ cups evaporated fat-free milk	4 ounces low-fat Monterey Jack cheese, cubed
1 garlic clove, minced	
1 teaspoon dried oregano	2 medium tomatoes, diced
Pepper to taste	Fresh parsley

In a food processor, blend corn and broth for 15 seconds. Over medium heat, simmer corn mixture in margarine in a pan for 5 minutes, stirring frequently. Blend in milk, garlic, oregano, pepper, and cinnamon, and bring to a boil. Reduce heat, add chilies, and simmer another 5 minutes. Remove soup from heat and stir in cheese until melted. Divide diced tomatoes among serving bowls, pour soup over tomatoes, and garnish with parsley. Serve immediately.

Chinese Rice Soup

6 Servings

3 cans (14½ ounces each) low-sodium chicken broth	1 cup thinly sliced celery
5½ cups water	¼ cup low-sodium soy sauce
2 cups cubed chicken breasts, cooked	½ teaspoon ground ginger
1 package frozen chopped spinach	1 cup quick-cooking rice, uncooked
	½ cup sliced radishes

In a large saucepan, combine all ingredients (except rice and radishes). Bring to a boil. Add rice and radishes, reduce heat, and simmer for 5 minutes, or until thoroughly heated, stirring occasionally. Serve with additional soy sauce.

Exchange Values Per Serving
1 Serving = 1 Cup
2¼ Meat
1 Starch
½ Vegetable

172 Calories
(12% from Fat)
2.3 gm Total Fat
0.6 gm Saturated Fat
39.7 mg Cholesterol
579 mg Sodium
16.6 gm Carbohydrates
2.0 gm Dietary Fiber
19.3 gm Protein
222 mg Potassium

Chicken and Vegetable Soup

10 Servings

4 cans (14½ ounces each) low-sodium chicken broth	1 cup fresh mushrooms, chopped
⅛ teaspoon pepper	1 can (6 ounces) low-sodium tomato juice
2 carrots	1 tablespoon chopped parsley
1 small onion, chopped	¼ teaspoon paprika
2 stalks celery, chopped	2 cups diced chicken breast, cooked

Place chicken broth in a pot and bring to a boil. Add the remaining ingredients (except chicken). Simmer gently for about 30 minutes or until the vegetables are tender. Add the chicken pieces and stir. Simmer another 10 minutes.

Exchange Values Per Serving
1 Serving = ¾ Cup
1½ Meat
½ Vegetable

71 Calories
(17% from Fat)
1.4 gm Total Fat
0.4 gm Saturated Fat
23.8 mg Cholesterol
76 mg Sodium
3.6 gm Carbohydrates
1.0 gm Dietary Fiber
10.6 gm Protein
218 mg Potassium

Gingered Parsnip and Chicken Soup

8 Servings

Exchange Values Per Serving
1 Serving = ¾ Cup
¼ Fat
1 Meat
4 Vegetable

132 Calories
(12% from Fat)
1.9 gm Total Fat
0.4 gm Saturated Fat
14.9 mg Cholesterol
64 mg Sodium
21.4 gm Carbohydrates
4.4 gm Dietary Fiber
8.1 gm Protein
448 mg Potassium

2   medium white onions
1   tablespoon low-fat margarine
8   medium parsnips, peeled and sliced
2   tablespoons grated fresh ginger, or
    1 tablespoon ground

Pepper to taste
4   cups low-sodium chicken broth
1   cup chopped chicken breast, cooked
Chopped parsley

Peel and roughly chop the onion. Sauté the onion in a heavy pan in margarine until translucent. Add the parsnips to the onion and sauté. Add the ginger and pepper. Stir for about 1 minute. Add the chicken broth and breast. Simmer until the parsnips become soft. Drain the mixture, reserving the liquid, and purée parsnips in a food processor. Return the purée to the liquid and simmer for 10 minutes. Adjust the seasonings and serve. Garnish with chopped parsley.

Cream of Chicken and Wild Rice Soup

10 Servings

Exchange Values Per Serving
1 Serving = 1 Cup
1 Meat
½ Milk
¾ Starch
½ Vegetable

131 Calories
(7% from Fat)
1.0 gm Total Fat
0.3 gm Saturated Fat
13.7 mg Cholesterol
161 mg Sodium
18.9 gm Carbohydrates
1.7 gm Dietary Fiber
11.3 gm Protein
344 mg Potassium

½   cup wild rice
1   tablespoon low-sodium soy sauce
1½ cups water
3   large garlic cloves, minced
1   medium onion, chopped
¼   cup low-sodium chicken broth
2   carrots, finely diced
6   stalks fresh asparagus, finely diced
½   cup all-purpose flour

5   cups low-sodium chicken broth
½   teaspoon dried thyme
1   bay leaf
    Minced parsley
    Pepper to taste
1   cup chopped chicken breast, cooked
4   cups fat-free milk

Cook the wild rice with the soy sauce and water in a covered pot. Sauté the garlic and onion in ¼ cup chicken broth in a large saucepan until tender. Add the carrots and asparagus and cook until tender. Mix in the flour and cook over low heat for approximately 10 minutes, stirring frequently. Pour in the chicken broth, using a wire whisk to blend until smooth. Add the seasonings and chicken breast. Slowly add the fat-free milk. Simmer for 20 minutes. Fold in the prepared rice and serve.

Turkey Chowder

10 Servings

½	cup chopped onion	¼	teaspoon ground black pepper
1	cup chopped celery	5	cups low-sodium chicken broth
1	garlic clove, minced	2	potatoes, peeled and cubed
2	tablespoons low-fat margarine	1	cup chopped carrots
2	tablespoons all-purpose flour	3	cups chopped turkey breast,
½	teaspoon salt substitute		cooked

Sauté the onion, celery, and garlic in the margarine in a pan. Add the flour, salt substitute, and pepper. Gradually add the broth, stirring constantly. Add the potatoes and carrots. Cover and simmer for 15 minutes, or until the vegetables are tender. Add the turkey and continue to cook over low heat for 10 minutes. This dish can be served over long grain and brown rice.

Exchange Values Per Serving
1 Serving = 1 Cup
¼ Fat
2 Meat
½ Starch
½ Vegetable

120 Calories
(12% from Fat)
1.5 gm Total Fat
0.3 gm Saturated Fat
34.9 mg Cholesterol
87 mg Sodium
10.7 gm Carbohydrates
1.2 gm Dietary Fiber
14.8 gm Protein
412 mg Potassium

Beef and Barley Soup

10 Servings

2	pounds round steak, cubed	1	cup chopped celery
	Nonstick cooking spray	⅔	cup barley
8	cups water		Parsley
3	low-sodium beef bouillon cubes	⅛	teaspoon pepper
2	cans (14½ ounces each) low-sodium peeled whole tomatoes	1	teaspoon dried basil
1	large onion, chopped	½	teaspoon low-sodium Worcestershire sauce
1	garlic clove, minced	½	teaspoon low-sodium soy sauce
1	cup chopped carrots		

Brown the round steak in a skillet coated with cooking spray. Stir in the water, bouillon cubes, undrained tomatoes, onion, and garlic. Simmer for 2 hours. Add the carrots, celery, barley, and seasonings. Continue to simmer for 30 more minutes or until vegetables are tender.

Exchange Values Per Serving
1 Serving = 1 Cup
3 Meat
½ Starch
1 Vegetable

201 Calories
(20% from Fat)
4.2 gm Total Fat
1.6 gm Saturated Fat
39.9 mg Cholesterol
270 mg Sodium
15.3 gm Carbohydrates
3.7 gm Dietary Fiber
23.1 gm Protein
523 mg Potassium

Spicy-Tangy Beef Soup

4 Servings

Exchange Values Per
Serving
1 Serving = 1 Cup
⅔ Fat
3 Meat
½ Starch
½ Vegetable

196 Calories
(28% from Fat)
6.0 gm Total Fat
2.5 gm Saturated Fat
53.3 mg Cholesterol
375 mg Sodium
11.9 gm Carbohydrate
1.2 gm Dietary Fiber
22.3 gm Protein
471 mg Potassium

1	can (14½ ounces) low-sodium beef or vegetable broth	½	teaspoon crushed red pepper
1½	cups water	1	ounce uncooked angel hair pasta, broken up (approx. ¼ cup)
1	cup chopped mushrooms	2	tablespoons cornstarch dissolved in ¼ cup water
1	cup julienned carrots		
2	tablespoons low-sodium soy sauce, divided	¾	pound beef round tip steaks, cooked
2	tablespoons red wine vinegar	¼	cup sliced green onions

In 3-quart saucepan combine broth, water, mushrooms, carrots, 1 tablespoon soy sauce, vinegar, and red pepper. Bring to a boil; reduce heat and simmer, uncovered, 5 minutes. Add pasta and continue simmering 5 additional minutes. Stir in cornstarch and bring to a boil. Cook and stir 1 minute. Stir beef into soup. Immediately remove from heat. Cover and let stand 5 minutes. Stir in remaining 1 tablespoon soy sauce and green onions. Serve immediately.

Beef Stew Base

8 Servings

Exchange Values Per
Serving
1 Serving = ½ Cup
3½ Meat
1 Vegetable

217 Calories
(42% from Fat)
9.8 gm Total Fat
4.0 gm Saturated Fat
62.7 mg Cholesterol
119 mg Sodium
5.3 gm Carbohydrates
1.4 gm Dietary Fiber
25.3 gm Protein
818 mg Potassium

2	pounds stew beef	1½	teaspoons salt-free seasoning
2	medium onions, sliced	⅛	teaspoon pepper
1	green bell pepper, chopped	1	tablespoon low-sodium Worcestershire sauce
¾	cup puréed whole tomatoes		Vegetable of choice
¾	cup water		

Preheat the oven to 350°. Place the beef, onions, and green pepper in a baking dish. Stir in the tomatoes, water, salt-free seasoning, pepper, Worcestershire sauce, and any vegetables desired for a baked beef stew. Bake for 1 hour or until the vegetables are tender. This stew can be served over rice as an entrée.

Family Beef Stew

8 Servings

1¼	pounds top round steak, cubed	1	teaspoon low-sodium soy sauce
1	tablespoon virgin olive oil	2	cups pared, cubed potatoes
¼	cup all-purpose flour	1	cup diced onions
⅛	teaspoon pepper	1	cup diced carrots
1	garlic clove, minced	1	teaspoon Italian seasoning
3	cups low-sodium vegetable broth		
1	teaspoon low-sodium Worcestershire sauce		

Brown the outside of the round steak cubes in oil. Drain on a paper towel. Combine the remaining ingredients in a large pot and bring to a boil. Lower the temperature to a simmer and cook for 1 hour. Add the meat and pan drippings to the pot and simmer for 30 more minutes. The stew is done when the vegetables are tender.

Exchange Values Per Serving
1 Serving = ¾ Cup
¼ Fat
2¼ Meat
1 Starch
½ Vegetable

201 Calories
(22% from Fat)
4.8 gm Total Fat
1.4 gm Saturated Fat
31.2 mg Cholesterol
109 mg Sodium
20.0 gm Carbohydrates
1.9 gm Dietary Fiber
18.3 gm Protein
722 mg Potassium

Lentil and Beef Soup

16 Servings

2	pounds lean pot roast	2	pounds lentils
⅓	cup low-sodium soy sauce	4	quarts water
2	carrots, diced	½	cup low-sodium chicken broth
4	ribs celery, diced		Pepper to taste
2	large Vidalia onions, chopped	2	tablespoons chopped parsley leaves
1	garlic clove, minced	1	can (28 ounces) whole tomatoes
⅓	virgin olive oil		

Chop the pot roast into 1-inch cubes. Place in a bowl and marinate in soy sauce overnight in the refrigerator.

Sauté the carrots, celery, onion, garlic, and meat in the olive oil in a soup kettle. Add the lentils, water, chicken broth, and seasonings, and simmer for 1½ to 2 hours. Purée the whole tomatoes in a food processor and add to the soup mixture. Serve hot.

Exchange Values Per Serving
1 Serving = ¾ Cup
2 Fat
3 Meat
2¼ Starch
1 Vegetable

394 Calories
(33% from Fat)
14.7 gm Total Fat
4.6 gm Saturated Fat
37.9 mg Cholesterol
366 mg Sodium
38.5 gm Carbohydrates
18.8 gm Dietary Fiber
27.9 gm Protein
802 mg Potassium

Italian Meatball Soup

4 Servings

Exchange Values Per Serving
1 Serving = 1 Cup
¼ Fat
2¼ Meat
1¼ Starch
1½ Vegetable

271 Calories
(29% from Fat)
8.6 gm Total Fat
2.7 gm Saturated Fat
52.9 mg Cholesterol
784 mg Sodium
26.6 gm Carbohydrates
2.5 gm Dietary Fiber
20.9 gm Protein
282 mg Potassium

2	cans (14½ ounces each) low-sodium chicken-with-rice soup	
2¾	cups water	
⅓	cup chopped onion	
¼	cup chopped carrot	
¼	cup chopped celery	
1	large garlic clove, minced	
2	tablespoons chopped parsley	
½	pound lean ground turkey	

3   tablespoons Parmesan cheese
2   tablespoons breadcrumbs
¼   cup egg substitute
⅛   teaspoon pepper
1   tablespoon all-purpose flour
1   can (14½ ounces) low-sodium peeled whole tomatoes, drained and chopped

In a large saucepan, combine soup, water, onion, carrot, celery, garlic, and parsley. Bring to a boil and reduce heat. Simmer for 10 minutes, stirring occasionally.

In a large bowl combine turkey, Parmesan cheese, breadcrumbs, egg substitute, and pepper. Shape into 48 small meatballs. Dust meatballs with flour. Add meatballs and tomatoes to simmering soup. Simmer 10 minutes more or until meatballs are cooked.

Family-Style Chili

8 Servings

Exchange Values Per Serving
1 Serving = ¾ Cup
¼ Fat
1½ Meat
½ Starch
1¾ Vegetable

179 Calories
(29% from Fat)
6.2 gm Total Fat
1.8 gm Saturated Fat
48.2 mg Cholesterol
277 mg Sodium
19.2 gm Carbohydrates
6.0 gm Dietary Fiber
14.1 gm Protein
662 mg Potassium

1   cup chopped onion
1   cup diced green bell pepper
1   pound ground turkey breast
½   cup low-sodium chicken broth
2   garlic cloves, minced
3   tablespoons chili powder

1½   teaspoons paprika
3   whole cloves
4   cups skinless low-sodium stewed tomatoes
1   can (15½ ounces) kidney beans

In a saucepan brown the onion, green pepper, and ground turkey in the chicken broth. Add the garlic, seasonings, and tomatoes. Cover and cook over low heat for about 1 hour. Add the kidney beans during the last 15 minutes of cooking time. This can be served in a bowl as soup or over pasta as a main dish.

Fish Soup

4 Servings

1 can (14½ ounces) tomatoes, diced
½ cup dry white wine
¼ cup chopped parsley
1 teaspoon crushed fresh basil leaves
1 can (10¾ ounces) low-sodium chicken broth

Pepper to taste
1 pound whitefish fillets, cut into 2-inch cubes

In a saucepan, simmer tomatoes, wine, parsley, and basil for about 2 minutes. Add remaining ingredients. Bring to a boil, reduce heat, and simmer for 10 minutes, or until fish flakes easily with a fork.

Exchange Values Per Serving
1 Serving = ¾ Cup
¼ Fat
3¼ Meat
1½ Vegetable

225 Calories
(29% from Fat)
6.7 gm Total Fat
1.0 gm Saturated Fat
68.1 mg Cholesterol
504 mg Sodium
8.2 gm Carbohydrates
2.1 gm Dietary Fiber
24.3 gm Protein
406 mg Potassium

Spicy Crab Soup

6 Servings

2 cups water
1 can (10¾ ounces) low-sodium chicken broth
2 cans (16 ounces each) low-sodium tomatoes, chopped and drained
¾ cup chopped celery
¾ cup diced onion
1 teaspoon salt-free seafood seasoning

¼ teaspoon lemon pepper
1 package (10 ounces) frozen chopped broccoli, thawed
1 package (10 ounces) frozen cut green beans, thawed
1 pound crabmeat, cooked, flaked, and cartilage removed

In a 6-quart soup pot combine the water, broth, tomatoes, celery, onion, seafood seasoning, and lemon-pepper. Bring to a boil and simmer for 20 to 30 minutes. Add the broccoli and beans and simmer for 10 minutes. Add the crabmeat and heat through. Serve immediately.

Exchange Values Per Serving
1 Serving = 1 Cup
¼ Fat
2½ Meat
2½ Vegetable

153 Calories
(7% from Fat)
1.2 gm Total Fat
0.2 gm Saturated Fat
57.4 mg Cholesterol
360 mg Sodium
14.3 gm Carbohydrates
4.5 gm Dietary Fiber
20.7 gm Protein
877 mg Potassium

Cajun Shrimp and Oyster Soup

6 Servings

Exchange Values Per Serving

1 Serving = 1½ Cups
1¼ Fat
2¾ Meat
1½ Starch
2 Vegetable

347 Calories

(24% from Fat)
8.9 gm Total Fat
1.4 gm Saturated Fat
158.4 mg Cholesterol
479 mg Sodium
37.4 gm Carbohydrates
5.2 gm Dietary Fiber
26.6 gm Protein
474 mg Potassium

2 quarts water	¾ cup chopped green bell pepper
2 slices lemon	¼ cup chopped parsley
2 dried red hot chilies	½ teaspoon dried thyme
1 large bay leaf	¼ teaspoon cayenne pepper
½ teaspoon dried thyme	¼ teaspoon hot sauce
Shrimp shells (reserved from shrimp)	1 can (14½ ounces) low-sodium peeled whole tomatoes, undrained
Oyster liquid (reserved from oysters)	1 package (10 ounces) frozen cut okra, thawed, or 1 pound fresh okra, stems removed and sliced
* * *	
2 tablespoons canola oil	1 pound medium shrimp, peeled and deveined (shells reserved to make stock)
2 tablespoons low-sodium chicken broth	
¼ cup all-purpose flour	1 pint shucked oysters, drained (liquid reserved to make stock)
1 cup chopped onion	
2 teaspoons minced garlic	2½ cups hot cooked brown rice

To make the stock: combine the water, lemon slices, chilies, bay leaf, thyme, shrimp shells, and oyster liquid in a large stockpot. Bring to a boil and cook at low, uncovered, until the mixture is reduced to 3 or 4 cups, about 30 minutes. Strain and discard the seasonings.

To make the roux: combine the stock, the oil, the broth, and the flour in a large heavy pan or Dutch oven. Cook and stir over medium-high heat until the mixture turns a dark, rich, red-brown color but is not scorched, about 20 to 30 minutes. Stir in the onion and garlic, and cook until soft, stirring constantly. Add the green pepper, parsley, thyme, cayenne pepper, and hot sauce. Stir and cook 5 minutes longer. Gradually whisk in about 2 cups of warm broth and the tomatoes. Return to a boil and simmer for 20 minutes, stirring occasionally. Add the okra and simmer just until the okra is tender, about 10 minutes. Add the shrimp and oysters. Simmer until the edges of the oysters curl and the shrimp is pink and opaque, about 5 to 10 minutes. Do not overcook the seafood. Remove from the heat. Mound the hot rice in soup dishes and ladle the gumbo over the top.

Hot, Hot Gumbo Chicken

6 Servings

⅓   cup all-purpose flour
    Pepper to taste
    Paprika to taste
4   boneless skinless split chicken
    breasts (about 5 ounces each)
3   tablespoons canola oil
1   cup chopped onion
1   cup chopped green bell pepper

2   cans (14½ ounces each) low-
    sodium peeled whole tomatoes
2   pounds frozen okra, or 1 pound
    fresh
8   drops hot sauce
3   cups cooked brown rice
    Chopped green onion and/or
    chopped fresh parsley.

Preheat oven to 350°. Mix the flour with pepper and paprika in a bowl. Dredge the chicken in the flour mixture and brown in hot oil in a large skillet, turning to brown all sides. Remove and place in a baking dish. Bake for 20 to 30 minutes or until juices run clear when chicken is pierced with a fork.

Sauté the onion and green pepper in the oil used for the chicken. Stir until limp but not brown. Add the tomatoes, okra, and hot sauce, and cook until tender. Place the chicken on a bed of rice and cover with the tomato and okra mixture. Garnish with chopped onion and parsley.

Exchange Values Per Serving
1 Serving = 1 Cup
1⅓ Fat
2 Meat
2 Starch
3 Vegetable

382 Calories
(23% from Fat)
9.5 gm Total Fat
1.0 gm Saturated Fat
54.9 mg Cholesterol
377 mg Sodium
43.4 gm Carbohydrates
7.9 gm Dietary Fiber
27.7 gm Protein
445 mg Potassium

Oyster Stew

6 Servings

1   large Vidalia onion, chopped
1   rib celery, chopped
1   small garlic clove, minced
1   tablespoon low-fat margarine

1   pint oysters with liquid
2   cups fat-free milk
⅛   teaspoon cayenne pepper
    Fresh parsley leaves

Sauté the onion, celery, and garlic in the margarine. Add the oysters and liquid to the sautéed vegetables. Add the milk and pepper. Simmer, but do not boil. Garnish with the parsley.

Exchange Values Per Serving
1 Serving = ¾ Cup
½ Fat
1 Meat
¼ Milk
½ Vegetable

108 Calories
(26% from Fat)
3.2 gm Total Fat
0.9 gm Saturated Fat
45.1 mg Cholesterol
237 mg Sodium
10.7 gm Carbohydrates
0.8 gm Dietary Fiber
9.1 gm Protein
345 mg Potassium

Tuna Chowder

4 Servings

1 can (10¾ ounces) low-sodium chicken broth	1 cup chopped carrots
1 can (10¾ ounces) water	1 cup chopped celery
1 cup diced potatoes	½ cup frozen corn
1 pound yellowfin tuna steaks, skinned and cubed	½ teaspoon dried basil
	¼ teaspoon dried thyme
½ cup chopped onion	½ cup fat-free milk
	1 tablespoon chopped fresh parsley

Mix the chicken broth with water. Add the potatoes and simmer for 10 to 15 minutes, until tender. Remove the potatoes from the broth, reserving the liquid. Puree the cooked potatoes with ¼ cup of broth. Add the tuna, vegetables, seasonings, and puréed potatoes to the remaining broth in the saucepan. Simmer for 8 to 10 minutes, until the fish flakes easily. Stir in the milk and heat to serving temperature without boiling. Sprinkle with parsley just before serving.

Clam Chowder

8 Servings

½ cup chopped mushrooms	¼ cup low-fat margarine
1 cup chopped celery	¼ cup all-purpose flour
1 cup chopped onion	1 gallon fat-free milk
¼ cup low-fat margarine	2 cans (6½ ounces each) chopped clams, including juice
1 quart boiling water	
1 cup finely diced carrots	1 tablespoon chopped pimientos
1 cup diced potatoes	¼ cup dry white wine

Sauté the mushrooms, celery, and onion in ¼ cup margarine in a large heavy saucepan. Add the water, carrots, and potatoes. Simmer for 20 minutes, or until the vegetables are tender.

While the vegetables are simmering, make a roux by melting ¼ cup of margarine in a saucepan over medium heat. Stir in the flour and mix well. Add the fat-free milk and stir occasionally, until thickened. Set aside.

When the vegetables are tender, add the clams with their juice, the pimientos, and white wine. Add the white sauce. Cook 10 minutes longer. Serve piping hot.

Tofu Soup

6 Servings

8 ounces fresh tofu	1 can (10¾ ounces) cream of potato soup
½ cup water	
1 tablespoon dried onion	2 cups fat-free milk
½ teaspoon chicken bouillon granules	¾ cup shredded low-fat Swiss cheese
½ teaspoon dried basil	1 teaspoon dried parsley for garnish
1 package (10 ounces) frozen chopped broccoli	

Dry the tofu in cheesecloth or paper towels and cut into ½-inch cubes.

Combine the water, onion, bouillon granules, and basil in a saucepan. Bring to a boil. Stir in the frozen broccoli, and return to a boil. Reduce the heat, cover, and simmer for 5 minutes, or until tender. Do not drain. Stir in the cream of potato soup. Gradually add the milk and heat almost to a boil. Reduce the heat. Add the tofu and cheese, stirring until the cheese is melted. Top each serving with parsley for garnish.

Exchange Values Per Serving
1 Serving = ¾ Cup
½ Fat
1 Meat
½ Milk
1½ Vegetable

159 Calories
(34% from Fat)
5.7 gm Total Fat
2.8 gm Saturated Fat
13.9 mg Cholesterol
54 mg Sodium
13.4 gm Carbohydrates
2.4 gm Dietary Fiber
11.6 gm Protein
270 mg Potassium

Hearty Fruit Soup

8 Servings

1 can (29 ounces) light pear halves, cut into chunks	1½ cups raisins
	3 tablespoons brown sugar substitute
1 can (29 ounces) light sliced peaches	½ teaspoon grated lemon peel
1 cup unsweetened pineapple bits	¼ teaspoon ground allspice
¼ cup water	⅛ teaspoon ground cloves
½ teaspoon cornstarch	¼ teaspoon cinnamon

Drain the pears, peaches, and pineapples, reserving 1½ cups of the mixed juices.

Mix the water with the cornstarch and in a 4-quart saucepan over high heat combine the raisins, cornstarch mixture, brown sugar substitute, lemon peel, allspice, cloves, cinnamon, and reserved fruit juice. Bring to a boil, and reduce the heat. Cover and simmer for 10 minutes. Add the pears, peaches, and pineapple. Serve hot or cold.

Exchange Values Per Serving
1 Serving = ⅓ Cup
2½ Fruit

156 Calories
(1% from Fat)
0.3 gm Total Fat
0.1 gm Saturated Fat
0 mg Cholesterol
9 mg Sodium
40.9 gm Carbohydrates
4.4 gm Dietary Fiber
1.6 gm Protein
384 mg Potassium

Pineapple and Peach Soup

8 Servings

Exchange Values Per Serving
1 Serving = ½ Cup
1¼ Fruit
¼ Milk

133 Calories
(3% from Fat)
0.4 gm Total Fat
0.1 gm Saturated Fat
1.0 mg Cholesterol
46 mg Sodium
25.2 gm Carbohydrates
0.6 gm Dietary Fiber
3.9 gm Protein
425 mg Potassium

1½ pounds peaches	2 cups fat-free plain yogurt
½ fresh pineapple	2 packets artificial sweetener
1 cup unsweetened orange juice	½ cup dry white wine
1 cup unsweetened pineapple juice	Lime slices and mint leaves for
1 tablespoon lemon juice	garnish

Peel and pit the peaches. Purée the peaches and pineapple in a food processor until smooth. Add the juices, yogurt, sweetener, and wine, and blend well. Put the soup through a fine strainer. Serve chilled, garnished with lime slices and mint leaves.

Summer Strawberry and Burgundy Soup

8 Servings

Exchange Values Per Serving
1 Serving = 1 Cup
½ Fat
1 Fruit
¾ Milk
¼ Starch

186 Calories
(4% from Fat)
0.9 gm Total Fat
0.2 gm Saturated Fat
2.1 mg Cholesterol
87 mg Sodium
28.3 gm Carbohydrates
3.2 gm Dietary Fiber
7.7 gm Protein
687 mg Potassium

3 pints strawberries, washed and hulled	2 cups unsweetened orange juice
1 cup water	3 cups fat-free plain yogurt
4 packets artificial sweetener	1 cup fat-free milk
¼ cup all-purpose flour	Sliced strawberries
2 cups Burgundy wine	Mint leaves

Quarter the strawberries and in a saucepan cook over low heat in water for 10 minutes.

In a separate saucepan, over medium-high heat, combine the sugar substitute and flour. Stir in the wine and orange juice. Heat, stirring constantly until the mixture boils, approximately 10 minutes. Remove from the heat immediately and add the strawberries and cool. Purée in a blender or food processor and add the yogurt and fat-free milk. Chill before serving, and garnish with strawberries and mint leaves.

Salads

Orange Wilted-Spinach Salad with Pork

4 Servings

¼ cup water
2 tablespoons orange marmalade
2 tablespoons white wine vinegar
4 teaspoons low-sodium soy sauce
1 teaspoon sesame oil
¼ teaspoon freshly grated ginger, or
 ½ teaspoon ground

1 2-pound pork loin, trimmed
1 small red bell pepper, cut ¼ inch
 thick
8 cups torn spinach, washed
4 individual orange sections
3 tablespoons sesame seed

In a food processor combine the water, orange marmalade, vinegar, soy sauce, sesame oil, and ginger, and process until completely blended. Place pork loin in a sealable plastic bag and pour the sauce over the meat. Refrigerate overnight.

Preheat oven to 325°. Remove pork from the marinade, reserving the mixture, and place the pork in a baking dish. Bake covered for 1 to 1¼ hours or until a meat thermometer in the center registers 160° to 170°. Remove the pork loin, and place the remaining marinade into a nonstick frying pan. Add the red peppers, and cook for 1 minute covered. Then add spinach to the pan and cook for an additional minute or until just wilted.

Serve on 4 individual plates as follows: place greens to cover the bottom of the plate; arrange red pepper on greens, and add a ¼-inch slice of pork loin; top with a section of orange and sprinkle with sesame seed.

Spinach Salad

4 Servings

1   bunch spinach, stemmed and washed
¼   pound bean sprouts
¼   pound scallops, cooked
1   garlic clove, minced
⅛   teaspoon salt-free seasoning
1   tablespoon cider vinegar
⅛   cup sliced fresh mushrooms
⅛   tablespoon diced pimiento
    Dash of pepper

Toss all of the ingredients together in a salad bowl. Cover and chill before serving.

Spinach and Pomegranate Salad

8 Servings

1   pound spinach, stemmed and washed
2   oranges, peeled and sectioned
1   cup pomegranate seeds
2   tablespoons virgin olive oil
2   tablespoons unsweetened orange juice
1   tablespoon white balsamic vinegar
1   tablespoon honey
¼   teaspoon pepper
¼   teaspoon anise seed, crushed

In a large bowl combine spinach, oranges, and pomegranate seeds.

In a cup, whisk together remaining ingredients. Pour over salad and toss to coat. This great flavor combination is well worth the time spent extracting the pomegranate seeds.

Eggplant Salad

8 Servings

1 large eggplant	1 cup tomato purée
3 tablespoons virgin olive oil	½ cup chopped black olives
1 cup chopped onion	½ cup red wine vinegar
1 cup chopped celery	2 tablespoons sugar
1 cup chopped green bell pepper	

Cut the unpeeled eggplant into small cubes.

In a large skillet heat olive oil over moderately high heat. Sauté the eggplant, turning and stirring until nicely browned, about 10 minutes. Add the onion, celery, and green pepper, and cook until crisp-tender. Stir in the tomato purée, olives, vinegar, and sugar. Simmer uncovered for 10 minutes, stirring occasionally. Remove from heat. Cool and refrigerate.

This is great served with crackers, pita bread triangles, and even tortilla squares.

Exchange Values Per Serving
1 Serving = ½ Cup
1⅓ Fat
2 Vegetable

112 Calories
(48% from Fat)
6.4 gm Total Fat
0.9 gm Saturated Fat
0 mg Cholesterol
215 mg Sodium
13.7 gm Carbohydrates
3.3 gm Dietary Fiber
1.7 gm Protein
366 mg Potassium

Marinated Mushroom Salad

6 Servings

3 tablespoons virgin olive oil	8 ounces sliced mushrooms
3 tablespoons red wine vinegar	¼ cup pimiento strips
2 tablespoons chopped parsley	¼ cup sliced green onions
1 tablespoon lemon juice	3 cups alfalfa sprouts
1 teaspoon dried tarragon	3 cups shredded lettuce
⅛ teaspoon pepper	

In a medium bowl stir together oil, vinegar, parsley, lemon juice, tarragon, and pepper. Add mushrooms, pimiento and green onions; toss to coat evenly. Cover and refrigerate for several hours or overnight, stirring occasionally.

In a small bowl toss together sprouts and shredded lettuce. Form into a ring on serving plate. Place mushroom mixture in center of sprout ring. Pour any remaining marinade over mushrooms.

Exchange Values Per Serving
1 Serving = 1 Cup
1⅓ Fat
1 Vegetable

95 Calories
(63% from Fat)
7.3 gm Total Fat
1.0 gm Saturated Fat
0 mg Cholesterol
10.5 mg Sodium
6.0 gm Carbohydrates
2.4 gm Dietary Fiber
3.5 gm Protein
302 mg Potassium

Fresh Broccoli and Cauliflower Salad

8 Servings

Exchange Values Per Serving
1 Serving = 1 Cup
1¾ Fat
2 Vegetable

142 Calories
(56% from Fat)
9.5 gm Total Fat
0.8 gm Saturated Fat
0 mg Cholesterol
323 mg Sodium
12.4 gm Carbohydrates
2.1 gm Dietary Fiber
4.3 gm Protein
685 mg Potassium

1   bunch fresh broccoli, broken in florets
8   ounces fresh mushrooms, sliced
1   bunch fresh cauliflower, broken in florets
4   ounces fresh cherry tomatoes
⅓   cup safflower oil
1   cup fat-free Italian dressing
½   cup red wine vinegar
½   teaspoon dried parsley
½   teaspoon minced garlic
1   small onion, finely chopped
½   teaspoon poppy seed
    Dash of pepper

Mix the fresh vegetables in a large bowl. Spoon onto individual plates. Combine the oil, dressing, vinegar, parsley, garlic, onion, and poppy seed, and pour over fresh vegetables. Top with pepper as desired.

Green Bean Salad

4 Servings

Exchange Values Per Serving
1 Serving = ½ Cup
1⅓ Fat
1⅓ Vegetable

97 Calories
(59% from Fat)
7.0 gm Total Fat
0.5 gm Saturated Fat
0 mg Cholesterol
4 mg Sodium
9.7 gm Carbohydrates
2.2 gm Dietary Fiber
1.5 gm Protein
169 mg Potassium

1   package (10 ounces) frozen cut green beans
2   tablespoons canola oil
¼   cup water
¼   cup white wine vinegar with tarragon
1   teaspoon sugar
    Dash of pepper
⅛   teaspoon paprika
½   teaspoon Dijon mustard
½   teaspoon low-sodium Worcestershire sauce
1   garlic clove, minced (optional)
1   tablespoon finely chopped onion
2   teaspoons finely chopped parsley

Cook the green beans according to the package directions. Drain and set aside.

Combine the remaining ingredients and blend well. Pour the mixture over the green beans and refrigerate for a few hours or until ready to serve. To serve, drain the green beans and arrange on salad plates.

Celery Cole Slaw

4 Servings

3   cups finely shredded cabbage
3   tablespoons virgin olive oil
⅓   cup warm vinegar
1   tablespoon finely chopped onion

1   tablespoon chopped pimiento
2   packets artificial sweetener
½   teaspoon dry mustard
½   teaspoon celery seed

Toss the cabbage, oil, and warm vinegar in a bowl. Add the remaining ingredients and toss again. Cover and refrigerate for 2 hours or until time to serve.

Exchange Values Per Serving
1 Serving = 1 Cup
2 Fat
½ Vegetable

114 Calories
(62% from Fat)
10.7 gm Total Fat
1.5 gm Saturated Fat
0 mg Cholesterol
10 mg Sodium
4.8 gm Carbohydrates
1.6 gm Dietary Fiber
0.8 gm Protein
158 mg Potassium

Tangy Tomato Aspic

6 Servings

2   packages (.3 ounce each) sugar-free lemon gelatin
1½ cups boiling water
2   cups low-sodium tomato juice
1   bay leaf

1   rib celery, sliced
1   small onion, sliced
⅛   teaspoon pepper
¼   cup finely chopped celery

Dissolve the gelatin in boiling water. Heat the tomato juice in a saucepan, and simmer with the bay leaf, celery, onion, and pepper. Strain the tomato juice mixture and combine with the gelatin. Refrigerate until the mixture begins to thicken. Add the finely chopped celery and stir. Chill until firm. Cut into squares.

Exchange Values Per Serving
1 Serving = 1 Cup
1½ Vegetable

34.8 Calories
(3% from Fat)
0.1 gm Total Fat
0 gm Saturated Fat
0 mg Cholesterol
28 mg Sodium
8.2 gm Carbohydrates
1.8 gm Dietary Fiber
1.7 gm Protein
365 mg Potassium

Molded Cucumber Salad

6 Servings

Exchange Values Per
Serving
  1 Serving = ½-Inch Slice
  ⅔ Vegetable

41 Calories
  (4% from Fat)
  0.2 gm Total Fat
  0.1 gm Saturated Fat
  0.7 mg Cholesterol
  36 mg Sodium
  6.2 gm Carbohydrates
  0.9 gm Dietary Fiber
  4.3 gm Protein
  355 mg Potassium

1   package (¼ ounce) sugar-free unflavored gelatin
¼   cup cold water
¼   teaspoon salt substitute
⅛   teaspoon white pepper
¼   teaspoon finely chopped dill weed
2   tablespoons grated onion
2   large cucumbers, chilled
1   cup fat-free plain yogurt

In a saucepan soften the gelatin in the cold water. Heat the water to boiling to dissolve the gelatin. Cool to lukewarm. Add the salt substitute, pepper, dill weed, and onion. Thinly slice the cucumbers and add to the mix. Stir well. Add the yogurt to the mixture and pour into a mold. Refrigerate for 4 hours before serving.

Fresh Corn and Black-Eyed Pea Salad

6 Servings

Exchange Values Per
Serving
  1 Serving = 1 Cup
  2 Fat
  1 Starch
  ⅔ Vegetable

192 Calories
  (47% from Fat)
  10.5 gm Total Fat
  1.5 gm Saturated Fat
  0.5 mg Cholesterol
  40 mg Sodium
  23.0 gm Carbohydrates
  4.5 gm Dietary Fiber
  3.2 gm Protein
  394 mg Potassium

⅓   cup balsamic vinegar
1   tablespoon hot sweet mustard
¼   cup chopped fresh parsley
¼   teaspoon freshly ground black pepper
½   teaspoon Creole seasoning
¼   cup virgin olive oil
1½ cups fresh, frozen, or canned corn kernels
½   pound shelled fresh black-eyed peas, seasoned to taste
1   medium red bell pepper, chopped
1   medium Vidalia or red onion, chopped
3   ribs celery, chopped

Blend vinegar, mustard, parsley, pepper, and Creole seasoning in a bowl. Whisk in oil and set aside.

In a separate bowl combine corn, peas, bell pepper, onion, and celery. Toss vegetables with dressing and refrigerate until ready to serve, but no longer than 12 hours.

Couscous Vegetable and Feta Cheese Salad

8 Servings

1   cup dry couscous
1½ cups low-sodium chicken broth, boiling
3   red bell peppers, roasted, peeled, and diced
1   pound tomatoes, diced
1   cup sugar snap peas, cut in half
½   small cucumber, peeled and diced
2   green onions, finely diced
¼   cup chopped black olives
2   tablespoons dried parsley

1   cup crumbled feta cheese
¼   cup fresh lemon juice
1   teaspoon ground cumin
½   teaspoon chili flakes
    Salt to taste
    Black pepper, freshly cracked, to taste
1   garlic clove, minced
¼   cup virgin olive oil

To prepare the salad: place the couscous in a large saucepan and pour in the boiling broth. Cover and allow the mixture to stand for about 20 minutes, or until cool and all of the broth is absorbed. Gently toss the couscous with a fork. Add the red peppers, tomatoes, sugar snap peas, cucumber, onions, olives, parsley, and feta cheese. Toss gently.

To prepare the dressing: combine the lemon juice, cumin, chili flakes, salt, pepper, and garlic in a mixing bowl. Gradually whisk in the olive oil. Pour the dressing over the salad and toss well.

Exchange Values Per Serving
1 Serving = 1 Cup
2 Fat
½ Meat
1 Starch
1¾ Vegetable

253 Calories
(46% from Fat)
13.1 gm Total Fat
4.0 gm Saturated Fat
17.4 mg Cholesterol
297 mg Sodium
27.3 gm Carbohydrate
3.5 gm Dietary Fiber
7.8 gm Protein
336 mg Potassium

Old-Fashioned Potato Salad

6 Servings

2   cups diced potatoes, cooked
½   cup finely chopped onion
¼   cup finely cut celery
1   dill pickle, finely chopped

½   cup fat-free plain yogurt
1   tablespoon Dijon mustard
¾   teaspoon no-oil herb or Italian seasoning

In a medium bowl combine the potatoes, onion, celery, and pickle. In a small bowl, combine the yogurt, mustard, and seasoning. Add to the vegetables and mix carefully. Cover and refrigerate for several hours to allow the flavors to blend.

Exchange Values Per Serving
1 Serving = ½ Cup
½ Starch
⅓ Vegetable

66 Calories
(5% from Fat)
0.3 gm Total Fat
0.1 gm Saturated Fat
0.4 mg Cholesterol
86 mg Sodium
13.6 gm Carbohydrates
1.3 gm Dietary Fiber
2.6 gm Protein
289 mg Potassium

Skillet Apple Potato Salad

6 Servings

Exchange Values Per Serving
1 Serving = ½ Cup
⅓ Fat
½ Fruit
1 Vegetable

90 Calories
(17% from Fat)
1.9 gm Total Fat
0.5 gm Saturated Fat
8.0 mg Cholesterol
126 mg Sodium
17.5 gm Carbohydrates
2.1 gm Dietary Fiber
2.7 gm Protein
308 mg Potassium

4 medium red potatoes	1 tablespoon sugar
4 slices turkey bacon, diced	¼ teaspoon paprika
¼ cup chopped green onions	¼ teaspoon dry mustard
¼ cup chopped green bell pepper	3 large Golden Delicious apples, cored and coarsely diced
¼ cup water	
½ cup cider vinegar	

Wash the potatoes and cook with the skins on in boiling water just until tender. Drain and coarsely dice.

Sauté the bacon in a large, heavy skillet until crisp. Add the green onions and green pepper and sauté for a few minutes. Drain. Stir in the water, vinegar, sugar, paprika, and mustard. Heat to boiling. Add the potatoes and apples to the skillet and heat through, stirring gently. Serve immediately.

Pasta and Vegetable Salad

4 Servings

Exchange Values Per Serving
1 Serving = 1 Cup
½ Fat
3 Starch
½ Vegetable

252 Calories
(12% from Fat)
3.5 gm Total Fat
0.3 gm Saturated Fat
0 mg Cholesterol
25 mg Sodium
46.3 gm Carbohydrates
2.7 gm Dietary Fiber
9.1 gm Protein
379 mg Potassium

12 ounces medium shell macaroni	2 tablespoons red wine vinegar
1 small zucchini, cut into 1-inch julienne strips	1 tablespoon canola oil
½ cup shredded carrots	1 garlic clove, minced
1 cup steamed broccoli florets	½ teaspoon dried oregano
¼ cup diced pimientos	¼ teaspoon dried basil
2 tablespoons chopped Italian parsley	¼ teaspoon salt substitute
¼ cup fat-free plain yogurt	⅛ teaspoon pepper

Prepare the macaroni according to the package directions, without salt. Drain and combine in a large bowl the macaroni, zucchini, carrots, broccoli, pimientos, and Italian parsley. Combine in a separate bowl the remaining ingredients, and pour over the salad. Cover and chill about 1 hour.

Macaroni Salad

6 Servings

3 cups cooked macaroni, drained
⅓ cup thinly sliced celery
1 cup chopped green onions, cooked
1 cup chopped broccoli, cooked
1 cup chopped cauliflower, cooked

½ cup fat-free plain yogurt
1 tablespoon prepared mustard
¾ teaspoon no-oil herb or Italian seasoning

Combine in a large bowl the macaroni and vegetables. In a separate bowl combine the yogurt, mustard, and seasoning and mix well. Add to the vegetable and macaroni mixture and chill.

Exchange Values Per Serving
1 Serving = 1 Cup
1⅓ Starch
1 Vegetable

138 Calories
(6% from Fat)
0.9 gm Total Fat
0.2 gm Saturated Fat
0.4 mg Cholesterol
200 mg Sodium
26.8 gm Carbohydrates
2.8 gm Dietary Fiber
6.3 gm Protein
202 mg Potassium

Red Pepper and Pasta Salad

14 Servings

1 medium red bell pepper, seeded and cut into fourths
2 cups rotini, uncooked
2 cups fresh spinach, cut into thin strips
1 cup sliced zucchini

½ cup thinly sliced carrots
½ cup fat-free Italian dressing
2 tablespoons chopped fresh parsley
2 tablespoons lemon juice
1 teaspoon grated lemon peel
1 cup fat-free plain yogurt

Place the red pepper quarters on a broiler pan, skin side up. Broil 3 to 4 inches from the heat until the skin blackens, then remove from the broiler. Place in a plastic bag, and let stand for 10 minutes to steam. Peel the skin from the pepper, and cut into ½-inch pieces.

Cook the rotini according to the package directions. Drain and rinse with cold water. Combine all of the ingredients in a large bowl. Cover and refrigerate for several hours or overnight.

Exchange Values Per Serving
1 Serving = 1 Cup
½ Milk
2 Starch
⅔ Vegetable

237 Calories
(4% from Fat)
1.1 gm Total Fat
0.2 gm Saturated Fat
1.1 mg Cholesterol
397 mg Sodium
46.1 gm Carbohydrates
3.4 gm Dietary Fiber
10.9 gm Protein
504 mg Potassium

Layered Turkey and Broccoli Pasta Salad

10 Servings

Exchange Values Per Serving
1 Serving = ½ Cup
1 Fat
2 Meat
1½ Starch
1 Vegetable

270 Calories
(26% from Fat)
7.7 gm Total Fat
1.9 gm Saturated Fat
36.2 mg Cholesterol
98 mg Sodium
29.4 gm Carbohydrates
3.1 gm Dietary Fiber
21.2 gm Protein
658 mg Potassium

12 ounces cooked corkscrew pasta, drained
2   tablespoons virgin olive oil
1   pound fresh spinach, washed, stemmed, and torn into pieces
2   cups cooked turkey breast, cubed
1   bunch broccoli, blanched and broken into pieces
4   medium tomatoes, peeled, seeded, and chopped
    Ricotta Yogurt Dressing (page 260)

In a large bowl mix pasta with olive oil and chill.

In a large serving bowl, using half the total amount of each ingredient, alternate layers. Start with spinach, followed by pasta, turkey, broccoli, tomato, and Ricotta Yogurt Dressing. Repeat sequence using remaining half of each ingredient. Chill thoroughly before serving.

Steak and Roasted Vegetable Salad

4 Servings

Exchange Values Per Serving
1 Serving = 3¾ Cups salad and 3 tablespoons dressing
1½ Fat
3½ Meat
3¾ Vegetable

343 Calories
(28% from Fat)
10.9 gm Total Fat
4.6 gm Saturated Fat
75.7 mg Cholesterol
634 mg Sodium
32.3 gm Carbohydrate
7.7 gm Dietary Fiber
30.6 gm Protein
1,467 mg Potassium

    Nonstick cooking spray
1   medium zucchini, cut diagonally into 1-inch pieces
1   medium Japanese or baby eggplant, cut diagonally into 1-inch pieces
1   large red, yellow, or green bell pepper, cut into 1-inch strips
1   medium onion, cut into 1-inch wedges
16 small mushrooms, chopped
2   tablespoons balsamic vinegar
2   large garlic cloves, minced
1   teaspoon dried rosemary
¼   teaspoon pepper
1   pound boneless beef top loin steaks, cut 1-inch thick, all fat removed
¼   teaspoon salt-free seasoning
8   cups torn mixed salad greens
¾   cup fat-free Italian dressing

Preheat oven to 425°. Lightly coat a 15 x 10-inch jelly roll pan with cooking spray. Place vegetables in pan. Generously spray vegetables with cooking spray. Combine vinegar, garlic, rosemary, and pepper in a small bowl and drizzle over vegetables. Roast in oven for 30 to 35 minutes or until tender, stirring once.

Heat large nonstick skillet over medium heat until hot. Place beef steaks in skillet; cook 12 to 15 minutes for medium rare to medium doneness, turning once. Let stand 10 minutes. Season steaks with salt-free seasoning; carve crosswise into thin slices. To serve, place an equal amount of salad greens on each of four dinner plates. Arrange beef and roasted vegetables over salad greens. Serve immediately with dressing.

Chicken Pasta Salad

8 Servings

½   cup fat-free mayonnaise
3   tablespoons low-sodium soy sauce
2   tablespoons sherry
⅛   teaspoon ground ginger
¼   teaspoon pepper
1   cup cooked spiral pasta, drained
2   cups cooked boneless skinless chicken breasts, cut into bite-sized pieces

2   cups fresh snow peas, strings removed and blanched
2   green onions, sliced
½   cup water chestnuts, sliced
¼   cup toasted almonds, for garnish

In a small bowl combine the mayonnaise, soy sauce, sherry, ground ginger, and pepper. Set aside. In a separate bowl combine pasta, chicken, snow peas, green onions, and water chestnuts and toss with dressing mix. Refrigerate overnight. Sprinkle with toasted almonds before serving.

Exchange Values Per Serving
1 Serving = 1 Cup
½ Fat
1½ Meat
½ Starch
½ Vegetable

132 Calories
(22% from Fat)
3.2 gm Total Fat
0.6 gm Saturated Fat
29.8 mg Cholesterol
335 mg Sodium
11.1 gm Carbohydrates
1.8 gm Dietary Fiber
13.3 gm Protein
179 mg Potassium

Chutney Chicken Salad

8 Servings

    Lemon juice
1   Granny Smith apple, unpeeled and coarsely chopped
1   cup fat-free mayonnaise
½   cup mango chutney
8   boneless skinless split chicken breasts, cooked and cubed

2   ribs celery, coarsely chopped
4   green onions, coarsely chopped
½   cup sliced red seedless grapes
¼   cup chopped pecans, toasted
2   cups cooked brown rice

Sprinkle lemon juice over apple. In a small bowl thoroughly blend mayonnaise and chutney. In a large bowl combine chutney mixture with chicken, celery, onions, apple, grapes, pecans, and rice. Serve chilled.

Exchange Values Per Serving
1 Serving = 1 Cup
1 Fat
½ Fruit
3½ Meat
1 Starch

306 Calories
(23% from Fat)
7.7 gm Total Fat
1.2 gm Saturated Fat
72.3 mg Cholesterol
440 mg Sodium
29.8 gm Carbohydrates
2.5 gm Dietary Fiber
28.3 gm Protein
366 mg Potassium

Smoked Turkey Salad

4 Servings

Exchange Values Per Serving
1 Serving = 1 Cup
1⅔ Meat
2 Vegetable

140 Calories
(10% from Fat)
1.7 gm Total Fat
0.7 gm Saturated Fat
28.3 mg Cholesterol
1,009 mg Sodium
16.0 gm Carbohydrates
2.8 gm Dietary Fiber
17.4 gm Protein
788 mg Potassium

2　medium cucumbers
8　romaine or leaf lettuce leaves
12　ounces smoked turkey breast, julienne cut
2　large tomatoes, thinly sliced

½　cup diagonally-cut celery
½　cup fat-free plain yogurt
1　teaspoon sugar
1　tablespoon crumbled blue cheese

Seed cucumbers, if desired. Cut 1½ of the cucumbers into thin slices. Set aside the remaining cucumber for dressing. Arrange lettuce leaves on individual serving plates. Top with turkey, tomato slices, cucumber slices, and celery.

For dressing, shred enough of the remaining cucumber to make 6 tablespoons. Slice any remaining cucumber and arrange on serving plates. In a small bowl combine the shredded cucumber, yogurt, and sugar. Drizzle each serving with some of the cucumber dressing. Sprinkle with crumbled blue cheese.

Turkey Ham Salad

4 Servings

Exchange Values Per Serving
1 Serving = 1 Cup
1 Fat
1⅔ Meat
1½ Starch
1 Vegetable

251 Calories
(26% from Fat)
7.3 gm Total Fat
1.9 gm Saturated Fat
25.1 mg Cholesterol
684 mg Sodium
29.5 gm Carbohydrates
2.1 gm Dietary Fiber
17.5 gm Protein
509 mg Potassium

4　ounces corkscrew macaroni
⅓　cup red wine vinegar
2　tablespoons water
1　tablespoon virgin olive oil
2　teaspoons sugar
½　teaspoon Dijon mustard
½　teaspoon dried basil
⅛　teaspoon ground pepper

4　ounces turkey ham, cut into ½-inch cubes
¾　cup shredded low-fat Swiss cheese
2　medium tomatoes, seeded and chopped
1　cup sliced fresh mushrooms
　Lettuce leaves

Cook pasta according to package directions. Drain and rinse with cold water; drain again.

In a screw-top jar combine vinegar, water, oil, sugar, mustard, basil, and pepper. Cover and shake well to mix. Pour dressing over pasta; toss gently to coat. Cover and chill several hours.

In a salad bowl, combine the pasta mixture, turkey ham, cheese, tomatoes, and mushrooms. Toss gently to mix.

To serve, place the pasta mixture on lettuce-lined plates.

Potato and Salmon Salad

4 Servings

4 medium red potatoes
½ cup fat-free mayonnaise dressing
½ cup fat-free sour cream
2 tablespoons lemon juice
¼ cup finely chopped kosher dill
    pickles
4 tablespoons finely chopped white
    onion
2 cans (6 ounces each) boneless
    salmon
    Red-tip Bibb lettuce leaves
    Fresh dill for garnish

Preheat the oven to 350°. Wash and scrub potatoes. Wrap each potato in foil and bake for 35 to 45 minutes or until a fork inserts easily into the center. Let potatoes cool; cut potatoes into cubes.

In a large bowl combine mayonnaise, sour cream, lemon juice, pickles, and onion and stir. Crumble salmon and add to bowl. Add potato cubes and toss to combine. Serve on Bibb lettuce leaves. Sprinkle with fresh dill to garnish.

Exchange Values Per Serving
1 Serving = 1 Cup
2 Meat
1⅔ Vegetable

224 Calories
(28% from Fat)
7.0 gm Total Fat
1.8 gm Saturated Fat
56.1 mg Cholesterol
992 mg Sodium
19.5 gm Carbohydrates
1.6 gm Dietary Fiber
20.0 gm Protein
443 mg Potassium

Shrimp-Stuffed Tomato

4 Servings

4   medium tomatoes
2⅔ cups fat-free cottage cheese
¼   cup sliced green onions
¼   cup chopped fresh basil
2   tablespoons chopped fresh parsley
16 medium shrimp, cooked with
     tails on
4   tablespoons shrimp cocktail sauce

With a sharp knife, core the tomatoes. Place the tomatoes cored side down on a cutting board. Make 4 cuts almost through the tomatoes to divide into 8 sections. Open up and place 1 tomato on each plate. It will resemble a star.

In a medium bowl combine cottage cheese, green onions, basil, and parsley. Spoon mix among the tomatoes. Place 4 whole shrimp in a crisscross fashion on top of each tomato, and top with 1 tablespoon of cocktail sauce.

Exchange Values Per Serving
1 Serving = ½ Cup
    Topping
⅛ Fat
3⅓ Meat
⅓ Starch
1⅓ Vegetable

178 Calories
(5% from Fat)
0.9 gm Total Fat
0.1 gm Saturated Fat
62.3 mg Cholesterol
942 mg Sodium
17.6 gm Carbohydrates
1.8 gm Dietary Fiber
24.9 gm Protein
680 mg Potassium

Lemon-Dill Crabmeat Salad On Cucumber

6 Servings

Exchange Values Per Serving

1 Serving = ½ Cup
1 Meat
½ Vegetable

62 Calories

(9% from Fat)
0.6 gm Total Fat
0.1 gm Saturated Fat
26.7 mg Cholesterol
207 mg Sodium
5.3 gm Carbohydrates
0.9 gm Dietary Fiber
8.6 gm Protein
283 mg Potassium

½	pound fresh crabmeat, picked	⅛	teaspoon cayenne pepper
1	green onion, finely chopped	1	10- to 12-inch cucumber, scored
2	tablespoons chopped fresh dill		and sliced in ¼-inch rounds
1	teaspoon grated lemon peel		Paprika
¼	cup fat-free mayonnaise		Dill sprigs for garnish

Combine crabmeat, onion, dill, lemon peel, mayonnaise, and cayenne pepper; chill for 1 hour. Divide the cucumber rounds equally onto 6 plates. Mound crabmeat salad onto cucumber rounds, sprinkle with paprika, and garnish with a sprig of dill.

Satellite Beach Salad

6 Servings

Exchange Values Per Serving

1 Serving = 3 Ounces
    scallops with
    vegetables
2⅓ Meat
1 Starch
1 Vegetable

201 Calories

(6% from Fat)
1.3 gm Total Fat
0.5 gm Saturated Fat
37.4 mg Cholesterol
696 mg Sodium
22.8 gm Carbohydrate
1.7 gm Dietary Fiber
22.6 gm Protein
543 mg Potassium

1½	pounds calico or bay scallops	½	cup chopped water chestnuts
½	teaspoon salt substitute	½	cup finely chopped celery
1	teaspoon paprika	½	cup chopped green onions
1	teaspoon minced garlic	½	cup fat-free Caesar dressing
½	teaspoon white pepper	½	cup quartered artichoke hearts,
2	cups cooked ziti (or other pasta)		drained
1	cup chopped yellow bell pepper	¼	cup chopped red cabbage

Rinse scallops to remove any remaining shell particles. In a large bowl combine salt substitute, paprika, garlic, and pepper and mix well. Spread scallops close together in a single layer on a broiler pan and coat the tops with spice mixture. Broil scallops 4 to 6 inches from heat for 6 to 8 minutes or until they are opaque in the center. Remove from heat and cool in the refrigerator.

Combine pasta, bell pepper, water chestnuts, celery, onions, and dressing and mix well. Add cooled scallops to the pasta mixture. Garnish with the artichoke hearts and red cabbage.

Ybor City Fillets (page 191)

Wakulla Grilled Grouper (page 196)

Santa Rosa Shrimp (page 201)

Rock Shrimp and Oyster Maque Choux (page 203)

Tuna Salad

6 Servings

2 cans (7 ounces each) tuna, packed in water, drained
1 cup fat-free plain yogurt
2 kosher pickle spears, finely diced
½ cup finely cut celery

Pinch of garlic salt
Pinch of paprika
1 tablespoon Dijon mustard
Crisp lettuce

Combine all of the ingredients except the lettuce in a bowl. Mix well. Chill for 2 hours.

With an ice cream scoop, serve tuna salad on a lettuce leaf.

Exchange Values Per Serving
1 Serving = ½ Cup
2 Meat

106 Calories
(8% from Fat)
0.9 gm Total Fat
0.2 gm Saturated Fat
20.6 mg Cholesterol
431 mg Sodium
4.0 gm Carbohydrates
0.3 gm Dietary Fiber
19.8 gm Protein
307 mg Potassium

Fluffy Orange Yogurt Salad

8 Servings

1 can (20 ounces) pineapple chunks in pineapple juice, drained
1 can (15 ounces) mandarin orange segments, drained
1 cup nondairy fat-free whipped topping

½ cup fat-free orange or pineapple yogurt
2 bananas, sliced
8 Mint leaves for garnish

In a medium bowl combine pineapple and orange pieces. Mix the whipped topping and yogurt in a blender until fluffy. Gently toss the topping with the pineapple and orange pieces. Cover and place in the refrigerator for 2 hours or more. Just before serving gently add the bananas. Spoon into tall wine glasses and top with a mint leaf.

Exchange Values Per Serving
1 Serving = 1 Cup
2 Fruit

252 Calories
(12% from Fat)
3.5 gm Total Fat
0.3 gm Saturated Fat
0 mg Cholesterol
25 mg Sodium
46.3 gm Carbohydrates
2.7 gm Dietary Fiber
9.1 gm Protein
379 mg Potassium

Apple-Orange Cider Salad

8 Servings

Exchange Values Per Serving
1 Serving = 1 Cup
1 Fruit

82 Calories
(2% from Fat)
0.2 gm Total Fat
0 gm Saturated Fat
0 mg Cholesterol
67 mg Sodium
20.7 gm Carbohydrates
1.4 gm Dietary Fiber
1.6 gm Protein
218 mg Potassium

2 packages (.3 ounce each) sugar-free orange gelatin
4 cups apple cider
1 cup raisins
1 cup coarsely chopped apple
1 cup chopped celery
   Juice and grated peel of 1 lemon

In a saucepan heat 2 cups of cider over medium heat, and add the gelatin until dissolved. Stir in the raisins and allow the mixture to cool. Add the remaining cider. Chill until slightly thickened. Add the remaining ingredients and chill until set.

Traditional Holiday Cranberry Salad

16 Servings

Exchange Values Per Serving
1 Serving = ½-Inch Slice
½ Fat
⅓ Fruit

53 Calories
(35% from Fat)
2.3 gm Total Fat
0.2 gm Saturated Fat
0 mg Cholesterol
54 mg Sodium
7.0 gm Carbohydrates
1.5 gm Dietary Fiber
2.4 gm Protein
131 mg Potassium

3 packages (.3 ounce each) sugar-free cherry gelatin
2 cups boiling water
1 can (15¼ ounces) crushed pineapple in pineapple juice
2 tablespoons lemon juice
2 cups ground fresh cranberries
2 small oranges, unpeeled, seeded, and finely chopped
2 cups finely chopped celery
½ cup walnuts
   Nonstick cooking spray
   Lettuce leaves
   Orange peel twists

Dissolve gelatin in boiling water.

Drain pineapple, reserving liquid. Set pineapple aside. Add water to pineapple juice to measure 1 cup. Stir in lemon juice. Stir juice mixture into gelatin mixture; chill until consistency of unbeaten egg white. Add cranberries, oranges, celery, and walnuts to gelatin mixture; mix well. Pour into a lightly sprayed 10-cup mold. Chill until set. Unmold on lettuce leaves. Garnish with orange twists.

Fruit and Nut Curried Salad

8 Servings

1   head red leaf or romaine lettuce, torn
1   cup torn fresh spinach, well washed
1   cup grapes, halved and seeded
1   cup bean sprouts
1   can (11 ounces) mandarin orange sections, chilled and drained
¼   cup canola oil
¼   cup white wine vinegar
1   garlic clove, minced
2   tablespoons brown sugar substitute
2   tablespoons minced chives
1   tablespoon curry powder
1   teaspoon low-sodium soy sauce
¼   cup almond slivers, toasted

Combine in a large bowl the lettuce, spinach, grapes, bean sprouts, and mandarin oranges. Set aside.

Combine the oil, vinegar, garlic, brown sugar substitute, chives, curry powder, and soy sauce in a jar. Pour some dressing over salad, tossing lightly to coat. Scatter the almonds over the salad. Serve the remaining dressing with the salad or save for use later. Extra tablespoons are 1 fat exchange each.

Exchange Values Per Serving
1 Serving = ¾ Cup
1⅓ Fat
½ Fruit
⅓ Vegetable

121 Calories
(62% from Fat)
8.9 gm Total Fat
0.7 gm Saturated Fat
0 mg Cholesterol
33 mg Sodium
10.2 gm Carbohydrates
1.7 gm Dietary Fiber
2.0 gm Protein
215 mg Potassium

Tropical Fruit Salad

12 Servings

2   kiwi fruit, pared, halved lengthwise, and sliced
1½ cups quartered strawberries
1   fresh pineapple, cored and sliced in ¼-inch pieces (3 cups)
2   bananas, sliced
1   cup seedless grapes
4   apples, peeled, cored, and cubed
1   cup honeydew melon balls
1   cup cantaloupe melon balls
½   cup unsweetened pineapple juice
6   medium papayas, halved lengthwise and seeded
2   cups nondairy fat-free whipped topping
8   ounces fat-free pineapple yogurt

Combine the fruits in a bowl and add the pineapple juice. Strain and spoon into the papaya halves. In a separate bowl mix together the whipped topping and yogurt. Place a dollop of whipped mixture over each filled papaya and serve.

Exchange Values Per Serving
1 Serving = 1 Papaya Half with ½ Cup Fruit Mixture
⅓ Fat
3 Fruit

194 Calories
(10% from Fat)
2.2 gm Total Fat
1.5 gm Saturated Fat
0.6 mg Cholesterol
31 mg Sodium
44.0 gm Carbohydrates
5.7 gm Dietary Fiber
2.7 gm Protein
806 mg Potassium

Gingered Fruit Compote

4 Servings

Exchange Values Per
Serving
1 Serving = 1 Cup
1¾ Fruit

105 Calories
(5% from Fat)
0.6 gm Total Fat
0.2 gm Saturated Fat
0 mg Cholesterol
1.4 mg Sodium
26.5 gm Carbohydrates
3.2 gm Dietary Fiber
1.2 gm Protein
349 mg Potassium

1 apple, cored and sectioned	¼ cup unsweetened orange juice
1 orange, sectioned	2 teaspoons freshly grated ginger
1 banana, sliced	2 tablespoons nondairy whipped
1 cup seedless green grapes	topping or mint leaves for garnish

Combine the fruits and orange juice in a serving dish mixing well. Add the ginger and stir well. Refrigerate for at least 2 hours. Serve garnished with 2 tablespoons nondairy whipped topping or mint leaves.

Peaches and Cream Salad

8 Servings

Exchange Values Per
Serving
1 Serving = 1 Cup
¾ Fat
½ Fruit

105 Calories
(34% from Fat)
4.0 gm Total Fat
1.9 gm Saturated Fat
0.6 mg Cholesterol
55 mg Sodium
13.3 gm Carbohydrates
0.9 gm Dietary Fiber
4.0 gm Protein
180 mg Potassium

1 package (.3 ounce) sugar-free peach gelatin	1¾ cups nondairy fat-free whipped topping
1 cup boiling water	¼ cup chopped walnuts
⅓ cup sugar-free ginger ale	1 can (15 ounces) unsweetened sliced
½ cup fat-free plain yogurt	peaches, drained and chopped

Dissolve the gelatin in boiling water. Add cold ginger ale. Chill until slightly thickened. Blend the yogurt into the whipped topping and then fold into the peach gelatin. Stir in the walnuts and peaches (reserve 8 slices), and pour into a loaf pan. Chill until firm, approximately 4 hours. Unmold and garnish with reserved peach slices.

Very Orange Salad

6 Servings

½   cup white currants
2   tablespoons unsweetened orange
     juice
4   cups finely shredded carrots
1   cup unsweetened mandarin
     oranges, drained

¼   cup unsweetened crushed
     pineapple, drained
½   cup fat-free vanilla yogurt

Place the currants in a bowl. Pour the juice over the currants, and set aside for 5 minutes. Add the carrots, orange slices, and pineapple. Add yogurt and mix well.

Exchange Values Per Serving
  1 Serving = 1 Cup
  ½ Fruit
  1½ Vegetable

76 Calories
  (2% from Fat)
  0.2 gm Total Fat
  0.1 gm Saturated Fat
  0.3 mg Cholesterol
  42.0 mg Sodium
  17.6 gm Carbohydrates
  3.0 gm Dietary Fiber
  2.3 gm Protein
  388 mg Potassium

Orange Pineapple Salad

8 Servings

1   can (15 ounces) mandarin oranges
1   can (15¼ ounces) crushed
     pineapple in pineapple juice
2   packages (.3 ounce each) sugar-free
     orange gelatin

8   ounces nondairy fat-free whipped
     topping
8   ounces fat-free cottage cheese

Drain the juices from the oranges and pineapple into a saucepan. Heat to the boiling point, and remove from the heat. Mix in the gelatin, stirring until dissolved. When the gelatin has cooled, stir in the fruits, whipped topping, and cottage cheese. Refrigerate overnight before serving.

Exchange Values Per Serving
  1 Serving = 1 Cup
  ⅔ Fat
  ½ Fruit
  ⅔ Meat

137 Calories
  (25% from Fat)
  3.6 gm Total Fat
  3.6 gm Saturated Fat
  2.3 mg Cholesterol
  144 mg Sodium
  19.0 gm Carbohydrates
  0.9 gm Dietary Fiber
  5.5 gm Protein
  183 mg Potassium

Strawberry Gelatin Salad

8 Servings

**Exchange Values Per
Serving (without pecans)**
1 Serving = ¾ Cup
⅔ Fat
⅔ Fruit

121 Calories
(29% from Fat)
3.7 gm Total Fat
3.6 gm Saturated Fat
0 mg Cholesterol
56 mg Sodium
18.7 gm Carbohydrates
1.9 gm Dietary Fiber
1.9 gm Protein
189 mg Potassium

2   packages (.3 ounce each) sugar-free
    strawberry gelatin
2   cups boiling water
1   can (15¼ ounces) crushed
    pineapple in pineapple juice
2   packages (10 ounces each) frozen
    strawberries

½   cup pecans, optional
2   tablespoons lemon juice
8   ounces nondairy fat-free whipped
    topping
    Fresh strawberries

Dissolve the gelatin in the boiling water. Add the crushed pineapple (with juice), strawberries, pecans, and lemon juice. Pour into a 2-quart dish and refrigerate overnight. When set, combine the gelatin with half of the whipped topping in a blender, and whip until well blended. Spoon into tall wine glasses, top with the remaining topping and a fresh strawberry.

Orange-Cranberry Salad

8 Servings

**Exchange Values Per
Serving**
1 Serving = 1 Cup
1 Fat
⅔ Fruit
⅓ Meat

96 Calories
(39% from Fat)
4.6 gm Total Fat
0.3 gm Saturated Fat
0 mg Cholesterol
28 mg Sodium
12.6 gm Carbohydrates
3.6 gm Dietary Fiber
3.2 gm Protein
144 mg Potassium

2   large navel oranges
1   package (.3 ounce) sugar-free
    raspberry gelatin
1   cup hot water

1   package (16 ounces) fresh
    cranberries, washed and sorted
½   cup walnuts

In a small bowl, dissolve the gelatin in hot water. Peel and section oranges, reserving the peel. In food processor, combine gelatin, oranges, peel, cranberries, and walnuts. Pulse until all are coarsely chopped. Place in a glass bowl and chill for 1 hour before serving.

Breads

Herb Bread

16 Servings

1½ cups whole wheat flour
1 package (¼ ounce) quick-rise dry yeast
¼ cup nonfat dry milk
2 tablespoons sugar
½ teaspoon ground nutmeg
1 teaspoon dried sage
1 teaspoon celery seed or caraway seed

1 cup hot water (120°–130°)
2 tablespoons canola oil
¼ cup egg substitute, at room temperature
1½ cups all-purpose flour
Nonstick cooking spray
1 tablespoon low-fat margarine, melted

Combine in a large bowl whole wheat flour, yeast, milk, sugar, nutmeg, sage, and celery seed. Pour in hot water and add oil and egg substitute. Mix thoroughly. Gradually add all-purpose flour, ¼ cup at a time, to make moderately soft dough.

On a lightly floured surface knead until smooth, about 9 minutes. Or knead in mixer bowl using dough hook for 8 minutes. Place dough in bowl coated with cooking spray and turn to coat. Cover and allow to rise until doubled in bulk, 30 to 45 minutes.

Punch down dough and turn out onto floured surface. Knead 30 seconds to press out bubbles that have formed throughout dough. Shape dough into round or rectangular loaf and place in pan that has been coated with nonstick cooking spray. Cover with light cloth and allow to rise until almost doubled, about 30 minutes. Preheat oven to 375°. Bake loaf 30 to 35 minutes or until done. Brush hot loaf with melted margarine.

Exchange Values Per Serving
1 Serving = ½-Inch Slice
¼ Fat
¼ Milk
1¼ Starch

124 Calories
(17% from Fat)
2.4 gm Total Fat
0.3 gm Saturated Fat
0.8 mg Cholesterol
33 mg Sodium
21.3 gm Carbohydrates
1.9 gm Dietary Fiber
5.0 gm Protein
147 mg Potassium

Baked Potato Bread

(For Bread Machine)
16 Servings

Exchange Values Per Serving
1 Serving = ½-Inch Slice
½ Fat
¾ Starch

92 Calories
(30% from Fat)
3.1 gm Total Fat
0.3 gm Saturated Fat
13.4 mg Cholesterol
81.3 mg Sodium
13.5 gm Carbohydrate
0.6 gm Dietary Fiber
2.5 gm Protein
58 mg Potassium

½ cup fat-free milk	2 teaspoons sugar
3 tablespoons canola oil	½ teaspoon salt
1 egg	2 cups all-purpose flour
⅓ cup cooked baked potato, mashed	1½ teaspoons dry yeast
½ cup chopped red onion	

All ingredients should be at room temperature. Place ingredients into pan in the order suggested by the machine's manual. Set for a 2-pound loaf and bake as directed.

Cheesy Broccoli/Cauliflower Bread

(For Bread Machine)
16 Servings

Exchange Values Per Serving
1 Serving = ½-Inch Slice
⅓ Fat
¾ Starch

81 Calories
(19% from Fat)
1.7 gm Total Fat
0.4 gm Saturated Fat
1.1 mg Cholesterol
51.3 mg Sodium
12.7 gm Carbohydrate
0.7 gm Dietary Fiber
3.5 gm Protein
53.2 mg Potassium

¼ cup water	½ cup chopped broccoli
4 teaspoons canola oil	½ cup chopped cauliflower
1 egg white	½ teaspoon lemon pepper
1 teaspoon lemon juice	2 cups all-purpose flour
⅔ cup low-fat Cheddar cheese	1½ teaspoons dry yeast
3 tablespoons green onions	

All ingredients should be at room temperature. Place ingredients into pan in the order suggested by the machine's manual. Set fr a 2-pound loaf and bake as directed.

Whole Wheat Bread

32 Servings

2 cups fat-free milk	¼ cup egg substitute
¼ cup sugar	2 packages (¼ ounce each) dry yeast
⅓ cup canola oil	3 cups whole wheat flour
1 teaspoon salt	3 cups all-purpose flour
2 cups hot water	Nonstick cooking spray

Scald the milk in a pan and pour into a bowl with the sugar, oil, salt, and water. Cool until lukewarm. Add the egg substitute, yeast, and whole wheat flour. Turn out onto a floured surface and knead until elastic and smooth using the all-purpose flour. Place in a bowl that has been coated with nonstick cooking spray and spray the dough as well. Allow to double in size.

Punch down the dough and knead again. Form into loaves and/or rolls and let rise until double. Preheat the oven to 375°. Bake for 15 to 25 minutes. Bread should be brown and sound hollow when tapped on top. Remove from the pan immediately and cool on a wire rack.

Exchange Values Per Serving:
1 Serving = ½-Inch Slice or 1 Roll
½ Fat
1¼ Starch

115 Calories
(20% from Fat)
2.7 gm Total Fat
0.3 gm Saturated Fat
0.3 mg Cholesterol
85 mg Sodium
19.6 gm Carbohydrates
1.8 gm Dietary Fiber
3.7 gm Protein
99 mg Potassium

Whole Wheat Carrot Bread

(For Bread Machine)
16 Servings

2 tablespoons canola oil	1 teaspoon orange peel
2 tablespoons honey	½ teaspoon salt
½ cup fat-free cottage cheese	⅔ cup whole wheat flour
1 cup grated carrots	1⅓ cups all-purpose flour
1½ teaspoons dill weed	1½ teaspoons dry yeast
½ teaspoon dry mustard	

All ingredients should be at room temperature. Place ingredients into pan in the order suggested by the machine's manual. Set for a 2-pound loaf and bake as directed.

Exchange Values Per Serving
1 Serving = ½-Inch Slice
⅓ Fat
¾ Starch

88 Calories
(20% from Fat)
2.0 gm Total Fat
0.2 gm Saturated Fat
0.6 mg Cholesterol
99 mg Sodium
14.9 gm Carbohydrate
1.2 gm Dietary Fiber
3.0 gm Protein
70 mg Potassium

Golden Apple-Wheat Loaf

15 Servings

Exchange Values Per
Serving:
1 Serving = ½-Inch Slice
1 Fat
¼ Fruit
1 Starch

138 Calories
(33% from Fat)
5.2 gm Total Fat
0.4 gm Saturated Fat
0 mg Cholesterol
104 mg Sodium
20.2 gm Carbohydrates
1.2 gm Dietary Fiber
4.1 gm Protein
194 mg Potassium

1½ cups chopped Golden Delicious
     apples
¼   cup sugar
1   tablespoon brown sugar
1   teaspoon baking soda
1   teaspoon canola oil
1   cup sugar-free lemon-lime soda

4   egg whites, slightly beaten
1½ cups all-purpose flour
2½ teaspoons low-sodium baking
     powder
1   cup whole wheat flour
1   cup chopped walnuts
     Nonstick cooking spray

Combine the apples, sugar, brown sugar, baking soda, and oil in a large bowl.
Add the lemon-lime soda and mix. Add the egg whites. Sift the all-purpose
flour and baking powder together into a separate bowl. Stir in the whole
wheat flour.

Preheat the oven to 350°. Combine the apple mixture and the flour mixture. Fold in the walnuts. Turn into a 9 x 5-inch loaf pan sprayed with nonstick cooking spray. Bake for 1 hour. Remove from pan immediately and cool
on a wire rack.

Banana Bread

15 Servings

Exchange Values Per
Serving:
1 Serving = ½-Inch Slice
1 Fat
½ Fruit
1 Starch

141 Calories
(34% from Fat)
5.4 gm Total Fat
0.5 gm Saturated Fat
14.1 mg Cholesterol
47 mg Sodium
21.2 gm Carbohydrates
1.0 gm Dietary Fiber
2.4 gm Protein
199 mg Potassium

2   cups all-purpose flour
2   teaspoons low-sodium baking
     powder
½   teaspoon baking soda
½   teaspoon cinnamon
1½ cups sliced bananas (3 ripe
     bananas)

1   egg
⅓   cup canola oil
2   tablespoons sugar
½   cup unsweetened orange juice
     Nonstick cooking spray

Preheat oven to 350°. Combine the flour, baking powder, baking soda, and
cinnamon in a bowl. Stir to blend. Purée the bananas in a blender. Add the
bananas and remaining ingredients and mix well. Pour into a loaf pan that has
been sprayed with nonstick cooking spray. Bake for 40 to 50 minutes. Cool
on a wire rack.

Oat Bran Bread

20 Servings

2½ cups fat-free milk, scalded	3 cups oat flour
½ cup low-fat margarine	2 cups hot water
¼ cup honey	½ cup eggs substitute
2 packages (¼ ounces each) dry yeast	1 cup chopped nuts
1¾ cups oat bran	3 cups all-purpose flour

Combine the scalded milk, margarine, and honey in a bowl. Cool to lukewarm.

Combine the yeast, oat bran, and the oat flour in a separate bowl. Add hot water to yeast mixture. Whisk into the lukewarm liquid. Add the egg substitute and mix well. Add nuts; mix well. Add the all-purpose flour and mix well by hand. This will make a stiff dough. Turn dough out onto a floured surface and knead for approximately 10 minutes or until smooth in texture. Place in an oiled bowl, cover, and let rise until double in bulk, approximately 1 hour.

Punch down dough and form into 2 loaves. Place in loaf pans and allow to double in size. Preheat the oven to 375°. Bake for 30 to 35 minutes or until golden brown. Cool on a wire rack for at least 1 hour before slicing.

Exchange Values Per Serving:
1 Serving = ½-Inch Slice
1½ Fat
2 Starch

238 Calories
(28% from Fat)
7.9 gm Total Fat
0.9 gm Saturated Fat
0.6 mg Cholesterol
60 mg Sodium
35.6 gm Carbohydrates
4.1 gm Dietary Fiber
9.7 gm Protein
234 mg Potassium

Zucchini Bread

(For Bread Machine)
16 Servings

½ cup buttermilk	1 tablespoon sugar
1 tablespoon canola oil	½ teaspoon salt
½ cup grated zucchini	½ teaspoon lemon pepper
2 tablespoons chopped green onion	½ cup oatmeal
¼ cup chopped red bell pepper	2½ cups all-purpose flour
2 tablespoons grated Romano cheese	1½ teaspoons dry yeast

All ingredients should be at room temperature. Place ingredients into pan in the order suggested by the machine's manual. Set for a 2-pound loaf and bake as directed.

Exchange Values Per Servings
1 Serving = ½-Inch Slice
1 Starch

98 Calories
(13% from Fat)
1.4 gm Total Fat
0.2 gm Saturated Fat
0.7 mg Cholesterol
99 mg Sodium
18.2 gm Carbohydrate
1.0 gm Dietary Fiber
3.0 gm Protein
65 mg Potassium

Blackberry and Zucchini Bread

15 Servings

Exchange Values Per Serving:
1 Serving = ½-Inch Slice
¾ Fat
¼ Fruit
1½ Starch

164 Calories
(21% from Fat)
4.1 gm Total Fat
0.3 gm Saturated Fat
0 mg Cholesterol
97 mg Sodium
29.0 gm Carbohydrates
2.8 gm Dietary Fiber
4.0 gm Protein
210 mg Potassium

¼ cup canola oil
½ cup sugar
3 egg whites
1 tablespoon freshly grated orange peel
½ cup unsweetened orange juice
1½ cups whole wheat flour
1½ cups all-purpose flour

1 teaspoon baking soda
2 teaspoons low-sodium baking powder
1 can (16 ounces) blackberries, drained
1½ cups finely shredded zucchini
Nonstick cooking spray

Preheat oven to 350°. Combine all ingredients, except berries and zucchini, in a bowl, and mix until just blended. Fold in the berries and zucchini. Turn into a loaf pan sprayed with nonstick cooking spray and bake for 1½ hours. Check after the first 45 minutes to prevent browning too quickly. Cool on a wire rack.

Pumpkin-Apple Bread

15 Servings

Exchange Values Per Serving:
1 Serving = ½-Inch Slice
1 Fat
¼ Fruit
1 Starch

132 Calories
(35% from Fat)
5.2 gm Total Fat
0.4 gm Saturated Fat
0 mg Cholesterol
51 mg Sodium
19.4 gm Carbohydrates
1.3 gm Dietary Fiber
2.4 gm Protein
187 mg Potassium

⅓ cup canola oil
2 tablespoons sugar
2 egg whites
¾ cup canned pumpkin
2 cups all-purpose flour
1 tablespoon low-sodium baking powder

½ teaspoon baking soda
1 teaspoon cinnamon
½ cup unsweetened orange juice
2 large apples, peeled, cored, and cubed
Nonstick cooking spray

Preheat oven to 350°. Beat together in a large bowl the oil, sugar, egg whites, and pumpkin until light and fluffy. Combine the flour, baking powder, baking soda, and cinnamon in a separate bowl. Stir in the pumpkin mixture and the orange juice. Stir in the apple chunks. Pour into a loaf pan coated with nonstick cooking spray. Bake for 40 to 45 minutes. Cool on a wire rack.

Hot Apple Cinnamon Cereal

6 Servings

4   cups fat-free milk
½   cup brown sugar
½   teaspoon cinnamon
2   teaspoons low-fat margarine
2   cups rolled oats

2   cups peeled and chopped apples
¼   cup raisins
½   cup wheat germ
    Nonstick cooking spray

Preheat the oven to 350°. Combine in a pan the milk, brown sugar, and cinnamon. Scald over high heat. Combine with the remaining ingredients and pour into a 2-quart casserole dish that has been coated with nonstick cooking spray. Cover, and bake for 45 minutes or microwave for 10 minutes at full power. Stir several times.

Exchange Values Per Serving:
   1 Serving = 1 Cup
   ½ Fat
   1 Fruit
   ¾ Milk
   2¾ Starch

333 Calories
   (9% from Fat)
   3.4 gm Total Fat
   0.7 gm Saturated Fat
   2.9 mg Cholesterol
   105 mg Sodium
   66.6 gm Carbohydrates
   6.1 gm Dietary Fiber
   12.5 gm Protein
   659 mg Potassium

Breakfast Biscuits

12 Biscuits

3   cups all-purpose flour
⅓   cup sugar
1   tablespoon low-sodium baking powder

½   teaspoon baking soda
¾   cup low-fat margarine
1   cup low-fat buttermilk or fat-free milk

Combine flour, sugar, baking powder, and soda in a mixing bowl. Cut in margarine with a pastry blender until coarse crumbs form. Add milk, stirring until dry ingredients are moistened. Shape dough into a ball and knead lightly 4 or 5 times.

Preheat oven to 400°. Roll out dough to ½-inch thickness on a lightly floured surface. Cut into rounds with a biscuit cutter and place on ungreased baking sheets. Brush lightly with milk. Bake for 12 to 15 minutes.

Exchange Values Per Serving
   1 Serving = 1 Biscuit
   2 Starch

151 Calories
   (3% from Fat)
   0.5 gm Total Fat
   0.2 gm Saturated Fat
   0.8 mg Cholesterol
   168 mg Sodium
   32.3 gm Carbohydrates
   0.9 gm Dietary Fiber
   4.0 gm Protein
   199 mg Potassium

Buttermilk Biscuits

36 Biscuits

Exchange Values Per Serving
1 Serving = 1 Biscuit
¾ Starch

56 Calories
(2% from Fat)
0.2 gm Total Fat
0 gm Saturated Fat
0 mg Cholesterol
57 mg Sodium
12.0 gm Carbohydrates
0.8 gm Dietary Fiber
1.7 gm Protein
125 mg Potassium

4 cups all-purpose flour	½ teaspoon salt
2 tablespoons low-sodium baking powder	½ cup low-fat margarine
	1 pint low-fat buttermilk

Stir together the flour, baking powder, and salt in a large mixing bowl. Cut in the margarine until coarse, and gradually pour in the buttermilk. Stir, then knead quickly to make a stiff dough. Do not overwork.

Preheat the oven to 375°. Roll out dough to ½-inch thickness and cut into biscuits of the desired size. Bake for 18 minutes. The dough can be kept in the refrigerator for up to 6 hours after being cut.

Yogurt Drop Biscuits

16 Biscuits

Exchange Values Per Serving
1 Serving = 1 Biscuit
1 Starch

65 Calories
(3% from Fat)
0.2 gm Total Fat
0.1 gm Saturated Fat
0.3 mg Cholesterol
84 mg Sodium
13.4 gm Carbohydrates
0.5 gm Dietary Fiber
2.3 gm Protein
146 mg Potassium

1 tablespoon low-sodium baking powder	¼ cup fat-free plain yogurt
½ teaspoon salt	1 cup fat-free milk
2 cups sifted all-purpose flour	Nonstick cooking spray

Preheat the oven to 425°. Sift together the dry ingredients in a bowl. Stir in the yogurt and fat-free milk. Drop the batter into well-sprayed muffin tins, filling them ⅓ full. The batter will be very soft. Bake for about 10 minutes. The batter can be made ahead of time and refrigerated until needed.

Whole Wheat and Yogurt Biscuits

20 Biscuits

2 cups whole wheat flour
2 teaspoons low-sodium baking powder
⅓ teaspoon salt
3 tablespoons safflower oil
¼ cup fat-free milk
¼ cup fat-free plain yogurt
Nonstick cooking spray

Preheat oven to 400°. Sift together the dry ingredients in a bowl. Mix in the safflower oil and work by hand until the dough is the consistency of coarse meal. Add the milk and yogurt, and work into a dough. Place on a lightly floured board and roll to ½-inch thickness. Cut with a biscuit cutter. Place the biscuits on a baking sheet coated with nonstick cooking spray. Bake for 10 minutes or until golden brown.

Exchange Values Per Serving
1 Serving = 1 Biscuit
½ Starch

50 Calories
(16% from Fat)
0.9 gm Total Fat
0.1 gm Saturated Fat
0.1 mg Cholesterol
43 mg Sodium
9.3 gm Carbohydrates
1.5 gm Dietary Fiber
1.9 gm Protein
111 mg Potassium

Cranberry-Orange Biscuits

10 Biscuits

2 cups all-purpose flour
1 teaspoon low-sodium baking powder
⅛ teaspoon salt
3 tablespoons sugar
2 tablespoons vegetable shortening
⅔ cup low-fat buttermilk, lukewarm
2 tablespoons water, lukewarm
1 package (¼ ounce) dry yeast
½ cup cranberries, dried and crushed
¼ cup pure-fruit orange marmalade

Mix the all-purpose flour, baking powder, salt, and sugar in a bowl. Cut the vegetable shortening into the flour mixture until it looks grainy.

In a separate cup combine the buttermilk and water and dissolve the yeast in the liquid. Add slowly to the flour mixture to form a dough.

On a floured surface knead the cranberries and orange marmalade into the dough. It will be sticky at first, but it will improve as it mixes. Roll the dough to ½-inch thickness and cut biscuits. Place on a baking sheet coated with nonstick cooking spray and allow to rise for approximately 20 minutes. Preheat oven to 425°. Bake for 8 minutes or until golden brown.

Exchange Value Per Serving:
1 Serving = 1 Biscuit
½ Fat
1 Fruit
1½ Starch

175 Calories
(15% from Fat)
3.1 gm Total Fat
0.8 gm Saturated Fat
0 mg Cholesterol
36 mg Sodium
33.9 gm Carbohydrates
2.0 gm Dietary Fiber
4.1 gm Protein
179 mg Potassium

Lemon Zest Muffins

12 Muffins

Exchange Values Per Serving
1 Serving = 1 Muffin
1½ Starch

111 Calories
(5% from Fat)
0.6 gm Total Fat
0.2 gm Saturated Fat
1.3 mg Cholesterol
147 mg Sodium
23.1 gm Carbohydrates
0.6 gm Dietary Fiber
3.4 gm Protein
131 mg Potassium

1¾ cups all-purpose flour
¼ cup sugar
1 tablespoon grated lemon peel
1 teaspoon low-sodium baking powder
¾ teaspoon baking soda
8 ounces fat-free lemon yogurt

1 tablespoon pure no-sugar-added apple butter
1 tablespoon unsweetened applesauce
6 tablespoons low-fat margarine
¼ cup egg substitute
1 tablespoon fresh lemon juice
Nonstick cooking spray

In a large bowl blend flour, sugar, lemon peel, baking powder, and baking soda. Make a well in the center. In a separate bowl, whisk together yogurt, apple butter, applesauce, margarine, egg substitute, and lemon juice. Pour yogurt mixture into well in dry ingredients. Stir until just blended.

Preheat oven to 400°. Spoon dough into prepared muffin tins and bake for 20 minutes or until golden brown.

Lemon Buns

20 Buns

Exchange Values Per Serving
1 Serving = 1 Bun
¼ Fat
1½ Starch

127 Calories
(14% from Fat)
1.9 gm Total Fat
0.9 gm Saturated Fat
3.7 mg Cholesterol
188 mg Sodium
21.9 gm Carbohydrates
0.9 gm Dietary Fiber
4.9 gm Protein
90 mg Potassium

1 package (¼ ounce) dry yeast
1 teaspoon sugar
½ cup warm water (105°-115°)
¾ cup evaporated fat-free milk (105°-115°)
½ cup low-fat margarine

½ cup egg substitute
1 tablespoon grated lemon peel
1 teaspoon salt
4 cups all-purpose flour, divided
Lemon Butter (page 263)

Dissolve yeast and sugar in warm water in a bowl until bubbly. In a separate bowl combine warm milk, margarine, egg substitute, and lemon peel. Add dissolved yeast.

In food processor with plastic dough blade in place, combine salt and 3 cups of flour and pulse to blend. With machine running, add liquid mixture and process 20 seconds. Stop machine and add more flour, if needed, to form smooth, wet dough.

Turn dough out onto floured surface and knead a few times. Place dough in large, oiled bowl and turn to coat. Cover and allow to rise until doubled, about 1¼ hours. Gently punch dough down and knead lightly until smooth.

Divide into 20 equal pieces and roll each piece into a ball. Place buns on a greased 12-inch pan with sides just touching.

Preheat oven to 375°. Cover rolls loosely and allow to rise for twenty minutes or until doubled. Gently brush buns with Lemon Butter and bake for 35 minutes until brown.

Apple-Raisin Muffins

12 Muffins

2	cups all-purpose flour	¼	cup egg substitute	
2	teaspoons low-sodium baking powder	3	tablespoons canola oil	
½	teaspoon baking soda	½	cup unsweetened apple juice	
1	teaspoon cinnamon	1	cup unsweetened applesauce	
1	tablespoon sugar	⅓	cup raisins	
		¼	cup finely chopped pecans	

Preheat oven to 350°. Combine all of the ingredients in a bowl, mixing until just blended. Pour into prepared muffin tins. Bake for 20 minutes.

Exchange Values Per Serving
1 Serving = 1 Muffin
1 Fat
½ Fruit
1 Starch

156 Calories
(30% from Fat)
5.3 gm Total Fat
0.4 gm Saturated Fat
0.1 mg Cholesterol
65 mg Sodium
24.6 gm Carbohydrates
1.3 gm Dietary Fiber
3.1 gm Protein
190 mg Potassium

Blueberry-Banana Muffins

12 Muffins

1	cup whole wheat flour	⅓	cup canola oil	
1	cup all-purpose flour	4	tablespoons sugar	
1	teaspoon baking soda	3	egg whites	
2	teaspoons low-sodium baking powder	1	tablespoon lemon juice	
½	teaspoon cinnamon	½	cup unsweetened orange juice	
½	cup rolled oats	1	cup frozen blueberries	
		2	whole bananas, mashed	

Preheat oven to 350°. Combine all of the ingredients (except the berries and bananas) in a bowl; mix until just blended. Gently add the berries and bananas by hand with a wooden spoon. Spoon into prepared muffin tins. Bake for 20 minutes.

Exchange Values Per Serving
1 Serving = 1 Muffin
1¼ Fat
½ Fruit
1¼ Starch

188 Calories
(31% from Fat)
6.7 gm Total Fat
0.6 gm Saturated Fat
0 mg Cholesterol
121 mg Sodium
29.4 gm Carbohydrates
2.9 gm Dietary Fiber
4.2 gm Protein
265 mg Potassium

Apricot-Oat Bran Muffins

12 Muffins

Exchange Values Per Serving
1 Serving = 1 Muffin
¼ Fruit
¼ Meat
1 Starch

129 Calories
(13% from Fat)
1.9 gm Total Fat
0.1 gm Saturated Fat
0.2 mg Cholesterol
81 mg Sodium
25 gm Carbohydrates
2.1 gm Dietary Fiber
4.3 gm Protein
244 mg Potassium

2	cups oat bran cereal	½	cup fat-free milk
¼	cup wheat bran	1	tablespoon canola oil
½	cup whole wheat flour	⅓	cup honey
2½	teaspoons low-sodium baking powder		* * *
½	teaspoon cinnamon	1	cup all-purpose flour
½	cup diced dried apricots	¼	cup low-fat margarine
4	egg whites	3	tablespoons whole rolled oats
		½	teaspoon cinnamon

Preheat oven to 350°. Combine the brans, whole wheat flour, baking powder, cinnamon, and apricots in a large bowl. Add the egg whites, milk, oil, and honey, stirring until just blended. Pour into prepared muffin tins.

Combine in a separate bowl the all-purpose flour, margarine, oats, and cinnamon, mixing well. Sprinkle over the batter. Bake for 15 to 20 minutes.

Banana Muffins

12 Muffins

Exchange Values Per Serving
1 Serving = 1 Muffin
1¼ Fat
¼ Fruit
1½ Starch

179 Calories
(33% from Fat)
6.6 gm Total Fat
0.6 gm Saturated Fat
0.1 mg Cholesterol
85 mg Sodium
26.9 gm Carbohydrates
2.2 gm Dietary Fiber
3.8 gm Protein
162 mg Potassium

2	cups whole wheat flour	¼	cup unsweetened orange juice
2	teaspoons low-sodium baking powder	¼	cup water
½	teaspoon baking soda	2	large bananas, mashed
½	teaspoon cinnamon		* * *
¼	cup egg substitute	½	cup all-purpose flour
1	teaspoon vanilla extract	3	tablespoons low-fat margarine
⅓	cup canola oil	¼	teaspoon cinnamon
2	tablespoons sugar		Nonstick cooking spray

Preheat oven to 350°. Combine 2 cups of flour, baking powder, baking soda, and ½ teaspoon cinnamon in a mixing bowl. Stir to blend.

In a separate bowl combine the egg substitute, vanilla, oil, sugar, orange juice, water, and bananas, and blend until smooth. Pour the banana mixture into the dry ingredients and stir until just blended. Pour into prepared muffin tins.

Combine all-purpose flour, margarine, and ¼ teaspoon of cinnamon in a bowl, and sprinkle over the muffins. Bake for 15 minutes.

Blueberry Muffins

12 Muffins

½ cup all-purpose flour
½ cup whole wheat flour
2 teaspoons low-sodium baking powder
1 teaspoon baking soda
3 tablespoons sugar
1 teaspoon cinnamon
2 egg whites

1½ cups fat-free milk
2 tablespoons canola oil
1 cup frozen blueberries

*   *   *

½ cup all-purpose flour
½ cup low-fat margarine
1½ teaspoons cinnamon

Preheat oven to 400°. Combine ½ cup of all-purpose flour with the whole wheat flour in a large bowl. Add the baking powder, baking soda, sugar, and 1 teaspoon cinnamon.

In a separate bowl combine the egg whites, milk, and oil. Make a well in the center of the dry ingredients, and add the egg mixture. Stir until just combined. Fold in the blueberries carefully with a wooden spoon. Pour into muffin tins.

In a separate bowl combine ½ cup of all-purpose flour with the margarine and 1½ teaspoons of cinnamon. Sprinkle over the muffins. Bake for 20 to 25 minutes.

Exchange Values Per Serving
1 Serving = 1 Muffin
½ Fat
1 Starch

114 Calories
(20% from Fat)
2.6 gm Total Fat
0.2 gm Saturated Fat
0.6 mg Cholesterol
191 mg Sodium
19.8 gm Carbohydrates
1.8 gm Dietary Fiber
3.5 gm Protein
189 mg Potassium

Carrot Cake Muffins

12 Muffins

1½ cups whole wheat flour
1 teaspoon baking soda
1 tablespoon low-sodium baking powder
1 teaspoon ground cinnamon
1 egg
2 tablespoons canola oil

¼ cup raisins
¼ cup chopped walnuts
½ cup unsweetened orange juice
1 can (8 ounces) crushed pineapple in pineapple juice, undrained
1½ cups grated carrots

Preheat oven to 350°. Combine the flour, baking soda, baking powder, and cinnamon in a bowl. Add the remaining ingredients and stir to blend. Spoon into prepared muffin tins and bake for 20 to 25 minutes.

Exchange Values Per Serving
1 Serving = 1 Muffin
1 Fat
¼ Fruit
¾ Starch
¼ Vegetable

120 Calories
(32% from Fat)
4.5 gm Total Fat
0.5 gm Saturated Fat
17.7 mg Cholesterol
118 mg Sodium
18.4 gm Carbohydrates
2.8 gm Dietary Fiber
3.6 gm Protein
318 mg Potassium

Blackberry Corn Muffins

12 Muffins

Exchange Values Per
Serving
  1 Serving = 1 Muffin
  ½ Fruit
  1 Starch

124 Calories
  (4% from Fat)
  0.6 gm Total Fat
  0.1 gm Saturated Fat
  0.1 mg Cholesterol
  221 mg Sodium
  27.6 gm Carbohydrates
  2.4 gm Dietary Fiber
  3.2 gm Protein
  238 mg Potassium

1 cup plain white cornmeal	1 cup low-fat buttermilk
1 cup all-purpose flour	6 tablespoons low-fat margarine, melted
¼ cup sugar	
2½ teaspoons low-sodium baking powder	¼ cup egg substitute
1 tablespoon pure-fruit apple butter	1⅔ cups fresh or frozen blackberries
2 tablespoons unsweetened applesauce	½ teaspoon grated lemon peel

Preheat the oven to 400°. Blend together the cornmeal, flour, sugar, and baking powder in a bowl and set aside. In a separate bowl whisk together the apple butter, applesauce, buttermilk, melted margarine, and egg substitute. Make a well in the dry ingredients and pour in the liquids. Stir to blend. Fold in blackberries and lemon peel; fill prepared muffin tins. Bake for 20 to 25 minutes.

Cranberry-Orange Muffins

12 Muffins

Exchange Values Per
Muffin
  1 Serving = 1 Muffin
  ½ Fat
  ½ Starch

81 Calories
  (32% from Fat)
  2.9 gm Total Fat
  0.2 gm Saturated Fat
  0.1 mg Cholesterol
  63 mg Sodium
  11.6 gm Carbohydrates
  0.7 gm Dietary Fiber
  2.4 gm Protein
  151 mg Potassium

½ cup fresh or frozen cranberries	2 teaspoons low-sodium baking powder
¼ cup egg substitute	
½ cup unsweetened orange juice	½ teaspoon baking soda
1 tablespoon canola oil	1 tablespoon sugar
1 teaspoon grated orange peel	1 teaspoon vanilla extract
1 cup all-purpose flour	¼ cup chopped walnuts

Preheat the oven to 350°. Combine all of the ingredients in a bowl, stirring until just blended. Pour into prepared muffin tins, and bake for 20 minutes.

Black Jack Muffins

24 Muffins

2½	cups all-purpose flour	1	tablespoon sugar
1½	cups cornmeal	2	tablespoons fresh cilantro, chopped
4	teaspoons low-sodium baking powder	1	cup fresh corn kernels
1	teaspoon baking soda	¼	cup jalapeño peppers, diced
1½	cups assorted low-fat shredded cheeses (sharp Cheddar, Monterey Jack, or jalapeño cheese)	½	cup cooked black beans, drained
		2	eggs
		2	cups fat-free milk
		⅓	cup canola oil

Preheat oven to 350°. In a large mixing bowl combine the flour, cornmeal, baking powder, baking soda, cheese, sugar, cilantro, corn, peppers, and black beans. Mix well. Add the eggs, milk, and oil, stirring until well blended.

Spoon the batter into prepared muffin tins, ⅔ full. Bake for 35 minutes or until springy to the touch and no longer moist in the center.

Exchange Values Per Serving
1 Serving = 1 Muffin
⅔ Fat
1 Starch

148 Calories
(27% from Fat)
4.5 gm Total Fat
0.8 gm Saturated Fat
20.7 mg Cholesterol
139 mg Sodium
21.2 gm Carbohydrate
1.6 gm Dietary Fiber
5.9 gm Protein
174 mg Potassium

Oat Bran Muffins

6 Muffins

¾	cup whole wheat flour	½	teaspoon cinnamon
¾	cup oat bran cereal	3	tablespoons canola oil
2	tablespoons low-sodium baking powder	3	tablespoons honey
		¾	cup unsweetened orange juice

Preheat the oven to 375°. Combine the dry ingredients in a large bowl. Mix the oil, honey, and orange juice in a separate bowl. Make a well in the center of the dry ingredients and add the oil mixture. Stir until blended. Fill prepared muffin tins ¾ full. Bake for 15 minutes.

Exchange Values Per Muffin
1 Serving = 1 Muffin
1½ Fat
¼ Fruit
1 Starch

183 Calories
(35% from Fat)
7.6 gm Total Fat
0.6 gm Saturated Fat
0 mg Cholesterol
25 mg Sodium
28.6 gm Carbohydrates
2.6 gm Dietary Fiber
3.2 gm Protein
657 mg Potassium

Oat Bran-Banana Muffins

32 Muffins

Exchange Values Per Serving
1 Serving = 1 Muffin
1¼ Fat
¼ Fruit
¼ Meat
2¼ Starch

246 Calories
(26% from Fat)
7.5 gm Total Fat
0.8 gm Saturated Fat
0.1 mg Cholesterol
96 mg Sodium
39.9 gm Carbohydrates
5.8 gm Dietary Fiber
8 gm Protein
393 mg Potassium

4	cups whole wheat flour	¼	teaspoon grated nutmeg
4	cups all-purpose flour	4	tablespoons brown sugar
2	cups wheat bran	1	cup egg substitute
4	cups rolled oats	½	cup canola oil
2	tablespoons low-sodium baking powder	2	cups unsweetened orange juice
2	teaspoons baking soda	4	small bananas
2	teaspoons cinnamon	1	cup toasted unsalted sunflower seeds

Preheat the oven to 350°. Combine all of the ingredients in a mixing bowl, stirring until just blended. Do not over-stir. Pour into prepared muffin tins. Bake for 20 minutes.

Pumpkin-Apple Bran Muffins

12 Muffins

Exchange Values Per Serving
1 Serving = 1 Muffin
¾ Fat
¼ Fruit
1 Starch

102 Calories
(28% from Fat)
3.5 gm Total Fat
0.4 gm Saturated Fat
0 mg Cholesterol
42 mg Sodium
15.9 gm Carbohydrates
3.1 gm Dietary Fiber
4.0 gm Protein
279 mg Potassium

1	cup all-purpose flour	2	egg whites
½	cup bran	¾	cup unsweetened orange juice
1	teaspoon sugar	½	cup chopped apple
2	teaspoons low-sodium baking powder		* * *
½	teaspoon cinnamon	1	cup wheat germ
2	tablespoons canola oil	½	cup all-purpose flour
½	cup canned pumpkin	4	tablespoons low-fat margarine, melted

Preheat oven to 350°. Combine 1 cup of flour, bran, sugar, baking powder, and cinnamon in a large bowl. Add the oil, pumpkin, egg whites, orange juice, and apple, stirring until just blended. Spoon into prepared muffin tins.

Combine the wheat germ, ½ cup of flour, and the margarine in a bowl until the mixture resembles coarse crumbs. Sprinkle over the muffins. Bake for 15 to 20 minutes.

Oatmeal-Banana Muffins

12 Muffins

3 cups all-purpose flour	1 tablespoon sugar
¾ cup rolled oats	¼ cup egg substitute
1 tablespoon low-sodium baking powder	2 tablespoons canola oil
	1 cup unsweetened orange juice
½ teaspoon cinnamon	2 small bananas, chopped

Preheat oven to 350°. Combine the flour, oats, baking powder, cinnamon, and sugar in a bowl. Add the remaining ingredients. Stir until blended. Spoon into prepared muffin tins. Bake for 15 to 20 minutes.

Exchange Values Per Serving
1 Serving = 1 Muffin
½ Fat
½ Fruit
2 Starch

190 Calories
(15% from Fat)
3.2 gm Total Fat
0.3 gm Saturated Fat
0.1 mg Cholesterol
12 mg Sodium
35.6 gm Carbohydrates
2.0 gm Dietary Fiber
5.0 gm Protein
312 mg Potassium

Dried Fruit and Buttermilk Drop Scones

12 Scones

2½ cups all-purpose flour	2 tablespoons apple butter
¼ cup sugar	½ cup dried currants
4 teaspoons low-sodium baking powder	½ cup dried raisins
	½ cup dried cranberries
¼ teaspoon baking soda	½ cup dried blueberries
¼ cup egg substitute	½ cup dried apricots
1 cup low-fat buttermilk	Nonstick cooking spray
1 tablespoon canola oil	

Preheat oven to 400°. In a large bowl whisk together the flour, sugar, baking powder, and baking soda. In another bowl, whisk together egg substitute, buttermilk, oil, apple butter, and remaining fruits. Add wet mixture to dry ingredients with a wooden spoon. Mix until the dry ingredients are just moistened. The batter will be quite sticky.

Using an ice cream scoop, drop batter in 2½-inch mounds onto a baking sheet that has been sprayed with nonstick cooking spray. Bake until tops of scones are golden brown, 12 to 15 minutes.

Exchange Values Per Serving
1 Serving = 1 Scone
¼ Fat
1½ Fruit
1½ Starch

226 Calories
(7% from Fat)
1.9 gm Total Fat
0.2 gm Saturated Fat
0.1 mg Cholesterol
47 mg Sodium
50.3 gm Carbohydrates
3.2 gm Dietary Fiber
4.8 gm Protein
512 mg Potassium

Scottish Oat Cakes

12 Servings

Exchange Values Per Serving
1 Serving = 1 Oat Cake
¼ Fat
1¾ Starch

137 Calories
(12% from Fat)
1.8 gm Total Fat
0.3 gm Saturated Fat
0.1 mg Cholesterol
64 mg Sodium
25.4 gm Carbohydrates
3.1 gm Dietary Fiber
5.3 gm Protein
176 mg Potassium

4 cups rolled oats	½ cup low-fat margarine
¾ cup all-purpose flour	3 tablespoons fat-free milk
1½ teaspoons low-sodium baking powder	

Preheat the oven to 350°. Process the oats in a food processor until fine. Combine with the remaining ingredients in a bowl to form a stiff dough. Let the dough rest for 30 minutes. Roll out dough to ¼-inch thickness on a floured surface. Cut into circles and place on a baking sheet. Bake for 8 to 10 minutes or until golden brown.

Scottish Oat-Bran Toast

36 Servings

Exchange Values Per Serving
1 Serving = 1 Slice
½ Starch

47 Calories
(11% from Fat)
0.7 gm Total Fat
0.1 gm Saturated Fat
0 mg Cholesterol
21 mg Sodium
9.6 gm Carbohydrates
1.8 gm Dietary Fiber
2.0 gm Protein
78 mg Potassium

4 cups rolled oats	1½ teaspoons low-sodium baking powder
1 cup wheat bran	½ cup low-fat margarine
¾ cup all-purpose flour	3 tablespoons fat-free milk
½ teaspoon cinnamon	
½ teaspoon vanilla extract	

Preheat oven to 400°. Process the oats in a food processor until fine. Combine with the remaining ingredients in a bowl to form a stiff dough. Let the dough rest for 30 minutes.

Roll out dough to ¼-inch thickness on a floured surface. Cut into circles and place on a baking sheet. Bake for 4 to 8 minutes or until golden.

Buckwheat Buttermilk Pancakes

6 Pancakes

1   egg white
½   cup low-fat buttermilk
1   tablespoon canola oil
1¼   cups buckwheat flour
1   teaspoon sugar

1   teaspoon low-sodium baking powder
½   teaspoon baking soda
Nonstick cooking spray

Beat together the egg white, buttermilk, and oil in a bowl. Add the flour, sugar, baking powder, and baking soda. Stir until the ingredients are just blended. Pour the batter onto a hot, lightly sprayed griddle. Cook until bubbles form on the surface and the edges become dry. Turn and cook until golden brown.

Exchange Values Per Serving
1 Serving = 1 Pancake
½ Fat
1¼ Starch

118 Calories
(24% from Fat)
3.5 gm Total Fat
0.4 gm Saturated Fat
0 mg Cholesterol
123 mg Sodium
19.9 gm Carbohydrates
3.1 gm Dietary Fiber
4.1 gm Protein
274 mg Potassium

Buckwheat and Yogurt Pancakes

16 Pancakes

2   cups buckwheat flour
¼   teaspoon salt substitute
1   teaspoon baking soda
1½   cups low-fat buttermilk
½   cup fat-free plain yogurt

¼   cup egg substitute
1   teaspoon maple flavoring
1   tablespoon canola oil
Nonstick cooking spray

Combine the flour, salt substitute, and baking soda. Add the remaining ingredients. Pour onto a hot, lightly sprayed griddle and cook until brown, turning once. Serve hot.

Exchange Values Per Serving
1 Serving = 1 Pancake
¼ Fat
¾ Starch

74 Calories
(20% from Fat)
1.8 gm Total Fat
0.2 gm Saturated Fat
0.2 mg Cholesterol
135 mg Sodium
12.5 gm Carbohydrates
2.1 gm Dietary Fiber
3.2 gm Protein
160 mg Potassium

Cornmeal Griddle Cakes

18 Pancakes

Exchange Values Per Serving
1 Serving = 1 Pancake
¾ Fat
¾ Starch

94 Calories
(34% from Fat)
3.6 gm Total Fat
0.3 gm Saturated Fat
0.2 mg Cholesterol
17 mg Sodium
13 gm Carbohydrates
1.3 gm Dietary Fiber
2.5 gm Protein
245 mg Potassium

1	cup cornmeal	¼	cup egg substitute
1	cup all-purpose flour	1½	cups low-fat buttermilk
1	teaspoon salt substitute	½	cup fat-free plain yogurt
1⅓	tablespoons low-sodium baking powder	¼	cup canola oil
			Nonstick cooking spray

Mix the dry ingredients in a large bowl. Combine the egg substitute and milk in a small bowl, add the yogurt and whip. Add the milk mixture to the dry ingredients and stir to make a smooth batter. Stir in the canola oil. Bake on a hot, sprayed griddle, turning when the underside is browned and the batter is bubbly.

Old-Fashioned Corn Cakes

4 Servings

Exchange Values Per Serving
1 Serving = 1 Corn Cake
1¼ Fat
½ Milk
1¾ Starch

185 Calories
(22% from Fat)
4.6 gm Total Fat
0.4 gm Saturated Fat
0 mg Cholesterol
642 mg Sodium
31.1 gm Carbohydrates
4.7 gm Dietary Fiber
5.5 gm Protein
232 mg Potassium

1½	cups low-fat buttermilk	½	teaspoon salt
1	tablespoon safflower oil	¾	cup cornmeal
1	teaspoon baking soda	¼	cup all-purpose flour
1	egg white		Nonstick cooking spray

Combine all of the ingredients in a bowl and mix well. Drop by heaping tablespoons onto a hot griddle that has been coated with nonstick spray. Cook until golden on each side.

Cinnamon French Toast

4 Servings

8 egg whites
8 tablespoons fat-free milk
1 teaspoon vanilla extract
½ teaspoon cinnamon

8 slices day-old reduced-calorie white
   bread
   Nonstick cooking spray

Lightly beat together the egg whites, milk, vanilla, and cinnamon. Coat both sides of the bread with the egg white mixture. Place bread soaked in egg white mixture on a hot, lightly sprayed griddle. Cook until brown and crisp on both sides.

Exchange Values Per Serving
1 Serving = 2 Slices
¼ Fat
1 Meat
1½ Starch

146 Calories
(7% from Fat)
1.2 gm Total Fat
0.3 gm Saturated Fat
0.6 mg Cholesterol
378 mg Sodium
23.4 gm Carbohydrates
4.6 gm Dietary Fiber
12.1 gm Protein
185 mg Potassium

Oven-Baked Orange and Vanilla French Toast

4 Servings

   Butter-flavored nonstick cooking
   spray
¼ teaspoon cinnamon
1 teaspoon finely grated orange peel
⅓ cup fat-free evaporated milk
⅓ cup unsweetened orange juice

1 teaspoon vanilla extract
1 cup egg substitute
8 slices low-fat whole wheat or white
   bread
   Orange slices for garnish

Preheat oven to 325°. Spray a large baking dish with cooking spray. Sprinkle the bottom of the pan with the cinnamon and orange peel. Combine the milk, orange juice, vanilla, and egg substitute in a bowl. Dip bread slices into egg batter to coat each side. Place in baking dish and bake until browned or about 25 minutes. Garnish with orange slices.

Exchange Values Per Serving
1 Serving = 2 Slices
¼ Fat
½ Fruit
1 Meat
¼ Milk
1½ Starch

189 Calories
(15% from Fat)
3.3 gm Total Fat
0.6 gm Saturated Fat
1.4 mg Cholesterol
372 mg Sodium
29.4 gm Carbohydrates
6.5 gm Dietary Fiber
13.8 gm Protein
436 mg Potassium

Corn Bread Muffins

4 Muffins

Exchange Values Per Serving
1 Serving = 1 Muffin
1 Fruit
¾ Meat
1½ Starch

190 Calories
(6% from Fat)
1.2 gm Total Fat
0.1 gm Saturated Fat
0.2 mg Cholesterol
621 mg Sodium
36.7 gm Carbohydrates
1.5 gm Dietary Fiber
8.5 gm Protein
459 mg Potassium

1	cup plain white cornmeal	¼	cup egg substitute
2	tablespoons all-purpose flour	½	cup fat-free creamer
½	teaspoon sugar	½	cup fat-free cottage cheese
½	teaspoon onion powder	1	teaspoon hot sauce
2	teaspoons low-sodium baking powder		Nonstick cooking spray

Heat muffin tin inside preheated 425° oven. In a mixing bowl, whisk together cornmeal, flour, sugar, onion powder, and baking powder. Blend egg substitute, creamer, cottage cheese, and hot sauce in a separate bowl. Add the liquid mixture all at once to the dry mixture.

Remove the muffin tin from the oven and coat with cooking spray. Fill each cup ⅔ full with cornmeal mix.

Bake for 12 to 15 minutes or until golden brown.

Southern Corn Bread

12 Servings

Exchange Values Per Serving
1 Serving = 1 2-Inch Square
¼ Meat
1 Starch

106 Calories
(7% from Fat)
0.8 gm Total Fat
0.2 gm Saturated Fat
0.6 mg Cholesterol
135 mg Sodium
19.6 gm Carbohydrates
1.2 gm Dietary Fiber
4.8 gm Protein
249 mg Potassium

1	cup yellow cornmeal	1	cup fat-free milk
1	cup all-purpose flour	½	cup fat-free plain yogurt
1	tablespoon low-sodium baking powder	½	cup egg substitute
½	teaspoon salt		Nonstick cooking spray

Preheat oven to 400°. Mix all ingredients together in a large bowl and stir by hand until moist. Pour into a 9-inch baking dish that has been coated with cooking spray. Bake for 20 minutes.

Pepper Sweet Corn Bread

(For Bread Machine)
16 Servings

2	tablespoons canola oil	1	teaspoon paprika
½	cup water	½	teaspoon salt
1	egg	⅓	cup cornmeal
½	cup sweet corn	2	cups all-purpose flour
1	cup chopped red bell pepper	1½	teaspoons dry yeast

All ingredients should be at room temperature. Place ingredients into pan in the order suggested by the machine's manual. Set for a 2-pound loaf and bake as directed.

Exchange Values Per Servings
1 Serving = ½-Inch Slice
½ Fat
1 Starch

95 Calories
(22% from Fat)
2.3 gm Total Fat
0.3 gm Saturated Fat
13.3 mg Cholesterol
88 mg Sodium
16.0 gm Carbohydrate
1.0 gm Dietary Fiber
2.6 gm Protein
63 mg Potassium

Southern Corn Bread Stuffing

8 Servings

3	cups crumbled corn bread		Pepper
1	cup breadcrumbs	½	teaspoon rubbed sage
2	cups low-sodium chicken broth	½	teaspoon paprika
3	ribs celery, finely chopped	2	tablespoons low-fat margarine
1	large onion, finely chopped		Nonstick cooking spray
2	egg whites		

Preheat oven to 325°. Combine all of the ingredients (except margarine) in a bowl. Turn into a baking dish coated with nonstick cooking spray and dot the top with margarine. Cover and bake for 30 minutes. Remove the cover and cook 15 minutes longer.

Exchange Values Per Serving
1 Serving = ½ Cup
1 Fat
¼ Meat
2¼ Starch
¼ Vegetable

254 Calories
(21% from Fat)
6.1 gm Total Fat
1.0 gm Saturated Fat
25.5 mg Cholesterol
272 mg Sodium
41.3 gm Carbohydrates
2.1 gm Dietary Fiber
7.9 gm Protein
205 mg Potassium

Baked Grilled Cheese Sandwiches

4 Servings

Exchange Values Per Serving
1 Serving = 1 Sandwich
¼ Fat
1 Meat
1 Starch

119 Calories
(10% from Fat)
1.5 gm Total Fat
0.3 gm Saturated Fat
0.1 mg Cholesterol
345 mg Sodium
18.2 gm Carbohydrates
2.1 gm Dietary Fiber
9.6 gm Protein
242 mg Potassium

2   egg whites
2   tablespoons fat-free milk
2   dash of paprika
4   slices oat bran bread

Nonstick cooking spray
4   slices fat-free cheese
Kosher dill pickle

Preheat oven to 400°. With a whisk, mix in a shallow bowl the egg whites, fat-free milk, and paprika. Dip each side of the bread in the egg mixture and place on a baking sheet that has been coated with nonstick cooking spray. Bake until toasted brown on both sides. When golden brown, top each piece of bread with cheese and allow to melt slightly. Place on serving plates and top with kosher dill pickle slices.

Entrées

Holiday Beef Steaks with Vegetable Sauté and Hot Mustard Sauce

4 Servings

½	cup fat-free plain yogurt	1	pound boneless beef top loin steaks, cut 1-inch thick
1	teaspoon cornstarch		
¼	cup low-sodium beef broth	1	bag (16 ounces) frozen whole green beans
2	teaspoons coarse-grained mustard		
1	teaspoon horseradish	1	cup quartered large mushrooms
1	teaspoon spicy mustard	1	tablespoon low-fat margarine
½	teaspoon lemon pepper	¼	cup water

Combine the yogurt and cornstarch in a medium bowl and stir until blended. Stir in the beef broth, coarse-grained mustard, horseradish, and spicy mustard. Set aside.

Press an equal amount of lemon pepper into the surface of the steaks. Place the steaks on a rack in a broiler pan 3 to 4 inches from the heat. Broil the steaks about 15 minutes for rare, 20 minutes for medium, turning once.

Meanwhile cook the beans and mushrooms in margarine and water in a large frying pan over medium heat for 6 minutes, stirring occasionally, until the beans are tender. Cook the reserved sauce over medium-low heat for 5 minutes, stirring until the sauce is slightly thickened. Serve the steaks and vegetables with the sauce.

Exchange Values Per Serving
1 Serving = 1 Steak (3 Ounces)
¾ Fat
3½ Meat
1½ Vegetable

284 Calories
(44% from Fat)
14.0 gm Total Fat
5.8 gm Saturated Fat
77.1 mg Cholesterol
156 mg Sodium
11.0 gm Carbohydrates
3.0 gm Dietary Fiber
28.6 gm Protein
701 mg Potassium

Baked Beef Tenderloin with Vegetables

12 Servings

Exchange Values Per
Serving
   1 Serving = 4 Ounces
   1 Vegetable
   3 Meat

277 Calories
   (38% from Fat)
   11.6 gm Total Fat
   5.1 gm Saturated Fat
   95.3 mg Cholesterol
   276 mg Sodium
   8.3 gm Carbohydrates
   2.2 gm Dietary Fiber
   33.8 gm Protein
   815 mg Potassium

1   3 to 4-pound beef tenderloin roast
¼   cup low-sodium soy sauce
2   tablespoons low-sodium
    Worcestershire sauce
    Garlic to taste
2   onions, quartered

1   pound fresh mushrooms, sliced
4   to 6 ribs celery, sliced diagonally
6   carrots, cleaned and diced
1   lemon, thinly sliced
¼   cup water

Marinate the tenderloin overnight in a pan in the combined soy sauce, Worcestershire sauce, and garlic.

Preheat oven to 350°. Add the remaining ingredients to the pan. Cover and bake for 1½ hours.

Beef and Noodles

6 Servings

Exchange Values Per
Serving
   1 Serving = 1 Cup
   1¾ Meat
   2¾ Starch
   ½ Vegetable

326 Calories
   (18% from Fat)
   6.6 gm Total Fat
   2.3 gm Saturated Fat
   20.6 mg Cholesterol
   274 mg Sodium
   46.1 gm Carbohydrates
   2.8 gm Dietary Fiber
   19.7 gm Protein
   351 mg Potassium

1   pound extra lean ground beef, cut
    into 2 x 2½-inch strips
½   cup sliced white onion
1   garlic clove, minced
2   tablespoons low-sodium beef broth
1   can (6 ounces) mushrooms,
    drained
2   drops hot sauce
1   tablespoon low-sodium
    Worcestershire sauce

1   tablespoon low-sodium soy sauce
¼   teaspoon pepper
¼   teaspoon paprika
    Dash of grated nutmeg
1   can (10¾ ounces) low-sodium
    reduced-fat tomato soup
12 ounces yolkless wide noodles,
    cooked

Sauté the beef, onion, and garlic in broth in a skillet. When browned, add the mushrooms, hot sauce, Worcestershire sauce, soy sauce, seasonings, and soup. Simmer until the beef is tender. Serve over noodles.

Beef Bourguignon

12 Servings

1	4-pound boneless sirloin roast	1	green bell pepper, chopped
1	cup Burgundy or other dry red wine	1	pound pearl onions, peeled and chopped
1	cup water	½	teaspoon garlic powder
2	cans (10¾ ounces each) reduced-fat cream of mushroom soup	10	cherry tomatoes
1	package onion soup mix		Parsley sprigs
2	pounds fresh mushrooms, sliced	6	cups cooked brown rice

Preheat oven to 325°. Cut beef into 1½-inch cubes and place in a 2½-quart casserole dish. Combine wine, water, soup, and soup mix; stir well, and pour over beef. Stir in mushrooms. Cover and bake for 2 hours. Add green pepper, onions, garlic powder, and tomatoes; cover and bake an additional 30 minutes. Garnish with parsley sprigs and serve over rice.

Exchange Values Per Serving
1 Serving = 1 Cup
3 Meat
1½ Starch
2½ Vegetable

361 Calories
(21% from Fat)
8.2 gm Total Fat
3.2 gm Saturated Fat
78.1 mg Cholesterol
472 mg Sodium
36.8 gm Carbohydrates
3.5 gm Dietary Fiber
31.3 gm Protein
747 mg Potassium

Fall Apple Pot Roast

6 Servings

2	pounds beef blade pot roast	½	cup water
¼	cup all-purpose flour	1	acorn squash or 1 pound large winter squash
¼	teaspoon pepper	2	tart apples, cored and quartered
¼	cup low-sodium beef broth		
2	medium onions, sliced		

Trim the surface fat from the roast. Mix the flour and pepper together and rub the mixture all over the meat. Cook the meat in the broth in a Dutch oven, turning to brown on all sides. Pour off the excess drippings. Add the onions and cook until they are tender but not browned. Add the water. Cover and simmer for 2 hours.

Peel the squash and scrape off seeds and stringy pulp. Slice or cube the squash and add it to the pot roast along with the apples. Cover and simmer for 30 minutes longer or until the meat and vegetables are tender.

Exchange Values Per Serving
1 Serving = 1 Slice (4 Ounces)
¼ Fat
½ Fruit
5 Meat
¼ Starch
1¾ Vegetable

379 Calories
(37% from Fat)
15.5 gm Total Fat
6.8 gm Saturated Fat
120.2 mg Cholesterol
87 mg Sodium
22.1 gm Carbohydrates
3.2 gm Dietary Fiber
37.1 gm Protein
685 mg Potassium

Chinese Green Pepper Steak

6 Servings

Exchange Values Per Serving
1 Serving = 1 Cup
1¾ Fat
3½ Meat
2 Starch
2 Vegetable

414 Calories
(24% from Fat)
10.9 gm Total Fat
4.7 gm Saturated Fat
76.7 mg Cholesterol
620 mg Sodium
44.1 gm Carbohydrates
3.2 gm Dietary Fiber
30.7 gm Protein
679 mg Potassium

½ cup dry sherry	1½ cups low-sodium chicken broth
4 tablespoons low-sodium soy sauce	* * *
1½ pounds top sirloin beef, cut into ⅛-inch slices	2 tablespoons cornstarch
½ teaspoon pepper	¼ cup cold water
1 teaspoon grated fresh ginger	2 tablespoons low-sodium soy sauce
1 garlic clove, minced	4 cups steamed rice
2 pounds fresh green bell peppers, each cut diagonally into pieces	

Combine the sherry and soy sauce. Marinate the beef for at least 2 hours in the mixture. Place the marinade, pepper, ginger, and garlic in a heated wok. Stir to combine. Add the beef and stir fry for 3 minutes. Add the green peppers and mix well. Add the chicken broth. Stir to combine. Cook for 6 minutes. Combine the cornstarch, water, and soy sauce in a bowl. Add to the cooked beef mixture and stir continuously until the juice thickens. Serve with steamed rice.

Mom's Meatloaf

6 Servings

Exchange Values Per Serving
1 Serving = 1 Slice
(4 Ounces)
⅓ Fat
3¼ Meat
½ Vegetable

221 Calories
(43% from Fat)
10.5 gm Total Fat
3.0 gm Saturated Fat
89.8 mg Cholesterol
182 mg Sodium
7.2 gm Carbohydrates
1.1 gm Dietary Fiber
23.7 gm Protein
460 mg Potassium

2 pounds lean ground turkey	2 tablespoons chopped parsley
1 medium onion, peeled and chopped	1 teaspoon dried basil
½ cup low-sodium tomato sauce	½ teaspoon dried thyme
½ cup egg substitute	¼ teaspoon dried allspice
1 cup breadcrumbs	½ teaspoon pepper

Preheat oven to 350°. In a large mixing bowl combine turkey, onion, tomato sauce, and egg substitute. Mix well. Add remaining ingredients and combine thoroughly. Pat mixture into an 8- or 9-inch loaf pan; smooth surface with spatula. Bake for 1 hour. Serve hot or cold with toasted bread to make a great sandwich.

Beef Oriental

6 Servings

1½	pounds lean round steak
¼	teaspoon minced onion
¼	teaspoon minced garlic
1	tablespoon low-sodium soy sauce
¼	cup water
⅛	teaspoon coarsely ground pepper
1	low-sodium beef bouillon cube
1½	cups hot water
1	package (16 ounces) frozen broccoli

1	package (16 ounces) frozen cauliflower
½	cup raw carrot strips
2½	cups sliced fresh mushrooms
½	cup sliced water chestnuts
½	cup celery
4	cups cooked white rice

Preheat oven to 350°. Place the round steak in a baking pan. Sprinkle with onion, garlic, soy sauce, ¼ cup water, and pepper. Bake for 30 minutes. Cut into bite-sized pieces.

Dissolve the bouillon cube in 1½ cups hot water in a large pot. Add the frozen broccoli, cauliflower, carrots, mushrooms, water chestnuts, and celery. Bring to a boil and then simmer 15 minutes. Add the cubed steak to the vegetables, and simmer an additional 15 minutes. Serve over ⅔ cup of rice.

Exchange Values Per Serving
1 Serving = 1 Cup Beef Mix and ⅔ Cup Rice
½ Fat
4½ Meat
1¾ Starch
2½ Vegetable

381 Calories
(15% from Fat)
6.4 gm Total Fat
2.6 gm Saturated Fat
76.5 mg Cholesterol
199 mg Sodium
42.1 gm Carbohydrates
6.5 gm Dietary Fiber
38.6 gm Protein
769 mg Potassium

Round Steak in Wine Sauce

10 Servings

3	pounds round steak, about 1½ inches thick
1	teaspoon low-sodium Worcestershire sauce
1	teaspoon low-sodium soy sauce
2	tablespoons low-sodium chicken broth

1½	cups chopped onion
2	tablespoons brown mustard
1	cup sliced fresh mushrooms
¼	cup dry white wine
	White wine mixed with water

Four hours before cooking, marinate the steak in Worcestershire and soy sauces.

Sauté the steak in the broth in a large skillet. Add the remaining ingredients, cover, and simmer for 2 hours, adding 1 part wine and 1 part water to the meat as it cooks if it becomes too dry. The meat should be tender when done.

Exchange Values Per Serving
1 Serving = 4 Ounces
¾ Fat
5 Meat
½ Vegetable

233 Calories
(27% from Fat)
6.7 gm Total Fat
2.9 gm Saturated Fat
91.9 mg Cholesterol
111 mg Sodium
2.9 gm Carbohydrates
0.6 gm Dietary Fiber
37.1 gm Protein
424 mg Potassium

Poached Beef Tenderloin

6 Servings

Exchange Values Per Serving
1 Serving = 2 Slices
   (3 Ounces)
1¾ Fat
3½ Meat

217 Calories
(36% from Fat)
8.5 gm Total Fat
3.7 gm Saturated Fat
71.4 mg Cholesterol
75 mg Sodium
1.7 gm Carbohydrates
0.3 gm Dietary Fiber
25.4 gm Protein
456 mg Potassium

1½ pounds lean beef tenderloin roast Kitchen twine	1 cup dry red wine
1 can (10¾ ounces) low-sodium beef broth	2 garlic cloves, minced
	1 teaspoon diced marjoram leaves
4 cups water	4 peppercorns
	3 whole cloves

Tie the beef roast with kitchen twine at 2-inch intervals. In a deep pan brown the beef roast in broth over medium-high heat until all sides are browned. Pour off the drippings and reserve.

Combine the water, reserved drippings, wine, garlic, marjoram, peppercorns, and garlic cloves in a bowl. Pour over beef. Bring to a boil, reduce the heat to medium low, cover, and simmer for 10 minutes per pound. The temperature will register 130°. Do not overcook.

Remove the roast to a serving platter. Cover tightly with plastic wrap or aluminum foil and allow the roast to stand for 10 minutes before carving. The roast temperature will rise approximately 10° in temperature to 140° for rare. Remove the string and carve the roast into thin slices.

Stir-Fry Beef and Spinach with Noodles

4 Servings

Exchange Values Per Serving
1 Serving = 1¾ Cups
1 Fat
3½ Meat
2 Starch
1½ Vegetable

382 Calories
(20% from Fat)
8.5 gm Total Fat
3.2 gm Saturated Fat
69.1 mg Cholesterol
340 mg Sodium
44.2 gm Carbohydrate
4.7 gm Dietary Fiber
31.1 gm Protein
527 mg Potassium

1 pound beef round tip steaks, all fat removed	6 ounces uncooked thin spaghetti
¼ cup low-sodium hoisin sauce	2 cups fresh spinach, stems removed, thinly sliced
2 tablespoons low-sodium soy sauce	1 can (8 ounces) sliced water chestnuts, drained
1 tablespoon water	
1 teaspoon dark sesame oil	¼ cup sliced green onions
2 large garlic cloves, minced	2 tablespoons chopped red chili peppers
¼ teaspoon crushed red pepper	

Stack beef steaks and cut lengthwise in half and then crosswise into 1-inch wide strips. Place in a pan. Combine hoisin sauce, soy sauce, water, oil, garlic, and pepper in a bowl and pour half over beef. Cover and marinate in refrigerator 10 minutes. Reserve remaining marinade.

Cook pasta according to package directions; keep warm.

Remove beef from marinade. Heat large nonstick wok or skillet over medium-high heat until hot. Add beef (half at a time) and stir-fry 1 to 2 minutes or until outside surface is no longer pink. (Do not overcook). Remove from skillet with slotted spoon; keep warm.

In same skillet, combine pasta, spinach, water chestnuts, green onions, and reserved marinade; cook until spinach is wilted and mixture is heated through, stirring occasionally. Return beef to skillet; mix lightly. Garnish with chili peppers.

Beef Tenderloin with Herbed Tomato Sauce

8 Servings

2½ pounds center cut beef tenderloin, trimmed	¼ cup puréed tomatoes
½ teaspoon freshly ground pepper	¼ cup low-sodium soy sauce
½ teaspoon garlic powder	¼ cup balsamic vinegar
1 teaspoon paprika	1 teaspoon paprika
½ teaspoon celery salt	1 garlic clove, minced
¼ teaspoon rubbed sage	1 tablespoon dried basil
Nonstick cooking spray	1 teaspoon pepper freshly ground
	Lettuce leaves

Rub beef with ½ teaspoon pepper, garlic powder, paprika, celery salt, and sage. Refrigerate in a sealed plastic bag for 2 to 4 hours. Remove beef from the refrigerator 1 hour before cooking.

Preheat oven to 325°. Slice beef into thin medallion sizes, leaving the tenderloin together. Place in a baking pan that has been coated with nonstick cooking spray. Bake for 1 hour.

To make tomato sauce, combine the tomato purée, soy sauce, vinegar, and remaining spices in a medium mixing bowl. Remove the meat from the oven and brush the tomato herb sauce over the meat. Return to the oven and continue to bake for another hour or until the juices run clear and the center of meat reaches a temperature of 140° (rare) to 160° (well-done). Serve on a large platter, placing meat medallions in a circular fashion on top of lettuce leaves.

Exchange Values Per Serving
1 Serving = 3 Medallions
1½ Fat
4¼ Meat

235 Calories
(40% from Fat)
10.2 gm Total Fat
4.5 gm Saturated Fat
89.3 mg Cholesterol
460 mg Sodium
3.5 gm Carbohydrates
0.5 gm Dietary Fiber
30.9 gm Protein
533 mg Potassium

Pepper Steak

4 Servings

Exchange Values Per Serving
1 Serving = 4 Ounces
1½ Fat
3½ Meat
1 Vegetable

222 Calories
(39% from Fat)
9.5 gm Total Fat
4.1 gm Saturated Fat
57.0 mg Cholesterol
403 mg Sodium
6.5 gm Carbohydrates
1.5 gm Dietary Fiber
26.7 gm Protein
609 mg Potassium

½   cup water
2   low-sodium beef bouillon cubes
1   pound flank steak, cut very thin
1   small onion, sliced
1   can (4 ounces) mushrooms, drained
1   medium green bell pepper, cut into thin strips
1   tablespoon low-sodium Worcestershire sauce
1   tablespoon low-sodium soy sauce
    Pepper to taste

Boil water and dissolve bouillon cubes. Preheat oven to 350°. Place the steak strips in a baking pan and cover with bouillon mixture. Layer the onions, mushrooms, and green peppers over the steak. Sprinkle with Worcestershire and soy sauces and pepper to taste. Cover and bake for 20 minutes or until the vegetables and steak are tender. Serve with Steak Sauce (page 251).

Swedish Meatballs

4 Servings

Exchange Values Per Serving
1 Serving = 2 Large Meatballs
¼ Fat
1½ Meat
2 Vegetable

233 Calories
(25% from Fat)
6.6 gm Total Fat
1.6 gm Saturated Fat
38.2 mg Cholesterol
576 mg Sodium
27.6 gm Carbohydrates
2.0 gm Dietary Fiber
16.7 gm Protein
344 mg Potassium

½   pound ground turkey breast
¾   cup fat-free breadcrumbs
1   onion, diced
¼   cup egg substitute
1   teaspoon low-sodium Worcestershire sauce
1   tablespoon parsley flakes
1   teaspoon pepper
1   can (10¾ ounces) reduced-fat cream of celery soup
1   soup can (10¾ ounces) fat-free milk
    Nonstick cooking spray

Preheat oven to 350°. Combine the ground turkey, breadcrumbs, onion, egg substitute, Worcestershire sauce, and seasonings. Add ¼ cup of the soup to the mixture. Form into meatballs and place on a shallow baking sheet that has been coated with cooking spray. Bake until browned. Combine the remaining soup and the milk in a saucepan. Add the meatballs and heat through, about 15 minutes.

Swiss Steak

6 Servings

1	2-pound round steak
½	teaspoon pepper
1	teaspoon minced garlic
1	teaspoon onion powder
1	can (14½ ounces) low-sodium diced tomatoes, with liquid
1	small onion, minced
1	cup diced carrots
1	cup mushroom crowns
½	cup cold water

Preheat oven to 350°. Place the round steak in a baking pan. Sprinkle with pepper, garlic, and onion powder. Combine the tomatoes, onion, carrots, mushrooms, and water in a bowl. Pour over the steak. Cover and bake for 30 minutes. Uncover and cook for 10 minutes more. Test for doneness.

Exchange Values Per Serving
1 Serving = 4 Ounces
¾ Fat
5¾ Meat
1 Vegetable

265 Calories
(26% from Fat)
7.3 gm Total Fat
3.2 gm Saturated Fat
102.1 mg Cholesterol
123 mg Sodium
6.1 gm Carbohydrates
1.4 gm Dietary Fiber
41.4 gm Protein
514 mg Potassium

Sausage and Spinach Casserole

4 Servings

	Nonstick cooking spray
4	ounces smoked turkey sausage
2	medium carrots, thinly sliced
½	cup chopped white onion
2	garlic cloves, minced
8	cups torn spinach leaves
1	cup fat-free sour cream
½	cup cracker crumbs
4	tablespoons low-fat Monterey Jack cheese

Preheat oven to 350°. Coat a large frying pan with nonstick spray. Over medium heat, cook the sausage, carrots, onion, and garlic in the frying pan until the onion is tender. Add spinach and heat through. Remove from heat, add the sour cream, and pour into a casserole dish that has been coated with nonstick cooking spray. Sprinkle the top with cracker crumbs. Bake for 20 to 25 minutes or until bubbly and brown. Remove from the oven and top with cheese. Let sit for 5 minutes before serving.

Exchange Values Per Serving
1 Serving = 3-Inch Square
½ Fat
1 Meat
1½ Vegetable

214 Calories
(26% from Fat)
6.1 gm Total Fat
2.7 gm Saturated Fat
32.6 mg Cholesterol
514 mg Sodium
24.3 gm Carbohydrates
3.2 gm Dietary Fiber
15.4 gm Protein
698 mg Potassium

Stuffed Pork Roast with Mushrooms

8 Servings

Exchange Values Per Serving
1 Serving = 1 Slice
   (4 Ounces)
¼ Fat
3¾ Meat
¾ Starch
½ Vegetable

257 Calories
(34% from Fat)
9.5 gm Total Fat
2.8 gm Saturated Fat
75.3 mg Cholesterol
208 mg Sodium
12.0 gm Carbohydrates
1.1 gm Dietary Fiber
30.1 gm Protein
635 mg Potassium

½	pound mushrooms, including shiitake, cremini, and oyster	½	cup chopped roasted red peppers
4	green onions, sliced	½	teaspoon pepper
1	garlic clove, chopped	1	boneless pork loin roast, about 3 pounds
2	tablespoons low-fat margarine		Kitchen twine
1	cup plain breadcrumbs		

In a skillet over medium heat, cook mushrooms, green onions, and garlic in margarine 3 to 4 minutes, stirring occasionally, until lightly browned. Stir in breadcrumbs, roasted peppers, and pepper. Toss to combine.

Preheat oven to 450°. Prepare roast by laying open the butterflied meat and pound to a flat ⅔-inch thickness. Spread the bread/vegetable mixture over the roast and roll tightly. Secure with twine to maintain the roll. Place on a rack in a roasting pan. Roast 15 minutes at 450°, then reduce to 350° and continue roasting 45 minutes, or until meat thermometer registers 160°. Cover and let stand 10 to 15 minutes before carving.

Veal Provençale

8 Servings

Exchange Values Per Serving
1 Serving = 4 Ounces
2¾ Fat
4¼ Meat
½ Vegetables

284 Calories
(51% from Fat)
16.0 gm Total Fat
2.3 gm Saturated Fat
96.2 mg Cholesterol
78 mg Sodium
2.8 gm Carbohydrates
0.7 gm Dietary Fiber
29.5 gm Protein
418 mg Potassium

3	tomatoes	8	veal scaloppini (4 ounces each)
6	tablespoons canola oil		Pepper to taste
¼	cup low-sodium chicken broth	6	tablespoons dry white wine
3	green onions, chopped	½	bunch fresh basil, chopped

Chop the tomatoes after removing the skin and seeds. Set aside.

Heat the oil and chicken broth in a sauté pan. Sauté the green onions and veal. Add the pepper, tomatoes, wine, and basil. Cover the pan and cook over low heat until the liquid has reduced, about 5 minutes.

Veal Marsala

6 Servings

1½   pounds thinly sliced veal cutlets
¾   cup low-sodium chicken broth
1½   cups thinly sliced mushrooms

Pepper to taste
½   cup Marsala wine
Parsley for garnish

In a large skillet poach veal in broth just until tender, about 5 minutes. With a slotted spoon, remove veal to warmed serving platter. Drain off all but ¼ cup of broth from skillet. Add mushrooms, pepper, and wine. Simmer just until mushrooms are tender, about 3 minutes. Spoon mushroom sauce over veal; garnish with parsley sprigs.

Exchange Values Per Serving
1 Serving = 1 Cutlet
 (4 Ounces)
1¼ Fat
3¾ Meat

266 Calories
(52% from Fat)
14.9 gm Total Fat
5.8 gm Saturated Fat
100.8 mg Cholesterol
83 mg Sodium
1.6 gm Carbohydrates
0.3 gm Dietary Fiber
26.6 gm Protein
349 mg Potassium

POULTRY

Apricot Chicken

6 Servings

6   boneless skinless split chicken
     breasts (about 4 ounces each)
     Nonstick cooking spray
2   tablespoons low-fat margarine,
     melted

2   teaspoons salt-free seasoning
1   teaspoon garlic powder
½   cup unsweetened pure apricot
     preserves

Preheat oven to 350°. Place the chicken breasts in a baking dish coated with cooking spray and brush with melted margarine. Sprinkle with salt-free seasoning and garlic powder. Cover and bake for 45 minutes. Drain the excess fat and juice from the chicken and brush the apricot jam on each piece of chicken with a pastry brush. Return to the oven and bake an additional 15 minutes.

Exchange Values Per Serving
1 Serving = 1 Chicken
 Breast (4 Ounces)
½ Fat
3 Meat
1¼ Starch

206 Calories
(20% from Fat)
4.5 gm Total Fat
1.1 gm Saturated Fat
62.7 mg Cholesterol
113 mg Sodium
17.7 gm Carbohydrates
0.1 gm Dietary Fiber
23.0 gm Protein
228 mg Potassium

Apricot and Chicken Pasta

4 Servings

Exchange Values Per Serving
1 Serving = 1 Chicken Breast and 1 Cup Pasta
3 Meat
½ Milk
2¾ Starch

477 Calories
(16% from Fat)
8.3 gm Total Fat
1.6 gm Saturated Fat
65.0 mg Cholesterol
171 mg Sodium
62.4 gm Carbohydrates
5.0 gm Dietary Fiber
36.6 gm Protein
529 mg Potassium

4 boneless skinless split chicken breasts	⅛ teaspoon ground thyme
1 tablespoon low-fat margarine	1 cup evaporated fat-free milk
2 garlic cloves, minced	2 tablespoons sugarless apricot preserves
4 teaspoons balsamic vinegar	½ pound pasta, cooked
4 teaspoons cider vinegar	¼ cup sliced almonds, toasted
4 teaspoons white muscadine juice	Chopped chives
¼ teaspoon honey	

Cook chicken breasts in margarine in a skillet over medium-low heat 5 minutes on one side. Turn breasts. Spread garlic over breasts and cover tightly. Turn heat to low and cook 3 minutes.

Blend vinegars, muscadine juice, honey, and thyme in a bowl. Pour mixture over chicken, cover, and cook 3 more minutes. Turn chicken and reduce liquid to a glaze. Remove chicken. Add milk, raise heat to high and cook, stirring constantly, until sauce thickens. Blend in preserves.

To serve, toss pasta with almonds and place on platter. Arrange chicken breasts and sauce on pasta and top with chopped chives.

Baked Chicken and Rice

4 Servings

Exchange Values Per Serving
1 Serving = 1 Chicken Breast (4 Ounces)
½ Fat
3 Meat
1½ Starch

269 Calories
(12% from Fat)
3.6 gm Total Fat
1.2 gm Saturated Fat
65.9 mg Cholesterol
275 mg Sodium
27.6 gm Carbohydrates
0.6 gm Dietary Fiber
26.0 gm Protein
263 mg Potassium

8 boneless skinless split chicken breasts (about 4 ounces each)	⅔ cup dry white wine
¼ cup low-sodium chicken broth	1 tablespoon fresh parsley, chopped
1 medium onion, chopped	1 teaspoon paprika
Nonstick cooking spray	Pepper to taste
1 can (10¾ ounces) reduced-fat cream of chicken soup	1 tablespoon low-sodium soy sauce
	1 tablespoon lemon juice
	4 cups cooked rice

Preheat oven to 350°. Lightly brown the chicken breasts in chicken broth in a covered skillet. Place chicken in a medium-size baking dish coated with nonstick cooking spray. Add the onion to the broth in the skillet, and cook until tender, being careful not to brown. Add the soup, white wine, seasonings, soy sauce, and lemon juice. Blend thoroughly and pour over the chicken. Bake for about 45 minutes. Remove from the oven. Place the chicken on a bed of hot rice.

Cheese and Sesame Chicken

8 Servings

8   4-ounce boneless skinless split
    chicken breasts
1   cup fat-free milk
1   cup crushed fat-free cheese crackers
    Nonstick cooking spray

2   tablespoons sesame seed
    Paprika
    Garlic powder to taste
1   tablespoon low-fat margarine

Preheat oven to 350°. Soak the chicken in milk in a bowl. Roll chicken in cracker crumbs and place in a baking dish coated with nonstick cooking spray. Sprinkle with sesame seed, paprika and garlic powder, and drizzle with margarine. Cover and bake for 30 to 45 minutes, until tender and the juices run clear. Uncover for the last 5 to 10 minutes to give a crusty topping.

Exchange Values Per Serving
1 Serving = 1 Chicken
  Breast (4 Ounces)
½ Fat
3 Meat
½ Starch

183 Calories
(25% from Fat)
5.0 gm Total Fat
1.2 gm Saturated Fat
63.6 mg Cholesterol
172 mg Sodium
7.8 gm Carbohydrates
0.5 gm Dietary Fiber
25.2 gm Protein
262 mg Potassium

Baked Fried Chicken

4 Servings

4   boneless skinless split chicken
    breasts (about 5 ounces each)
½   cup fat-free milk
1½ cups puffed rice cereal, slightly
    crushed

    Paprika
    Butter-flavored nonstick cooking
    spray
2   tablespoons low-sodium chicken
    broth

Preheat oven to 350°. Wash the chicken breasts with water and then place in a bowl. Cover with milk.

In another bowl mix the cereal with the paprika and dredge the chicken evenly on each side, covering well. Place in a baking dish that has been coated with butter-flavored cooking spray. Sprinkle a small amount of chicken broth on each piece of chicken. Cover and bake for 30 minutes. Uncover the chicken and continue to bake for another 10 minutes or until browned.

Exchange Values Per Serving
1 Serving = 1 Chicken
  Breast (4 Ounces)
2¾ Meat
½ Starch

142 Calories
(17% from Fat)
2.5 gm Total Fat
0.8 gm Saturated Fat
57.1 mg Cholesterol
68 mg Sodium
6.3 gm Carbohydrates
0.1 gm Dietary Fiber
22.0 gm Protein
227 mg Potassium

Chicken Rosemary

4 Servings

Exchange Values Per Serving
  1 Serving = 1 Chicken
    Breast (4 Ounces)
  3 Meat
  ¾ Starch

176 Calories
  (19% from Fat)
  3.5 gm Total Fat
  0.8 gm Saturated Fat
  62.9 mg Cholesterol
  166 mg Sodium
  9.9 gm Carbohydrates
  0.7 gm Dietary Fiber
  25.1 gm Protein
  189 mg Potassium

4   boneless skinless split chicken breasts
¼   cup low-sodium chicken broth
½   cup breadcrumbs
    Nonstick cooking spray
1   teaspoon crushed fresh rosemary

Preheat oven to 350°. Dip each piece of chicken in bowl of chicken broth, then roll in breadcrumbs. Place in a shallow baking pan that has been coated with cooking spray. Sprinkle lightly with rosemary leaves. Add a small amount of water to cover the bottom of the pan. Cover with foil and bake for 40 minutes. Remove the foil and place under the broiler for a few seconds to brown the chicken.

Chicken à l'Orange

8 Servings

Exchange Values Per Serving
  1 Serving = 1 Chicken
    Breast (4 Ounces)
  1¼ Fruit
  3 Meat

205 Calories
  (12% from Fat)
  2.8 gm Total Fat
  0.8 gm Saturated Fat
  62.7 mg Cholesterol
  56 mg Sodium
  20.0 gm Carbohydrates
  0.8 gm Dietary Fiber
  24.2 gm Protein
  528 mg Potassium

8   boneless skinless split chicken breasts
⅛   teaspoon pepper
1   teaspoon ground ginger
1   orange, sliced
    Nonstick cooking spray
1   cup unsweetened orange juice concentrate, thawed
1   cup unsweetened orange juice
2   tablespoons honey
    Peel of 2 oranges, slivered
1   tablespoon all-purpose flour

Preheat oven to 350°. Rub each piece of chicken with the pepper, ginger, and orange slices. Place the chicken in a baking dish that has been coated with cooking spray. With a pastry brush, brush the chicken breasts with orange juice concentrate. Cover and cook for 20 minutes. Remove from the oven and turn and brush the other side of the chicken breasts. Return chicken to the oven for an additional 15 to 20 minutes.

To make orange sauce, combine remaining juice and honey. Pour the juice mixture into a saucepan. Add the slivered orange peels and flour, and cook until thickened.

When chicken is done, remove it from the oven and serve topped with orange sauce.

Chicken Breasts with Cranberry Chutney

8 Servings

8   boneless skinless split chicken
    breasts
2   tablespoons canola oil
1   tablespoon low-fat margarine
3   tablespoons all-purpose flour
1   tablespoon curry powder

½   cup low-sodium chicken broth
1¼ cups evaporated fat-free milk
    Cranberry Chutney (page 265) or
    whole berry cranberry sauce
4   cups cooked rice
8   slices turkey bacon, crumbled

Sauté chicken in canola oil in a skillet until just firm, not browned. Remove chicken from pan. Add margarine to pan and blend in flour. Cook 3 minutes. Add curry powder and blend. Add chicken broth and stir until smooth. Add milk and cook until thickened. Blend in Cranberry Chutney and stir well. Return chicken to pan, cover, and cook over low heat until chicken is done, about 15 minutes. Serve over rice and top with crumbled turkey bacon.

Exchange Values Per Serving
1 Serving = 1 Chicken
   Breast (4 Ounces)
1½ Fat
3 Meat
1½ Starch

357 Calories
(25% from Fat)
9.5 gm Total Fat
1.9 gm Saturated Fat
73.3 mg Cholesterol
271 mg Sodium
35.4 gm Carbohydrates
1.2 gm Dietary Fiber
30.3 gm Protein
387 mg Potassium

Chicken Popovers

6 Servings

2   egg whites
1   cup fat-free milk
1   cup all-purpose flour
2   tablespoons low-fat margarine
1½ cups finely chopped chicken,
    cooked
½   cup finely chopped celery

½   cup fat-free mayonnaise
2   tablespoons fat-free Italian
    Parmesan salad dressing
1   teaspoon Dijon mustard
2   green onions, finely chopped
    Salt-free seasoning
    Paprika

Preheat oven to 375°. Beat together the egg whites, milk, flour, and margarine in a bowl. Pour into a nonstick deep muffin or popover pan, filling the cups ⅔ full. Bake for 20 to 25 minutes. Do not open the oven while cooking or these will collapse.

Combine the chicken, celery, mayonnaise, dressing, mustard, and onions in a bowl. Stir well. Sprinkle with salt-free seasoning and paprika to taste. Open each popover and stuff with the chicken mixture.

Exchange Values Per Serving
1 Serving = 1 Popover
   filled with ½ Cup
   Stuffing
¾ Fat
1½ Meat
1 Starch

199 Calories
(22% from Fat)
4.8 gm Total Fat
1.2 gm Saturated Fat
28.7 mg Cholesterol
292 mg Sodium
22.1 gm Carbohydrates
0.9 gm Dietary Fiber
15.2 gm Protein
228 mg Potassium

Lemon Pepper Chicken

4 Servings

Exchange Values Per Serving
1 Serving = 1 Chicken Breast
⅓ Fat
¾ Fruit
3½ Meat
¾ Vegetable

200 Calories
(14% from Fat)
3.2 gm Total Fat
0.9 gm Saturated Fat
72.3 mg Cholesterol
67 mg Sodium
15.8 gm Carbohydrate
1.9 gm Dietary Fiber
27.2 gm Protein
384 mg Potassium

2 teaspoons low-sodium chicken broth	¼ teaspoon red pepper flakes
⅓ cup minced onion	¼ teaspoon poppy seeds
1 garlic clove, minced	1 lemon
1½ cups applesauce	Apple juice, if needed
½ teaspoon pepper	4 boneless skinless split chicken breasts

Heat the broth in a medium saucepan. Add the onion and garlic. Sauté for 5 minutes or until soft. Reduce heat. Add applesauce. Stir well. Add seasonings, lemon juice, and peel. Simmer uncovered for 20 minutes, stirring occasionally. If mixture is too thick, add a few tablespoons of apple juice.

Grill the chicken for seven minutes over hot coals. Brush with sauce. Cook 5 minutes. Turn meat and baste again. Cook 5 more minutes. Chicken should be cooked through but not dry. Remove from grill. Cut at an angle into slices. Fan slices on a plate and serve with additional sauce.

Chicken Teriyaki

4 Servings

Exchange Values Per Serving
1 Serving = 1 Chicken Breast (4 Ounces) with 1 Cup Vegetables
½ Fruit
3 Meat
½ Vegetable

171 Calories
(15% from Fat)
2.8 gm Total Fat
0.8 gm Saturated Fat
62.7 mg Cholesterol
57 mg Sodium
12.5 gm Carbohydrates
1.7 gm Dietary Fiber
23.8 gm Protein
405 mg Potassium

4 boneless skinless split chicken breasts	¼ cup chopped water chestnuts
2 cups water	¼ cup snow peas
½ cup chopped green bell pepper	1 can (15¼ ounces) pineapple chunks in pineapple juice, drained
¼ cup chopped mushrooms	¼ cup low-sodium teriyaki sauce

Boil the chicken breasts in 2 cups of water until the meat is tender. Add the vegetables and pineapple, and bring to a rapid boil. Reduce the heat, add teriyaki sauce, and simmer for 30 minutes or until the vegetables are tender. Serve over cooked seasoned rice (not included in analysis).

Chicken Tarragon

8 Servings

8	boneless skinless split chicken breasts (about 4 ounces each)		Pepper to taste
1½	teaspoons chopped fresh tarragon	6	tablespoons low-sodium chicken broth
1	tablespoon white wine vinegar		Nonstick cooking spray
⅔	cup all-purpose flour	18	medium mushroom caps

Marinate the chicken breasts in a pan with tarragon and white wine vinegar. Cover and refrigerate for 2 hours.

Preheat oven to 350°. Drain the marinade and dredge chicken in flour. Pepper to taste. Brown in a skillet with chicken broth. Remove and place in baking dish coated with nonstick spray. Sauté mushrooms in the same skillet. Pour over the chicken breasts. Cover and bake for 35 to 40 minutes.

Exchange Values Per Serving
1 Serving = 1 Chicken Breast (4 Ounces)
3 Meat
½ Starch

164 Calories
(16% from Fat)
2.9 gm Total Fat
0.8 gm Saturated Fat
62.8 mg Cholesterol
61 mg Sodium
8.5 gm Carbohydrates
0.4 gm Dietary Fiber
24.3 gm Protein
246 mg Potassium

Citrus Broiled Chicken

8 Servings

8	boneless skinless split chicken breasts (about 4 ounces each), cut into pieces	½	cup hot water
		1	tablespoon canola oil
	* * *	1	tablespoon brown prepared mustard
¼	cup lemon juice	¼	teaspoon dried thyme
¼	cup sugar-free orange marmalade	¼	teaspoon crushed fresh marjoram
¼	cup sugar-free apricot jelly		

Place the chicken pieces in a 5-quart Dutch oven. Add enough water to cover completely. Bring to a boil, then reduce the heat. Cover and simmer for 10 minutes. Remove from the heat and drain off the liquid.

To make the marinade, combine in a small bowl the remaining ingredients. Place the chicken pieces in a large, shallow non-metal container. Pour the marinade over the chicken and place in the refrigerator for 2 to 4 hours, basting several times. Drain the chicken and reserve the marinade.

When ready to cook, place the chicken on a grill 4 to 6 inches from medium-hot coals, and brush with marinade. Cook for 20 to 30 minutes or until the chicken is tender, turning and brushing frequently with marinade.

Exchange Values Per Serving
1 Serving = 1 Chicken Breast (4 Ounces)
½ Fat
3 Meat
¾ Starch

189 Calories
(21% from Fat)
4.5 gm Total Fat
0.9 gm Saturated Fat
62.7 mg Cholesterol
89 mg Sodium
13.8 gm Carbohydrates
0.2 gm Dietary Fiber
23.1 gm Protein
212 mg Potassium

Louisiana Creole Barbecue Sauce

32 Servings

Exchange Values Per Serving
1 Serving = 3
   Tablespoons
¼ Vegetable

11 Calories
(35% from Fat)
0.5 gm Total Fat
0.1 gm Saturated Fat
0 mg Cholesterol
56 mg Sodium
1.6 gm Carbohydrates
0.3 gm Dietary Fiber
0.3 gm Protein
52 mg Potassium

1 cup finely chopped white onion	1 tablespoon low-sodium soy sauce
2 tablespoons low-fat margarine	2 tablespoons brown mustard
4 large tomatoes, skinned and diced (about 2 cups)	8 drops hot sauce
¼ cup white wine vinegar	1 garlic clove, minced
¼ cup lemon juice	1 bay leaf
3 tablespoons low-sodium Worcestershire sauce	¾ teaspoon chili powder
	2 tablespoons brown sugar substitute

Sauté the onion in low-fat margarine in a skillet until tender. Add the remaining ingredients (except the brown sugar substitute) and bring to a boil. Reduce the heat to a simmer for 20 minutes. Remove from heat and allow to cool. When cooled to slightly warm, add the brown sugar substitute and stir well. Serve over beef or chicken. This can be refrigerated and used later.

Gingered Lime Chicken

4 Servings

Exchange Values Per Serving
1 Serving = 1 Chicken
   Breast (4 Ounces)
¼ Fat
4½ Meat
1½ Starch

304 Calories
(13% from Fat)
4.4 gm Total Fat
1.2 gm Saturated Fat
94.2 mg Cholesterol
90 mg Sodium
25.4 gm Carbohydrates
0.9 gm Dietary Fiber
37.9 gm Protein
337 mg Potassium

½ teaspoon pepper	¼ cup low-sodium chicken broth
2 large garlic cloves, minced	Nonstick cooking spray
1 tablespoon fresh minced ginger	Juice of 1 lime
1 cup all-purpose flour	Parsley
6 boneless skinless split chicken breasts (about 4 ounces each)	Lime wedges

Preheat oven to 350°. Combine pepper, garlic, and ginger in a bowl with the flour. Coat the chicken well in the flour mixture. Heat the broth in a frying pan and cook the chicken until lightly brown on both sides. Remove chicken and place in a baking dish coated with nonstick spray. Squeeze the lime juice over breasts. Cover and bake for 30 minutes. Remove the cover and bake an additional 10 minutes. Remove and place on a serving dish. Garnish with parsley and lime wedges.

Poultry and Rice Pilaf

12 Servings

- 2 cups low-sodium chicken broth
- 2 cups long grain white rice, uncooked
- ½ teaspoon cinnamon
- ¼ teaspoon pepper
- 3 tablespoons pine nuts
- 8 boneless skinless split chicken breasts (about 4 ounces each)
- 2 tablespoons low-sodium chicken broth
- ½ garlic clove, minced
- Juice of ½ lemon
- 1 teaspoon dried oregano
- Parsley for garnish

Preheat oven to 350°. Combine the 2 cups broth, rice, cinnamon, pepper, and pine nuts in a pan. Cook for 5 minutes over low heat, stirring often. Reduce the heat and simmer for 20 minutes or until the rice is done.

Place chicken in a foil-lined pan. Combine the 2 tablespoons chicken broth with the garlic, lemon, and oregano; brush on the chicken. Seal the foil. Bake for 30 minutes. Uncover for the last 10 minutes. Serve the hot rice mixture on a large platter topped with chicken pieces. Garnish with parsley.

Exchange Values Per Serving
- 1 Serving = 1 Chicken Breast (4 Ounces) with ½ Cup Rice
- ⅓ Fat
- 2 Meat
- 1½ Starch

212 Calories
- (15% from Fat)
- 3.3 gm Total Fat
- 0.9 gm Saturated Fat
- 42.5 mg Cholesterol
- 57 mg Sodium
- 25.6 gm Carbohydrates
- 0.6 gm Dietary Fiber
- 18.5 gm Protein
- 179 mg Potassium

Stir-Fry Chicken

4 Servings

- 1 cup low-sodium chicken broth
- 2 tablespoons low-sodium soy sauce
- 2 tablespoons low-sodium Worcestershire sauce
- ¼ teaspoon garlic powder
- ½ cup chopped onion
- 1 cup diced celery
- 2 cups cooked chicken
- 1 can (6 ounces) bean sprouts
- 1 can (8 ounces) bamboo shoots
- 1 can (8 ounces) sliced water chestnuts
- 1 can (4 ounces) sliced mushrooms
- 1 package (6 ounces) frozen snow peas
- Hot cooked rice

Heat the broth in a large saucepan until simmering. Add the soy sauce, Worcestershire sauce, garlic powder, onion, and celery. Cook for about 5 or 6 minutes. Add the remaining ingredients (except the rice), and cook for 10 minutes. Serve over hot rice.

Exchange Values Per Serving
- 1 Serving = 1 Heaping Cup with ½ Cup Rice
- 2¾ Meat
- 1½ Starch
- 2¾ Vegetable

313 Calories
- (10% from Fat)
- 3.3 gm Total Fat
- 1.0 gm Saturated Fat
- 54.9 mg Cholesterol
- 702 mg Sodium
- 43.2 gm Carbohydrates
- 6.1 gm Dietary Fiber
- 28.2 gm Protein
- 645 mg Potassium

Kiwi Chicken

8 Servings

Exchange Values Per Serving
1 Serving = 1 Chicken
    Breast (4 Ounces)
1 Fat
½ Fruit
2¾ Meat
½ Starch

197 Calories
(29% from Fat)
6.2 gm Total Fat
1.0 gm Saturated Fat
56.9 mg Cholesterol
65 mg Sodium
12.3 gm Carbohydrates
1.5 gm Dietary Fiber
22.2 gm Protein
310 mg Potassium

½   cup all-purpose flour
    White pepper to taste
    Paprika to taste
8   boneless skinless split chicken
    breasts (about 5 ounces each)
2   tablespoons canola oil

1   can (14½ ounces) low-sodium
    chicken broth
4   garlic cloves, minced
4   kiwi fruit
    Chopped parsley

Preheat oven to 350°. Mix flour and seasonings in a bowl. Dredge the chicken in flour mixture. Sauté the chicken in hot oil in a skillet until golden brown. Place in a Dutch oven. Pour broth over chicken, rub the garlic cloves on the chicken, leaving them in the pot. Peel and slice the kiwi and arrange around the chicken. Cover and bake for 1 hour or until the chicken is tender. Sprinkle with chopped parsley and serve from the Dutch oven.

Southern Chicken Fry

4 Servings

Exchange Values Per Serving
1 Serving = 1 Chicken
    Breast (4 Ounces)
1 Fat
3 Meat
1 Starch

245 Calories
(25% from Fat)
6.6 gm Total Fat
1.4 gm Saturated Fat
63.2 mg Cholesterol
73 mg Sodium
18.8 gm Carbohydrates
1.6 gm Dietary Fiber
25.5 gm Protein
267 mg Potassium

4   boneless skinless split chicken
    breasts (about 4 ounces each)
¼   cup low-fat buttermilk
½   cup yellow cornmeal
3   tablespoons all-purpose flour

¼   cup chopped fresh parsley
¼   teaspoon freshly ground pepper
2   tablespoons virgin olive oil
    Nonstick cooking spray

Preheat oven to 350°. Place chicken in a large bowl and pour buttermilk over chicken. Turn to coat evenly. In a large plastic bag combine the cornmeal, flour, parsley, and pepper, and mix well. Add chicken one piece at a time and coat.

Place a skillet on medium heat and add olive oil. Place chicken into oil and cook on medium until slightly browned on each side. Remove from pan and drain well.

Place chicken in a baking pan that has been coated with cooking spray. Cover and bake for 30 to 40 minutes or until chicken is tender. Remove cover during last 10 minutes of baking.

Vegetable and Chicken Outdoor Bake

4 Servings

1	pound cooked chicken breasts, diced	2	ribs celery, chopped
1	bunch fresh broccoli, chopped	1	medium onion, chopped
1	bunch fresh cauliflower, chopped	2	carrots, diced
		2	tablespoons low-fat margarine

Combine all of the ingredients (except the margarine) in a large piece of foil (dull side out). Sprinkle with melted margarine and seal all edges of the foil. Place on a hot grill and cover. Grill for 20 to 25 minutes, turning after ten minutes.

Exchange Values Per Serving

1 Serving = 1 Cup
¾ Fat
4½ Meat
3½ Vegetable

284 Calories
(21% from Fat)
6.6 gm Total Fat
1.6 gm Saturated Fat
87.3 mg Cholesterol
242 mg Sodium
18.1 gm Carbohydrates
7.4 gm Dietary Fiber
39.2 gm Protein
1,098 mg Potassium

Asparagus in a Chicken Blanket

6 Servings

1½	pounds boneless skinless chicken breasts, cut into 12 slices	½	cup low-sodium chicken broth
			Juice of one lemon
12	stalks fresh asparagus, cooked	3	tablespoons chopped fresh parsley
1	egg white, lightly beaten		Pinch of pepper
	* * *		Lemon slices for garnish
¼	cup dry white wine		Parsley for garnish

Preheat oven to 350°. Trim all fat from chicken. Pound chicken slices as thinly as possible. Place 1 stalk of asparagus in center of each chicken slice; roll compactly. Seal each chicken roll by brushing with egg white and pressing edges together.

To prepare sauce, heat wine in a non-aluminum saucepan. Add chicken broth, lemon juice, chopped parsley, and pepper. Simmer 1 minute. Place chicken rolls in large shallow baking dish. Top with wine sauce and lemon slices. Cover dish tightly with foil. Bake chicken rolls for 30 to 40 minutes or until chicken is tender. Serve garnished with parsley.

Exchange Values Per Serving

1 Serving = 2 Rolled Breasts
½ Fat
3 Meat

143 Calories
(18% from Fat)
2.8 gm Total Fat
0.8 gm Saturated Fat
63.0 mg Cholesterol
75 mg Sodium
2.3 gm Carbohydrates
0.8 gm Dietary Fiber
24.5 gm Protein
309 mg Potassium

Stuffed Chicken Breasts

2 Servings

Exchange Values Per Serving
1 Serving = 1 Rolled Breast
1⅓ Fat
⅓ Fruit
3 Meat

218 Calories
(26% from Fat)
6.3 gm Total Fat
1.7 gm Saturated Fat
64.4 mg Cholesterol
202 mg Sodium
9.0 gm Carbohydrates
1.0 gm Dietary Fiber
25.5 gm Protein
262 mg Potassium

2 boneless skinless split chicken breasts	1 tablespoon breadcrumbs
½ cup chopped Golden Delicious apples	1 tablespoon low-fat margarine
	¼ cup dry white wine
2 tablespoons shredded, low-fat Cheddar cheese	5 tablespoons water
	1½ teaspoons cornstarch
	Chopped parsley

Flatten the chicken breasts between sheets of waxed paper to ¼-inch thickness. Combine the apple, cheese, and breadcrumbs in a bowl, and divide between the chicken breasts. Roll up each chicken breast and secure with toothpicks.

Melt the margarine in a 7-inch skillet and brown the chicken in the margarine. Add the wine and ¼ cup water, cover, and simmer for 15 to 20 minutes or until the chicken is no longer pink. Remove the chicken from the pan.

Combine remaining water with the cornstarch in a bowl and stir into the juices in the pan. Cook and stir until thickened. Pour the gravy over the chicken and garnish with parsley.

Zesty Chicken Italiano

8 Servings

Exchange Values Per Serving
1 Serving = 1 Cup
½ Fat
2 Meat
1½ Starch
1½ Vegetable

248 Calories
(19% from Fat)
5.4 gm Total Fat
2.0 gm Saturated Fat
36.3 mg Cholesterol
608 mg Sodium
30.7 gm Carbohydrates
4.1 gm Dietary Fiber
19.7 gm Protein
575 mg Potassium

2 tablespoons low-fat margarine	1½ teaspoons oregano
1 pound boneless skinless chicken breasts, cut into 1-inch pieces	½ teaspoon lemon pepper
1 garlic clove, minced	⅛ teaspoon cayenne pepper (optional)
1½ cups thinly sliced zucchini	8 ounces capellini or vermicelli, uncooked
1½ cups sliced fresh mushrooms	½ cup grated Parmesan cheese
1 can (15 ounces) low-sodium tomato sauce	
1 can (14½ ounces) low-sodium peeled whole tomatoes, undrained and quartered	

Melt the margarine in a large skillet. Sauté the chicken pieces until lightly browned. Add the garlic, zucchini, and mushrooms, and sauté for 2 minutes. Stir in the remaining ingredients (except the pasta and Parmesan cheese), and simmer uncovered for 10 minutes to blend the flavors and thicken the sauce.

Meanwhile, cook the pasta according to package directions. Drain. Serve the hot cooked pasta with the sauce. Sprinkle with Parmesan cheese.

Chicken with Onion Marinade

4 Servings

4 boneless skinless split chicken breasts
⅓ cup all-purpose flour
   Nonstick cooking spray

½ cup chopped onion
1 lemon, thinly sliced
1 cup low-sodium chicken broth
2 tablespoons chopped parsley

With a meat mallet, pound each chicken breast half to ¼-inch thickness. Coat with flour. In a large skillet coated with cooking spray, cook chicken 5 minutes on each side. Meat should be golden brown. Remove from pan. Add onion; stirring frequently, cook 1 minute, scraping pan. Return chicken to the pan. Top with lemon slices. Add chicken broth. Cover and simmer about 5 minutes or until chicken is cooked throughout. Sprinkle with parsley.

Exchange Values Per Serving
1 Serving = 1 Chicken Breast (4 Ounces)
3 Meat
½ Starch
½ Vegetable

181 Calories
(16% from Fat)
3.2 gm Total Fat
1.0 gm Saturated Fat
63.6 mg Cholesterol
84 mg Sodium
13.0 gm Carbohydrates
2.0 gm Dietary Fiber
25.3 gm Protein
281 mg Potassium

Herbed Marinated Chicken

6 Servings

½ cup Dijon mustard
2 tablespoons fresh lemon juice
2 cups dry white wine
2 teaspoons dried basil
1 teaspoon dried oregano
½ teaspoon dried thyme

½ teaspoon dried chervil
½ teaspoon dried tarragon

*   *   *

6 boneless skinless split chicken breasts (about 4 ounces each)

To make marinade, blend mustard and lemon juice in a bowl. Gradually stir in wine. Add herbs and blend thoroughly.

Place chicken in large shallow bowl; pour marinade evenly over chicken. Cover and chill several hours. Preheat oven to 350°. Remove chicken from marinade and place on a broiler pan. Bake for 20 minutes or until chicken is tender.

Exchange Values Per Serving
1 Serving = 1 Chicken Breast (4 Ounces)
1 Fat
3 Meat

162 Calories
(20% from Fat)
3.6 gm Total Fat
0.8 gm Saturated Fat
62.7 mg Cholesterol
309 mg Sodium
1.9 gm Carbohydrates
0.3 gm Dietary Fiber
23.6 gm Protein
253 mg Potassium

Oven-Baked Chicken Livers

4 Servings

Exchange Values Per
Serving
  1 Serving = 4 Ounces
  ½ Fat
  1½ Meat
  ⅓ Starch
  ½ Vegetable

119 Calories
  (22% from Fat)
  2.9 gm Total Fat
  1.0 gm Saturated Fat
  294 mg Cholesterol
  54 mg Sodium
  9.2 gm Carbohydrates
  0.6 gm Dietary Fiber
  13.4 gm Protein
  165 mg Potassium

1 pound chicken livers	½ cup low-sodium chicken broth
½ cup fat-free milk	1 medium onion, slivered
1½ cups puffed rice cereal, crushed	Paprika
Nonstick cooking spray	

Preheat oven to 350°. Soak the chicken livers in milk in a bowl. Roll in cereal and place in a baking dish that has been coated with cooking spray. Pour the broth and onion over the livers and sprinkle with paprika. Cover and bake for 1 hour or until tender.

Turkey Frittata

4 Servings

Exchange Values Per
Serving
  1 Serving = ½ Cup
  1 Fat
  4⅕ Meat
  1¾ Vegetable

259 Calories
  (33% from Fat)
  9.6 gm Total Fat
  2.3 gm Saturated Fat
  25.7 mg Cholesterol
  516 mg Sodium
  11.7 gm Carbohydrates
  1.9 gm Dietary Fiber
  31.6 gm Protein
  1,064 mg Potassium

Nonstick cooking spray	3 cups egg substitute
1 cup finely chopped red potatoes	¼ cup fat-free milk
½ cup crumbled turkey sausage	1 teaspoon dried oregano
½ cup finely chopped red bell pepper	¼ teaspoon pepper
¼ cup chopped white onion	

In a deep frying pan coated with nonstick cooking spray, cook the potatoes, covered, over medium heat about 5 minutes or until lightly brown and tender. Add sausage, red pepper, and onion, and continue to cook an additional 3 minutes, or until the sausage is cooked through. Remove from heat.

Arrange the vegetables so that they are in equal portions across the bottom of the skillet. In a bowl combine the egg substitute, milk, oregano, and pepper. Return the frying pan to medium heat and pour the egg mixture over the vegetables. Let stand over medium heat and as the edges set, lift the edges to distribute more of the egg mixture as it cooks. Continue to cook until the egg has set. Remove from the heat and let stand for 5 minutes. Slice into wedges and serve warm.

Herbed Turkey

16 Servings

2	10- to 15-pound turkey breasts	1	teaspoon pepper
7	garlic cloves	½	teaspoon dried thyme leaves
	Nonstick cooking spray	½	teaspoon rubbed sage
2	bay leaves	½	teaspoon dried oregano
6	tablespoons low-sodium chicken	½	teaspoon dried marjoram
	broth	½	teaspoon dried basil

Preheat oven to 350°. Rinse and dry the turkey breasts. Rub the skin with a clove of the garlic and lightly coat surface with cooking spray. Stuff the cavity with the bay leaves and garlic cloves. Heat the chicken broth in a saucepan and add the remaining ingredients. Place 1 tablespoon of herbed mixture in the cavities. Brush the remaining mixture over the skin. Bake for 1½ to 2 hours.

Exchange Values Per Serving
1 Serving = 1 Slice (4 Ounces)
4 Meat

223 Calories
(38% from Fat)
9.0 gm Total Fat
2.6 gm Saturated Fat
81.7 mg Cholesterol
69 mg Sodium
0.5 gm Carbohydrates
0 gm Dietary Fiber
32.8 gm Protein
333 mg Potassium

Spicy Turkey Jambalaya

6 Servings

1½	teaspoons garlic powder	4	ribs celery, chopped
1½	teaspoons paprika	2	garlic cloves, minced
½	teaspoon ground white pepper	2	cups smoked turkey sausage, cut
½	teaspoon dried thyme, crushed		¼ inch thick
¼	teaspoon pepper	1	can (14½ ounces) low-sodium
¼	teaspoon ground cumin		chicken broth
¼	teaspoon ground red pepper	½	cup water
1	teaspoon canola oil	1	cup cooked and chopped turkey
4	medium onions, chopped	2	cups long grain rice
2	medium green bell peppers, chopped	3	whole tomatoes, chopped

Combine all dry spices together in a small bowl and set aside.

Heat the oil in a frying pan over medium heat. Add onion, green pepper, celery, garlic, and sausage. Sprinkle the dry spice mix over the vegetables and sausage and stir. Cook uncovered for 10 minutes, stirring frequently. Add chicken broth, water, chopped turkey, and rice. Bring to a boil. Reduce heat, cover, and simmer for 30 minutes or until the rice is tender. Stir in the tomatoes and heat through.

Exchange Values Per Serving
1 Serving = 1 Cup
½ Fat
1¾ Meat
1 Starch
2⅓ Vegetable

239 Calories
(26% from Fat)
7.0 gm Total Fat
1.8 gm Saturated Fat
38.7 mg Cholesterol
427 mg Sodium
29.8 gm Carbohydrates
3.3 gm Dietary Fiber
15.4 gm Protein
545 mg Potassium

Ground Turkey Parmigiana

4 Servings

Exchange Values Per Serving
1 Serving = 1 Patty with
1 Cup Spaghetti
2 Fat
2¾ Meat
2¾ Starch

470 Calories
(36% from Fat)
19.0 gm Total Fat
5.3 gm Saturated Fat
74.8 mg Cholesterol
210 mg Sodium
47.9 gm Carbohydrates
8.4 gm Dietary Fiber
28.0 gm Protein
278 mg Potassium

2	tablespoons all-purpose flour	1⅓	cups low-fat low-sodium spaghetti sauce
	Salt-free seasoning		
1	pound lean, ground turkey	2	ounces low-fat mozzarella cheese
1	tablespoon canola oil	4	cups whole wheat spaghetti,
1	tablespoon low-fat margarine		cooked without salt

Preheat oven to 350°. Mix the flour and seasoning in a bowl. Make 4 turkey patties approximately ¼ inch thick and dredge in the seasoned flour. Be sure that both sides are well covered.

In a saucepan heat oil and margarine. Place turkey patties into the hot oil mix and sprinkle with seasoned flour. Cook until golden brown, turn, and continue to cook the other side until golden brown as well. Remove and drain well.

Place 1 cup of pasta on an ovenproof plate. Place a turkey patty in the center of the pasta. Spoon spaghetti sauce equally over each patty. Cover with mozzarella cheese and bake for 10 minutes. Serve immediately.

Thanksgiving Herbed Turkey

23 Servings

Exchange Values Per Serving
1 Serving = 1 Slice
   (4 Ounces)
4⅓ Meat

239 Calories
(43% from Fat)
11.0 gm Total Fat
3.2 gm Saturated Fat
93.0 mg Cholesterol
80 mg Sodium
0.7 gm Carbohydrates
0.2 gm Dietary Fiber
32.0 gm Protein
336 mg Potassium

1	12-pound turkey	2	garlic cloves, minced
6	fresh thyme sprigs	1	medium onion, quartered
4	fresh rosemary sprigs	2	ribs celery, cut into 4 pieces
4	fresh sage sprigs		Nonstick cooking spray
½	teaspoon salt-free seasoning		

Clean turkey, removing giblets and neck. Rinse in cold water; pat dry. Remove excess fat. Starting at the neck, loosen the skin from the meat with your fingers. Continue this throughout the body cavity and drumsticks.

Preheat oven to 325°. Arrange a thyme sprig beneath the skin on both drumsticks. On the chest cavity place 2 sprigs of thyme, rosemary, and sage. Gently press the skin down onto the herbs. Sprinkle the internal cavity with the salt-free seasoning and garlic, reserving a small amount for the external chest area. Place the onion and celery and a sprig of thyme, sage, and rosemary inside the chest cavity. Truss opening together.

Place turkey in a roasting pan and coat the outside of the turkey with cooking spray. Sprinkle salt-free seasoning and garlic on the outside of the turkey as well. Cover the bottom of the pan with water. Seal loosely with aluminum foil. Place in oven and bake for 2 hours. Uncover and continue to bake for an additional hour or until a meat thermometer registers 170°. Let stand for 20 minutes after cooking before carving.

Turkey with Cranapple Sauce

8 Servings

1	pound boneless skinless split turkey breasts	
	Nonstick cooking spray	
2	teaspoons thyme	
	Pepper to taste	
2	medium onions, quartered	
2	garlic cloves, minced	

2   cups coarsely chopped red apples

1   tablespoon low-fat margarine
3   cups unsweetened cranapple juice
¼   cup cornstarch
1   cup whole berry cranberry sauce
1   tablespoon orange peel

Exchange Values Per Serving
   1 Serving = 3 Ounces
      Turkey with ½ Cup
      Cranapple Sauce
   1 Fat
   1 Fruit
   3½ Meat
   ⅓ Starch
   ½ Vegetable

279 Calories
   (23% from Fat)
   7.2 gm Total Fat
   2.0 gm Saturated Fat
   62.9 mg Cholesterol
   82 mg Sodium
   21.1 gm Carbohydrates
   2.1 gm Dietary Fiber
   25.0 gm Protein
   352 mg Potassium

Preheat oven to 350°. Coat surface of turkey breasts with cooking spray. Rub one teaspoon of thyme inside and outside of each turkey breast and sprinkle with pepper. Place onion and garlic inside each breast cavity. Place the breasts skin side up on the rack in a roasting pan. Bake for 2½ to 3 hours or until the internal temperature reaches 170° and the turkey is tender. Let the turkey stand for 15 minutes before slicing.

To make Cranapple Sauce, sauté apples in margarine in a skillet and set aside. Add the cranapple juice to the cornstarch in a medium saucepan, and blend well. Add the cranberry sauce and orange peel. Cook over medium heat until the mixture boils and thickens, stirring constantly. Add the apples and stir until thoroughly heated. Serve with turkey.

Cranberry Turkey Steaks

4 Servings

Exchange Values Per Serving
1 Serving = 4 Ounces
1 Fruit
3¾ Meat

220 Calories
(4% from Fat)
0.9 gm Total Fat
0.3 gm Saturated Fat
79.1 mg Cholesterol
71 mg Sodium
20.2 gm Carbohydrates
1.3 gm Dietary Fiber
31.7 gm Protein
445 mg Potassium

4   turkey breast tenderloins
½   cup whole berry cranberry sauce
1   medium navel orange, sliced
1   tablespoon brown sugar
Orange slices and cranberries for garnish

Rinse turkey tenderloins and pat dry. In a food processor, place cranberry sauce and orange slices. Process until smooth. Stir the brown sugar into the cranberry/orange mixture.

Place the turkey tenderloins on a grill. Grill turkey until all pink is turned to white. Turn once during cooking. When tenderloins appear done, brush with cranberry sauce. Serve immediately. Garnish with orange slices and whole cranberries.

Italian Turkey Fest

8 Servings

Exchange Values Per Serving
1 Serving = 1 Cup
1 Fat
2½ Meat
1⅓ Starch
3 Vegetable

297 Calories
(20% from Fat)
6.8 gm Total Fat
1.7 gm Saturated Fat
55.3 mg Cholesterol
134 mg Sodium
34.9 gm Carbohydrates
5.1 gm Dietary Fiber
24.7 gm Protein
893 mg Potassium

1½   pounds lean ground turkey breast
1   cup minced onion
3   cups water
1   garlic clove, minced
2   cans (10¾ ounces) low-sodium tomato purée
1   can (6 ounces) low-sodium tomato paste
1   teaspoon low-sodium soy sauce
1   teaspoon low-sodium Worcestershire sauce
2   teaspoons Italian seasoning
1   teaspoon chili powder
4   cups cooked spaghetti

Brown the ground turkey and onions in a large pan. Add the water and remaining ingredients (except spaghetti). Stir to combine, and simmer for 30 minutes. Serve over cooked spaghetti.

Fish Amandine

6 Servings

½ cup slivered almonds
1½ pounds bluefish, boned and
    cleaned
1 tablespoon low-fat margarine,
    melted

½ teaspoon chopped parsley
    Paprika, pepper
    Lemon wedges

Preheat oven to 350°. Arrange the almonds in a single layer on a baking sheet and bake for 4 to 5 minutes or until golden brown. Place the fish in an ungreased baking pan. Arrange the toasted almonds on top of the fish. Drizzle melted margarine over the fish and almonds. Sprinkle with parsley, paprika and pepper to taste. Bake for 20 to 25 minutes, or until the fish flakes easily. Serve with a lemon wedge on top of each piece.

Exchange Values Per Serving
1 Serving = 6 Equal
  Pieces
1½ Fat
3½ Meat

202 Calories
  (47% from Fat)
  10.4 gm Total Fat
  1.7 gm Saturated Fat
  66.9 mg Cholesterol
  91.7 mg Sodium
  1.9 gm Carbohydrates
  1.0 gm Dietary Fiber
  24.5 gm Protein
  488 mg Potassium

Cornflake-Breaded Baked Fish

4 Servings

1 pound fish fillets (sole, flounder,
    or perch)
    Juice of 1 lemon
    Dash freshly ground pepper

1 tablespoon canola oil
⅓ cup cornflake cereal crumbs
    Nonstick cooking spray

Preheat oven to 350°. Wash and dry the fish fillets, and cut into serving size pieces, allowing for shrinkage. Rub each piece with lemon juice. Season to taste, then coat each piece lightly with oil.

Dredge the fillets in cornflake crumbs. Arrange in a single layer in a baking dish that has been coated with cooking spray. Bake for 30 minutes or until the fish flakes.

Exchange Values Per Serving
1 Serving = ¼ Pound
  Fillet
¾ Fat
3½ Meat
⅓ Starch

162 Calories
  (28% from Fat)
  4.8 gm Total Fat
  0.6 gm Saturated Fat
  54.4 mg Cholesterol
  171 mg Sodium
  6.6 gm Carbohydrates
  0 gm Dietary Fiber
  22.0 gm Protein
  428 mg Potassium

Quick and Easy Zesty Fish

4 Servings

4	4-ounce flounder fillets Nonstick cooking spray	½	teaspoon dried Italian seasoning
1½	cups stewed tomatoes, coarsely chopped		

Preheat oven to 400°. Place fish in a 8-inch square baking dish coated with cooking spray; spoon tomatoes over fish. Sprinkle with Italian seasoning. Bake for 12 to 15 minutes or until the fish flakes easily with a fork.

Ale-Poached Sea Bass with Pimiento Sauce

4 Servings

1½	pounds black sea bass fillets	2	tablespoons low-fat margarine
1	cup water	2	tablespoons all-purpose flour
1	cup light beer	1	can (10¾ ounces) low-sodium chicken broth
1	small onion, sliced		
1	teaspoon low-sodium Worcestershire sauce	3	tablespoons chopped pimiento
		1	teaspoon curry powder
3	peppercorns	1	teaspoon lemon juice
1	garlic clove, minced	¾	teaspoon sugar

Remove the skin and bones from fish. Combine the water, beer, onion, Worcestershire sauce, peppercorns, and garlic in a 10-inch skillet and bring to a gentle boil. Place the fillets in the poaching liquid, cover, and simmer for 5 to 10 minutes or until the fish flakes easily when tested with a fork. Carefully remove the fish to a warm platter.

To make pimiento sauce, melt the margarine in a medium saucepan. Stir in the flour. Add the chicken broth gradually and cook until thick and smooth, stirring constantly. Add the pimento, curry powder, lemon juice, and sugar and heat through. Pour the sauce over the fish and serve.

Broiled Fish Steaks and Herbs

4 Servings

1 tablespoon low-fat margarine	1½ pounds fish steaks
1 tablespoon finely chopped parsley	Nonstick cooking spray
¾ teaspoon celery salt	¼ cup white wine
½ teaspoon crumbled oregano leaves	1 tablespoon lemon juice
¼ teaspoon white pepper	Fresh parsley for garnish

Preheat oven to 350°. Melt the margarine in a small saucepan and add parsley, celery, salt, oregano, and pepper. Arrange the fish in a baking dish that has been coated with nonstick spray and brush the herb butter over the fish. Pour the white wine and lemon juice over the fish. Cover and bake for 30 minutes. Uncover and bake 5 more minutes. The fish should flake easily with a fork when done. Garnish with parsley.

Exchange Values Per Serving
1 Serving = 1 Fillet (4 Ounces)
1⅓ Fat
5 Meat

230 Calories
(34% from Fat)
8.2 gm Total Fat
2.2 gm Saturated Fat
66.3 mg Cholesterol
467 mg Sodium
0.6 gm Carbohydrates
0.1 gm Dietary Fiber
33.8 gm Protein
515 mg Potassium

Ybor City Fillets

4 Servings

1½ pounds Tilefish fillets	2 teaspoons minced garlic
½ cup diced yellow bell pepper	1 teaspoon black pepper
½ cup diced green bell pepper	1 teaspoon salt-free seasoning
2 cups cooked yellow rice	1 teaspoon ground cumin
1 tablespoon paprika	

Cut fish into approximately 2-inch cubes. Mix bell peppers with cooked rice in a pan; keep warm. In mixing bowl combine paprika, garlic, pepper, salt-free seasoning, cumin, and fish. Mix ingredients until fish is coated well.

Place fish on a lightly oiled broiler pan, and broil 4 to 6 inches from heat for 5 to 6 minutes on each side. Fish is done when it flakes easily when tested with a fork and is opaque in the center. Serve immediately with yellow rice and bell peppers.

Exchange Values Per Serving
1 Serving = 6 Ounces Fish with ½ Cup Rice and Peppers
⅓ Fat
5 Meats
1⅓ Starch
½ Vegetable

288 Calories
(15% from Fat)
4.6 gm Total Fat
0.9 gm Saturated Fat
85.1 mg Cholesterol
94 mg Sodium
27.0 gm Carbohydrate
1.4 gm Dietary Fiber
32.9 gm Protein
886 mg Potassium

Fish Bake

4 Servings

½ cup enriched cornmeal	1 pound cod, halibut or sole fillets,
¼ teaspoon grated nutmeg	cut into 4 equal fillets
½ teaspoon paprika	Nonstick cooking spray
¼ teaspoon pepper	2 tablespoons low-fat margarine,
¼ cup egg substitute	melted
2 tablespoons fat-free milk	

Exchange Values Per Serving
1 Serving = 1 Fillet
½ Fat
3⅓ Meat
¾ Starch

207 Calories
(20% from Fat)
4.5 gm Total Fat
0.9 gm Saturated Fat
53.9 mg Cholesterol
161 mg Sodium
14.1 gm Carbohydrates
1.4 gm Dietary Fiber
26.1 gm Protein
539 mg Potassium

Preheat oven to 350°. Combine the cornmeal, nutmeg, paprika, and pepper in a bowl. In a separate bowl, combine the egg and milk. Coat the fish in the milk mixture and dredge in the cornmeal mixture. Place in a shallow pan coated with nonstick cooking spray. Drizzle with melted margarine. Bake for 15 to 20 minutes or until golden brown.

Baked Flounder with Orange Sauce

4 Servings

⅔ cup unsweetened orange juice from concentrate	Cayenne pepper to taste
1 tablespoon grated orange peel	4 4-ounce flounder fillets
1 teaspoon freshly grated nutmeg	Nonstick cooking spray
Salt-free seasoning	1 whole orange sliced into rounds
	Ground nutmeg

Exchange Values Per Serving
1 Serving = 1 Fillet
(4 Ounces)
½ Fruit
3½ Meat

141 Calories
(11% from Fat)
1.6 gm Total Fat
0.4 gm Saturated Fat
54.4 mg Cholesterol
92 mg Sodium
8.9 gm Carbohydrates
1.1 gm Dietary Fiber
22.0 gm Protein
550 mg Potassium

Preheat oven to 450°. To make orange sauce, combine the orange juice, peel, nutmeg, salt-free seasoning, and pepper in a bowl and set aside.

Lay fish fillets on a baking dish that has been coated with cooking spray. Spoon equal amounts of orange nutmeg sauce over each fillet. Bake, covered, for 15 minutes. Uncover and bake an additional 5 minutes. Place each fillet on a plate, top with a orange slice, and sprinkle with nutmeg.

Flounder and Vegetable Bake

2 Servings

8	ounces flounder fillets	¼	cup chopped onion
4	ounces evaporated fat-free milk	½	cup sliced mushrooms
	Paprika to taste	2	ribs celery, chopped
	Pepper to taste	1	cup chopped cauliflower
	Salt substitute to taste	1	cup chopped broccoli
½	tablespoon lemon juice	1	cup julienne-cut carrots
	Nonstick cooking spray		

Marinate the fish fillets in milk in a bowl for 15 minutes. Drain. Preheat oven to 350°. Sprinkle the fillets with paprika, pepper, salt substitute, and lemon juice. Place in a foil tent inside a baking dish coated with nonstick spray. Cover with the vegetables and bake for 15 to 20 minutes or until tender.

Exchange Values Per Serving
1 Serving = 4 Ounces
½ Milk
3½ Meat
3 Vegetable

216 Calories
(8% from Fat)
2.1 gm Total Fat
0.5 gm Saturated Fat
56.5 mg Cholesterol
239 mg Sodium
21.6 gm Carbohydrates
5.5 gm Dietary Fiber
29.4 gm Protein
1,290 mg Potassium

Trout with Pecan Sauce

4 Servings

4	tablespoons low-fat margarine	4	4-ounce trout fillets
2	tablespoons canola oil	¼	cup pecan halves
¼	cup evaporated fat-free milk	2	tablespoons fresh lemon juice
½	cup all-purpose flour	2	tablespoons finely chopped fresh parsley
	Salt-free seasoning		

Melt 2 tablespoons margarine with oil in a large, heavy skillet. Place the milk in a bowl. In another bowl mix the flour and salt-free seasoning. Coat trout in milk and then dredge in seasoned flour. Sauté trout in oil and margarine until golden on one side, about 8 minutes. Turn and cook 8 minutes longer. Remove trout to warm platter and sprinkle with salt seasoning.

Empty and wipe out skillet, then add remaining 2 tablespoons of margarine. Sauté pecans in margarine, shaking pan, until margarine turns golden brown. Add lemon juice to pan, then pour pecan sauce over trout. Sprinkle with fresh parsley.

Exchange Values Per Serving
1 Serving = 1 Fillet
    (4 Ounces)
4½ Fat
3½ Meat
¾ Starch

350 Calories
(51% from Fat)
20.0 gm Total Fat
2.8 gm Saturated Fat
65.2 mg Cholesterol
181 mg Sodium
15.8 gm Carbohydrates
1.0 gm Dietary Fiber
26.7 gm Protein
523 mg Potassium

Trout Bake

6 Servings

Exchange Values Per
Serving
   1 Serving = 1 Fillet
      (4 Ounces)
   1½ Fat
   3½ Meat

217 Calories
   (42% from Fat)
   9.9 gm Total Fat
   1.6 gm Saturated Fat
   65.5 mg Cholesterol
   85 mg Sodium
   5.1 gm Carbohydrates
   0.5 gm Dietary Fiber
   25.8 gm Protein
   508 mg Potassium

3 8-ounce trout fillets, halved	Nonstick cooking spray
1 cup fat-free milk	¼ cup almond slivers, toasted
1 cup puffed rice cereal	
4 tablespoons low-sodium chicken broth	

Soak the trout in the milk in a bowl for 1 hour before cooking. Drain.

Preheat oven to 350°. In a separate bowl combine the rice cereal and broth. Dredge the trout in cereal mixture and place in a baking dish that has been coated with nonstick cooking spray. Sprinkle the fillets with almonds. Bake uncovered for 30 minutes or until the fish flakes easily.

Salmon Mousse

6 Servings

Exchange Values Per
Serving
   1 Serving = 1-Inch Slice
   1½ Meat

114 Calories
   (40% from Fat)
   5.3 gm Total Fat
   1.0 gm Saturated Fat
   30.5 mg Cholesterol
   238 mg Sodium
   4.2 gm Carbohydrates
   0.2 gm Dietary Fiber
   13.5 gm Protein
   151 mg Potassium

1 package (¼ ounce) sugar-free unflavored gelatin	½ teaspoon black pepper
½ cup cold water	¼ teaspoon paprika
1 can (7½ ounces) skinned and boned red salmon, drained	¼ teaspoon garlic powder
1 cup fat-free plain yogurt	Salad greens
1 tablespoon fresh lemon juice	6 whole cherry tomatoes
1 teaspoon dried dill weed	Parsley sprigs
	Lemon or lime wedges

In a small saucepan sprinkle gelatin over cold water. Stir constantly over low heat until gelatin dissolves, about 3 minutes. Remove from heat and cool.

Place gelatin mixture, salmon, yogurt, lemon juice, and seasonings in a large bowl. Stir until blended. Pour salmon mixture into a 1-quart mold. Cover and chill at least 4 hours. Unmold mousse onto serving plate. Garnish with salad greens, tomatoes, parsley, and lemon or lime wedges.

Mostaccioli al Forno (page 214), Manicotti with Eggplant-Tomato Relish (page 216)

Lemon Pepper Chicken (page 176), Shrimp with Oriental Ginger Apple Barbecue Sauce (page 252), Ham with Mustard Garlic Apple-cue Sauce (page 253)

FACING PAGE: *Manicotti with Ratatouille Sauce (page 217), Savory Jumbo Shells (page 214)*

Light and Easy Poundcake (page 292)

Spicy Salmon Cakes

4 Servings

6	ounces canned salmon	¼	teaspoon hot pepper sauce
½	cup egg substitute	2	tablespoons all-purpose flour
½	cup seasoned breadcrumbs	1	tablespoon canola oil
½	cup sliced green onions		Lemon wedges
1	tablespoon Dijon mustard		

In a medium bowl combine the salmon, egg substitute, breadcrumbs, green onions, mustard, and hot pepper sauce. Form into 4 patties. Dredge patties in flour to coat both sides. Drizzle oil onto hot griddle and cook patties for 5 minutes on each side or until browned. Serve with lemon wedges.

Exchange Values Per Serving
1 Serving = 1 Patty
1 Fat
1¾ Meat
1 Starch

216 Calories
(37% from Fat)
9.0 gm Total Fat
1.2 gm Saturated Fat
19.0 mg Cholesterol
881 mg Sodium
18.1 gm Carbohydrates
1.2 gm Dietary Fiber
15.9 gm Protein
311 mg Potassium

Stuffed Sole with Lemon-Mustard Sauce

4 Servings

4	4-ounce sole (or flounder) fillets	¼	cup plain fat-free yogurt
4	teaspoons low-fat margarine, soft	¼	cup fat-free sour cream
¼	teaspoon dried tarragon	1	teaspoon lemon juice
	Large spinach leaves	½	teaspoon Dijon mustard
	Nonstick cooking spray	½	teaspoon finely shredded lemon peel
		1	tablespoon finely snipped parsley

Preheat oven to 350°. Divide fish into 8 equal portions, combining and piecing the fillets as necessary. Combine the margarine and tarragon. Spread each portion with ⅛ of the margarine mixture; place 1 or 2 spinach leaves on top. Roll up fillets and secure with a wooden toothpick. Place rolls in an 8 x 8 x 2-inch baking dish coated with nonstick spray. Cover with foil and bake for 15 to 20 minutes or until the fish flakes.

For the sauce, combine the yogurt, sour cream, lemon juice, mustard, and lemon peel in a bowl. Place in a microwave and heat on high for 1 minute, or warm in saucepan over medium heat. Stir once during cooking process. Do not boil. Stir in parsley. Spoon sauce on individual plates and place fish rolls on the sauce.

Exchange Values Per Serving
1 Serving = 1 Fillet
½ Fat
3½ Meat

150 Calories
(21% from Fat)
3.4 gm Total Fat
0.7 gm Saturated Fat
56.0 mg Cholesterol
186 mg Sodium
4.9 gm Carbohydrates
0.4 gm Dietary Fiber
23.7 gm Protein
549 mg Potassium

Broiled Peppered Swordfish

4 Servings

Exchange Values Per Serving
1 Serving = 1 Steak
1⅓ Fat
3½ Meat
½ Vegetable

187 Calories
(41% from Fat)
8.3 gm Total Fat
1.8 gm Saturated Fat
44.2 mg Cholesterol
239 mg Sodium
3.6 gm Carbohydrates
1.3 gm Dietary Fiber
22.9 gm Protein
343 mg Potassium

4	4-ounce swordfish steaks
1	tablespoon low-sodium soy sauce
1	tablespoon virgin olive oil
2	tablespoons lemon juice
1	tablespoon black peppercorns, crushed
1	tablespoon green peppercorns, crushed
1	tablespoon red peppercorns, crushed

Serve with Green Onion Cream Sauce (page 251)

Preheat broiler to 475°. Season steaks with soy sauce, olive oil, and lemon juice. Combine peppercorns and sprinkle tops of swordfish steaks with mixture. Press pepper firmly into surface of fish. Place on broiler pan, peppered side up, and broil to desired degree of doneness, 4 to 6 minutes, depending on the thickness. To serve, place 1 tablespoon of warmed Green Onion Cream Sauce on plate and place the swordfish steak in the center.

Wakulla Grilled Grouper

4 Servings

Exchange Values Per Serving
1 Serving = 6 Ounces Grouper with Orange and Lettuce
⅓ Fat
1 Fruit
5 Meat
¾ Vegetable

270 Calories
(13% from Fat)
3.9 gm Total Fat
0.7 gm Saturated Fat
62.9 mg Cholesterol
106 mg Sodium
23.4 gm Carbohydrate
5.6 gm Dietary Fiber
36.1 gm Protein
1,356 mg Potassium

1½	pounds grouper fillets
⅓	cup unsweetened orange juice
1	tablespoon virgin olive oil
1	tablespoon honey
½	teaspoon salt-free seasoning
4	medium oranges, peeled
2	heads iceberg lettuce
¾	cup chopped green onions
½	cup fresh basil leaves, chopped
¼	teaspoon white pepper

Cut grouper into four equal portions. Combine orange juice, olive oil, honey, and salt-free seasoning in a shallow container and mix. Coat fish with marinade and keep in refrigerator one hour, turning once.

Slice oranges into ¼-inch rounds and arrange three on a plate. Peel outer leaves from lettuce and discard; slice remaining lettuce into ½-inch rounds. Place lettuce rounds and onions on orange slices and arrange basil leaves on lettuce. Season with white pepper.

Grill grouper, basting with marinade. Place grilled fish over salad and serve immediately.

Orange Roughy in Lemon Wine Sauce

4 Servings

2   tablespoons chopped green onions
2   teaspoons chopped fresh parsley
1   teaspoon low-sodium
    Worcestershire sauce
½   teaspoon lemon peel
½   cup dry white wine
1   tablespoon fresh lemon juice

1   teaspoon arrowroot
½   cup low-fat buttermilk
4   4-ounce orange roughy fillets
    Nonstick cooking spray
    White wine for broiling
1   cup seedless red grapes
1   tablespoon finely chopped almonds

Combine green onions, parsley, Worcestershire, lemon peel, wine, and lemon juice in a skillet. Bring to a boil and reduce to ½ cup. Combine arrowroot with buttermilk and add to sauce, stirring constantly until slightly thickened; then set aside.

Preheat broiler. Place fish fillets in a baking dish coated with cooking spray and add ⅛-inch white wine. Broil fish 3 to 5 minutes. Remove from broiler, pour sauce over fish, add grapes, and sprinkle with almonds. Broil until sauce bubbles and fish begins to flake, about 1 more minute.

Exchange Values Per Serving
1 Serving = 1 Fillet
    (4 Ounces)
¾ Fat
½ Fruit
2½ Meat

157 Calories
(14% from Fat)
2.4 gm Total Fat
0.4 gm Saturated Fat
23.8 mg Cholesterol
121 mg Sodium
10.6 gm Carbohydrates
0.7 gm Dietary Fiber
18.5 gm Protein
527 mg Potassium

Very Orange Roughy

4 Servings

2   whole oranges
4   4-ounce orange roughy fillets
    Nonstick cooking spray
2   teaspoons low-fat margarine,
    melted

½   teaspoon salt-free seasoning
    Orange slices for garnish

Peel the oranges, removing white from the edges. Cut the oranges into ¼-inch slices and set aside.

Place the fish on a broiling rack that has been coated with cooking spray. Combine the melted margarine and salt-free seasoning in a bowl. Brush each fillet with the margarine mix. Arrange orange slices on broiler. Broil for 4 to 5 minutes or until the fish will flake. Place on individual plates. Garnish with orange slices.

Exchange Values Per Serving
1 Serving = 1 Fillet
    (4 Ounces)
⅓ Fat
½ Fruit
2⅓ Meat

117 Calories
(14% from Fat)
1.8 gm Total Fat
0.2 gm Saturated Fat
22.7 mg Cholesterol
94 mg Sodium
7.7 gm Carbohydrates
1.6 gm Dietary Fiber
17.3 gm Protein
459 mg Potassium

Hot Tuna and Potato Bake

6 Servings

Exchange Values Per Serving
1 Serving = 1 Cup
3 Meat
½ Milk
1 Starch
⅓ Vegetable

267 Calories
(5% from Fat)
1.5 gm Total Fat
0.5 gm Saturated Fat
32.1 mg Cholesterol
509 mg Sodium
29.2 gm Carbohydrates
2.1 gm Dietary Fiber
33.3 gm Protein
849 mg Potassium

3   cans (6 ounces) water-packed tuna, drained
1   can (4 ounces) sliced mushrooms, drained
1   tablespoon low-sodium Worcestershire sauce
½   teaspoon hot sauce
2   tablespoons vinegar
3   cups cooked and diced potatoes
¼   cup low-sodium chicken broth
¼   cup thinly sliced onion
¼   cup thinly sliced celery
¼   cup all-purpose flour
1   teaspoon dry mustard
2   cups fat-free milk
1   cup fat-free plain yogurt

Preheat oven to 350°. Combine the tuna, mushrooms, Worcestershire sauce, and hot sauce in a bowl. In a separate bowl, combine the vinegar and potatoes.

Warm the chicken broth in a sauté pan and simmer the onion and celery until tender. Add the flour and dry mustard, and remove from the heat. Gradually add the milk and yogurt, and stir until combined.

Place ½ of the potatoes in a large casserole dish. Top with half of the tuna mixture and half of the sauce mixture. Repeat the layers. Bake for 35 minutes.

Tuna and Noodle Casserole

4 Servings

Exchange Values Per Serving
1 Serving = 3-Inch Square
½ Fat
3 Meat
½ Starch
1⅓ Vegetable

206 Calories
(15% from Fat)
3.3 gm Total Fat
0.7 gm Saturated Fat
41.3 mg Cholesterol
402 mg Sodium
15.1 gm Carbohydrates
1.9 gm Dietary Fiber
28.3 gm Protein
1,008 mg Potassium

1½   cups no-yolk wide noodles, broken into 1-inch pieces
¾   teaspoon salt substitute
6   cups water
¼   cup finely chopped celery
¼   cup finely chopped onion
4   teaspoons low-fat margarine
Dash of white pepper
2   cups low-sodium canned tomatoes, crushed
2   cans (6 ounces) tuna packed in water, drained
Nonstick cooking spray
Grated Parmesan cheese

Preheat oven to 350°. Cook the noodles in 6 cups of water with salt substitute. Drain and rinse in cold water.

Sauté the celery and onion in margarine in a skillet. When the vegetables are tender, add the pepper, tomatoes, and tuna. Add the sautéed mixture to the noodles and place in a baking dish coated with cooking spray. Sprinkle the top with Parmesan cheese. Bake for 30 minutes.

Tuna Potato Casserole

4 Servings

1½ cups no-yolk wide noodles, cooked	1 tablespoon low-sodium Worcestershire sauce
1 can (6 ounces) tuna packed in water, drained	½ teaspoon hot sauce
4 ounces peas	1 cup cubed potatoes, cooked
½ cup canned mushrooms, drained	¼ cup chopped celery
4 ounces evaporated fat-free milk	Nonstick cooking spray
2 tablespoons onion flakes	10 fat-free cheese crackers, crushed
Dash of pepper	

Preheat oven to 350°. Combine all of the ingredients (except the cracker crumbs) in a bowl and place in a casserole dish coated with nonstick spray. Sprinkle the top with the crumbs. Bake covered for 30 to 40 minutes, until the potatoes are tender. Uncover for the last 10 minutes of cooking time to brown the top.

Exchange Values Per Serving
1 Serving = 1 Cup
1½ Meat
2 Starch
½ Vegetable

248 Calories
(4% from Fat)
1.0 gm Total Fat
0.2 gm Saturated Fat
16.0 mg Cholesterol
403 mg Sodium
38.2 gm Carbohydrates
4.6 gm Dietary Fiber
21.4 gm Protein
600 mg Potassium

Pimiento Tuna in a Pepper Cup

6 Servings

3 medium red bell peppers, halved and seeded	1 tablespoon fresh chopped parsley
2 cans (6 ounces each) tuna packed in water, drained	1 tablespoon finely chopped and seeded jalapeño pepper
1 cup finely chopped celery	1 tablespoon lemon juice
¼ cup sliced green onions	2 tablespoons fat-free mayonnaise
¼ cup diced pimiento	1 tablespoon Dijon mustard

Place pepper halves on plates. In a bowl mix all ingredients. When well blended, spoon into bell pepper shells.

Exchange Values Per Serving
1 Serving = 1 Pepper Half
2 Meat
1 Vegetable

104 Calories
(8% from Fat)
0.9 gm Total Fat
0.2 gm Saturated Fat
19.8 mg Cholesterol
342 mg Sodium
6.2 gm Carbohydrates
1.7 gm Dietary Fiber
17.8 gm Protein
342 mg Potassium

Grilled Tuna with Citrus-Sage Marinade

4 Servings

Exchange Values Per Serving
1 Serving = 1 Fillet (4 Ounces)
1½ Fat
3½ Meat

200 Calories
(37% from Fat)
8.1 gm Total Fat
1.3 gm Saturated Fat
51.0 mg Cholesterol
42 mg Sodium
3.8 gm Carbohydrates
0.5 gm Dietary Fiber
26.8 gm Protein
561 mg Potassium

2 teaspoons dried sage	¼ cup virgin olive oil
1 tablespoon lemon peel	4 3-ounce tuna fillets
1 tablespoon orange peel	10 fresh sage leaves
¼ cup fresh lemon or lime juice	Fresh sage leaves for garnish
¼ cup unsweetneed orange juice from concentrate	Lemon, lime, and orange slices for garnish

To make marinade, combine sage, peels, and juices. Whisk in oil.

To prepare the fish, score each fillet on both sides. Place in glass dish and cover with the marinade. Marinate for at least 3 hours.

Prepare grill and put a bundle of 10 fresh sage leaves on coals. Cook fish until flaky, 5 to 7 minutes per side. Baste fish with marinade while cooking. Garnish with sage leaves and fresh citrus slices before serving.

Catfish with Angel Hair Pasta

6 Servings

Exchange Values Per Serving
1 Serving = 1 Fillet (4 Ounces)
1 Fat
2½ Meat
2 Starch
½ Vegetable

359 Calories
(31% from Fat)
12.5 gm Total Fat
2.6 gm Saturated Fat
53.3 mg Cholesterol
448 mg Sodium
36.1 gm Carbohydrates
1.7 gm Dietary Fiber
25.4 gm Protein
599 mg Potassium

6 4-ounce catfish fillets Nonstick cooking spray	½ teaspoon freshly ground black pepper
2 medium green onions, chopped	¼ teaspoon cayenne pepper
2 garlic cloves, minced	½ teaspoon dried oregano
¼ cup low-fat margarine	½ teaspoon dried basil
1 bay leaf, crushed	¾ pound angel hair pasta, cooked and drained
1 tablespoon fresh lemon juice	
1 can (14½ ounces) low-sodium stewed tomatoes, crushed	

Preheat oven to 325°. Pat catfish fillets dry with a paper towel and place in a baking dish that has been coated with nonstick cooking spray. Sauté green onions and garlic in margarine in a skillet until tender. Add bay leaf, lemon juice, tomatoes, pepper, cayenne, oregano, and basil. Cook until heated. Pour sauce over catfish and bake, uncovered, until fish is flaky, about 20 minutes. Divide pasta among 6 plates and place a fillet with sauce over each nest of pasta.

Baked Spicy Shrimp

4 Servings

Salt substitute to taste
1½ pounds shrimp, peeled and
    deveined
 2 tablespoons canola oil
 1 garlic clove, minced
 ¼ cup chopped green onions
 ¼ cup chopped green bell pepper

 ½ cup dry white wine
 8 drops hot sauce
 ¼ teaspoon ground mustard
    Juice of 1 lemon
    Nonstick cooking spray
 ½ cup soft fat-free breadcrumbs

Preheat oven to 350°. Sprinkle salt substitute over the shrimp on all sides. Heat the oil in a 12-inch skillet over moderate heat. Add the shrimp, garlic, onions, and green pepper. Sauté for 2 to 3 minutes. Reduce the heat and stir in the wine, seasonings, and lemon juice. Cover and simmer for 5 minutes.

Place the shrimp in a single layer in a 1-quart baking dish coated with cooking spray. Pour the sauce evenly over the tops of the shrimp and top with crumbs. Bake for 15 minutes or until tender.

Exchange Values Per Serving
1 Serving = ½ Cup
1¾ Fat
3¾ Meat

227 Calories
(34% from Fat)
8.4 gm Total Fat
0.8 gm Saturated Fat
242.1 mg Cholesterol
307 mg Sodium
5.0 gm Carbohydrates
0.7 gm Dietary Fiber
26.7 gm Protein
301 mg Potassium

Santa Rosa Shrimp

6 Servings

1½ pounds shrimp, peeled and
    deveined
 2 tablespoons minced garlic
 1 tablespoon lime juice
 1 teaspoon ground thyme
 1 teaspoon salt-free seasoning
 ½ teaspoon white pepper

    Nonstick cooking spray
 2 cups fresh corn kernels
 1 cup chopped green bell pepper
 1 cup chopped red bell pepper
 ½ cup chopped onion
 1 large tomato, cut in 8 pieces

Drain shrimp of excess water. In large mixing bowl combine shrimp, garlic, lime juice, thyme, salt-free seasoning, and white pepper and mix well.

Lightly coat a large skillet with cooking spray and cook shrimp on medium high for 6 to 8 minutes, stirring occasionally. Remove shrimp from skillet. In same skillet combine corn, bell peppers, and onion. Cook on medium until corn is tender. Add shrimp and tomatoes to skillet and cook until shrimp are opaque in the center.

Exchange Values Per Serving
1 Serving = 4 Ounces
    Shrimp with
    Vegetables
2½ Meat
¾ Starch
1 Vegetable

177 Calories
(9% from Fat)
1.8 gm Total Fat
0.3 gm Saturated Fat
161.4 mg Cholesterol
329 mg Sodium
21.9 gm Carbohydrate
3.4 gm Dietary Fiber
20.5 gm Protein
468 mg Potassium

Shrimp and Olive Pasta

4 Servings

Exchange Values Per Serving
1 Serving = 1 Cup
⅓ Fruit
2 Meats
2 Starch

270 Calories
(13% from Fat)
3.8 gm Total Fat
0.1 gm Saturated Fat
121 mg Cholesterol
476.8 mg Sodium
38.3 gm Carbohydrates
1.3 gm Dietary Fiber
20.7 gm Protein
320.1 mg Potassium

12	ounces shrimp	2	teaspoons capers
6	tablespoons unsweetened orange juice from concentrate	2	tablespoons puréed tomato
			Dash of coarsely ground pepper
10	pitted black olives, halved	8	ounces angel hair pasta, cooked
4	garlic cloves, minced		Parmesan cheese (optional)
2	tablespoons salt-free seasoning		Crumbled feta cheese (optional)

Peel and devein shrimp.

In a medium skillet combine the orange juice, olives, garlic, salt-free seasoning, capers, tomato purée, and pepper. Bring to a boil over medium heat. Add shrimp and cook 2 to 4 minutes or until the shrimp turn pink. Divide the pasta between 4 deep bowls and distribute the shrimp mix equally among the bowls. Top with Parmesan or crumbled feta cheese.

Lemon Shrimp

6 Servings

Exchange Values Per Serving
1 Serving = 1 Cup
1¾ Meat
1½ Starch
½ Vegetable

188 Calories
(6% from Fat)
1.2 gm Total Fat
0.3 gm Saturated Fat
107.8 mg Cholesterol
340 mg Sodium
28.4 gm Carbohydrates
2.5 gm Dietary Fiber
15.4 gm Protein
404 mg Potassium

2	tablespoons cornstarch	1½	cups bias-sliced celery
1	teaspoon sugar	1	medium green bell pepper, cut into strips
2	teaspoons chicken bouillon granules	2	cups sliced fresh mushrooms
⅛	teaspoon pepper	1	package (6 ounces) frozen pea pods, thawed and drained
1	cup water	¼	cup sliced green onions
1	teaspoon finely shredded lemon peel	1	pound shrimp, peeled
3	tablespoons lemon juice	2½	cups hot cooked rice
	Nonstick cooking spray		Lemon slices

Combine cornstarch, sugar, bouillon granules, and pepper in a bowl. Stir in water, lemon peel, and lemon juice. Set aside.

Coat a large skillet with cooking spray. Stir-fry celery for 1 minute. Add green pepper; stir-fry for 1 minute. Add mushrooms, pea pods, and onions. Stir-fry for 1 to 2 minutes more or until vegetables are crisp tender. Remove from skillet.

Add half of the shrimp to the skillet. Stir-fry for 2 to 3 minutes or till shrimp turn pink. Remove shrimp. Stir-fry remaining shrimp for 2 to 3 minutes. Return all shrimp to the skillet. Stir lemon mixture and add to center of skillet. Cook and stir until thickened and bubbly. Cook and stir for 1 minute longer. Return vegetables to pan. Cook and stir for 1 minute or until heated throughout. Serve immediately over rice and garnish with lemon slices.

Rock Shrimp and Oyster Maque Choux

6 Servings

4 slices turkey bacon	1 cup oyster liquid (add water if necessary)
1 large onion, finely chopped	
1 teaspoon minced garlic	¼ teaspoon cayenne pepper
½ cup chopped green bell pepper	½ pound peeled and deveined rock shrimp
2 cups corn	
2½ cups canned low-sodium peeled tomatoes, chopped and drained (reserve liquid)	½ pint oysters, drained (reserve liquid)

Fry the turkey bacon until crispy in a heavy 4-quart skillet. Drain the fat. Add the onion, garlic, and green pepper, and cook until the onion is translucent but not brown. Stir in the corn and tomatoes. Add the tomato liquid, reserved oyster liquid, and cayenne pepper. Simmer for 10 minutes or until the corn is tender. Add the shrimp and oysters and cook for 2 minutes or until the edges of the oysters begin to curl. Serve at once.

Exchange Values Per Serving
1 Serving = 1 Cup
⅓ Fat
1¾ Meat
1 Starch
1 Vegetable

180 Calories
(23% from Fat)
4.7 gm Total Fat
1.3 gm Saturated Fat
107.3 mg Cholesterol
370 mg Sodium
19.7 gm Carbohydrates
2.5 gm Dietary Fiber
16.6 gm Protein
508 mg Potassium

Shrimp and Mushrooms

4 Servings

Exchange Values Per Serving
1 Serving = 1 Cup Shrimp with Sauce; ¾ Cup Rice
⅓ Fat
1¾ Meat
1½ Starch
¾ Vegetable

209 Calories
(13% from Fat)
2.9 gm Total Fat
0.6 gm Saturated Fat
86.2 mg Cholesterol
393 mg Sodium
28.7 gm Carbohydrates
1.6 gm Dietary Fiber
15.8 gm Protein
233 mg Potassium

1	tablespoon low-fat margarine	½	cup water, divided
1½	cups shrimp, drained and rinsed	¼	teaspoon grated nutmeg
½	cup chopped celery		Dash of pepper
2	tablespoons minced onion	1	teaspoon low-sodium soy sauce
1	can (7 ounces) sliced mushrooms, drained	½	cup low-sodium beef broth
1	tablespoon cornstarch	2	cups cooked rice

Melt the margarine in a large skillet. Add the shrimp and cook for 4 to 6 minutes, stirring often. Add the celery, onion, and mushrooms. Cook, stirring over high heat, for about 1½ to 2 minutes.

Combine the cornstarch and water in a bowl. Add the nutmeg, pepper, soy sauce, and broth, and pour over the shrimp mixture, cooking and stirring until thick and clear. Spoon the shrimp over the rice.

Broiled Scallops with Spinach

6 Servings

Exchange Values Per Serving
1 Serving = 6 Ounces
1 Fat
1 Meat
½ Vegetable

103 Calories
(18% from Fat)
2.1 gm Total Fat
0.4 gm Saturated Fat
18.4 mg Cholesterol
287 mg Sodium
4.1 gm Carbohydrates
1.5 gm Dietary Fiber
11.1 gm Protein
501 mg Potassium

1½	pounds scallops	1	pound fresh spinach
1	cup plus 2 tablespoons dry white wine	½	cup low-sodium chicken broth
6	tablespoons fresh lemon juice		Lemon slices for garnish

Preheat the broiler. Rinse scallops with cold running water to remove any shell particles. Blend wine and lemon juice in small bowl. Soak scallops in juice for 1 hour in the refrigerator. Meanwhile remove stems from spinach leaving only the leafy part. In a pan cook spinach in chicken broth over low heat until wilted/blanched.

Broil scallops on a baking sheet just until opaque and crisp, about 5 minutes. Form a circle on each plate with spinach, then place scallops in the center. Serve with lemon slices as a garnish.

Perfect Orange Scampi

4 Servings

3	garlic cloves, minced
2	teaspoons canola oil
⅛	teaspoon white pepper
2	pounds medium fresh shrimp, peeled and deveined
⅔	cup unsweetened orange juice
2	tablespoons lemon juice
4	teaspoons chopped fresh chives
2	teaspoons cornstarch

Sauté garlic in oil in a large skillet until tender. Stir in pepper. Add shrimp and cook over medium heat 3 to 5 minutes, stirring occasionally. Drain off liquid and discard.

Combine juices, chives, and cornstarch in a small saucepan, stirring well. Bring mixture to a boil; cook 1 minute, stirring constantly. Add orange sauce to shrimp, stirring well.

Exchange Values Per Serving
1 Serving = 1 Cup
½ Fat
⅓ Fruit
½ Meat

213 Calories
(18% from Fat)
4.1 gm Total Fat
0.5 gm Saturated Fat
322.9 mg Cholesterol
372 mg Sodium
7.1 gm Carbohydrates
0.2 gm Dietary Fiber
35.2 gm Protein
401 mg Potassium

Seafood Stuffed Eggplant

6 Servings

3	medium eggplants
1½	bunches green onions, chopped
1	pound medium shrimp, peeled
1½	teaspoons dried basil
1½	teaspoons dried oregano
3	tablespoons low-fat margarine
2	tablespoons fresh lemon juice
2	tablespoons white wine
1	pound fresh crabmeat, picked
½	cup all-purpose flour
1½	cups evaporated fat-free milk
	Parmesan cheese

Preheat oven to 350°. Cut eggplants in half lengthwise, score flesh, and place in a baking dish. Bake eggplants until tender, 30 to 40 minutes.

Sauté green onions, shrimp, basil, and oregano in margarine in a skillet until done, about 3 to 5 minutes. Scoop out eggplant flesh, reserving shells. Combine eggplant with shrimp mixture and cook in saucepan over medium heat until eggplant is soft. Add lemon juice and wine. Gently fold in crabmeat.

In a bowl whisk together flour and milk into a paste and gradually blend into eggplant mixture until desired consistency is reached. Stuff reserved eggplant shells with cooked mixture. Bake stuffed eggplants at 350° until heated through, about 30 minutes. Top with Parmesan cheese during the last 5 minutes of cooking.

Exchange Values Per Serving
1 Serving = 1 Slice Eggplant
¾ Fat
2⅓ Meat
½ Starch
4 Vegetable

237 Calories
(18% from Fat)
4.9 gm Total Fat
1.0 gm Saturated Fat
117.1 mg Cholesterol
200 g Sodium
29.7 gm Carbohydrates
8.1 gm Dietary Fiber
19.9 gm Protein
936 mg Potassium

Crab Imperial

6 Servings

Exchange Values Per Serving
1 Serving = 1 Cup
¾ Fat
2½ Meat
⅓ Starch

168 Calories
(30% from Fat)
5.5 gm Total Fat
1.0 gm Saturated Fat
71.6 mg Cholesterol
523 mg Sodium
10.0 gm Carbohydrates
0.8 gm Dietary Fiber
19.4 gm Protein
524 mg Potassium

1	pound cooked crabmeat	⅛	teaspoon cayenne pepper
½	cup chopped pimiento	1	teaspoon dry mustard
½	cup finely chopped celery		Salt substitute
2	slices crustless fat-free bread		Juice of ½ lemon
2	egg whites (or egg substitute), beaten		Nonstick cooking spray
1	cup fat-free plain yogurt		Paprika
	Dash of low-sodium Worcestershire sauce		

Preheat oven to 400°. Combine the crab meat, pimiento, and celery in a mixing bowl. Crumble the slices of bread and add to the mixture. Gently add the egg whites, yogurt, Worcestershire sauce, cayenne, mustard, salt substitute, and lemon juice. Place in a casserole dish that has been coated with cooking spray. Top with a sprinkle of paprika. Bake for 15 to 20 minutes, until lightly brown.

Italian Crab Cakes

4 Servings

Exchange Values Per Serving
1 Serving = 2 Cakes
2 Fat
3¾ Meat
½ Starch

243 Calories
(44% from Fat)
11.8 gm Total Fat
1.7 gm Saturated Fat
106 mg Cholesterol
778 mg Sodium
8.5 gm Carbohydrates
0.6 gm Dietary Fiber
25.4 gm Protein
423 mg Potassium

1	tablespoon finely chopped green bell pepper	1	tablespoon fat-free mayonnaise
4	tablespoons finely chopped green onions	6	tablespoons Italian breadcrumbs
2	tablespoons canola oil	1	teaspoon Dijon mustard
1	pound fresh lump crabmeat	¼	teaspoon black pepper
¼	cup egg substitute	¼	teaspoon cayenne pepper
			Nonstick cooking spray

Sauté green pepper and onions in canola oil in a skillet until soft. Drain and mix with crabmeat, egg substitute, mayonnaise, breadcrumbs, mustard, and black and cayenne pepper in a bowl. Chill 20 minutes. Form chilled mixture into 8 flat cakes.

Place cakes in a single layer in a skillet that has been coated with cooking spray. Brown on each side over medium heat for about 5 to 8 minutes or until golden brown and heated through. Serve warm with Dijon Sauce (page 254).

Angel Pasta with Crab

4 Servings

8	ounces angel hair pasta	2	garlic cloves, minced
1	pound asparagus, chopped, half of the tops reserved for garnish	1½	cups low-sodium chicken broth
		¼	cup canned tomatoes, diced
2	medium carrots, cut matchstick style	1	tablespoon fresh basil
		12	ounces fresh or imitation crabmeat
2	teaspoons virgin olive oil	¼	teaspoon pepper
2	tablespoons sliced green onions		

Cook the pasta according to directions. In the last 2 to 3 minutes of cooking, add the asparagus and the carrots. Drain the pasta and vegetables and set aside.

Heat oil in a shallow frying pan. Cook the green onions and garlic in this pan for 1 to 2 minutes or until crisp tender. Stir in broth, tomato, and basil. Bring to a boil. Add crabmeat and cook an additional 2 to 3 minutes until crab is done. Add pepper.

In a large bowl, toss together the pasta, vegetables, and sauce. Divide onto 4 plates and top with reserved asparagus tops and basil leaves if desired.

Exchange Values Per Serving
1 Serving = 1 Cup
2 Bread
½ Fat
2½ Meat
2 Vegetable

328 Calories
(15% from Fat)
5.7 gm Total Fat
0.9 gm Saturated Fat
86.5 mg Cholesterol
508 mg Sodium
42.2 gm Carbohydrates
4.8 gm Dietary Fiber
28.7 gm Protein
859 mg Potassium

Lettuce-Baked Lobster Tails

6 Servings

6	lobster tails (½ pound each) Nonstick cooking spray	10	to 12 lettuce leaves, rinsed and drained
½	cup low-sodium chicken broth	6	teaspoons low-fat margarine, melted
½	teaspoon garlic powder Paprika		

Preheat oven to 400°. Fan-cut lobster tails by cutting off the under shell, leaving the tail fan and upper shell in place. Place the lobster shell-side down on a baking sheet coated with nonstick spray.

Combine chicken broth with garlic powder in a bowl and brush the lobster meat. Sprinkle with paprika. Cover the tails completely with damp lettuce leaves and bake for 15 to 20 minutes or until the lobster meat is opaque white and tender. Serve the lobster with small melted margarine containers at each setting.

Exchange Values Per Serving
1 Serving = 1 Lobster Tail
1⅓ Fat
6¾ Meat

286 Calories
(29% from Fat)
8.9 gm Total Fat
4.1 gm Saturated Fat
172.7 mg Cholesterol
1,466 mg Sodium
3.7 gm Carbohydrates
0.4 gm Dietary Fiber
45.6 gm Protein
825 mg Potassium

Skewered Seafood

6 Servings

Exchange Values Per Serving
1 Serving = 2 Skewers
⅓ Fat
2¾ Meat
1½ Vegetable

140 Calories
(8% from Fat)
1.2 gm Total Fat
0.2 gm Saturated Fat
107.5 mg Cholesterol
132 mg Sodium
8.3 gm Carbohydrates
2.1 gm Dietary Fiber
21.0 gm Protein
595 mg Potassium

12	ounces shelled shrimp	24	cherry tomatoes
12	ounces cod (or other fish) fillets, cut into large pieces	1	tablespoon lemon juice
6	green bell peppers, cut into large squares	½	cup dry white wine

Preheat oven to 350°. Alternate shrimp and fish with vegetables on 12 skewers, beginning and ending with tomatoes. Blend lemon juice and wine in a bowl; brush over each skewer. Bake until fish is opaque. Place skewers under broiler for 1 to 2 minutes before serving.

Leek and Mussel Poach

8 Servings

Exchange Values Per Serving
1 Serving = 1 Hearty Cup
½ Fat
4½ Meat
⅓ Vegetable

239 Calories
(13% from Fat)
3.2 gm Total Fat
0.8 gm Saturated Fat
98.4 mg Cholesterol
374.4 mg Sodium
9.3 gm Carbohydrates
0.7 gm Dietary Fiber
36.4 gm Protein
776 mg Potassium

½	cup julienne-cut celery	2	pounds haddock or cod
½	cup julienne-cut carrots	½	cup fat-free milk
½	cup julienne-cut zucchini	¼	cup all-purpose flour
1	cup water (reserved from cooking vegetables)	¼	teaspoon grated nutmeg
1	cup dry white wine		Pepper to taste
½	cup finely sliced leeks or green onions		Paprika to taste
		¼	cup low-sodium chicken broth
4	dozen mussels	2	tablespoons chopped fresh parsley

Cook the julienne vegetables in a large saucepan in water until tender but still firm. Drain and reserve 1 cup of water. Set the vegetables aside.

Bring the water, wine, and sliced leeks (or green onions) to a simmer in a saucepan. Scrub and debeard the mussels, and add to the leeks. Cover and steam. Continue to steam for 5 minutes after the mussels have opened. Remove about half from their shells and reserve the rest for garnish.

Strain the liquid from the steaming mussels into a large skillet and add the fish. Cover and gently simmer for 8 to 10 minutes, until the fish flakes easily. Transfer to an ovenproof platter and keep warm. Reduce the liquid quickly to ½ cup. Add the milk, flour, seasonings, and broth, whisking constantly. Add the shelled mussels and parsley, and heat through. Pour the sauce over the fish, top with the vegetables, and garnish with the remaining mussels.

Pasta Primavera with Zucchini and Roasted Red Peppers

8 Servings

2 tablespoons virgin olive oil
3 garlic cloves, minced
4 green onions, finely chopped
½ pound fettuccine noodles, cooked
1 cup zucchini, blanched
1 cup snow peas, blanched
½ pound fresh asparagus, ½-inch pieces, blanched
2 red bell peppers, roasted, peeled, seeded, and julienne-cut

1 yellow bell pepper, roasted, peeled, seeded, and julienne-cut
3 tablespoons chopped fresh basil
1 teaspoon lemon pepper seasoning
2 ounces Parmesan cheese
¼ cup chopped fresh parsley
Salt-free seasoning

In a large skillet heat oil and add garlic and green onions. Cook over medium heat for 1 minute. Add fettuccine and all other ingredients, seasoning to taste. Heat until thoroughly warmed and serve.

Exchange Values Per Serving
1 Serving = 1 Cup
½ Starch
1 Fat
½ Meat
½ Vegetable

126 Calories
(41% from Fat)
5.8 gm Total Fat
1.8 gm Saturated Fat
14.2 mg Cholesterol
171 mg Sodium
13.1 gm Carbohydrates
2.8 gm Dietary Fiber
5.6 gm Protein
283 mg Potassium

Parmesan Linguine with Garlic

4 Servings

4 teaspoons low-sodium chicken broth
1 cup chopped zucchini
⅓ cup chopped onion
2 garlic cloves, minced

¼ pound fresh mushrooms, sliced
Dash of crushed red pepper flakes
8 ounces linguine, prepared as directed, omitting salt
2 tablespoons Parmesan cheese

Heat the chicken broth in a skillet. Add zucchini, onion, and garlic. Sauté for approximately 4 minutes. Add the mushrooms and red pepper flakes. Cook and stir for another 3 minutes. In a large bowl add the cooked vegetables to the linguine and toss. Sprinkle with Parmesan cheese.

Exchange Values Per Serving
1 Serving = 1 Cup
3 Starch
⅓ Meat
½ Vegetable

256 Calories
(8% from Fat)
2.2 gm Total Fat
0.8 gm Saturated Fat
2.5 mg Cholesterol
65 mg Sodium
48.7 gm Carbohydrates
5.3 gm Dietary Fiber
10.1 gm Protein
264.4 mg Potassium

Vegetable Lasagna I

6 Servings

Exchange Values Per Serving
1 Serving = 3-inch Square
1 Starch
½ Fat
1 Meat
1 Vegetable

190 Calories
(17% from Fat)
3.5 gm Total Fat
0.7 gm Saturated Fat
6.6 mg Cholesterol
339 mg Sodium
26.8 gm Carbohydrates
2.3 gm Dietary Fiber
12.9 gm Protein
309 mg Potassium

6 ounces lasagna noodles	¼ teaspoon dried oregano
1 tablespoon canola oil	¼ teaspoon dried basil
1 medium onion, chopped	¼ teaspoon garlic powder
1 garlic clove, minced	¼ teaspoon black pepper
½ cup chopped zucchini	¼ teaspoon crushed dried red pepper
½ cup chopped broccoli	1½ cups fat-free ricotta cheese
1 pound canned plum tomatoes, chopped and drained (reserve liquid)	Nonstick cooking spray
	2 tablespoons grated Parmesan cheese

Prepare lasagna noodles according to package directions, but do not add salt to cooking water. Drain noodles and place in a single layer on a large tray.

Preheat oven to 350°. Heat oil in a large skillet and sauté onion and garlic until golden brown. Add zucchini, broccoli, tomatoes, tomato liquid, and seasonings. Simmer, covered, for 10 minutes, stirring occasionally.

To assemble lasagna, layer vegetable sauce, noodles, and ricotta cheese in round 2-quart baking dish coated with cooking spray, beginning and ending with sauce. Sprinkle with Parmesan cheese. Bake for 25 minutes.

Vegetable Lasagna II

6 Servings

Exchange Values Per Serving
1 Serving = 3-Inch Square
2 Starch
1 Fat
1½ Meat
1 Vegetable

260 Calories
(22% from Fat)
6.6 gm Total Fat
1.5 gm Saturated Fat
10.3 mg Cholesterol
807 mg Sodium
33.2 gm Carbohydrates
4.6 gm Dietary Fiber
18.6 gm Protein
765 mg Potassium

6 individual lasagna noodles (regular or no-boil)	⅓ cup chopped onion
2 teaspoons canola oil	1 cup fat-free ricotta cheese
8 ounces halved and sliced zucchini	¼ cup finely grated Parmesan cheese
8 ounces halved and sliced summer squash	¼ teaspoon pepper
2 cups sliced mushrooms	Nonstick cooking spray
⅓ cup chopped green bell pepper	2 cups low-fat pasta sauce
⅓ cup chopped red bell pepper	1 cup fat-free mozzarella cheese
	1 medium tomato, seeded and chopped

Cook the lasagna noodles according to package instructions.

Preheat oven to 350°. Heat oil in a large frying pan. Add zucchini, squash, mushrooms, red and green peppers, and onion. Sauté over medium heat for 6 to 10 minutes or until tender. In a separate bowl, combine the ricotta cheese, Parmesan cheese, and pepper.

Coat a baking dish with nonstick cooking spray. Place 3 lasagna noodles on bottom of pan. Top with cheese mixture, ½ of the vegetable mixture, ½ of the sauce, and ½ of the mozzarella cheese. Place the other layer of lasagna noodles on top and add the other ½ of the vegetable mix, sauce, and mozzarella. Bake for approximately 30 to 45 minutes. Sprinkle the top with the chopped tomato.

Vegetarian Lasagna

8 Servings

1	pound fresh spinach	½	teaspoon dried rosemary
10	lasagna noodles	¼	teaspoon dried sage
	* * *	¼	teaspoon chopped oregano
2	cups sliced fresh mushrooms		Nonstick cooking spray
1	cup grated carrots	2	cups fat-free cottage cheese
½	cup chopped onion	16	ounces low-fat Monterey Jack
1	tablespoon canola oil		cheese, sliced
1	can (10¾ ounces) low-sodium,	2	tablespoons grated Parmesan
	tomato, purée		cheese
½	teaspoon chopped basil		

Rinse the spinach well. Steam the spinach by heating in a covered saucepan with only the water drops that cling to the leaves after rinsing. Reduce the heat when the steam forms and cook 3 to 4 minutes more.

Cook the lasagna noodles in unsalted water in a pot and drain.

Preheat oven to 375°. To make sauce, cook the mushrooms, carrots, and onion in a saucepan in hot oil until tender, but not brown. Stir in the tomatoes and herbs. Simmer for at least 20 minutes.

In a baking dish coated with cooking spray, layer as follows: lasagna noodles, cottage cheese, spinach, Monterey Jack cheese, and sauce mixture. Repeat the layers, reserving several cheese slices for the top. Then sprinkle the top with Parmesan cheese. Bake for 30 minutes. Let the lasagna cool for 10 minutes before serving.

Exchange Values Per Serving
  1 Serving = 3-Inch
    Square
  1 Starch
  1½ Fat
  2 Meat
  1½ Vegetable

358 Calories
  (33% from Fat)
  13.1 gm Total Fat
  7.6 gm Saturated Fat
  46.7 mg Cholesterol
  752 mg Sodium
  29.4 gm Carbohydrates
  3.8 gm Dietary Fiber
  31.9 gm Protein
  675 mg Potassium

Spinach Parmesan Lasagna

8 Servings

Exchange Values Per Serving
1 Serving = 1 Rolled
    Lasagna Noodle
1 Starch
½ Meat
2 Vegetable

150 Calories
(7% from Fat)
1.2 gm Total Fat
0.4 gm Saturated Fat
3.7 mg Cholesterol
189 mg Sodium
26.2 gm Carbohydrates
3.9 gm Dietary Fiber
10.2 gm Protein
690 mg Potassium

2 bunches spinach	Nonstick cooking spray
¼ pound mushrooms, sliced	2 cups low-sodium, puréed whole
1 cup fat-free cottage cheese	tomatoes
¼ teaspoon grated nutmeg	½ teaspoon dried basil
⅛ teaspoon pepper	½ teaspoon dried oregano
1 garlic clove, minced	2 tablespoons grated Parmesan
½ cup sliced onion	cheese
8 lasagna noodles, cooked	

Preheat oven to 350°. Steam the spinach until limp. Chop and mix with the mushrooms, cottage cheese, nutmeg, pepper, garlic, and onion in a bowl. Line each noodle with 2 to 3 tablespoons of this mixture, roll up, and place standing on end in a shallow baking pan coated with cooking spray.

Combine the remaining ingredients (except the Parmesan cheese) and pour over the noodles. Sprinkle lightly with Parmesan cheese. Bake for 20 minutes.

Old-Fashioned Macaroni and Cheese

6 Servings

Exchange Values Per Serving
1 Serving = 1 Cup
1 Starch
⅓ Fat
½ Meat

142 Calories
(19% from Fat)
3.0 gm Total Fat
1.1 gm Saturated Fat
6.2 mg Cholesterol
296 mg Sodium
20.1 gm Carbohydrates
0.7 gm Dietary Fiber
8.4 gm Protein
148 mg Potassium

1½ cups fat-free milk	Nonstick cooking spray
1½ tablespoons all-purpose flour	¼ cup fat-free cheese cracker crumbs
1½ tablespoons low-fat margarine	Pinch of pepper
¾ cup grated low-fat American cheese	Pinch of paprika
2 cups macaroni, cooked	

Preheat oven to 375°. To make a white sauce, combine the milk, flour, and margarine in a saucepan over low heat. Add the grated cheese, stirring constantly. Cook until the cheese has melted and the sauce boils. Remove from heat.

Alternate layers of macaroni and cheese sauce in a baking dish coated with nonstick spray. Cover the top with cheese cracker crumbs. Sprinkle with pepper and paprika for taste. Bake until the mixture bubbles and the crumbs turn brown.

Old-Fashioned Beef, Macaroni, and Tomato Casserole

6 Servings

⅔ cup uncooked macaroni
3 cups water
1 pound lean ground beef
¼ cup finely chopped onion
1 tablespoon finely chopped celery
¼ cup finely chopped green bell pepper
1 tablespoon low-sodium Worcestershire sauce

1 tablespoon low-sodium soy sauce
1 cup canned low-sodium tomatoes, crushed
1 cup low-sodium tomato juice
⅛ teaspoon pepper
¼ teaspoon dried basil
1 teaspoon parsley flakes

Cook the macaroni in water until tender. Drain and rinse with cold water. Set aside. Combine the ground beef, onion, celery, green pepper, and Worcestershire and soy sauces in a frying pan. Cook until the beef is browned and the vegetables are tender. Combine the tomatoes, tomato juice, pepper, basil, and parsley in a large pan. Add the ground beef mixture and bring to a boil. Reduce to a simmer and stir in the macaroni. Simmer until warmed throughout.

Exchange Values Per Serving
1 Serving = 1 Cup
½ Starch
2 Meat
¾ Vegetable

193 Calories
(33% from Fat)
7.1 gm Total Fat
2.8 gm Saturated Fat
27.5 mg Cholesterol
324 mg Sodium
13.8 gm Carbohydrates
1.1 gm Dietary Fiber
18.0 gm Protein
489 mg Potassium

Mostaccioli al Forno

8 Servings

Exchange Values Per Serving
1 Serving = 3-Inch
    Square
1 Starch
½ Fat
2⅔ Meat
½ Vegetable

227 Calories
(23% from Fat)
5.8 gm Total Fat
2.5 gm Saturated Fat
18.1 mg Cholesterol
1,187 mg Sodium
20.3 gm Carbohydrates
3.8 gm Dietary Fiber
22.9 gm Protein
704 mg Potassium

1	package (10 ounces) frozen chopped spinach	¼	teaspoon pepper
2	cups fat-free ricotta cheese	8	ounces mostaccioli, uncooked
6	egg whites, lightly beaten		Nonstick cooking spray
⅔	cup grated Parmesan cheese	1	jar (26 ounces) low-fat, low-sodium spaghetti sauce
1	cup shredded fat-free mozzarella cheese, divided	2	tablespoons grated Parmesan cheese
⅓	cup chopped fresh parsley		

Cook the spinach for 1 minute according to package directions. Drain and press out the excess moisture. Combine the spinach, ricotta cheese, egg whites, Parmesan cheese, ⅔ cup mozzarella cheese, parsley, and pepper in a bowl. Set aside.

Preheat oven to 350°. Cook the mostaccioli according to the package directions. Drain and combine with 2½ cups of spaghetti sauce. Arrange half of the mostaccioli in the bottom of an 11 x 7 x 2-inch pan or 9-inch square baking dish coated with cooking spray. Layer the spinach evenly over the mostaccioli, and cover with the remaining mostaccioli. Spread the remaining sauce over the top, and sprinkle with the remaining mozzarella and Parmesan cheeses. Bake for 35 to 40 minutes.

Savory Jumbo Shells

6 Servings

Exchange Values Per Serving
1 Serving = 2 Stuffed
    Shells
1 Starch
1⅔ Fat
3 Meat
½ Vegetable

327 Calories
(34% from Fat)
12.4 gm Total Fat
4.7 gm Saturated Fat
51.0 mg Cholesterol
708 mg Sodium
24.2 gm Carbohydrates
2.2 gm Dietary Fiber
29.0 gm Protein
495 mg Potassium

12	to 14 jumbo pasta shells, uncooked	¼	teaspoon pepper
3	tablespoons sliced green onions		
2	tablespoons low-fat margarine	3	tablespoons low-fat margarine
1	package (10 ounces) frozen chopped spinach, thawed and well drained	1	garlic clove, minced
		3	tablespoons all-purpose flour
1	cup diced cooked chicken	1½	teaspoon low-sodium, chicken bouillon granules
1	cup diced cooked turkey	⅛	teaspoon pepper
½	cup grated Parmesan cheese	2	cups fat-free milk
4	egg whites, beaten	½	cup grated Parmesan cheese
¾	teaspoon Italian seasoning		

Cook the shells according to package directions. Meanwhile combine the onions, margarine, spinach, chicken, turkey, Parmesan cheese, egg whites, seasoning, and pepper in a mixing bowl. Fill each shell with about 3 table-spoons of mixture.

Preheat oven to 350°. To make cheese sauce, melt 3 tablespoons of margarine in a saucepan. Add the garlic and sauté for 1 minute. Stir in the flour, bouillon granules, and pepper until well-blended. Gradually stir in the milk, and cook, stirring constantly until thickened. Reduce the heat to low and stir in the cheese until melted.

Pour 1 cup of cheese sauce into a 9-inch round baking dish. Place the shells in the baking dish, and cover with the remaining sauce. Bake for 20 to 25 minutes. If desired, broil for 3 to 5 minutes or until lightly browned. Serve immediately.

Spicy Manicotti

6 Servings

6 manicotti shells	1 can (14½ ounces) low-sodium
2 cups fat-free cottage cheese	peeled whole tomatoes
¼ cup chopped parsley	1 can (6 ounces) low-sodium tomato
1 small onion, diced	paste
1 egg white	½ cup shredded low-fat mozzarella
¼ garlic clove, minced	cheese
¼ teaspoon Italian seasoning	

Cook the manicotti according to package directions, omitting salt. Drain and set aside.

Preheat oven to 350°. Combine the cottage cheese, parsley, onion, egg white, garlic, and seasoning in a medium bowl and mix until well blended. Stuff cheese mixture into the shells.

Purée together the whole tomatoes and tomato paste in a blender. Spoon some sauce into the bottom of a baking dish and arrange the stuffed shells on top. Cover the centers of each shell with sauce and sprinkle with shredded cheese. Cover and bake for 20 to 25 minutes.

Exchange Values Per Serving
1 Serving = 1 Manicotti Shell
⅔ Starch
2 Meat
2 Vegetable

193 Calories
(11% from Fat)
2.3 gm Total Fat
1.1 gm Saturated Fat
11.9 mg Cholesterol
363 mg Sodium
26.2 gm Carbohydrates
2.9 gm Dietary Fiber
17.9 gm Protein
537 mg Potassium

Manicotti with Eggplant-Tomato Relish

10 Servings

Exchange Values Per Serving

1 Serving = 3-Inch Square
1 Starch
½ Fat
2 Meat
1 Vegetable

234 Calories
(17% from Fat)
4.5 gm Total Fat
1.2 gm Saturated Fat
36.8 mg Cholesterol
349 mg Sodium
26.3 gm Carbohydrates
2.0 gm Dietary Fiber
21.7 gm Protein
477 mg Potassium

1 pound lean ground turkey breast	Nonstick cooking spray
¼ cup finely chopped onion	* * *
¼ cup finely chopped celery	1½ cups diced peeled eggplant
½ cup tomato paste	2 tablespoons chopped onion
½ cup fat-free ricotta cheese	½ cup water
¼ cup seasoned breadcrumbs	2 tablespoons tomato paste
4 egg whites, lightly beaten	2 tablespoons water
1 teaspoon minced garlic	1 tablespoon low-fat margarine
10 manicotti shells	2 tablespoons chopped fresh parsley
3 tablespoons low-fat margarine	2 tablespoons sliced ripe black olives
3 tablespoons all-purpose flour	¼ teaspoon dried oregano
⅛ teaspoon pepper	¼ teaspoon dried thyme
2½ cups fat-free milk	¼ cup diced fresh tomato
¼ cup grated Parmesan cheese	

Brown the ground turkey with the onion and celery in a large skillet. Remove from the heat and stir in the tomato paste. Cool. Add the ricotta cheese, breadcrumbs, egg whites, and garlic.

Preheat oven to 350°. Cook manicotti according to package directions. Cool in a single layer on waxed paper for easier handling. Using a teaspoon, generously fill the shells with meat mixture. Melt the margarine in a saucepan. Stir in the flour and pepper. Gradually add the milk, cooking and stirring until thick and bubbly. Blend in the Parmesan cheese. Spoon 1½ cups of sauce into a 11 x 7 x 2-inch baking dish coated with nonstick cooking spray. Arrange the filled manicotti in the baking dish. Cover with aluminum foil and bake for 30 to 35 minutes or until hot and bubbly.

To make eggplant-tomato relish, combine the eggplant and onion in a small saucepan. Simmer in ½ cup of water for about 3 minutes or until tender. Drain. Combine the tomato paste with 2 tablespoons of water. Add to the eggplant mixture, and stir in the remaining ingredients.

To serve, spoon the manicotti onto a serving plate and serve with the remaining sauce and eggplant-tomato relish.

Manicotti with Ratatouille Sauce

6 Servings

6	manicotti shells, cooked	2	cups thinly sliced zucchini
1	cup fat-free mozzarella cheese	½	teaspoon dried oregano
¼	cup grated Parmesan cheese	½	teaspoon dried basil
2	egg whites, lightly beaten	¼	teaspoon dried marjoram
¼	cup chopped fresh parsley	¼	teaspoon pepper
⅛	teaspoon pepper	1	can (15 ounces) low-sodium tomato sauce
2	tablespoons low-sodium chicken broth	1	can (14½ ounces) low-sodium stewed tomatoes
2	cups diced, peeled eggplant		Nonstick cooking spray
1	cup sliced onion		Grated Parmesan cheese (optional)
1	cup green bell pepper strips		
2	garlic cloves, minced		

Cook the manicotti according to package directions. Drain, and cool in a single layer on wax paper for easier handling. Combine the cheeses, egg whites, parsley, and pepper in a mixing bowl. Spoon or pipe cheese mixture through a pastry tube into the manicotti. Set aside.

Preheat oven to 350°. In a large saucepan sauté in chicken broth, eggplant, onion, green pepper, and garlic for 5 minutes. Blend in the zucchini, seasonings, tomato sauce, and stewed tomatoes, and simmer uncovered for 5 minutes or until the vegetables are tender. Remove from heat.

Spoon half of the mixture into a 12 x 7½-inch baking dish coated with nonstick spray. Place the manicotti over the sauce mixture. Top with the remaining sauce mixture. Bake for 20 to 25 minutes or until hot and bubbly. Serve with Parmesan cheese.

Exchange Values Per Serving
1 Serving = 1 Manicotti Shell
1 Starch
1⅓ Meat
2 Vegetable

190 Calories
(9% from Fat)
2.0 gm Total Fat
0.9 gm Saturated Fat
7.1 mg Cholesterol
282 mg Sodium
29.7 gm Carbohydrates
4.9 gm Dietary Fiber
13.9 gm Protein
641 mg Potassium

Orange Curried Rice and Mushrooms

6 Servings

Exchange Values Per
Serving
  1 Serving = ⅔ Cup
  1½ Starch
  ⅓ Fruit
  ⅓ Vegetable

146 Calories
  (4% from Fat)
  0.7 gm Total Fat
  0.2 gm Saturated Fat
  0.8 mg Cholesterol
  25 mg Sodium
  31.3 gm Carbohydrates
  1.0 gm Dietary Fiber
  3.5 gm Protein
  168 mg Potassium

½   cup chopped onion
½   cup sliced mushrooms
1¼ cups low-sodium chicken broth, divided

2   teaspoons curry powder
1   cup uncooked rice
1   cup unsweetened orange juice

Sauté the onions and mushrooms in ¼ cup chicken broth in a skillet until soft. Stir in the curry powder and rice. Cook and stir for 2 minutes. Add the remaining ingredients and stir with a fork. Bring to a boil. Lower the heat, cover, and simmer for 20 minutes.

Orange Wild Rice with Currants and Apples

8 Servings

Exchange Values Per
Serving
  1 Serving = ⅔ Cup
  ⅔ Starch
  1 Fruit
  ⅔ Fat

151 Calories
  (23% from Fat)
  4.1 gm Total Fat
  0.6 gm Saturated Fat
  0 mg Cholesterol
  5 mg Sodium
  28.1 gm Carbohydrates
  2.8 gm Dietary Fiber
  2.1 gm Protein
  223 mg Potassium

2   cups brown and wild rice, cooked
1   cup dried currants
4   tablespoons chopped fresh parsley
2   tablespoons orange peel
1   Granny Smith apple, diced
2   tablespoons virgin olive oil

2   tablespoons unsweetened orange juice
Pepper to taste
Nonstick cooking spray
Freshly grated Parmesan cheese
Fresh parsley for garnish

Preheat oven to 350°. In a mixing bowl, combine cooked rice, currants, parsley, peel, apple, oil, orange juice, and pepper. Place mixture in a casserole dish that has been coated with nonstick cooking spray, cover with foil, and cook for about 20 minutes. Sprinkle with cheese and garnish with parsley.

Broccoli and Rice Casserole

8 Servings

¼ cup chopped onion	½ cup fat-free milk
¼ cup low-sodium chicken broth	1 cup shredded low-fat Cheddar cheese
2 packages (10 ounces each) frozen chopped broccoli, cooked	
1 cup rice, cooked	2 teaspoons pepper
1 can (10¾ ounces) reduced-fat cream of celery soup	Nonstick cooking spray
	2 tablespoons Parmesan cheese

Preheat oven to 350°. Sauté the onion in the broth in a skillet.

Combine all of the ingredients (except the Parmesan cheese) in a sprayed casserole dish. Sprinkle with Parmesan cheese. Cover and bake for 30 minutes.

Exchange Values Per Serving
1 Serving = ⅔ Cup
⅓ Starch
⅓ Fat
½ Meat
1½ Vegetable

105 Calories
(20% from Fat)
2.4 gm Total Fat
1.2 gm Saturated Fat
6.1 mg Cholesterol
292 mg Sodium
13.9 gm Carbohydrates
2.6 gm Dietary Fiber
7.9 gm Protein
202 mg Potassium

Brown Rice Broccoli Casserole

8 Servings

2½ cups brown rice, cooked	½ teaspoon pepper
2 egg whites	1 cup croutons
1 small onion, chopped	½ cup fat-free milk
1 bunch fresh broccoli, chopped	Nonstick cooking spray
1 cup fat-free cottage cheese	2 tablespoons Parmesan cheese

Preheat oven to 350°. In a bowl combine the rice, egg whites, onion, broccoli, cottage cheese, pepper, croutons, and milk and mix with a wooden spoon. Pour into a casserole dish that has been sprayed with nonstick spray. Sprinkle the top with Parmesan cheese and bake for 30 to 40 minutes until tender.

Exchange Values Per Serving
1 Serving = ⅔ Cup
1 Starch
⅔ Meat
1 Vegetable

144 Calories
(9% from Fat)
1.6 gm Total Fat
0.5 gm Saturated Fat
4.0 mg Cholesterol
190 mg Sodium
23.3 gm Carbohydrates
3.5 gm Dietary Fiber
10.0 gm Protein
307 mg Potassium

Brown Rice with Scallions

4 Servings

Exchange Values Per Serving
1 Serving = ⅔ Cup
2 Starch

162 Calories
(7% from Fat)
1.4 gm Total Fat
0.2 gm Saturated Fat
1.0 mg Cholesterol
34 mg Sodium
34.4 gm Carbohydrates
2.3 gm Dietary Fiber
5.0 gm Protein
34.5 mg Potassium

1¼ cups water	2 cups quick-cooking brown rice
1 cup low-sodium chicken broth	½ cup chopped green onions

In a saucepan bring the water and broth to a boil. Add rice, cover, simmer 10 minutes or until the water and broth is absorbed. Remove from heat and add green onions.

Creamy Rice Casserole with Chili Peppers

8 Servings

Exchange Values Per Serving
1 Serving = ⅔ Cup
1⅓ Starch
⅛ Fat
1½ Meat
½ Vegetable

222 Calories
(7% from Fat)
1.7 gm Total Fat
0.3 gm Saturated Fat
10.1 mg Cholesterol
708 mg Sodium
32.9 gm Carbohydrates
0.9 gm Dietary Fiber
16.4 gm Protein
192 mg Potassium

1 medium onion, chopped	¼ teaspoon pepper
2 tablespoons low-fat margarine	8 ounces green chili peppers, divided
4 cups cooked rice	Nonstick cooking spray
1 cup fat-free sour cream	8 ounces low-fat Cheddar cheese,
1 cup fat-free cottage cheese	shredded

Preheat oven to 325°. Sauté onion in margarine in a skillet. Combine sautéed onion with cooked rice, sour cream, cottage cheese, and pepper. Reserve half of the green chilies and add remaining chilies to rice mixture. Place rice mixture in 2½-quart casserole dish that has been coated with nonstick cooking spray. Sprinkle with Cheddar cheese and reserved chilies. Bake for 20 minutes.

Black-Eyed Peas and Wild Rice

4 Servings

1   cup uncooked wild rice
2   cups water
1   tablespoon low-sodium soy sauce
1   bunch green onions, chopped

1   vegetable bouillon cube
1   package (10 ounces) frozen black-eyed peas
2   tablespoons low-fat margarine

Bring the first 5 ingredients to a boil in a pan, reduce the heat, and cook for 20 minutes. Add the peas and margarine to the rice mixture and bring back to a boil. Reduce the heat and cook for an additional 14 to 20 minutes.

Exchange Values Per Serving
1 Serving = ⅔ Cup
3 Starch
½ Fat

283 Calories
(12% from Fat)
3.8 gm Total Fat
0.8 gm Saturated Fat
0 mg Cholesterol
217 mg Sodium
51.6 gm Carbohydrates
7.6 gm Dietary Fiber
12.7 gm Protein
453 mg Potassium

Mexican Black Beans and Rice

6 Servings

1   medium red onion, chopped
2   tablespoons medium-hot chili powder
1   teaspoon dried oregano
2   garlic cloves, minced
1   tablespoon canola oil
¾   cup long-grain rice
1   can (14½ ounces) low-sodium chicken broth

½   cup chopped carrot
1   large tomato, chopped
½   cup chopped zucchini
1   can (15½ ounces) black beans, drained and rinsed
2   tablespoons snipped parsley

Cook the onion, chili powder, oregano, and garlic in a frying pan with hot canola oil for approximately 3 minutes. Stir in the rice and brown over medium heat. Stir constantly. Add the broth and carrot. Bring to a boil. Reduce heat to medium and cover. Cook for approximately 10 minutes, there will still be liquid present at this point. Add tomato, zucchini, beans, and parsley. Cover and cook an additional 5 to 10 minutes until all liquid is absorbed and the rice is tender.

Exchange Values Per Serving
1 Serving = 1 Cup
1⅔ Starch
½ Fat
½ Meat
1 Vegetable

198 Calories
(18% from Fat)
4.1 gm Total Fat
0.6 gm Saturated Fat
1.4 mg Cholesterol
291 mg Sodium
34.0 gm Carbohydrates
6.1 gm Dietary Fiber
7.6 gm Protein
220 mg Potassium

New Year's Black-eyed Peas

8 Servings

Exchange Values Per Serving
1 Serving = 1 Cup
2 Starch
⅓ Fat
⅔ Meat
½ Vegetable

226 Calories
(21% from Fat)
5.4 gm Total Fat
1.4 gm Saturated Fat
26.5 mg Cholesterol
655 mg Sodium
36.7 gm Carbohydrates
4.2 gm Dietary Fiber
9.6 gm Protein
324 mg Potassium

1   cup chopped turkey ham
1   cup finely chopped onion
½   cup finely chopped celery
½   teaspoon hot sauce
1   tablespoon canola oil

2   cans (15 ounces each) black-eyed peas
3   cups cooked rice
    Mustard greens and turkey ham for garnish

Sauté turkey ham, onions, celery, and hot sauce in oil in a skillet over medium heat for 3 to 5 minutes, stirring frequently, until the onions and celery are soft but not browned. Combine black-eyed peas, turkey ham mixture and rice, then heat.

Garnish with thin slices of turkey ham and mustard greens.

Stuffed Spuds

4 Servings

Exchange Values Per Serving
1 Serving = 1 Potato
2 Starch
½ Meat
½ Vegetable

212 Calories
(7% from Fat)
1.8 gm Total Fat
1.0 gm Saturated Fat
4.7 mg Cholesterol
158 mg Sodium
40.1 gm Carbohydrates
3.4 gm Dietary Fiber
10.3 gm Protein
809 mg Potassium

4   6-ounce baking potatoes
1   cup chopped broccoli
¼   cup fat-free plain yogurt
¼   cup chopped pimiento

¼   teaspoon garlic powder
3   ounces low-fat Cheddar cheese, grated

Scrub potatoes, dry, prick with a fork, and wrap each in a paper towel. Place in microwave oven and cook on high for 15 minutes. Turn and test for doneness. May need an additional 15 minutes depending on size of spuds. (Potatoes can also be baked in the oven at a temperature of 400° for 1 hour or until tender).

In a medium bowl combine broccoli, yogurt, pimiento and garlic powder. Set aside. When potatoes are done, make an X on the top of the potato. Press the sides of the potato together to loosen the inside. Scoop out the inside of the potatoes and add to the broccoli mixture. Mix all ingredients well with a wooden spoon. Restuff the potatoes and top with Cheddar cheese. Return the potatoes to the oven or microwave just long enough to melt the cheese.

Stuffed Baked Potatoes

12 Servings

6 6-ounce baking potatoes
½ cup low-sodium chicken broth
1 cup fat-free plain yogurt
1 tablespoon minced onion
   Paprika to taste

Pepper to taste
Fat-free cheese cracker crumbs
¼ cup crumbled turkey bacon,
   cooked

Preheat oven to 350°. Scrub the potatoes, prick with a fork, and bake until tender (approximately 1 hour). When they are done, split them lengthwise and scoop out the insides. While potato is still hot, in a bowl whip together with the broth, yogurt, and seasonings. Spoon the mixture back into the shells. Sprinkle the tops with the cracker crumbs and bacon. Return to the oven and bake for an additional 10 minutes.

Exchange Values Per Serving
1 Serving = ½ Stuffed Potato
1 Starch
⅓ Fat

115 Calories
(10% from Fat)
1.3 gm Total Fat
0.4 gm Saturated Fat
4.7 mg Cholesterol
115 mg Sodium
22.3 gm Carbohydrates
1.4 gm Dietary Fiber
4.1 gm Protein
403 mg Potassium

Spinach-Stuffed Baked Potatoes

6 Servings

6 large Yukon gold potatoes
3 tablespoons fat-free milk
3 tablespoons fat-free sour cream
   White pepper to taste
1 package (10 ounces) frozen
   chopped spinach, thawed

Paprika
2 tablespoons grated Parmesan
   cheese

Preheat oven to 350°. Scrub potatoes, prick with a fork, and bake for 1¼ to 1½ hours or until tender. Cut in half lengthwise and scoop out insides. Mash potato in a bowl until no lumps remain. Gradually add milk and sour cream. Beat after each addition. Add pepper to taste.

Drain spinach well, pressing out excess liquid. Stir spinach into potato mixture; spoon or pipe into potato shells. Sprinkle with paprika and Parmesan cheese and bake for an additional 10 minutes.

Exchange Values Per Serving
1 Serving = 1 Stuffed Potato
3 Starch
½ Vegetable

239 Calories
(3% from Fat)
0.7 gm Total Fat
0.3 gm Saturated Fat
1.6 mg Cholesterol
76.0 mg Sodium
52.8 gm Carbohydrates
4.8 gm Dietary Fiber
7.0 gm Protein
1,071 mg Potassium

Baked Fluffy Potatoes

8 Servings

Exchange Values Per Serving
1 Serving = ½ Stuffed
  Potato
1½ Starch
½ Fat
⅔ Meat

186 Calories
(22% from Fat)
4.6 gm Total Fat
2.7 gm Saturated Fat
10.4 mg Cholesterol
279 mg Sodium
27.3 gm Carbohydrates
1.7 gm Dietary Fiber
9.4 gm Protein
535 mg Potassium

4   large baking potatoes, washed and pierced
1   cup fat-free plain yogurt
1   tablespoon low-fat margarine
½   teaspoon dried thyme
½   teaspoon dried oregano
1   cup Parmesan cheese

Bake the potatoes at 400° for 30 minutes or until tender. Remove from the oven and slice each in half. Hollow the potato out and retain the skins. Whip together the potato, yogurt, margarine, thyme, and oregano. Spoon back into the potato skins. Place on a baking sheet and sprinkle each with Parmesan cheese. Place back in the oven and bake until golden brown.

Cheesy Whipped Potatoes

6 Servings

Exchange Values Per Serving
1 Serving = ⅔ Cup
2½ Starch
⅔ Meat
⅓ Vegetable

241 Calories
(4% from Fat)
1.2 gm Total Fat
0.6 gm Saturated Fat
5.0 mg Cholesterol
172 mg Sodium
47.6 gm Carbohydrates
4.3 gm Dietary Fiber
10.6 gm Protein
906 mg Potassium

3   pounds potatoes, cooked, peeled, and whipped
½   cup low-sodium chicken broth
6   ounces fat-free cottage cheese
1   green bell pepper, chopped
½   cup shredded low-fat Cheddar cheese
1½   tablespoons grated Parmesan cheese

Preheat oven to 350°. Whip the cooked potatoes with the broth, cottage cheese, green pepper, and Cheddar cheese in a bowl. Place in a baking dish and top with Parmesan cheese. Bake for 30 minutes, until golden brown.

Cheesy Scalloped Potatoes

8 Servings

2½ cups fat-free milk
 6 medium potatoes, sliced
    Nonstick cooking spray
 ¼ cup diced onions
 ¼ cup diced celery
    Paprika

3 tablespoons all-purpose flour
3 tablespoons fat-free plain yogurt
⅛ teaspoons pepper
2 tablespoons Parmesan cheese
2 tablespoons low-fat margarine

Scald the milk in a pan and allow to cool to lukewarm. Place a layer of sliced potatoes in the bottom of a baking pan coated with cooking spray. Sprinkle with half the onion, celery, and paprika.

Preheat oven to 350°. To the milk, add the flour, yogurt, and pepper. Pour half on the first layer of potatoes and sprinkle with Parmesan cheese. Repeat the layers of potatoes, celery, and onion. Sprinkle with paprika, and cover with the remaining yogurt sauce. Sprinkle with Parmesan. Dot the top of the potatoes with margarine. Cover and bake for 30 minutes. Uncover and bake for 50 more minutes or until potatoes are tender.

Exchange Values Per Serving
1 Serving = ⅔ Cup
1⅓ Starchs
½ Fat

148 Calories
(11% from Fat)
1.9 gm Total Fat
0.6 gm Saturated Fat
2.1 mg Cholesterol
100 mg Sodium
27.5 gm Carbohydrates
2.1 gm Dietary Fiber
5.6 gm Protein
552 mg Potassium

Roasted New Potatoes with Herbs

6 Servings

20 new potatoes, halved
    Nonstick cooking spray
1½ teaspoons dried rosemary

¾ teaspoon dried thyme
1 tablespoon salt-free seasoning
½ teaspoon garlic powder

Preheat oven to 400°. Place potatoes skin side up on a baking sheet coated with cooking spray. Coat potatoes evenly with cooking spray and sprinkle with herbs. Bake for 45 minutes, stirring occasionally. Serve hot.

Exchange Values Per Serving
1 Serving = 3 Potatoes
4⅔ Vegetable

122 Calories
(2% from Fat)
0.2 gm Total Fat
0 gm Saturated Fat
0 mg Cholesterol
6 mg Sodium
24.5 gm Carbohydrates
3.4 gm Dietary Fiber
4.4 gm Protein
977 mg Potassium

Fruity Sweet Potatoes

8 Servings

Exchange Values Per Serving
1 Serving = ⅔ Cup
1½ Starch

116 Calories
(5% from Fat)
0.7 gm Total Fat
0.2 gm Saturated Fat
0.1 mg Cholesterol
23 mg Sodium
26.1 gm Carbohydrates
2.7 gm Dietary Fiber
1.8 gm Protein
201 mg Potassium

4 medium sweet potatoes, unpeeled	1 tablespoon chopped pineapple
1 teaspoon low-fat margarine	Pinch of cinnamon
¼ cup unsweetened pineapple juice	Pinch of grated nutmeg
2 tablespoons low-sodium chicken broth	Pinch of allspice
	Nonstick cooking spray

Preheat oven to 375°. Boil the potatoes in a pan until tender, about 30 minutes, and remove the skins. In a large bowl mash the pulp. Add the margarine. Add the fruit juice and broth, and whip until fluffy. Add the chopped pineapple and spices, and transfer to a 1-quart baking dish coated with nonstick spray. Bake for 30 minutes or until lightly browned.

Sweet Potato Coins

4 Servings

Exchange Values Per Serving
1 Serving = ½ Cup
2⅔ Starch
⅔ Fat

211 Calories
(17% from Fat)
3.9 gm Total Fat
0.4 gm Saturated Fat
0 mg Cholesterol
22 mg Sodium
41.8 gm Carbohydrates
4.5 gm Dietary Fiber
2.8 gm Protein
316 mg Potassium

3 medium sweet potatoes	1 tablespoon canola oil
Nonstick cooking spray	½ teaspoon salt-free seasoning

Preheat oven to 450°. Peel potatoes and cut crosswise into ¼-inch thick rounds.

Coat a baking dish with cooking spray. Place potato coins in the dish overlapping slightly. Combine oil and salt-free seasoning in a bowl. Brush lightly each coin. Cover and bake for approximately 10 minutes. Uncover and cook an additional 5 minutes. Turn out onto a paper towel to drain. Serve immediately.

Nutty Couscous Pilaf

6 Servings

1½	cups low-sodium chicken broth	¾	cup spinach, washed and shredded
1	garlic clove, minced	½	cup grated carrots
1	cup couscous	2	tablespoons almond slivers, toasted
¼	cup crumbled turkey bacon, cooked		

Combine the chicken broth and garlic in a 1½-quart saucepan. Bring to a boil. Stir in couscous and turkey bacon. Remove from heat. Cover and let stand for 5 minutes. Fluff with a fork. Stir in spinach, carrots, and almond slivers.

Exchange Values Per Serving
1 Serving = ⅔ Cup
1½ Starch
½ Fat
½ Meat

158 Calories
(21% from Fat)
3.6 gm Total Fat
0.8 gm Saturated Fat
9.1 mg Cholesterol
161 mg Sodium
24.6 gm Carbohydrates
2.1 gm Dietary Fiber
6.6 gm Protein
137 mg Potassium

Fruited Couscous

8 Servings

1	small onion, finely chopped	1	cup chopped dried apricots
1	garlic clove, minced	1	cup chopped dried pears
½	teaspoon ground ginger	½	cup sliced almonds, toasted
2	tablespoons low-fat margarine	2	tablespoons lemon juice
2½	cups low-sodium chicken broth	2	tablespoons honey
2	cups couscous	2	tablespoons chopped fresh mint
1	cup chopped pitted dates		

In a saucepan over medium heat, cook onion, garlic, and ginger in margarine for 5 minutes, or until tender. Add broth and bring to a boil. Stir in couscous, dates, apricots, and pears. Cover and remove from heat. Let stand 5 minutes or until broth is absorbed. Stir in remaining ingredients.

Exchange Values Per Serving
1 Serving = 1 Cup
2 Starch
⅔ Fat
2⅔ Fruit

402 Calories
(12% from Fat)
5.6 gm Total Fat
0.9 gm Saturated Fat
1.2 mg Cholesterol
77 mg Sodium
83.4 gm Carbohydrates
7.9 gm Dietary Fiber
9.4 gm Protein
638 mg Potassium

Oriental Oat Pilaf

6 Servings

Exchange Values Per Serving
1 Serving = ¾ Cup
⅓ Fat
½ Vegetable
1 Starch

130 Calories
(18% from Fat)
2.7 gm Total Fat
0.6 gm Saturated Fat
0.6 mg Cholesterol
250 mg Sodium
20.2 gm Carbohydrates
4.0 gm Dietary Fiber
7.0 gm Protein
275 mg Potassium

1 tablespoon low-fat margarine	2 egg whites
1 cup sliced mushrooms	2 tablespoons low-sodium soy sauce
½ cup chopped red bell pepper	1 cup low-sodium chicken broth
½ cup sliced green onions	1 package (6 ounces) frozen pea pods, thawed
½ cup chopped celery	
1¾ cups quick-cooking or old-fashioned oats	

Melt the margarine in a skillet over medium heat. Add the mushrooms, pepper, onions, and celery, and sauté for 2 to 3 minutes. In a bowl, mix the oats, egg whites, and soy sauce. Coat the oats well, then add to the vegetable mixture. Cook for an additional 5 minutes or until lightly browned. Add the chicken broth and pea pods, and cook until the liquid is absorbed and the vegetables are tender.

Golden Mediterranean Pilaf

8 Servings

Exchange Values Per Serving
1 Serving = ⅔ Cup
⅔ Fat
½ Fruit
1⅔ Starch

201 Calories
(19% from Fat)
4.3 gm Total Fat
0.6 gm Saturated Fat
1.4 mg Cholesterol
110 mg Sodium
36.7 gm Carbohydrates
0.9 gm Dietary Fiber
4.1 gm Protein
120 mg Potassium

3 cups low-sodium chicken broth	½ cup seedless golden raisins
1½ cups uncooked long grain white rice	½ teaspoon ground turmeric
2 tablespoons canola oil	½ teaspoon curry powder
	1 tablespoon low-sodium soy sauce

Bring the chicken broth to a boil in a 1-quart saucepan. In another medium saucepan combine the rice, canola oil, raisins, turmeric, curry, and soy sauce. Pour the chicken broth over the rice mix. Cover and cook over low heat for 20 minutes or until all of the liquid is absorbed and the rice is tender.

Vegetables

Steamed Vegetables

8 Servings

5 large carrots, peeled	1 tablespoon fresh lemon juice
4 medium new potatoes, quartered	⅛ teaspoon pepper
12 Brussels sprouts, halved	
1 tablespoon low-fat margarine, melted	

Place the carrots and potatoes in a steamer over 2 inches of boiling water. Cover and cook for 6 minutes. Add the Brussels sprouts, cover, and continue to cook for 5 to 7 minutes, or until the vegetables are tender. Combine the margarine, lemon juice, and pepper in a bowl. Toss with the steamed vegetables.

Exchange Values Per Serving
1 Serving = 1 Cup
2 Vegetable

56 Calories
(18% from Fat)
1.2 gm Total Fat
0.2 gm Saturated Fat
0 mg Cholesterol
35 mg Sodium
10.5 gm Carbohydrates
2.5 gm Dietary Fiber
1.8 gm Protein
386 mg Potassium

Creamed Vegetables

12 Servings

2 tablespoons low-fat margarine	5 carrots, diagonally sliced
2 tablespoons all-purpose flour	3 ribs celery, diagonally sliced
1½ cups evaporated fat-free milk	1 red onion, chopped
2 tablespoons dry sherry	1 bag (16 ounces) frozen green peas, thawed
1 teaspoon dried tarragon	
¼ teaspoon pepper	

In a large saucepan over medium heat, melt margarine. Stir in flour to form paste. Cook, stirring for 1 minute. Gradually whisk in milk, sherry, tarragon, and pepper. Stir in carrots, celery, and onion, reduce heat to low and simmer 10 minutes until crisp tender. Stir in peas and cook 5 minutes.

Exchange Values Per Serving
1 Serving = ⅔ Cup
½ Fat
⅓ Starch
⅔ Vegetable

79 Calories
(13% from Fat)
1.1 gm Total Fat
0.2 gm Saturated Fat
2.5 mg Cholesterol
101 mg Sodium
12.1 gm Carbohydrates
2.8 gm Dietary Fiber
4.1 gm Protein
193 mg Potassium

Roasted Vegetables

12 Servings

4 carrots, cut into large chunks	1 large red bell pepper, thickly sliced
1 bulb fennel, trimmed and cut into thin wedges	10 garlic cloves, peeled
	¼ teaspoon coarsely ground pepper
1 pound Yukon Gold potatoes, quartered	1 teaspoon salt-free seasoning
	2 tablespoons virgin olive oil
1 large red onion, cut into wedges	1 teaspoon grated orange peel

Preheat oven to 225°. In a roasting pan, toss together carrots, fennel, potatoes, onion, red pepper, garlic, and seasoning.

In a small bowl, whisk together the olive oil and orange peel. Pour over the vegetables and toss to coat. Roast 1½ hours, turning occasionally, until tender.

Lemon Artichoke Hearts and Mushrooms

4 Servings

8 to 10 artichoke hearts	¼ cup sherry
1 pound fresh mushrooms, sliced	1 teaspoon fresh lemon juice
2 tablespoons low-fat margarine	Pepper to taste
1 garlic clove, minced	Parsley to taste
1½ teaspoons cornstarch	

Drain and quarter artichokes, reserving liquid. Sauté artichokes and mushrooms in margarine with garlic in a saucepan.

Blend cornstarch with sherry, lemon juice, and reserved artichoke liquid in a pan. Heat liquid mixture, stirring constantly until smooth and clear. Add pepper and parsley. Combine liquid mixture with sautéed artichokes and mushrooms and heat gently before serving.

Fresh Asparagus Rice Pilaf

4 Servings

1½	cups water	⅛	teaspoon lemon pepper
1	tablespoon low-sodium soy sauce	½	cup long-grain rice
½	cup green onions, sliced	½	cup chopped water chestnuts
1	teaspoon chicken bouillon granules	1	cup chopped asparagus
½	teaspoon lemon peel, shredded	⅛	cup lemon peels for garnish

In a medium saucepan, combine the water, soy sauce, onions, chicken bouillon, lemon peel, and pepper. Bring to a boil. Stir in rice and water chestnuts, reduce heat. Cover and cook for approximately 20 to 25 minutes until all liquid is absorbed. When rice has 10 minutes cooking time left, stir in the asparagus. Serve with thin strips of lemon peel placed on top of each serving.

Exchange Values Per Serving
1 Serving = ½ Cup
1 Starch
1 Vegetable

111 Calories
(4% from Fat)
0.5 gm Total Fat
0.1 gm Saturated Fat
0.2 mg Cholesterol
417 mg Sodium
23.8 gm Carbohydrates
1.8 gm Dietary Fiber
3.3 gm Protein
185 mg Potassium

Asparagus and Basil

6 Servings

2	tablespoons low-fat margarine	1	teaspoon lemon juice
¼	teaspoon dried basil	2	pounds asparagus, cooked
	Pepper to taste		

Melt the margarine in a saucepan. Add the basil, pepper, and lemon juice. Pour over the asparagus and serve hot.

Exchange Values Per Serving
1 Serving = 2-3 Spears
1 Fat
2 Vegetable

103 Calories
(46% from Fat)
6.0 gm Total Fat
1.1 gm Saturated Fat
0 mg Cholesterol
67 mg Sodium
10.4 gm Carbohydrates
4.8 gm Dietary Fiber
5.2 gm Protein
620.7 mg Potassium

Grilled Asparagus

6 Servings

1   pound fresh asparagus, cut into 6-inch lengths

½   cup Dijon Vinaigrette (page 262)
Herbs for garnish

Preheat grill. Arrange asparagus in grill basket with tips toward outer edges of basket. (Asparagus layer can be doubled, if necessary). Brush asparagus with Dijon Vinaigrette. Grill 3 minutes, turn, and brush. Cook 3 more minutes or until asparagus is crisp tender, being careful not to burn. Serve hot, at room temperature, or chilled. Sprinkle with fresh herbs on plate.

Exchange Values Per Serving
1 Serving = 2 Spears
⅔ Starch
⅔ Vegetable

51 Calories
(3% from Fat)
0.2 gm Total Fat
0 gm Saturated Fat
0 mg Cholesterol
85 mg Sodium
10.8 gm Carbohydrates
1.6 gm Dietary Fiber
1.7 gm Protein
206 mg Potassium

Broccoli with Cream Sauce

8 Servings

4   packages (10 ounces each) frozen broccoli spears

2   tablespoons low-fat margarine

2   tablespoons minced onion

16   ounces fat-free sour cream

2   teaspoons sugar

½   teaspoon red wine vinegar

½   teaspoon paprika

Cook broccoli according to package directions (omitting salt).

Melt margarine in a heavy skillet; sauté onion until tender. Remove from heat; stir in sour cream, sugar, red wine vinegar, and paprika. Arrange broccoli on a serving dish. Spoon sauce over broccoli.

Exchange Values Per Serving
1 Serving = 3 Large Spears with 2 Tablespoons Sauce
⅓ Fat
1½ Vegetable

130 Calories
(12% from Fat)
1.9 gm Total Fat
0.4 gm Saturated Fat
5.0 mg Cholesterol
108 mg Sodium
21.4 gm Carbohydrates
4.3 gm Dietary Fiber
8.4 gm Protein
510 mg Potassium

Baked Broccoli

8 Servings

2   packages (10 ounces each) frozen chopped broccoli
1   can (10¾ ounces) reduced-fat cream of mushroom soup
½   cup fat-free plain yogurt
¼   cup egg substitute
1   small onion, grated

1   cup shredded low-fat Cheddar cheese
    Nonstick cooking spray
1   cup fat-free cheese cracker crumbs
2   tablespoons low-sodium chicken broth

Preheat oven to 350°. Cook or steam the broccoli slightly in a pan. Drain and combine with the soup, yogurt, egg substitute, onion, and cheese. Place in a 2-quart casserole dish coated with nonstick spray. Spoon the cracker crumbs over the broccoli, then sprinkle with chicken broth. Bake for 30 to 35 minutes.

Exchange Values Per Serving
    1 Serving = ⅔ Cup
    ½ Fat
    ½ Meat
    ½ Starch
    1½ Vegetable

117 Calories
    (20% from Fat)
    2.6 gm Total Fat
    1.0 gm Saturated Fat
    5.3 mg Cholesterol
    363 mg Sodium
    15.3 gm Carbohydrates
    2.9 gm Dietary Fiber
    9.1 gm Protein
    258 mg Potassium

Broccoli and Herbs

6 Servings

2   cups low-sodium chicken broth
3   pounds broccoli, lightly steamed
½   cup chopped onion
1   teaspoon minced garlic

1   teaspoon dried marjoram
1   bay leaf
½   teaspoon salt-free seasoning

Bring the chicken broth to a boil in a large skillet with a lid. Add all of the ingredients. Cook covered for 10 to 15 minutes or until the broccoli is tender. Drain and serve.

Exchange Values Per Serving
    1 Serving = 3-4 Spears
    2½ Vegetable

77 Calories
    (12% from Fat)
    1.3 gm Total Fat
    0.4 gm Saturated Fat
    1.3 mg Cholesterol
    92 mg Sodium
    12.9 gm Carbohydrates
    6.5 gm Dietary Fiber
    7.6 gm Protein
    645 mg Potassium

Broccoli and Mushroom Casserole

8 Servings

Exchange Values Per Serving
1 Serving = 3-Inch Square
½ Fat
⅔ Meat
½ Starch
1½ Vegetable

152 Calories
(14% from Fat)
2.5 gm Total Fat
1.0 gm Saturated Fat
7.2 mg Cholesterol
419 mg Sodium
22.1 gm Carbohydrates
2.8 gm Dietary Fiber
11.4 gm Protein
341 mg Potassium

2　cups rice, cooked
Nonstick cooking spray
2　packages (10 ounces each) frozen chopped broccoli
1　can (10¾ ounces) reduced-fat cream of mushroom soup

1　cup fat-free plain yogurt
1　cup shredded low-fat American cheese
1　medium onion, chopped
½　cup egg substitute

Preheat oven to 350°. Spread the rice in the bottom of a casserole dish. Steam the broccoli in a small amount of water for 5 minutes or until crisp tender. Spoon over the rice. Mix together the remaining ingredients in a bowl and pour over the broccoli. Bake for 30 to 35 minutes. Cut into 8 equal portions.

Broccoli Turkey Casserole

8 Servings

Exchange Values Per Serving
1 Serving = 3-Inch Square
½ Fat
1½ Meat
½ Starch
1 Vegetable

163 Calories
(27% from Fat)
5.1 gm Total Fat
1.5 gm Saturated Fat
54.6 mg Cholesterol
234 mg Sodium
15.4 gm Carbohydrates
5.7 gm Dietary Fiber
16.5 gm Protein
318 mg Potassium

2　packages (10 ounces each) frozen chopped broccoli
2　cans (10¾ ounces each) low-sodium turkey broth
2　cups diced cooked turkey
½　teaspoon rubbed sage
½　cup chopped onion

½　cup chopped celery
1　egg
2　cups fat-free bread, cut into chunks
Nonstick cooking spray
2　tablespoons low-fat margarine, melted

Preheat oven to 350°. Toss together all of the ingredients (except the melted margarine). Pour into a casserole dish coated with nonstick spray and pour the margarine over the top. Cover and bake for 35 to 40 minutes. Uncover and bake an additional 15 minutes or until the vegetables are tender.

Brussels Sprouts with Chive Sauce

10 Servings

4 shallots, chopped
¼ cup dry white wine
4 teaspoons low-sodium chicken
    broth
1¼ cups evaporated fat-free milk
5 sprigs watercress

3 tablespoons cold water
1 tablespoon finely chopped chives
5 tablespoons low-fat margarine at
    room temperature
1 tablespoon fresh lemon juice
2 pounds Brussels sprouts, steamed

Gently boil shallots and wine, uncovered, in a pan until nearly all wine has evaporated. Remove from heat. In another pan, mix broth and milk. Boil, uncovered, until mixture is rich and creamy. Remove from heat.

In a food processor, blend softened shallots, watercress, cold water, chives, and margarine for 30 seconds. Add cream mixture and lemon juice and blend until smooth, 30 seconds. Serve over Brussels sprouts.

Exchange Values Per Serving
1 Serving = 1 Cup
  Sprouts with 2
  Tablespoons Sauce
1½ Fat
2 Vegetable

129 Calories
(42% from Fat)
6.4 gm Total Fat
0.1 gm Saturated Fat
1.2 mg Cholesterol
122 mg Sodium
13.3 gm Carbohydrates
3.5 gm Dietary Fiber
5.8 gm Protein
498 mg Potassium

Creole Cabbage

4 Servings

5 cups chopped cabbage
1 large onion, chopped
1 teaspoon minced garlic
1 green bell pepper, chopped
2 tablespoons low-fat margarine
1 can (14½ ounces) low-sodium
    peeled whole tomatoes

1 teaspoon sugar
    Pepper to taste
    Nonstick cooking spray
1 cup shredded low-fat Cheddar
    cheese

Boil the cabbage in water for 10 minutes. Drain well and set aside.

Preheat oven to 325°. Sauté the onions, garlic, and green pepper in the margarine. Add the tomatoes with juice, sugar, and pepper, and simmer for 5 minutes or more. Combine this mixture with the cabbage and place in a baking dish that has been coated with nonstick spray. Sprinkle with cheese and bake for about 20 minutes or until the cheese melts.

Exchange Values Per Serving
1 Serving = 1 Cup
1 Fat
⅔ Meat
2½ Vegetable

138 Calories
(31% from Fat)
5.1 gm Total Fat
1.8 gm Saturated Fat
5.9 mg Cholesterol
348 mg Sodium
14.4 gm Carbohydrates
4.3 gm Dietary Fiber
10.8 gm Protein
422 mg Potassium

Golden Carrots

6 Servings

Exchange Values Per Serving
1 Serving = ½ Cup
1 Fruit
2 Vegetable

114 Calories
(7% from Fat)
0.9 gm Total Fat
0.2 gm Saturated Fat
0 mg Cholesterol
86 mg Sodium
26.5 gm Carbohydrates
4.1 gm Dietary Fiber
1.9 gm Protein
420 mg Potassium

4	cups thinly sliced carrots	½	cup golden raisins
1	cup unsweetened orange juice	2	teaspoons low-fat margarine
1	cup water	½	teaspoon vanilla extract
2	teaspoons grated lemon peel	¼	teaspoon ground mace

Combine the carrots, juice, water, and lemon peel in a medium saucepan; bring to a boil. Cover, reduce heat, and simmer 10 to 12 minutes or just until tender. Remove from heat, drain carrots, reserving ¼ cup of liquid. Stir reserved liquid, raisins, margarine, vanilla, and mace together with carrots.

Sweet Carrots with Dill or Basil

4 Servings

Exchange Values Per Serving
1 Serving = ⅔ Cup
⅓ Fat
2½ Vegetable

80 Calories
(19% from Fat)
1.8 gm Total Fat
0.3 gm Saturated Fat
0 mg Cholesterol
74 mg Sodium
15.5 gm Carbohydrates
3.7 gm Dietary Fiber
1.6 gm Protein
440 mg Potassium

1	pound carrots	½	cup unsweetened orange juice
½	cup water	½	teaspoon vanilla extract
1	tablespoon low-fat margarine	2	teaspoons dill seed or sweet basil

Cut the carrots into diagonal slices. Steam or boil in ½ cup water for 10 minutes in a large saucepan. Drain and add the margarine, orange juice, vanilla, and dill or basil. Simmer 10 to 15 minutes more, until the carrots are tender.

Cauliflower with Broccoli Sauce

6 Servings

1 large cauliflower, in florets, cooked
   or steamed
   Nonstick cooking spray
1 large bunch broccoli, blanched
2 tablespoons low-fat margarine

½ cup fat free sour cream
½ cup Parmesan cheese
   Pepper to taste
½ cup seasoned breadcrumbs

Preheat oven to 325°. Place cauliflower in 1½-quart baking dish coated with nonstick spray. Chop broccoli coarsely and purée in a food processor with margarine and sour cream. Add Parmesan cheese. Season with pepper. Cover cauliflower with broccoli purée and sprinkle top with breadcrumbs. Bake 20 minutes.

Exchange Values Per Serving
1 Serving = ⅔ Cup
½ Fat
⅓ Starch
1½ Vegetable

117 Calories
(26% from Fat)
3.5 gm Total Fat
1.2 gm Saturated Fat
5.0 mg Cholesterol
345 mg Sodium
15.5 gm Carbohydrates
3.3 gm Dietary Fiber
6.8 gm Protein
432 mg Potassium

Crumbly Cauliflower

8 Servings

1 head cauliflower
¼ cup low-sodium chicken broth
½ teaspoon pepper
1 cup fat-free cheese cracker crumbs
½ cup diced green bell pepper
1 can (14½ ounces) low-sodium
   peeled whole tomatoes

1 medium onion, chopped
   Nonstick cooking spray
1½ cups shredded low-fat Cheddar
   cheese

Preheat oven to 350°. Wash the cauliflower and remove the leaves. Break into florets. Boil for 5 minutes using no salt. Combine the broth, pepper, and cracker crumbs in a large mixing bowl. Stir in the green pepper, tomatoes, onion, and cauliflower. Pour into a 2-quart casserole dish that has been sprayed with nonstick spray. Sprinkle the top with Cheddar cheese. Bake for 1 hour. Serve hot.

Exchange Values Per Serving
1 Serving = 1 Cup
½ Meat
½ Starch
1½ Vegetable

106 Calories
(18% from Fat)
2.1 gm Total Fat
1.1 gm Saturated Fat
5.0 mg Cholesterol
246 mg Sodium
14.2 gm Carbohydrates
2.7 gm Dietary Fiber
8.4 gm Protein
391 mg Potassium

Cheesy Scalloped Cucumbers

6 Servings

Exchange Values Per Serving
1 Serving = ⅔ Cup
⅓ Fat
½ Meat
⅓ Starch
1 Vegetable

93 Calories
(18% from Fat)
2.0 gm Total Fat
1.0 gm Saturated Fat
4.8 mg Cholesterol
195 mg Sodium
12.2 gm Carbohydrates
2.4 gm Dietary Fiber
8.0 gm Protein
308 mg Potassium

3   slices fat-free bread
Nonstick cooking spray
3   large cucumbers, peeled and sliced ⅓ to ½ inch thick
Pepper to taste
Salt substitute to taste
½   cup low-sodium chicken broth
2   tablespoons minced onion
¾   cup fat-free milk
1   cup shredded low-fat Cheddar cheese

Preheat oven to 350°. Crumble one slice of bread into a baking dish that has been coated with nonstick cooking spray. Arrange about half the cucumber slices over the bread and sprinkle with pepper and salt. Mix broth, onion, and milk in a bowl. Cover cucumber layer with half of the broth mixture. Repeat for 2 more layers, then sprinkle the top with Cheddar cheese. Bake for 30 minutes or until browned.

Stuffed Eggplant

4 Servings

Exchange Values Per Serving
1 Serving = 1-inch Slice
½ Fat
½ Starch
3½ Vegetable

131 Calories
(23% from Fat)
3.5 gm Total Fat
0.8 gm Saturated Fat
3.0 mg Cholesterol
421 mg Sodium
23.2 gm Carbohydrates
4.8 gm Dietary Fiber
3.5 gm Protein
452 mg Potassium

1   large eggplant
½   cup water
¼   cup chopped onion
1   tablespoon low-fat margarine
1   can (10½ ounces) reduced-fat cream of mushroom soup
1   teaspoon low-sodium
Worcestershire sauce
1   cup fine butter-flavored fat-free cracker crumbs, divided
Nonstick cooking spray
1   cup finely chopped parsley
1½   cups water

Preheat oven to 375°. Slice off one side of the eggplant. Remove the pulp to within ½ inch of the skin. Dice the pulp and place in a saucepan. Add ½ cup of water, and simmer until the eggplant is tender. Drain. Sauté the onion in margarine in a skillet until golden brown. Mix onion, mushroom soup, Worcestershire sauce, and all of the cracker crumbs (except 2 tablespoons) together with the eggplant pulp.

Fill the eggplant shell with the mixture. Place the eggplant in a shallow baking pan that has been coated with cooking spray. Sprinkle the top with the reserved crumbs and parsley. Pour 1½ cups of water into the baking pan. Bake for 1 hour, until piping hot.

Cajun Green Beans

6 Servings

1	pound fresh French-style green beans
	Water as needed
½	cup chopped green bell pepper
½	cup chopped celery

½	cup chopped onion
2	tablespoons low-fat margarine
1	tablespoon chopped pimiento
⅓	cup chili sauce
1	teaspoon paprika

Cook the beans in water in a pan until tender. Drain. Sauté the green pepper, celery, and onion in margarine in a skillet until tender. Add the seasonings and beans, and stir until just heated through.

Exchange Values Per Serving
1 Serving = ⅔ Cup
½ Fat
⅓ Starch
1½ Vegetable

66.8 Calories
(25% from Fat)
2.1 gm Total Fat
0.4 gm Saturated Fat
0 mg Cholesterol
260 mg Sodium
11.7 gm Carbohydrates
3.4 gm Dietary Fiber
2.2 gm Protein
295 mg Potassium

French Green Beans Amandine

4 Servings

1	low-sodium chicken bouillon cube
⅓	cup boiling water
1	package (10 ounces) frozen French-style green beans

1	tablespoon slivered almonds
1	tablespoon low-fat margarine

Dissolve the bouillon cube in the boiling water. Add the green beans and boil until tender. In a separate pan sauté the almonds in margarine until brown. Drain the beans and almonds, and toss together.

Exchange Values Per Serving
1 Serving = ½ Cup
½ Fat
1 Vegetable

48 Calories
(45% from Fat)
2.6 gm Total Fat
0.4 gm Saturated Fat
0.2 mg Cholesterol
316 mg Sodium
5.5 gm Carbohydrates
1.8 gm Dietary Fiber
1.7 gm Protein
138 mg Potassium

French Green Bean and Rice Casserole

4 Servings

1   large onion, chopped
2   tablespoons low-fat margarine
½   cup uncooked rice
1   bag (16 ounces) low-sodium French-style green beans
⅛   teaspoon pepper
1   can (14½ ounces) low-sodium peeled whole tomatoes
⅓   cup water
1   teaspoon salt-free seasoning

Sauté the onions in margarine until brown. Add the remaining ingredients. Cook, covered, for 30 minutes.

Apples and Onions Side Dish

4 Servings

4   teaspoons low-fat margarine
2   onions, sliced
4   medium-size firm apples, cored and sliced
Pepper to taste
Salt substitute to taste
½   teaspoon freshly squeezed lemon juice

Heat the margarine in a large skillet, and add the onions and apples. Cook, turning occasionally until the apples and onions are tender. Season to taste. Stir in the lemon juice. Serve hot as a side dish.

Baked Italian Onions

6 Servings

6   onions
    Nonstick cooking spray
6   tablespoons fat-free Italian salad
    dressing, not creamy

¾   cup Parmesan cheese

Preheat oven to 350°. Peel and wash the onions. Slice the ends evenly so they sit straight. Score each onion in a cross like fashion leaving the outer ring intact. Place in an aluminum foil square that has been coated with coating spray. Pull the foil up around the onion leaving the top exposed, not sealed (tulip-fashioned). Spoon one tablespoon of salad dressing over each onion and sprinkle the top with 2 tablespoons of Parmesan cheese. Bake in a pan for 1 hour.

Exchange Values Per Serving
1 Serving = 1 Onion
½ Fat
⅔ Meat
2 Vegetable

104 Calories
(34% from Fat)
3.9 gm Total Fat
2.5 gm Saturated Fat
9.8 mg Cholesterol
381 mg Sodium
11.0 gm Carbohydrates
2.0 gm Dietary Fiber
6.5 gm Protein
206 mg Potassium

Stuffed Peppers

8 Servings

4   large bell peppers
    Nonstick cooking spray
1   pound ground turkey breast
1   cup chopped onions
1   tablespoon minced parsley
½   teaspoon dried oregano

1   can (6 ounces) low-sodium tomato
    paste
½   cup water
¾   cup shredded low-fat Cheddar
    cheese
1   cup cooked brown and wild rice

Preheat oven to 350°. Cut the tops off the bell peppers and remove the seeds. Hollow out and wash well. Place in a baking pan that has been coated with nonstick spray.

Brown the ground turkey with the onion, parsley, and oregano in a skillet. Add the tomato paste and water, and stir well. Spoon into the bell peppers and sprinkle with shredded cheese. Bake for 15 to 20 minutes.

Exchange Values Per Serving
1 Serving = ½ Stuffed
  Pepper
⅔ Fat
2 Meats
⅓ Starch
2 Vegetable

182 Calories
(26% from Fat)
5.3 gm Total Fat
1.6 gm Saturated Fat
39.1 mg Cholesterol
121 mg Sodium
16.9 gm Carbohydrates
3.2 gm Dietary Fiber
17.4 gm Protein
552 mg Potassium

Sautéed Cream Spinach

4 Servings

Exchange Values Per Serving
1 Serving = ⅔ Cup
½ Fat
¾ Vegetable

84 Calories
(41% from Fat)
4.1 gm Total Fat
1.2 gm Saturated Fat
3.7 mg Cholesterol
229 mg Sodium
7.6 gm Carbohydrates
3.1 gm Dietary Fiber
5.7 gm Protein
673 mg Potassium

2   tablespoons low-fat margarine
1   garlic clove, minced
1   pound fresh spinach, stemmed, washed, drained
¼   cup fat-free sour cream
2   tablespoons grated Parmesan cheese

Heat margarine over medium-high heat in a skillet. Add garlic and spinach, reduce heat, and simmer, covered, 5 to 7 minutes. During the last minute or two of cooking, add sour cream and Parmesan cheese. Blend well.

Spinach Casserole

6 Servings

Exchange Values Per Serving
1 Serving = ⅔ Cup
½ Fat
1 Meat
⅔ Starch
1 Vegetable

142 Calories
(29% from Fat)
4.8 gm Total Fat
2.0 gm Saturated Fat
10.6 mg Cholesterol
414 mg Sodium
15.5 gm Carbohydrates
3.4 gm Dietary Fiber
11.4 gm Protein
437 mg Potassium

2   packages (10 ounces each) frozen chopped spinach
2   ounces fat-free cream cheese
2   ounces feta cheese, crumbled
½   cup fat-free milk
½   cup egg substitute
2   tablespoons green onion, finely chopped
    Nonstick spray coating
¾   cup breadcrumbs
1   tablespoon grated Parmesan cheese
2   teaspoons low-fat margarine

Preheat oven to 350°. Cook spinach according to package directions. Drain in a colander. Place spinach in a saucepan. Over medium heat stir cream cheese and feta cheese into the spinach until cream cheese is melted. Stir in the milk, egg substitute, and onion.

Coat a 1½-quart casserole with nonstick cooking spray. Pour spinach mixture into the casserole dish. Toss together the breadcrumbs, Parmesan cheese, and melted margarine in a bowl. Sprinkle on top of spinach mixture. Bake covered for 40 minutes. Remove cover and continue to cook for an additional 10 minutes.

Summer Squash Casserole

6 Servings

3	to 4 medium yellow squash, sliced about ¼ inch thick		Nonstick cooking spray
3	medium tomatoes, sliced about ¼ inch thick	½	cup fat-free plain yogurt
½	cup thinly sliced onion	½	cup shredded low-fat Cheddar cheese
		2	teaspoons salt-free seasoning

Preheat oven to 350°. Layer half the vegetables in a sprayed 2-quart casserole. Spread the yogurt over the vegetables. Combine the cheese and salt-free seasonings in a bowl. Sprinkle half the cheese mixture over the yogurt. Top with the remaining vegetables and then the cheese mixture. Bake for 30 minutes.

Exchange Values Per Serving
1 Serving = 3-inch Square
⅓ Meat
⅓ Starch
1 Vegetable

64 Calories
(14% from Fat)
1.1 gm Total Fat
0.5 gm Saturated Fat
2.3 mg Cholesterol
83 mg Sodium
9.5 gm Carbohydrates
2.5 gm Dietary Fiber
5.8 gm Protein
540 mg Potassium

Apple-Stuffed Squash with Cinnamon

4 Servings

2	butternut, buttercup, or acorn squash		Cinnamon
	Nonstick cooking spray		Pepper to taste
2	large tart apples, cored and sliced	1	teaspoon sugar
½	onion, chopped	2	teaspoons low-fat margarine

Preheat oven to 350°. Split the squash in half. Scoop out the seeds and place cut side down in a shallow baking dish that has been coated with nonstick spray. Pour in hot water to a depth of ½ inch. Bake until partly tender, about 20 minutes for butternut or buttercup squash, 30 to 45 minutes for acorn squash.

Turn the squash cut sides up. Arrange a quarter of the apple slices and some of the onion in the cup of each squash half. Sprinkle lightly with cinnamon, and pepper to taste. Sprinkle ¼ teaspoon of the sugar over each half and dot with ½ teaspoon margarine. Add hot water to the dish, if necessary, to bring the depth to ½ inch again.

Return to the oven and bake for 20 to 30 minutes longer, until both the squash and the apple are tender.

Exchange Values Per Serving
1 Serving = ½ Stuffed Squash
1 Fruit
3½ Vegetable

166 Calories
(7% from Fat)
1.5 gm Total Fat
0.3 gm Saturated Fat
0 mg Cholesterol
30 mg Sodium
40.9 gm Carbohydrates
6.3 gm Dietary Fiber
2.1 gm Protein
892 mg Potassium

Spaghetti Squash and Vegetables

8 Servings

1 medium spaghetti squash
   Nonstick cooking spray
6 large tomatoes, diced
1 large onion, coarsely chopped

1 tablespoon Italian seasoning
2 cups mixed fresh vegetables such as broccoli, cauliflower, and carrots, cooked

Preheat oven to 350°. Split the spaghetti squash in half. Scoop out the seeds and place cut side down on a baking sheet coated with cooking spray. Bake for 35 to 45 minutes. Scoop out with a fork. It will come out in strands like spaghetti. Drain if needed. Set aside.

Mix the tomatoes, onion, and seasoning in a pan and bring to a boil, then reduce the heat to a simmer. Cook for approximately 25 minutes. Before serving, add the cooked vegetables to the sauce. Serve over the spaghetti squash.

Exchange Values Per Serving
1 Serving = ⅔ Cup
2½ Vegetable

55 Calories
(9% from Fat)
0.6 gm Total Fat
0.1 gm Saturated Fat
0 mg Cholesterol
30 mg Sodium
12.1 gm Carbohydrates
3.0 gm Dietary Fiber
2.0 gm Protein
395 mg Potassium

Broiled Tomatoes

6 Servings

6 small fresh tomatoes, not too ripe
½ cup fat-free cheese crackers
½ cup grated Parmesan cheese

⅛ cup minced parsley
¼ cup low-fat margarine

Slice the tomatoes ½-inch thick, discarding the ends. Place on broiler pan. Mix the remaining ingredients and place an equal portion of the mixture on the top of each tomato slice. Broil for 5 minutes until hot, and serve immediately.

Exchange Values Per Serving
1 Serving = 2 Slices
⅔ Fat
½ Meat
⅓ Starch
⅔ Vegetable

86 Calories
(42% from Fat)
4.2 gm Total Fat
0.9 gm Saturated Fat
2.1 mg Cholesterol
323 mg Sodium
8.2 gm Carbohydrates
1.2 gm Dietary Fiber
4.9 gm Protein
247 mg Potassium

Spicy Cherry Tomatoes with Avocado

4 Servings

20	cherry tomatoes	1	tablespoon lemon juice
2	medium avocados	1	tablespoon minced onion
2	teaspoons low-sodium Worcestershire sauce	6	to 10 drops hot sauce
		2	tablespoons fat-free plain yogurt

Slice the tops off the cherry tomatoes. Hollow out the insides of the small tomatoes and reserve the pulp. Turn the tomatoes over and drain for 20 minutes.

Peel the avocados, then mash in a food processor. Mix the remaining ingredients including the pulp from the tomatoes until light and smooth. Fill the tomatoes with the mixture.

Exchange Values Per Serving
1 Serving = 4 Tomatoes
½ Fruit
3 Fat
1 Vegetable

190 Calories
(68% from Fat)
15.7 gm Total Fat
2.5 gm Saturated Fat
0.1 mg Cholesterol
51.6 mg Sodium
13.5 gm Carbohydrates
6.1 gm Dietary Fiber
3.3 gm Protein
852 mg Potassium

Baked Zucchini and Cheese

4 Servings

2	medium zucchini, sliced very thin	1	small Vidalia onion, sliced very thin
¼	cup egg substitute		Nonstick cooking spray
1	teaspoon seasoned mustard	1	tomato, sliced thin
⅛	teaspoon ground white pepper	⅓	cup Parmesan cheese
⅛	teaspoon grated nutmeg		

Preheat oven to 350°. Drain and dry the zucchini. Combine the egg substitute, mustard, pepper, nutmeg, and onion in a bowl. Add the zucchini and stir gently. Pour into a casserole dish that has been coated with cooking spray. Place the tomato slices on top and sprinkle with Parmesan cheese. Cover and bake for 30 to 40 minutes or until done.

Exchange Values Per Serving
1 Serving = 1 Cup
½ Meat
⅔ Vegetable

66 Calories
(29% from Fat)
2.3 gm Total Fat
1.1 gm Saturated Fat
3.9 mg Cholesterol
138 mg Sodium
7.0 gm Carbohydrates
2.0 gm Dietary Fiber
5.8 gm Protein
413 mg Potassium

Stuffed Zucchini Shells

4 Servings

Exchange Values Per Serving
1 Serving = 1 Stuffed
   Zucchini
½ Fat
⅓ Meat
¾ Starch
6 Vegetable

258 Calories
(13% from Fat)
3.7 gm Total Fat
1.1 gm Saturated Fat
0.2 mg Cholesterol
248 mg Sodium
42.6 gm Carbohydrates
8.7 gm Dietary Fiber
15.2 gm Protein
887 mg Potassium

2	large zucchini (about 1½ pounds)	¾	cup rice, cooked
1	medium onion, finely chopped	2	tablespoons chopped parsley
2	teaspoons low-fat margarine	1	teaspoon dried basil
¼	pound fresh mushrooms, chopped	½	teaspoon pepper
12	ounces vegetable (or soy) patty, crumbled	¼	cup egg substitute
			Nonstick cooking spray

Preheat oven to 350°. Trim edges off zucchini, then slice them in half lengthwise. Using a kitchen spoon, scoop out the center of each half, leaving the shell with sides about ¼-inch thick.

Parboil shells for about 10 minutes. Drain carefully and set aside.

In a large skillet, sauté onion in margarine until limp. Add mushrooms to skillet and cook for 5 minutes. Add crumbled vegetable (or soy) patty and warm. Remove from heat and stir in rice, parsley, basil, and pepper. Let cool briefly, then stir in the egg substitute. Divide mixture evenly among the 4 zucchini halves in a pan that has been coated with cooking spray. Bake for 30 minutes.

Zucchini Casserole

4 Servings

Exchange Values Per Serving
1 Serving = ⅔ Cup
1 Starch
⅓ Vegetable

123 Calories
(14% from Fat)
2.2 gm Total Fat
0.7 gm Saturated Fat
2.8 mg Cholesterol
189 mg Sodium
21.2 gm Carbohydrates
4.2 gm Dietary Fiber
8.2 gm Protein
815 mg Potassium

6	zucchini squash		Nonstick cooking spray
3	ounces fat-free plain yogurt	½	cup fat-free breadcrumbs
⅛	teaspoon garlic powder	2	tablespoons Parmesan cheese
⅛	cup minced onion	⅛	teaspoon paprika

Preheat oven to 350°. Slice the squash into 2-inch pieces. Cook in a small amount of boiling water in a pan for 8 to 10 minutes. Drain the zucchini well, and mix in the yogurt, garlic, and onion. Place in a sprayed casserole dish and top with breadcrumbs and Parmesan cheese. Sprinkle with paprika. Bake for 30 minutes.

Zucchini Ricotta Casserole

4 Servings

1 small onion, diced
½ pound zucchini, chopped
1 tablespoon low-fat margarine
3 tablespoons all-purpose flour
   Dash of salt substitute
   Dash of pepper
   Dash of paprika

¾ cup egg substitute
1 pound fat-free ricotta cheese
¼ cup shredded low-fat Cheddar
   cheese
   Dash of grated nutmeg
   Nonstick cooking spray

Preheat oven to 350°. Sauté the onion and zucchini in margarine in a skillet. Stir in flour. Add the salt substitute, pepper, and paprika. Remove from the heat, add the remaining ingredients, and mix well. Bake in a 1½-quart casserole dish coated with nonstick spray for 35 to 40 minutes.

Exchange Values Per Serving
  1 Serving = ⅔ Cup
  ½ Fat
  3 Meat
  ½ Starch
  ½ Vegetable

178 Calories
  (18% from Fat)
  3.6 gm Total Fat
  0.9 gm Saturated Fat
  11.3 mg Cholesterol
  507 mg Sodium
  12.7 gm Carbohydrates
  1.3 gm Dietary Fiber
  23.4 gm Protein
  572 mg Potassium

Unsalted Dill Pickles

15 Servings

2 cloves garlic, peeled and halved
10 peppercorns
4 large sprigs dill
2 pounds small cucumbers

2 cups cider vinegar
1 cup water
3 tablespoons salt substitute

Sterilize two 1-quart jars. In each jar, place 1 clove garlic, 5 peppercorns, and 2 sprigs dill. Closely pack cucumbers in jars.

Combine vinegar, water, and salt substitute in medium saucepan, bring to a boil. Pour over cucumbers covering them completely. Cover and refrigerate 1 week before serving. Makes 2 quarts.

Exchange Values Per Serving
  1 Serving = 1 Spear
  ½ Vegetable

15.7 Calories
  (6% from Fat)
  0.1 gm Total Fat
  0 gm Saturated Fat
  0 mg Cholesterol
  3 mg Sodium
  4.2 gm Carbohydrates
  0.7 gm Dietary Fiber
  0.5 gm Protein
  1,570 mg Potassium

Vegetable Rice Pie

6 Servings

Exchange Values Per Serving
1 Serving = 1 Cup
⅛ Fat
1⅛ Meat
¾ Starch
¾ Vegetable

143 Calories
(12% from Fat)
1.9 gm Total Fat
0.5 gm Saturated Fat
4.9 mg Cholesterol
273 mg Sodium
19.1 gm Carbohydrates
1.9 gm Dietary Fiber
12.2 gm Protein
342 mg Potassium

	Nonstick cooking spray	½	cup chopped carrots
½	cup brown and wild rice	1	cup shredded low-fat mozzarella cheese
1¼	cups water		
1	tablespoon low-fat margarine	½	cup plain fat-free yogurt
2	egg whites, slightly beaten	2	egg whites
1	cup chopped zucchini	1	teaspoon freshly snipped mint sprigs
1	cup sliced mushrooms		
½	cup chopped white onion	1	medium tomato, thinly sliced
½	cup chopped celery heart	2	tablespoons grated Parmesan cheese

Preheat oven to 350°. Coat a 9-inch pie plate with nonstick cooking spray.

In a medium saucepan combine the rice and water. Bring to a boil; reduce heat. Simmer, covered, for about 40 minutes or until rice is tender. Stir in margarine and 2 egg whites. Press into the prepared pie plate.

Coat a large skillet with nonstick cooking spray. Cook the zucchini, mushrooms, onion, celery, and carrots until tender. Sprinkle half of the mozzarella cheese onto the rice crust; top with the vegetable mixture and then top with the remaining mozzarella cheese. Stir together the yogurt, the remaining 2 egg whites, and the mint. Pour over cheese and bake uncovered for 30 minutes or until set.

Arrange tomato slices on top of the pie and sprinkle with Parmesan cheese. Bake for 2 to 3 minutes longer or until the tomatoes are heated through.

Salsas, sauces, dressings, and spreads

Mexican Salsa

16 Servings
A family favorite with nachos!

2	medium tomatoes	⅓	cup green chili salsa
2	garlic cloves, crushed	2	tablespoons diced jalapeños
⅓	cup chopped onion		
1	teaspoon low-sodium Worcestershire sauce		

Place tomatoes in a small shallow pan. Broil under medium heat. Turn the tomatoes on all sides until the skins are blistered and burnt and the tomatoes are cooked through, 10 to 15 minutes. Cool.

Place the tomatoes in a blender or food processor fitted with the metal blade. Add the remaining ingredients and mix until blended. Refrigerate for several hours before serving. This may be stored in the refrigerator for several months.

Exchange Values Per Serving
1 Serving = 1 Tablespoon
Free

7 Calories
(7% from Fat)
0.1 gm Total Fat
0 gm Saturated Fat
0 mg Cholesterol
0 mg Sodium
1.6 gm Carbohydrates
0.3 gm Dietary Fiber
0.2 gm Protein
45 mg Potassium

Monterey Jack Salsa

16 Servings
Kids' favorite!

Exchange Values Per Serving
1 Serving = 2
  Tablespoons
⅓ Fat
⅓ Meat
⅓ Vegetable

43 Calories
(56% from Fat)
2.7 gm Total Fat
0 gm Saturated Fat
3.8 mg Cholesterol
168 mg Sodium
2.4 gm Carbohydrates
0.3 gm Dietary Fiber
2.3 gm Protein
67 mg Potassium

1 can (4¼ ounces) green chilies, chopped
1 can (4¼ ounces) black olives, chopped
4 green onions, chopped
¼ pound low-sodium, low-fat Monterey Jack cheese, melted
1 tomato chopped
½ cup fat-free Italian Parmesan salad dressing
¼ cup chopped fresh cilantro
Fat-free tortilla chips

Blend all ingredients (except chips) in a bowl. Serve with warm tortilla chips.

Tartar Sauce

24 Servings
Great on any whitefish.

Exchange Values Per Serving
1 Serving = 1
  Tablespoon
Free

16 Calories
(3% from Fat)
0.1 gm Total Fat
0 gm Saturated Fat
0.2 mg Cholesterol
159 mg Sodium
3.2 gm Carbohydrates
0.2 gm Dietary Fiber
0.9 gm Protein
66 mg Potassium

¾ cup chili sauce
1 cup fat-free plain yogurt
1 tablespoon grated onion
¼ cup minced kosher dill pickle spears
1 teaspoon lemon juice
1 teaspoon low-sodium Worcestershire sauce
½ teaspoon low-sodium soy sauce
½ teaspoon horseradish

Combine all of the ingredients in a bowl and blend well. Serve with seafood or a seafood salad.

Steak Sauce

4 Servings
Serve over thinly sliced steak such as Pepper Steak (page 168).

2 tablespoons dry sherry	Dash of pepper
1 tablespoon low-fat margarine	1 tablespoon snipped parsley
1 teaspoon dry mustard	
1 teaspoon low-sodium Worcestershire sauce	

In a small saucepan, combine the sherry, margarine, dry mustard, Worcestershire sauce, and pepper. Heat until bubbly. Stir in the parsley.

Exchange Values Per Serving
1 Serving = 1 Tablespoon

23 Calories
(65% from Fat)
1.7 gm Total Fat
0.3 gm Saturated Fat
0 mg Cholesterol
49 mg Sodium
0.6 gm Carbohydrates
0.1 gm Dietary Fiber
0.3 gm Protein
24 mg Potassium

Green Onion Cream Sauce

Makes 32 Servings
This sauce can be served over any fish.

1 cup clam juice	1 bunch green onions, tops only, chopped
1 cup white wine	
1½ cups evaporated fat-free milk	

Combine juice and wine and simmer over high heat until reduced to ½ cup, about 10 minutes. Add milk and continue cooking until reduced to 1 cup, about 10 minutes. Pour into a food processor, add green onions, and let mix sit for 5 minutes. Purée until smooth, strain, and refrigerate.

Exchange Values Per Serving
1 Serving = 1 Tablespoon

23 Calories
(2% from Fat)
0.1 gm Total Fat
0 gm Saturated Fat
0.4 mg Cholesterol
421 mg Sodium
2.8 gm Carbohydrates
0 gm Dietary Fiber
1.5 gm Protein
62 mg Potassium

Yogurt and Dill Seafood Sauce

8 Servings

Serve with fish, shrimp, or any seafood. Especially good with salmon steaks.

Exchange Values Per Serving

1 Serving = 3
Tablespoons

11 Calories
(7% from Fat)
0.1 gm Total Fat
0 gm Saturated Fat
0.3 mg Cholesterol
28 mg Sodium
1.7 gm Carbohydrates
0.1 gm Dietary Fiber
1.1 gm Protein
57 mg Potassium

½ cup fat-free plain yogurt
1 tablespoon lemon juice
1 teaspoon Dijon mustard
1 tablespoon finely chopped fresh dill

1 tablespoon grated onion
½ cup finely chopped cucumber, well drained

In a blender combine all of the ingredients until well blended. Chill. Serve with fish, shrimp, or any seafood dish.

Shrimp with Oriental Ginger Apple Barbecue Sauce

6 Servings

Exchange Value Per Servings

1 Serving = 4 Ounces
Shrimp with Sauce
⅓ Fat
⅓ Fruit
3½ Meat
½ Vegetable

164 Calories
(15% from Fat)
2.7 gm Total Fat
0.5 gm Saturated Fat
172.4 mg Cholesterol
438 mg Sodium
9.3 gm Carbohydrate
1.0 gm Dietary Fiber
24.2 gm Protein
317 mg Potassium

1 tablespoon low-sodium chicken broth
¼ cup minced onion
1 garlic clove, minced
3 tablespoons grated fresh ginger-root (2-inch piece)
1 tablespoon sesame seed

1 cup applesauce
3 tablespoons low-sodium soy sauce
2 tablespoons dry sherry
¼ teaspoon ground pepper
   Apple juice or water, if needed
1½ pounds shrimp

Heat the broth in a medium saucepan. Add the onion, garlic, and ginger. Sauté for 10 minutes or until lightly brown. Add sesame seed and cook for one minute to toast lightly. Reduce heat. Add applesauce. Stir well. Add soy sauce, sherry, and pepper. Simmer uncovered for 20 minutes, stirring occasionally. If mixture is too thick, add a few tablespoons of apple juice or water.

Peel and devein shrimp. Thread on skewers. Brush with sauce. Grill until pink and just cooked through, about 10 minutes. Baste and turn every two minutes. Serve with remaining sauce.

Cucumber Sauce for Fish, Meats, or Vegetables

35 Servings
Especially good in the summer served with grilled meat.

2 cups minced cucumbers, seeds removed	¼ cup minced onion
2 teaspoons salt substitute	¼ cup chopped fresh dill
2 cups fat-free plain yogurt	1 teaspoon sugar
1 cup low-fat margarine	¼ cup chopped fresh parsley
1 tablespoon lemon juice	White pepper

Place the cucumbers in a large bowl, add the salt substitute, and blend well. Place in a sieve and drain for 20 minutes. Press the cucumbers against the sieve to squeeze out the excess moisture. Place the yogurt in a mixing bowl, stir in the margarine and then the lemon juice. Add the remaining ingredients and mix well. Stir in the cucumbers.

Exchange Values Per Serving
1 Serving = 2 Tablespoons
9 Fat
1½ Milk
2 Vegetable

31 Calories
(67% from Fat)
44.8 gm Total Fat
9.1 gm Saturated Fat
4.4 mg Cholesterol
1,287 mg Sodium
31.8 gm Carbohydrates
1.9 gm Dietary Fiber
17.6 gm Protein
3,138 mg Potassium

Ham with Mustard Garlic Apple-cue Sauce

8 Servings

1 tablespoon low-sodium chicken broth	1½ cups applesauce
¼ cup minced onion	1 to 2 tablespoons apple cider vinegar
5 garlic cloves, minced	1 tablespoon brown sugar
2 tablespoons Dijon mustard	1½ pounds precooked turkey ham slices
½ teaspoon dry mustard	
2 tablespoons regular prepared mustard	

Heat the broth in a medium saucepan. Add the onion and garlic. Sauté for 3 minutes or until soft. Add mustards and cook for 1 minute or until well heated. Reduce heat. Add applesauce. Stir well. Add vinegar and sugar. Simmer uncovered for 20 minutes, stirring occasionally. If mixture is too thick, add a few tablespoons of apple juice or water. Brush turkey ham slices with sauce and grill or broil until heated. Serve with remaining sauce.

Exchange Values Per Serving
1 Serving = 4 Ounces Turkey Ham with Sauce
½ Fruit
2⅔ Meat
½ Vegetable

208 Calories
(34% from Fat)
8.0 gm Total Fat
2.3 gm Saturated Fat
76.2 mg Cholesterol
1,296 mg Sodium
14.9 gm Carbohydrate
1.2 gm Dietary Fiber
20.4 gm Protein
359 mg Potassium

Lemon-Dijon Mustard Sauce

6 Servings
Serve over any combination of cooked or steamed vegetables.

½	cup water	2	teaspoons low-sodium chicken bouillon granules
2	tablespoons lemon juice		
4	teaspoons Dijon mustard	¼	teaspoon garlic powder
2	teaspoons cornstarch		

In a saucepan, combine water, lemon juice, mustard, cornstarch, bouillon granules, and garlic powder. Cook and stir over medium heat until thick and bubbly. Cook and stir 1 minute more.

Dijon Sauce

20 Servings
Use as a sauce with crab cakes and baked fish dishes.

½	cup fat-free plain yogurt	1	tablespoon finely chopped onion
3	tablespoons Dijon mustard	2	tablespoons dill relish
¼	cup fat-free mayonnaise	2	teaspoons balsamic vinegar

Whisk together all ingredients in a bowl. Serve at room temperature. Refrigerate sauce if not using immediately.

Simple Horseradish Sauce

16 Servings
This mild topping is perfect for shrimp and fish.

1   cup tomato purée
½   cup fat-free sour cream

2   tablespoons horseradish
2   teaspoons fresh lemon juice

Thoroughly blend all ingredients in a bowl and chill.

Exchange Values Per Serving
1 Serving = 1 Tablespoon

16 Calories
(2% from Fat)
0 gm Total Fat
0 gm Saturated Fat
0.6 mg Cholesterol
69 mg Sodium
3.1 gm Carbohydrates
0.3 gm Dietary Fiber
0.8 gm Protein
88 mg Potassium

Pea and Horseradish Sauce

16 Servings
Serve with fish or thinly sliced beef.

1   package (10 ounces) frozen deluxe tiny tender peas
⅓   cup fat-free plain yogurt
⅓   cup fat-free mayonnaise
2   tablespoons fat-free milk

1   teaspoon dry mustard
1   teaspoon prepared horseradish
¼   teaspoon pepper
1   can (4 ounces) sliced mushrooms, drained

Cook peas according to package directions and drain.

Stir together the yogurt, mayonnaise, milk, dry mustard, horseradish, and pepper in a bowl. Stir in peas and mushrooms. Cover and chill before serving.

Exchange Values Per Serving
1 Serving = 2 Tablespoons

20 Calories
(7% from Fat)
0.2 gm Total Fat
0 gm Saturated Fat
0.1 mg Cholesterol
88 mg Sodium
3.3 gm Carbohydrates
1.1 gm Dietary Fiber
1.4 gm Protein
41 mg Potassium

Lemon-Garlic Vinegar

64 Servings

Store vinegar in pretty corked bottles, or pour into colorful bottles to make wonderful gifts. Many large discount stores sell fancy bottles without lids, and hardware stores carry corks.

1	quart white wine vinegar
2	garlic cloves, minced

Peel of 2 lemons

Combine the vinegar, lemon peel, and garlic in a crock or jar. (Do not use a metal lid.) Let stand covered for 3 to 4 weeks in a dark, warm cabinet. Strain and pour into clean bottles.

Exchange Values Per Serving

1 Serving = 1 Tablespoon

1 Calorie

(5% from Fat)
0 gm Total Fat
0 gm Saturated Fat
0 mg Cholesterol
2 mg Sodium
0.2 gm Carbohydrates
0.1 gm Dietary Fiber
0.1 gm Protein
3 mg Potassium

Red Raspberry Mint Vinegar

96 Servings

This is a fresh and tart vinegar.

3	cups fresh red raspberries	2	cups dry red wine
4	cups apple cider vinegar	6	(3- to 4-inch) fresh mint sprigs

Thoroughly rinse the fresh raspberries with cold water. Drain well. In a large bowl combine the raspberries, vinegar, and red wine. Cover and let stand overnight.

In a saucepan, heat the vinegar mixture to boiling. Boil, uncovered, for about 3 minutes. Strain mixture, discarding the solids. Place two sprigs of mint in three 16-ounce bottles. Using a funnel, pour the hot vinegar over the mint in the bottles. Cover tightly or cork. Store in a cool dark place for 2 to 4 weeks before using.

Exchange Values Per Serving

1 Serving = 1 Tablespoon

6 Calories

(4% from Fat)
0 gm Total Fat
0 gm Saturated Fat
0 mg Cholesterol
2 mg Sodium
0.6 gm Carbohydrates
0.3 gm Dietary Fiber
0.1 gm Protein
12 mg Potassium

House Salad with Dream Pepper Dressing

3 Servings

½ head iceberg lettuce
½ head romaine lettuce
2 to 3 jumbo onions, sliced into rings
2 to 3 green bell peppers, sliced into rings
2 to 3 cucumbers, sliced into rings
3 tomato wedges
4 cups fat-free mayonnaise
1 cup water

1½ tablespoons Parmesan cheese
2½ teaspoons peppercorns
½ teaspoon salt-free seasoning
Dash of hot sauce
2½ teaspoons vinegar
1 tablespoon diced onion
Dash of garlic powder
2½ teaspoons lemon juice
1 teaspoon low-sodium soy sauce

Hand break the lettuces and mix. Chill. When ready to serve place on each of 3 salad plates 1 cup of lettuce, 1 ring of onion, 1 ring of green pepper, 1 ring of cucumber, and a tomato wedge.

Mix the remaining ingredients in a blender on high until thoroughly blended. Ladle over the lettuce by the tablespoon.

Exchange Values Per Serving
1 Serving = 2 Cups

375 Calories
(6% from Fat)
2.2 gm Total Fat
0.8 gm Saturated Fat
2.5 mg Cholesterol
2,384 mg Sodium
74.7 gm Carbohydrates
9.3 gm Dietary Fiber
7.6 gm Protein
1,195 mg Potassium

Buttermilk-Style Dressing

12 Servings

This salad dressing improves with time and is best made the day before it is to be used.

½ cup fat-free plain yogurt
1 cup fat-free cottage cheese
¼ cup finely chopped onion

2 tablespoons finely chopped parsley
1 garlic clove, minced
½ teaspoon paprika

Whip the yogurt and cottage cheese together in a bowl until smooth and the consistency of mayonnaise. Add the remaining ingredients, stir well, and refrigerate.

Exchange Values Per Serving
1 Serving = 2 Tablespoons

22 Calories
(2% from Fat)
0.1 gm Total Fat
0 gm Saturated Fat
1.0 mg Cholesterol
92 mg Sodium
2.3 gm Carbohydrates
0.1 gm Dietary Fiber
2.9 gm Protein
72 mg Potassium

Buttermilk Blue Cheese Dressing

8 Servings
This wonderful blend of flavors is a salad-lover's favorite.

Exchange Values Per Serving
1 Serving = 2 Tablespoons
1 Fat
1½ Meat

77 Calories
(78% from Fat)
6.8 gm Total Fat
2.0 gm Saturated Fat
7.0 mg Cholesterol
138 mg Sodium
1.4 gm Carbohydrates
0 gm Dietary Fiber
2.9 gm Protein
32 mg Potassium

¼   cup egg substitute
3   garlic cloves
½   cup canola oil
½   cup low-fat buttermilk
½   teaspoon white pepper

¼   teaspoon cayenne pepper
8   ounces fat-free plain yogurt
8   ounces crumbled blue cheese
2   green onions, tops only, finely chopped

In a food processor, blend egg substitute and garlic until smooth. With the machine running, add oil slowly in a thin stream. Add buttermilk, peppers, and yogurt. Process a few seconds more until well mixed. Remove to bowl and add cheese and green onions. Break up large lumps of cheese, but maintain chunky texture. Refrigerate.

Blue Cheese Dressing

16 Servings
This salad dressing is best made a day ahead and allowed to sit to improve flavor.

Exchange Values Per Serving
1 Serving = 2 Tablespoons

35 Calories
(50% from Fat)
2.0 gm Total Fat
1.3 gm Saturated Fat
5.5 mg Cholesterol
108 mg Sodium
1.8 gm Carbohydrates
0 gm Dietary Fiber
2.6 gm Protein
70 mg Potassium

1   cup fat-free plain yogurt
½   cup low-fat buttermilk
¾   cup blue cheese

1   teaspoon celery seed
¼   teaspoon salt-free seasoning
¼   teaspoon dried tarragon

In a mixing bowl combine the yogurt and buttermilk. Stir in the blue cheese, celery seed, and spices. Transfer to a storage container. Cover and refrigerate.

Cottage Cheese Ranch Dressing

10 Servings
Prepare the night before and all the flavor will blend together by the next day.

1   cup fat-free cottage cheese
¼   cup fat-free milk
2   teaspoons low-sodium
    Worcestershire sauce

1   tablespoon powdered ranch
    dressing

Mix all of the ingredients for 2 to 3 minutes in a blender or until the mixture has a smooth consistency. Place in a covered storage container and chill until ready to use.

Exchange Values Per Serving
1 Serving = 2
   Tablespoons

25 Calories
 (23% from Fat)
 0.6 gm Total Fat
 0.1 gm Saturated Fat
 1.6 mg Cholesterol
 125 mg Sodium
 1.8 gm Carbohydrates
 0 gm Dietary Fiber
 2.9 gm Protein
 59 mg Potassium

Herbed Spice Dressing

4 Servings
This salad dressing is best if refrigerated overnight before using.

2   tablespoons fat-free plain yogurt
2   tablespoons fat-free mayonnaise
½   teaspoon garlic powder
½   teaspoon chopped parsley

1   teaspoon Parmesan cheese
½   teaspoon Italian seasoning
    Pinch of pepper

Blend all of the ingredients together and refreigerate.

Exchange Values Per Serving
1 Serving = 1
   Tablespoon

13 Calories
 (13% from Fat)
 0.2 gm Total Fat
 0.1 gm Saturated Fat
 0.6 mg Cholesterol
 68 mg Sodium
 1.9 gm Carbohydrates
 0 gm Dietary Fiber
 0.8 gm Protein
 27 mg Potassium

Ricotta Yogurt Dressing

16 Servings
Great on romaine and spinach leaves.

**Exchange Values Per
Serving**
1 Serving = 2
Tablespoons

21 Calories
(27% from Fat)
0.6 gm Total Fat
0.4 gm Saturated Fat
2.6 mg Cholesterol
22 mg Sodium
2.0 gm Carbohydrates
0 gm Dietary Fiber
1.9 gm Protein
55 mg Potassium

1 cup fat-free plain yogurt	¼ cup chopped fresh basil
½ cup fat-free ricotta cheese	½ teaspoon sugar
2 tablespoons white wine vinegar	1 teaspoon salt-free seasoning
4 garlic cloves, minced	Pepper to taste

Blend all ingredients in a bowl and chill.

Apple Bread Dressing

8 Servings

**Exchange Values Per
Serving**
1 Serving = ½ Cup
¾ Fat
¼ Fruit
2½ Starch
¼ Vegetable

247 Calories
(14% from Fat)
3.9 gm Total Fat
0.8 gm Saturated Fat
0 mg Cholesterol
604 mg Sodium
45.4 gm Carbohydrates
2.4 gm Dietary Fiber
7.3 gm Protein
216 mg Potassium

4 cups breadcrumbs	¼ teaspoon ground pepper
1 cup chopped celery	¼ teaspoon ground sage
1 small onion, chopped	¼ teaspoon dried marjoram
1 tablespoon chopped fresh parsley	¼ teaspoon dried thyme
1 garlic clove, minced	⅛ teaspoon dried basil
1 cup low-sodium turkey broth	Nonstick cooking spray
2 apples, peeled, cored, and diced	

Preheat oven to 350°. Combine all of the ingredients in a bowl. Stir with a wooden spoon. Pour into a casserole pan coated with nonstick cooking spray. Bake for 35 to 40 minutes. Use to stuff turkey, chicken, or Cornish hens.

Mushroom Dressing

8 Servings

2	pounds mushrooms, chopped	1	small white onion, chopped
4	cups corn bread crumbs	1	garlic clove, minced
4	teaspoons safflower oil	2	teaspoons herb seasoning
1	cup red wine vinegar	1½	cups low-sodium chicken broth
2	teaspoons white pepper	1	teaspoon rubbed sage
1	cup chopped celery		Nonstick cooking spray

Preheat oven to 350°. Combine all of the ingredients in a large bowl. Turn out into a baking dish that has been coated with nonstick cooking spray. Bake covered for 35 to 40 minutes. Uncover and continue to bake until the top is browned and onions and celery are tender.

Exchange Values Per Serving
1 Serving = ½ Cup
1¾ Fat
¼ Meat
2 Starch
1¼ Vegetable

317 Calories
(28% from Fat)
9.9 gm Total Fat
1.4 gm Saturated Fat
34 mg Cholesterol
153 mg Sodium
46.8 gm Carbohydrates
3.8 gm Dietary Fiber
9.2 gm Protein
634 mg Potassium

Chicken-Apple Dressing

8 Servings

2	tablespoons low-fat margarine	¼	teaspoon pepper
¼	cup chopped onion	½	cup cubed chicken
½	cup chopped celery	¾	cup low-sodium chicken broth
8	slices day-old or toasted bread, cubed	½	cup egg substitute
		1	cup diced peeled apples
1	teaspoon rubbed sage		

Preheat oven to 325°. Melt the margarine in a skillet and sauté the onion and celery until tender. Combine with the breadcrumbs in a large bowl. Add the seasonings and cubed chicken. Moisten with chicken broth as desired. Stir in the egg substitute and apples. Bake for 30 to 40 minutes, or stuff poultry and bake accordingly.

Exchange Values Per Serving
1 Serving = ½ Cup
¼ Fat
¼ Fruit
½ Meat
1 Starch

119 Calories
(17% from Fat)
2.3 gm Total Fat
0.5 gm Saturated Fat
8.0 mg Cholesterol
202 mg Sodium
17.8 gm Carbohydrates
2.1 gm Dietary Fiber
7.1 gm Protein
192 mg Potassium

Dijon Vinaigrette

20 Servings
Great over mixed greens.

Exchange Values Per
Serving
1 Serving = 1
    Tablespoon

28 Calories
(90% from Fat)
2.9 gm Total Fat
0.4 gm Saturated Fat
0 mg Cholesterol
19 mg Sodium
0.7 gm Carbohydrates
0.1 gm Dietary Fiber
0.1 gm Protein
10 mg Potassium

¼   cup virgin olive oil
6   tablespoons fresh lemon juice
1   tablespoon Dijon mustard

1   teaspoon freshly ground pepper
2   garlic cloves, minced

Thoroughly blend all ingredients in a bowl. Store in a clean jar.

Lemon Herbs

12 Servings
Use this seasoning mix on all meats and vegetables. You'll never buy store mixes again.

Exchange Values Per
Serving
1 Serving = 1 to 2
    Teaspoons

4 Calories
(17% from Fat)
0.1 gm Total Fat
0 gm Saturated Fat
0 mg Cholesterol
1 mg Sodium
0.9 gm Carbohydrates
0.6 gm Dietary Fiber
0.2 gm Protein
24 mg Potassium

Peel of 2 large lemons
1   tablespoon dried thyme
1   tablespoon dried savory

1   tablespoon dried marjoram
1   tablespoon rubbed sage
1   tablespoon dried basil

Preheat oven to 300°. Finely shred the lemon peel. Spread the peel in a shallow baking pan. Dry in oven for about 10 minutes, stirring occasionally.

In a small mixing bowl combine thyme, savory, marjoram, sage, basil, and dried lemon peel. Mix together thoroughly. Store in an airtight container. Crush seasoning before using.

Lemon Butter

15 Servings
Brush on the top of Lemon Buns (page 146).

¼ cup low-fat margarine, melted
1½ teaspoons grated lemon peel

1 teaspoon fresh lemon juice

Blend all ingredients together in a bowl. Store in a small clean jar.

Exchange Values Per Serving
1 Serving = 1 Teaspoon

13 Calories
(97% from Fat)
1.5 gm Total Fat
0.3 gm Saturated Fat
0 mg Cholesterol
36 mg Sodium
0.1 gm Carbohydrates
0 gm Dietary Fiber
0 gm Protein
2 mg Potassium

Pear-Apple Butter

36 Servings
Can be used as a sugar agent in recipes or served with warm rolls.

1 pound pears, peeled, quartered, and cored
1 pound Rome apples, peeled, quartered, and cored
1 can (12 ounces) frozen concentrated apple juice

1 tablespoon lemon juice
1 teaspoon orange peel, finely shredded
¼ teaspoon ground ginger
¼ teaspoon ground cinnamon

Preheat oven to 300°. In a large saucepan bring the pears, apples, and frozen concentrate to a boil. Reduce heat and simmer, covered, about 20 minutes or until the pears and apples are tender. Place the pear-apple mix, one half at a time, into a blender or food processor and blend until the mixture is smooth.

Pour into a 9 x 9 x 2-inch baking pan. Stir in the lemon juice, orange peel, ginger, and cinnamon. Bake for 2 to 2½ hours or until thick enough to be spooned. Stir every half hour of cooking. Serve warm or cold on biscuits or toast. (Can also be used in recipes as a substitute for sugar).

Exchange Values Per Serving
1 Serving = 2 Tablespoons

19 Calories
(4% from Fat)
0.1 gm Total Fat
0 gm Saturated Fat
0 mg Cholesterol
1 mg Sodium
4.9 gm Carbohydrates
0.6 gm Dietary Fiber
0.1 gm Protein
43 mg Potassium

Cinnamon-Raisin Spread

10 Servings

Kid's favorite for spreading on hot bread or French toast in the morning.

4 ounces Neufchâtel cheese, softened	¼ teaspoon cinnamon
2 tablespoons chopped raisins	2 teaspoons fat-free milk
1 tablespoon brown sugar	

In a small bowl stir together the cheese, raisins, sugar, and cinnamon. Stir in enough milk to make the mixture spreadable. Cover and refrigerate to store.

Exchange Values Per Serving
1 Serving = 1 Tablespoon

41 Calories
(56% from Fat)
2.7 gm Total Fat
1.7 gm Saturated Fat
8.7 mg Cholesterol
47 mg Sodium
3.4 gm Carbohydrates
0.1 gm Dietary Fiber
1.3 gm Protein
35 mg Potassium

Dried Fruit Chutney

64 Servings

This chutney is a delicious complement to chicken or pork.

2 cups dried cranberries (or any other dried fruit such as cherries)	¼ cup minced fresh ginger
1¼ cups sugar	6 tablespoons unsweetened apple juice
¾ cup distilled white vinegar	3 tablespoons lemon juice
¼ cup chopped celery	½ teaspoon crushed red pepper flakes

Combine berries, sugar, vinegar, celery, ginger, juices, and red pepper in a large saucepan over medium heat. Cook 8 to 10 minutes after sugar dissolves, stirring frequently.

Allow to cool to room temperature, cover, and refrigerate.

Exchange Values Per Serving
1 Serving = 1 Tablespoon
⅓ Starch
½ Fruit

42 Calories
(9% from Fat)
0.5 gm Total Fat
0.1 gm Saturated Fat
0 mg Cholesterol
2 mg Sodium
10.2 gm Carbohydrates
1.8 gm Dietary Fiber
0.2 gm Protein
52 mg Potassium

Cranberry Chutney

40 Servings

This chutney is wonderful served over curried chicken or pork, and even better over warmed Brie.

1 can (10 ounces) whole cranberries	1 onion, chopped
Peel of 1 lemon	½ red, green, or yellow bell pepper,
¼ cup raisins	chopped
1 teaspoon grated ginger	½ cup apple cider vinegar
1 teaspoon dry mustard	¼ cup brown sugar
1 Granny Smith apple, peeled and	½ teaspoon salt
diced	1 garlic clove, minced

In a saucepan combine all ingredients. Simmer, stirring frequently, until mixture thickens, about 1 hour. Cool and store in refrigerator until ready to serve.

Exchange Values Per Serving
1 Serving = 1 Tablespoon
Free

24 Calories
(2% from Fat)
0.1 gm Total Fat
0 gm Saturated Fat
0 mg Cholesterol
32 mg Sodium
6.1 gm Carbohydrates
0.4 gm Dietary Fiber
0.1 gm Protein
27 mg Potassium

Crock-Pot Applesauce

8 Servings

You can make this chunky or blend well to make it thin.

2 pounds Rome Beauty apples (about	½ teaspoon cinnamon
10 small)	¼ teaspoon grated nutmeg
2 tablespoons lemon juice	1 teaspoon vanilla extract
1 cup water	

Peel and thinly slice the apples. Place in Crock-Pot. Combine the lemon juice and water in a bowl, and pour over the apples. Cover and cook until the apples are very soft and tender. Pour from the Crock-Pot into a large bowl. With a wooden spoon mix the spices and vanilla with the apples. Pack into jars, cover, and store in the refrigerator. Serve warm or chilled.

Exchange Values Per Serving
1 Serving = 1 Cup
1 Fruit

70 Calories
(5% from Fat)
0.4 gm Total Fat
0.1 gm Saturated Fat
0 mg Cholesterol
0.1 mg Sodium
17.9 gm Carbohydrates
3.2 gm Dietary Fiber
0.2 gm Protein
137 mg Potassium

Applesauce

4 Servings

This can be served alone or over halved warm muffins. It is also great warmed and served over vanilla-flavored frozen yogurt.

Exchange Values Per
Serving
   1 Serving = 1 Cup
   2 Fruit

113 Calories
   (5% from Fat)
   0.7 gm Total Fat
   0.2 gm Saturated Fat
   0 mg Cholesterol
   0 mg Sodium
   29.0 gm Carbohydrates
   4.0 gm Dietary Fiber
   0.3 gm Protein
   221 mg Potassium

8 small cooking apples	1 teaspoon cinnamon
1 cup water	½ teaspoon grated nutmeg

Peel, core, and slice the apples. Place in a deep pot. Add the water and bring to a boil. Simmer until the apples are tender. With a potato masher, crush the apples until they reach a lumpy consistency. Remove from heat and add cinnamon and nutmeg. Stir well and place in jars. Refrigerate.

Maple Syrup

12 Servings

Serve hot or cold on pancakes or waffles. This syrup is also good drizzled over corn bread!

Exchange Values Per
Serving
   1 Serving = 1
      Tablespoon
   Free

7 Calories
   (0% from Fat)
   0 gm Total Fat
   0 gm Saturated Fat
   0 mg Cholesterol
   0 mg Sodium
   1.4 gm Carbohydrates
   0 gm Dietary Fiber
   0 gm Protein
   1 mg Potassium

1¼ cups cold water	1 teaspoon maple flavoring
1 tablespoon cornstarch	10 packets artificial sweetener

Put the water, cornstarch, and flavoring in a saucepan. Bring to a boil. Remove from heat and allow to cool. Add the artificial sweetener. Stir well until dissolved. Stir before serving.

Kids' Meals

Turkey Sausage Pizza

4 Servings

½ pound ground lean turkey sausage
3 garlic cloves
1 cup low-fat mozzarella cheese
1 Southern Pizza Crust, baked (page 268)
1 large green tomato, peeled and thinly sliced

1 large red tomato, peeled and thinly sliced
2 tablespoons coarsely chopped fresh basil or 2 teaspoons dried
   Hot red pepper flakes to taste

Preheat oven to 450°. Cook turkey sausage in a skillet until the meat is just brown. Drain.

In a food processor, finely mince garlic. Add mozzarella cheese to processor to finely chop and blend ingredients together. Spread cheese mixture over Southern Pizza Crust. Arrange tomato slices and sausage on top of the cheese. Lightly sprinkle with basil and pepper flakes. Bake for 15 to 20 minutes.

Exchange Values Per Serving
1 Serving = 2 Slices
1½ Starch
1 Fat
2½ Meat
½ Vegetable

321 Calories
(33% from Fat)
12.0 gm Total Fat
5.2 gm Saturated Fat
62.7 mg Cholesterol
786 mg Sodium
31.0 gm Carbohydrates
1.7 gm Dietary Fiber
22.8 gm Protein
326 mg Potassium

Nacho Pizzas

8 Servings

Nonstick cooking spray
8 6-inch flour or corn tortillas

*   *   *

¼ pound plum tomatoes, diced
¼ cup chopped cilantro
2 tablespoons diced red onion
1 tablespoon lime juice
½ teaspoon hot sauce

1½ pounds ground lean turkey
1 medium red onion, halved and cut in strips
4 large jalapeño peppers, seeded and sliced
¾ cup low-fat Monterey Jack cheese,
¾ cup low-fat Cheddar cheese

In a frying pan or flat skillet that has been coated with nonstick cooking spray, brown the tortillas on each side over medium heat. Let cool completely; store in an airtight container at room temperature.

To make salsa, mix tomatoes, cilantro, onion, lime juice, and hot sauce in a bowl. The salsa can be made a day or so ahead of time.

Preheat oven to 375°. In a skillet, brown the ground turkey, adding water if the meat begins to stick. Add onion strips and continue to cook until the onion is tender. Add jalapeños and cook for an additional 2 minutes.

Place tortillas on a flat baking sheet and sprinkle Cheddar cheese on top. Then add a layer of the onion and turkey mix and top with Monterey Jack cheese. Bake for 3 to 4 minutes or until cheese melts. Serve with salsa on the side.

Southern Pizza Crust

Four 12-Inch Pizza Crusts

2 packages (¼ ounce each) dry yeast
¼ cup sugar
1¼ cups warm water (105-115°)
2½ cups all-purpose flour

1½ teaspoons salt
1 cup plain yellow cornmeal
Nonstick cooking spray

Combine yeast, sugar, and water in a bowl and allow to stand until bubbly, about 5 minutes. In the food processor, with plastic dough blade in place, add 2 cups flour, salt, and cornmeal. With the machine running add the yeast mixture and process for 30 to 40 seconds. Remove dough from processor and knead by hand a few times on a floured surface. Add a small amount of flour as needed to have a smooth but not dry dough. Place dough in bowl that has been coated with cooking spray. Spray top of the dough as well. Cover and let rise until doubled in bulk, about 1 hour. Punch down dough, then allow to rise 1 more hour.

Preheat oven to 500°. Divide the dough into 4 equal balls. Press 1 ball of dough into a 12-inch pizza pan. Bake until brown, about 5 to 10 minutes. This dough may be stored in the freezer if not needed right away.

Whole Wheat Pizza Crust

One 12-Inch Pizza Crust

¾ cup all-purpose flour, divided	½ teaspoon salt
½ cup whole wheat flour	½ cup warm water (115–120°)
2 tablespoons cornmeal	1 teaspoon canola oil
1 package (¼ ounce) dry yeast	Nonstick cooking spray

In a small mixing bowl stir together ½ cup of the all-purpose flour, whole wheat flour, cornmeal, yeast, and salt. Stir in water and canola oil. Beat by hand until mixture forms a ball. On a lightly floured surface, knead in remaining flour to make a moderately stiff dough that is smooth and elastic. (Knead no longer than 8 minutes.) Cover and let dough rest for 10 minutes.

Coat a 12-inch pizza pan with nonstick cooking spray. On a lightly floured surface roll the dough to a 13-inch circle. Transfer to the pizza pan and roll edges under to fit. Cover and let rise for 30 minutes.

Preheat oven to 425°. Add toppings of your choice and bake for 15 to 17 minutes.

Exchange Values Per Serving
1 Serving = ¼ 12-Inch Pizza or 2 of 8 Slices
2 Starch
⅓ Fat

163 Calories
(10% from Fat)
1.9 gm Total Fat
0.2 gm Saturated Fat
0 mg Cholesterol
293 mg Sodium
31.5 gm Carbohydrates
3.1 gm Dietary Fiber
6.1 gm Protein
103 mg Potassium

Parmesan Pizza Crust

One 12-Inch Pizza Crust

Exchange Values Per Serving
1 Serving = ¼ 12-Inch
   Pizza or 2 of 8 Slices
⅓ Fat
2 Starch

185 Calories
(11% from Fat)
2.3 gm Total Fat
0.5 gm Saturated Fat
1.2 mg Cholesterol
176 mg Sodium
34.0 gm Carbohydrates
1.5 gm Dietary Fiber
7.3 gm Protein
37 mg Potassium

1½ cups all-purpose flour, divided
2 tablespoons Parmesan cheese
1 package (¼ ounce) dry yeast
¼ teaspoon salt
½ cup warm water (115-120°)
1 teaspoon canola oil
Nonstick cooking spray

In a mixing bowl, combine 1 cup of the flour, Parmesan cheese, yeast, and salt. Stir in the water and oil, mixing to make a round dough ball. On a lightly floured surface knead in the remaining flour to make a moderately stiff dough that is smooth and elastic. (Knead no longer than 8 minutes.) Cover and let rest for 10 minutes.

Coat a 12-inch pizza pan with cooking spray. On a floured surface roll the dough to a 13-inch circle. Transfer to the pizza pan and turn under the edges to fit the pan. Cover and let rise for 30 minutes.

Preheat oven to 425°. Put toppings of choice on pizza crust and bake for 15 to 17 minutes.

Turkey Burgers

4 Servings

Exchange Values Per Serving
1 Serving = 1 Burger
2⅓ Starch
½ Fat
3½ Meat
⅔ Vegetable

391 Calories
(31% from Fat)
13.5 gm Total Fat
3.5 gm Saturated Fat
89.9 mg Cholesterol
684 mg Sodium
38.3 gm Carbohydrates
5.4 gm Dietary Fiber
30.7 gm Protein
613 mg Potassium

16 ounces ground lean turkey
1 medium white onion, chopped
1 medium green bell pepper, chopped
¼ cup dry breadcrumbs
1 teaspoon hot chili sauce
4 teaspoons low-sodium soy sauce
2 teaspoons salt-free seasoning
½ cup egg substitute
Nonstick cooking spray
4 whole wheat buns

Combine the ground turkey, onion, peppers, breadcrumbs, chili sauce, soy sauce, salt-free seasoning, and egg substitute in a bowl. Form into 4 equal-sized hamburger patties approximately ½ inch thick. Place on a broiler pan that has been coated with nonstick cooking spray. Broil for 10 to 12 minutes at about 3 to 4 inches from the heat. Turn once during cooking. Burgers are done when the juices run clear. Place on buns and garnish with your choice of toppings.

Greek Turkey Burger

6 Servings

2	cups shredded lettuce	1	garlic clove, minced
1	cucumber, seeded and chopped	1	teaspoon dried oregano
1	cup fat-free plain yogurt	½	teaspoon dried basil
1	tablespoon sesame seeds, toasted	¼	teaspoon dried rosemary
1½	pounds ground lean turkey	6	pita pockets
½	cup chopped onion		

Combine the lettuce, cucumber, yogurt, and sesame seeds in a mixing bowl to make a relish. Place in a serving bowl and set aside.

Mix the turkey, onion, garlic, oregano, basil, and rosemary in a bowl. Form into 6 patties approximately ½ inch thick. Broil about 3 to 4 inches from the heat for 8 to 10 minutes or until the juices run clear. Place in pita pockets and top with relish.

Exchange Values Per Serving
1 Serving = 1 Burger
(with pita pocket)
2 Starch
½ Fat
2¾ Meat
⅔ Vegetable

383 Calories
(27% from Fat)
11.1 gm Total Fat
2.9 gm Saturated Fat
90.3 mg Cholesterol
465 mg Sodium
40.1 gm Carbohydrates
2.5 gm Dietary Fiber
29.0 gm Protein
586 mg Potassium

Spicy Fries

4 Servings

1½	pounds (4 medium) yellow potatoes	Nonstick cooking spray
4	teaspoons canola oil	½ teaspoon salt-free seasoning
		⅛ teaspoon ground red pepper

Preheat oven to 450°. Slice potatoes lengthwise into ⅛-inch slices. Rinse in cold water. Combine the potatoes and oil in a large bowl and toss to coat. On a baking pan coated with nonstick cooking spray, arrange potatoes in a single layer. Bake uncovered for 15 minutes or until golden brown and crisp. Sprinkle with salt-free seasonings.

Exchange Values Per Serving
1 Serving = 12 Fries
1½ Starch
1 Fat

156 Calories
(26% from Fat)
4.7 gm Total Fat
0.4 gm Saturated Fat
0 mg Cholesterol
6 mg Sodium
26.9 gm Carbohydrates
1.9 gm Dietary Fiber
2.4 gm Protein
487 mg Potassium

Chicken Tacos

4 Servings

Exchange Values Per
Serving
 1 Serving = 2 Tacos
 1⅓ Starch
 1¾ Fat
 3 Meat
 2 Vegetable

354 Calories
 (35% from Fat)
 14.3 gm Total Fat
 2.7 gm Saturated Fat
 62.6 mg Cholesterol
 712 mg Sodium
 29.6 gm Carbohydrates
 5.8 gm Dietary Fiber
 29.8 gm Protein
 580 mg Potassium

1   package (16 ounces) frozen broccoli, cauliflower, and carrots
8   taco shells
1   can (10 ounces) tomatoes with green chilies
½   teaspoon chicken bouillon granules
¼   teaspoon red pepper flakes

Nonstick cooking spray
1   tablespoon canola oil
2   cups boneless skinless chicken breast, diced
½   cup low-fat Cheddar cheese, shredded

Thaw broccoli, cauliflower, and carrots by running hot water over vegetables in a colander. Cut any large pieces into smaller pieces. Warm the taco shells according to the package directions. Stir together the tomatoes, chicken bouillon, and red pepper flakes in a bowl and set aside.

Coat a large skillet with nonstick cooking spray. Stir fry vegetables for 3 to 5 minutes or until tender. Remove from the skillet and set aside. In the same skillet add 1 tablespoon of oil and cook the chicken until meat is white. Push the chicken to one side of the skillet. Stir the tomato mixture into the skillet. Heat through. Stir in the vegetables and continue to heat. When all ingredients are heated through, spoon into taco shells and top with cheese.

Sloppy Joe Pitas

4 Servings

Exchange Values Per
Serving
 1 Serving = 1 Pita
 3 Starch
 2¾ Meat
 ½ Vegetable

404 Calories
 (24% from Fat)
 11.4 gm Total Fat
 3.1 gm Saturated Fat
 89.6 mg Cholesterol
 823 mg Sodium
 50.9 gm Carbohydrates
 7.3 gm Dietary Fiber
 28.4 gm Protein
 941 mg Potassium

1   pound ground lean turkey
1   small onion, chopped
⅓   cup chopped celery
1   can (6 ounces) low-sodium tomato paste
¼   cup catsup

1   tablespoon vinegar
2   teaspoons low-sodium Worcestershire sauce
½   teaspoon dry mustard
⅛   teaspoon pepper
4   whole wheat pita pockets

Combine turkey, onion, and celery in a large glass mixing bowl or baking dish. Stir to crumble turkey meat. Cover tightly and microwave at high 5½ to 6½ minutes or until beef is browned, stirring at 2 minute intervals. Drain. Stir in remaining ingredients (except pita). Cover and microwave at high 3 to 4 minutes or until mixture is thoroughly heated. Fill each pita pocket with ⅓ cup of meat sauce.

Chocolate and Banana Bars

8 Servings

1	package (¼ ounce) sugar-free unflavored gelatin
¼	cup hot water
2	packets (approx. 1 ounce each) sugar-free fat-free instant chocolate pudding
4	cups fat-free milk
1	teaspoon vanilla extract
16	reduced-fat graham crackers
2	medium bananas, sliced
½	cup nondairy whipped topping

In a small cup sprinkle gelatin over hot water. Gelatin will dissolve more easily if stirred for about 2 to 4 minutes. Prepare pudding with fat-free milk in a bowl. Add dissolved gelatin and vanilla to the pudding, stirring until well blended.

Arrange 8 graham crackers in a single layer in the bottom of a 11 x 7-inch dish. Spread with half the pudding and half the banana slices, and repeat layering, ending with pudding. Cover with whipped topping.

Exchange Values Per Serving
1 Serving = 1 Slice (3 Inches)
1⅔ Starch
⅔ Fat
½ Fruit

172 Calories
(21% from Fat)
4.0 gm Total Fat
1.7 gm Saturated Fat
9.2 mg Cholesterol
355 mg Sodium
25.7 gm Carbohydrates
0.7 gm Dietary Fiber
8.0 gm Protein
310 mg Potassium

Ice Cream Peaches with Gingersnaps

4 Servings

4	gingersnaps, crushed
1	teaspoon sugar
⅛	teaspoon cinnamon
3	cans (15 ounces each) lighr peach halves packed
2	tablespoons low-fat margarine, melted
4	scoops fat-free peach or vanilla frozen yogurt

Combine gingersnap crumbs, sugar, and cinnamon in a bowl.

Place peach halves in a 1½-quart casserole dish. Fill each peach cavity with crumb mixture and drizzle with margarine. Cover and microwave on high 3 to 4 minutes. Serve peaches in stemmed glasses and top with a scoop of yogurt.

Exchange Values Per Serving
1 Serving = ⅔ Cup
1½ Starch
½ Fat
½ Vegetable

184 Calories
(17% from Fat)
3.7 gm Total Fat
0.8 gm Saturated Fat
1.5 mg Cholesterol
182 mg Sodium
33.6 gm Carbohydrates
0.9 gm Dietary Fiber
5.5 gm Protein
295 mg Potassium

Creamy Sherbet

6 Servings

This is my kids' favorite! Pour sherbet mixture into disposable waxed cups with a popsicle stick in the center and let them freeze. To pop out the frozen dessert, warm between your hands and peel the cup off to make a popsicle!

Exchange Values Per Serving
1 Serving = 1 Cup
1 Starch
½ Milk

178 Calories
(3% from Fat)
0.5 gm Total Fat
0.3 gm Saturated Fat
4.2 mg Cholesterol
174 mg Sodium
29.7 gm Carbohydrates
1.4 gm Dietary Fiber
10.6 gm Protein
541 mg Potassium

2   envelopes (¼ ounce each) sugar-free fruit punch drink mix
3   cups fat-free milk
3   cups fat-free vanilla yogurt
1   cup fresh raspberries

Dissolve drink mix in milk in a bowl. Blend in yogurt. Place in freezer.

When mixture is partially firm, whip at high speed in a blender. Fold in raspberries. Pour into 6 individual cups and freeze.

You can substitute strawberries, blueberries, or grapes for the raspberries.

Banana-Grape Supreme

6 Servings

Exchange Values Per Serving
1 Serving = ¾ Cup
1½ Fruit

107 Calories
(10% from Fat)
1.3 gm Total Fat
0.9 gm Saturated Fat
0 mg Cholesterol
18.1 mg Sodium
25.6 gm Carbohydrates
1.8 gm Dietary Fiber
2.4 gm Protein
388 mg Potassium

1   envelope (¼ ounce) sugar-free unflavored gelatin
½   cup cold water
3   small ripe bananas
6   tablespoons lemon juice
1   cup unsweetened orange juice
1   cup seedless grapes
1   cup fat-free whipped topping
6   seedless grapes, cut in half, for garnish

In a small saucepan sprinkle gelatin over water. Stir over low heat until gelatin dissolves. Remove from heat.

Peel bananas and mash in small bowl. Immediately blend in lemon juice. In a large shallow bowl mix gelatin mixture, banana mixture, orange juice, and 1 cup grapes. Chill until mixture is syrupy and slightly thickened. Blend in an electric blender until light and fluffy. Stir in whipped topping by hand. Spoon into stemmed dessert dishes. Chill. Top with grape halves.

Pineapple and Orange Yogurt Freeze

4 Servings

2 cups fresh or drained canned pineapple chunks	¼ teaspoon vanilla extract
½ cup mandarin oranges, drained	1 cup fat-free plain yogurt
	1 cup fat-free whipped topping

In a food processor or blender process pineapple, oranges, and vanilla until smooth. Add yogurt, process briefly, just enough to mix. Scrape down sides of work bowl with a spatula. Place in freezer for 30 minutes.

Place bowl back on processor and pulse once to mix slightly; add whipped topping. Pulse once or twice to incorporate. Scrape the bowl sides again and pulse once or twice again. Spoon evenly into 6-ounce custard bowls or fluted glasses. Cover and freeze 1 to 2 hours or until firm.

Exchange Values Per Serving
1 Serving = ¾ Cup
¾ Fruit
½ Milk

94 Calories
(13% from Fat)
1.7 gm Total Fat
1.2 gm Saturated Fat
1.1 mg Cholesterol
70 mg Sodium
19.4 gm Carbohydrates
1.2 gm Dietary Fiber
4.7 gm Protein
290 mg Potassium

Desserts

Baked Apples with Raisins

6 Servings

6	small baking apples, such as Rome Beauty or Winesap Grated nutmeg Cinnamon
6	teaspoons unsweetened orange juice, divided
6	tablespoons seedless raisins, divided Water

Preheat oven to 400°. Core apples. Pare upper third of each apple to prevent skin from splitting. Place apples in shallow baking dish; sprinkle with nutmeg and cinnamon. Fill each apple with 1 teaspoon of orange juice and 1 tablespoon of raisins. Pour water (¼ inch deep) into baking dish. Cover dish with aluminum foil. Bake for 45 to 50 minutes or until apples are tender.

Exchange Values Per Serving
1 Serving = 1 Whole Apple
2 Fruit

115 Calories
(4% from Fat)
0.6 gm Total Fat
0.1 gm Saturated Fat
0 mg Cholesterol
1 mg Sodium
29.8 gm Carbohydrates
4.2 gm Dietary Fiber
0.6 gm Protein
247 mg Potassium

Orange Baked Apples and Pears

8 Servings

Exchange Values Per
Serving
  1 Serving = 2 Wedges
  1⅓ Fruit
  ½ Starch

100 Calories
  (3% from Fat)
  0.3 gm Total Fat
  0 gm Saturated Fat
  0 mg Cholesterol
  7 mg Sodium
  26 gm Carbohydrates
  2.4 gm Dietary Fiber
  0.6 gm Protein
  173 mg Potassium

2 medium Golden Delicious apples	4 tablespoons orange marmalade
2 medium ripe pears	½ cup hot water
½ cup raisins	Fat-free vanilla frozen yogurt

Preheat oven to 350°. Peel and core the apples and pears and cut into 8 wedges each. Add raisins and orange marmalade to hot water, and blend.

   In a 1½-quart baking dish place the pears and apples. Pour the orange and raisin mixture over the apples and pears. Cover and bake for 45 minutes or until tender. Serve warm with fat-free vanilla frozen yogurt.

Crispy Cheesy Apples

12 Servings

Exchange Values Per
Serving
  1 Serving = ½ Apple
  ½ Fat
  ½ Fruit
  ⅓ Meat
  1 Starch

146 Calories
  (19% from Fat)
  3.1 gm Total Fat
  1.0 gm Saturated Fat
  2.3 mg Cholesterol
  166 mg Sodium
  26.4 gm Carbohydrates
  1.9 gm Dietary Fiber
  3.7 gm Protein
  88 mg Potassium

6 cups pared, sliced apples	¼ cup low-fat margarine
Nonstick cooking spray	¼ cup fat-free cheese cracker crumbs
1 teaspoon cinnamon	1 cup shredded low-fat Cheddar
½ cup apple cider	cheese
⅔ cup all-purpose flour	

Preheat oven to 350°. Arrange the apples in a baking dish coated with cooking spray. Sprinkle with cinnamon and pour the cider over the apples. Combine the flour, margarine, cracker crumbs, and cheese in a bowl. Mix until of the consistency of a streusel. Sprinkle the top of the apples with this mixture. Bake for 1 hour or until the apples are tender.

Old-Fashioned Apple Crunch

6 Servings

1 cup oats	1 tablespoon all-purpose flour
½ cup all-purpose flour	1 teaspoon cinnamon
2 teaspoons cinnamon, divided	1 tablespoon unsweetened orange
½ cup low-fat margarine	juice from concentrate
3 cups chopped apples	2 packets artificial sweetener

Preheat oven to 350°. Mix the oats, ½ cup of flour, 1 teaspoon cinnamon, and margarine in a bowl until crumbly. Place ½ of the mixture in the bottom of a baking pan. Combine the apples, flour, 1 teaspoon cinnamon, juice, and sweetener in a bowl. Spread over the oat mixture. Cover with the remainder of the oat mixture. Bake for 45 minutes.

Exchange Values Per Serving
1 Serving = ⅔ Cup
1½ Fat
½ Fruit
1 Starch

195 Calories
(38% from Fat)
8.5 gm Total Fat
1.7 gm Saturated Fat
0 mg Cholesterol
183 mg Sodium
17.4 gm Carbohydrates
3.2 gm Dietary Fiber
3.6 gm Protein
135 mg Potassium

Fluffy Fruit Flan

6 Servings

1 can (15¼ ounces) pineapple chunks, in pineapple juice	½ cup fat-free vanilla yogurt
2 egg whites	Ground cinnamon

Preheat oven to 350°. Drain pineapple and spread evenly in 8-inch pie plate or flan pan. Beat egg whites until soft peaks form; blend with yogurt. Spoon mixture over pineapple chunks. Bake 15 minutes. Sprinkle with cinnamon. Serve warm.

Exchange Values Per Serving
1 Serving = 1 Slice
½ Fruit

59 Calories
(0% from Fat)
0 gm Total Fat
0 gm Saturated Fat
0.6 mg Cholesterol
30 mg Sodium
11.9 gm Carbohydrates
1.2 gm Dietary Fiber
2.7 gm Protein
126 mg Potassium

Winter Fruit Medley

8 Servings

Exchange Values Per Serving
1 Serving = ¾ Cup
⅓ Fat
1¾ Fruit

124 Calories
(16% from Fat)
2.4 gm Total Fat
1.7 gm Saturated Fat
0 mg Cholesterol
3 mg Sodium
27.5 gm Carbohydrates
3.3 gm Dietary Fiber
1.2 gm Protein
340 mg Potassium

1	medium pineapple, cored and cubed		Juice of 1 lemon
1	orange, peeled and sectioned	⅓	cup unsweetened orange juice
1½	cups halved seeded dark grapes, or seedless grapes	2	bananas
1	large red apple, cored and cubed	½	cup grated, fresh coconut (optional)

In a large serving bowl, combine pineapple cubes, orange sections, grapes, and apple cubes. Combine juices. Pour over fruit and toss to mix well. Chill. When ready to serve, peel and slice bananas. Add to bowl and mix lightly. Top with grated coconut.

Streusel Topping

8 Servings

Exchange Values Per Serving
1 Serving = 1 Tablespoon
½ Fat
½ Starch

57 Calories
(44% from Fat)
2.8 gm Total Fat
0.6 gm Saturated Fat
0 mg Cholesterol
68 mg Sodium
7.1 gm Carbohydrates
0.3 gm Dietary Fiber
0.9 gm Protein
11 mg Potassium

½	cup all-purpose flour	¼	cup low-fat margarine
½	teaspoon cinnamon	2	teaspoons sugar

Combine all of the ingredients in a bowl until the mixture resembles coarse crumbs. Sprinkle over any fruit pie before baking.

Blueberry Slump

4 Servings

Nonstick cooking spray
3   cups blueberries
¼   cup unsweetened orange juice from concentrate
1   packet artificial sweetener
½   teaspoon cinnamon

1   cup all-purpose flour
2   teaspoons low-sodium baking powder
1   tablespoon sugar
½   cup fat-free milk
3   tablespoons low-fat margarine

Preheat oven to 350°. Coat a casserole dish with cooking spray. Place the blueberries in dish and top with the orange juice. Combine the sweetener and cinnamon in a bowl, and sprinkle over the berries.

In a separate bowl combine all of the dry ingredients and make a well in the center. Add the milk and begin working by hand. Add the margarine and continue to work by hand. Drop by spoonfuls onto the blueberries. Bake for 20 minutes or until golden brown. Serve warm.

Exchange Values Per Serving
1 Serving = ¾ Cup
¾ Fat
1 Fruit
1⅔ Starch

245 Calories
(18% from Fat)
4.9 gm Total Fat
0.9 gm Saturated Fat
0.6 mg Cholesterol
128 mg Sodium
46.9 gm Carbohydrates
3.9 gm Dietary Fiber
5.2 gm Protein
466 mg Potassium

Crumbly Peaches

6 Servings

3   cups sliced peaches, fresh or frozen
2   cups oat bran
½   cup oat flakes
½   cup whole wheat flour
¼   cup slivered almonds

2   tablespoons sugar
¼   teaspoon cinnamon
½   cup low-fat margarine
1   teaspoon butter-flavored extract

Preheat oven to 375°. Place the peaches in a square casserole dish. Combine the dry ingredients in a bowl and then add the margarine and extract. Work by hand until crumbly. Spread over the peaches and bake for 35 minutes or until golden.

Exchange Values Per Serving
1 Serving = ¾ Cup
2 Fat
½ Fruit
1⅔ Starch

251 Calories
(36% from Fat)
12.3 gm Total Fat
2.2 gm Saturated Fat
0 mg Cholesterol
183 mg Sodium
41.0 gm Carbohydrates
8.0 gm Dietary Fiber
8.3 gm Protein
409 mg Potassium

Pears with Raspberry Sauce

6 Servings

Exchange Values Per Serving
1 Serving = 1 Pear
1¾ Fruit

107 Calories
(5% from Fat)
0.7 gm Total Fat
0 gm Saturated Fat
0 mg Cholesterol
0 mg Sodium
17.3 gm Carbohydrates
4.8 gm Dietary Fiber
1.0 gm Protein
265 mg Potassium

6   small firm ripe pears
4   cups cold water
¼   cup lemon juice

1   cup unsweetened raspberries, fresh or frozen
½   cup unsweetened orange juice
2   tablespoons lime juice
3   packets artificial sweetener

Peel the pears, leaving the stems. Cut a thin slice off the bottom of each so they will stand upright. Place the pears in a large saucepan, and add the cold water and lemon juice. Bring to a boil, reduce the heat and simmer, covered, for 10 to 15 minutes. Drain. Place in a baking dish, cover, and chill for 3 hours or overnight.

For the raspberry sauce, place the raspberries, orange juice, lime juice, and sugar substitute in a blender container. Blend on high speed for 1 minute. Strain to remove the seeds, if desired. To serve, place the pears in serving dishes and pour the raspberry sauce over the pears.

Strawberry and Orange Pops

6 Servings

Exchange Values Per Serving
1 Serving = 1 Pop
½ Fruit

30 Calories
(3% from Fat)
0.1 gm Total Fat
0 gm Saturated Fat
0 mg Cholesterol
5 mg Sodium
9.8 gm Carbohydrates
1.1 gm Dietary Fiber
0.5 gm Protein
157 mg Potassium

2   cups mashed unsweetened strawberries, fresh or frozen
1   cup unsweetened orange juice

½   cup sugar-free red-colored soda
6   packets artificial sweetener
1   teaspoon fresh lemon or lime juice

Blend all of the ingredients in a bowl with a wire whisk or in a food processor. Divide the mixture among six 5-ounce paper cups. Place in the freezer and allow to partially freeze. Place a plastic spoon or popsicle stick in the center of each serving. Freeze solid. To serve, remove from the freezer and allow to warm for a few minutes at room temperature. Tear the paper cup off and enjoy.

Fruit and Yogurt Parfaits

4 Servings

1 cup fat-free lemon custard yogurt
1 tablespoon grated orange peel
1 orange, peeled and cut into bite-sized pieces

1 banana, sliced
1 apple, cored and cut into bite-sized pieces

In a small bowl combine yogurt and orange peel. Chill. To serve, layer fruit and yogurt mixture in 4 parfait glasses.

Exchange Values Per Serving
1 Serving = ¾ Cup
1 Fruit
½ Starch

120 Calories
(3% from Fat)
0.4 gm Total Fat
0.1 gm Saturated Fat
1.0 mg Cholesterol
42 mg Sodium
27.1 gm Carbohydrates
2.6 gm Dietary Fiber
3.8 gm Protein
359 mg Potassium

Cranberry and Pineapple Sherbet

8 Servings

1 package (.3 ounce) sugar-free raspberry gelatin
1 cup low-calorie cranberry juice cocktail, boiling

1 cup cold low-calorie cranberry juice cocktail
1 cup crushed unsweetened pineapple
1 cup evaporated fat-free milk

Dissolve the gelatin in the boiling cranberry juice in a pan. Add the remaining cold juice and beat with an electric beater or wire whisk until well blended. Add the pineapple and milk and mix well. Freeze in a shallow pan until crystals form about 1 inch from the edge of the pan. This takes about 1½ hours. Beat until creamy. Return the mixture to the pan and freeze, stirring occasionally, until the mixture is frozen but slightly mushy, about 1½ to 2 hours.

Exchange Values Per Serving
1 Serving = ½ Cup
⅛ Fruit
⅛ Milk

50 Calories
(2% from Fat)
0.1 gm Total Fat
0 gm Saturated Fat
1.2 mg Cholesterol
66 mg Sodium
9.4 gm Carbohydrates
0.3 gm Dietary Fiber
3.2 gm Protein
159 mg Potassium

Yogurt Pudding

4 Servings

Exchange Values Per Serving
1 Serving = ½ Cup
⅓ Fat
½ Milk

106 Calories
(11% from Fat)
1.2 gm Total Fat
1.1 gm Saturated Fat
2.2 mg Cholesterol
459 mg Sodium
17.0 gm Carbohydrates
0 gm Dietary Fiber
6.0 gm Protein
263 mg Potassium

1 package (approx. 1 ounce) sugar-free fat-free instant vanilla pudding	1 cup fat-free plain yogurt
1 cup fat-free milk	½ cup nondairy fat-free whipped topping
2 packets artificial sweetener	

Whip the vanilla pudding and milk with a mixer in a bowl. Add the sweetener and yogurt and spoon into wine glasses. Top each with 2 tablespoons of nondairy whipped topping.

Apple Gelatin Dessert

10 Servings

Exchange Values Per Serving
1 Serving = 1-inch Slice
1½ Fat
½ Fruit
3¾ Meat
1 Starch

371 Calories
(33% from Fat)
15.2 gm Total Fat
6.2 gm Saturated Fat
0.2 mg Cholesterol
1,228 mg Sodium
38.8 gm Carbohydrates
1.7 gm Dietary Fiber
31.3 gm Protein
343 mg Potassium

6 packages (.3 ounce) sugar-free strawberry gelatin	1 packet artificial sweetener
5 cups boiling water	½ cup fat-free plain yogurt
3 cups diced apples	1 cup nondairy fat-free whipped topping
2 bananas, diced	⅛ teaspoon cinnamon
1 cup unsweetened crushed pineapple	½ cup chopped nuts

Dissolve the gelatin in the boiling water in a bowl. Cool until slightly thickened. Add the apples, bananas, and pineapple, and stir until well blended. Pour into a 9 x 13-inch pan and chill until firm.

For the topping, whip the sweetener, yogurt, and nondairy topping together in a bowl. Add the cinnamon and blend well. Spoon over the top and sprinkle with chopped nuts.

Apricot Cookies

16 Servings

½ cup low-fat margarine
¼ cup sugar
¼ cup sugar-free apricot preserves
¼ cup unsweetened orange juice from concentrate
¼ cup water

1 teaspoon vanilla extract
¼ cup egg substitute
2 cups all-purpose flour
2 teaspoons low-sodium baking powder

Preheat oven to 350°. Combine all of the ingredients in a large bowl. Chill for 2 hours.

Roll into balls and place on a cookie sheet, press down, and flatten slightly. Bake for 10 to 12 minutes.

Exchange Values Per Serving
1 Serving = 1 Cookie
½ Fat
1 Starch

109 Calories
(25% from Fat)
3.1 gm Total Fat
0.6 gm Saturated Fat
0 mg Cholesterol
77 mg Sodium
18.1 gm Carbohydrates
0.6 gm Dietary Fiber
2.2 gm Protein
105 mg Potassium

Cranberry-Orange Bar Cookies

24 Servings

1 cup crushed or chopped cranberries
2 oranges, ground with skins
¼ cup unsweetened crushed pineapple
¼ cup light brown sugar
¼ cup unsweetened apple butter
⅔ cup low-fat margarine

½ cup egg substitute
2 teaspoons vanilla extract
4 cups all-purpose flour
2 teaspoons low-sodium baking powder
1 teaspoon baking soda

Preheat oven to 350°. Combine all of the ingredients in a bowl. Press evenly into a 13 x 9-inch baking pan. Bake for 12 to 15 minutes or until firm. Cut into bars while hot. Remove from the pan when cool.

Exchange Values Per Serving
1 Serving = 1 Cookie
½ Fat
1 Starch

124 Calories
(19% from Fat)
2.7 gm Total Fat
0.5 gm Saturated Fat
0 mg Cholesterol
122 mg Sodium
22.0 gm Carbohydrates
1.1 gm Dietary Fiber
2.8 gm Protein
121 mg Potassium

Oat Bran Cookies

32 Servings

½ cup low-fat margarine
½ cup dark or light brown sugar
¼ cup egg substitute
2 cups oats
1½ cups oat bran
1 cup all-purpose flour
1 cup unsweetened applesauce
½ teaspoon low-sodium baking powder
1 teaspoon cinnamon
¼ teaspoon ground cloves
¼ teaspoon ground allspice
¼ cup fat-free milk
¼ cup unsweetened orange juice from concentrate
½ cup chopped walnuts

Preheat oven to 350°. Combine all of the ingredients in a bowl and mix well. Drop by spoonfuls onto an ungreased baking sheet and bake for 10 to 15 minutes.

Peanut Butter Cookies

32 Servings

½ cup low-fat margarine
¼ cup sugar
¼ cup reduced-fat peanut butter
¼ cup unsweetened orange juice from concentrate
¼ cup water
1 teaspoon vanilla extract
¼ cup egg substitute
2 cups all-purpose flour
2 teaspoons low-sodium baking powder

Combine all of the ingredients in a large bowl. Chill for 2 hours. Preheat oven to 350°. Roll into balls and place on a baking sheet. Press down with a fork. Bake for 10 to 12 minutes.

Rolled Sugar Cookies

36 Servings

½ cup low-fat margarine
½ cup sugar
1 teaspoon vanilla extract
¼ cup egg substitute
2 cups all-purpose flour

½ cup unsweetened orange juice form concentrate
2 teaspoons low-sodium baking powder

Preheat oven to 350°. Cream together the margarine, sugar, vanilla, and egg substitute in a bowl. Add the flour, orange juice, and baking powder until workable and not sticky. Roll on a floured surface and cut into shapes. Place on an ungreased baking sheet. Bake until lightly browned.

Exchange Values Per Serving
1 Serving = 1 Cookie
⅓ Fat
½ Starch

51 Calories
(24% from Fat)
1.4 gm Total Fat
0.3 gm Saturated Fat
0 mg Cholesterol
34 mg Sodium
8.6 gm Carbohydrates
0.2 gm Dietary Fiber
1.0 gm Protein
49 mg Potassium

Blueberry Crêpe

1 Serving

½ cup blueberries, fresh or frozen
1 teaspoon vanilla extract
1 teaspoon low-fat margarine
1 packet artificial sweetener
1 egg white

¼ cup fat-free plain yogurt
1 slice fat-free white bread, cubed
Pinch of ground cinnamon
½ teaspoon vanilla extract

Combine the blueberries and vanilla in a saucepan. Barely cover with water and bring to a slow boil over medium heat. Cook uncovered, stirring often, until the consistency of preserves. Remove from the heat, add margarine, and stir. Cover and let cool for five minutes. Add the envelope of sugar substitute.

Combine the egg white, yogurt, bread cubes, cinnamon, and vanilla in a blender jar. Blend until smooth. Heat a 10-inch nonstick skillet over low heat and pour in the contents of the blender, tilting the pan to spread evenly. Lift the edges with rubber spatula; turn only when brown-flecked (or the pancake may tear). Cook the other side. Spread the fruit in the center and roll up.

Exchange Values Per Serving
1 Serving = 1 Crêpe
½ Fat
⅔ Fruit
⅔ Meat
½ Milk
1 Starch

204 Calories
(15% from Fat)
3.3 gm Total Fat
0.7 gm Saturated Fat
1.4 mg Cholesterol
313 mg Sodium
31.5 gm Carbohydrates
2.7 gm Dietary Fiber
10.4 gm Protein
312 mg Potassium

Pear Cobbler

6 Servings

Exchange Values Per Serving
1 Serving = 2/3 Cup
1⅓ Fat
1⅔ Fruit
⅔ Starch

229 Calories
(28% from Fat)
7.5 gm Total Fat
0.5 gm Saturated Fat
0.5 mg Cholesterol
20 mg Sodium
40.7 gm Carbohydrates
4.4 gm Dietary Fiber
3.4 gm Protein
393 mg Potassium

6 pears, peeled, cored, and sliced	3 tablespoons chopped walnuts
3 tablespoons firmly packed brown sugar	1½ teaspoons sugar
1 tablespoon lemon juice	1 teaspoon low-sodium baking powder
¼ teaspoon cinnamon	⅓ cup evaporated fat-free milk
⅛ teaspoon ground ginger	2 tablespoons canola oil
⅓ cup all-purpose flour	

Preheat oven to 400°. In a medium bowl mix together pears, brown sugar, lemon juice, cinnamon, and ginger. Turn into a 10 x 6 x 1¾-inch baking dish. In a medium bowl stir together flour, walnuts, granulated sugar, and baking powder. Stir in milk and oil just until ingredients are moistened. Drop by teaspoonfuls onto pear mixture. Bake for 25 minutes or until lightly browned.

Apple-Cranberry Cobbler

8 Servings

Exchange Values Per Serving
1 Serving = 2/3 Cup
2 Fat
1 Fruit
1½ Starch

258 Calories
(39% from Fat)
11.7 gm Total Fat
1.7 gm Saturated Fat
0 mg Cholesterol
141 mg Sodium
36.9 gm Carbohydrates
4.4 gm Dietary Fiber
3.7 gm Protein
194 mg Potassium

3 cups peeled chopped cooking apples	1 tablespoon lemon juice
2 cups cranberries	1 teaspoon cinnamon
¼ cup pure unsweetened apple butter	½ teaspoon grated nutmeg
¼ cup sugar	½ cup low-fat margarine
¼ cup apple juice from concentrate	1½ cups uncooked oatmeal
¼ cup all-purpose flour	⅓ cup all-purpose flour
	½ cup chopped pecans

Preheat oven to 350°. Combine the apples, cranberries, apple butter, sugar, apple juice, ¼ cup of flour, lemon juice, and spices in a bowl. Set aside.

Combine the margarine, oatmeal, ⅓ cup of flour, and the pecans in a large bowl. Reserve ¼ cup of the mixture, and press the rest into the bottom and sides of a 9-inch pie plate. Add the apple and cranberry mixture. Sprinkle the top with the reserved oatmeal mix. Bake for 45 minutes. The cobbler should be bubbly when done.

Graham Cracker Crust

6 Servings

4	tablespoons low-fat margarine	¼	teaspoon cinnamon
1¼	cups finely crumbled fat-free graham crackers		

Preheat oven to 350°. Melt the margarine and mix with the graham cracker crumbs and cinnamon in a bowl. Press firmly into a 9-inch pie pan on the sides and the bottom. Bake for 5 minutes.

Exchange Values Per Serving
1 Serving = ⅙ Pie
⅔ Fat
1 Starch

123 Calories
(25% from Fat)
3.7 gm Total Fat
0.7 gm Saturated Fat
0 mg Cholesterol
118 mg Sodium
20.7 gm Carbohydrates
2.7 gm Dietary Fiber
3.6 gm Protein
3 mg Potassium

Oat Bran Pie Crust

6 Servings

1	cup whole wheat flour	3	tablespoons sugar-free lemon-lime soda
½	cup oat bran cereal		Nonstick cooking spray
¼	cup low-fat margarine		

Combine the flour and bran cereal in a bowl. Stir in the margarine and crumble by hand while adding the soda. Form into a ball and roll out between 2 sheets of wax paper. Place in a pie pan lightly coated with cooking spray and prick with a fork.

Exchange Values Per Serving
1 Serving = 2 Tablespoons (1 Slice)
⅔ Fat
1 Starch

113 Calories
(32% from Fat)
4.2 gm Total Fat
0.8 gm Saturated Fat
0 mg Cholesterol
123 mg Sodium
17.2 gm Carbohydrates
2.9 gm Dietary Fiber
3.2 gm Protein
97 mg Potassium

Pumpkin Pie in a Graham Cracker Crust

6 Servings

Exchange Values Per Serving
1 Serving = 1 Slice
¾ Fat
½ Meat
½ Milk
1½ Starch

230 Calories
(18% from Fat)
4.8 gm Total Fat
1.1 gm Saturated Fat
2.7 mg Cholesterol
241 mg Sodium
36.2 gm Carbohydrates
5.0 gm Dietary Fiber
13.5 gm Protein
462 mg Potassium

1 package (¼ ounce) unflavored gelatin
1 teaspoon ground ginger
½ teaspoon grated nutmeg
   Pinch of ground cloves
½ cup egg substitute

1 can (13 ounces) evaporated fat-free milk
1 can (16 ounces) pumpkin
8 packets sugar substitute
1 9-inch Graham Cracker Crust (p. 289)

Mix the gelatin and spices in a medium saucepan. Beat the egg substitute and milk together in a bowl and pour into the dry ingredients. Let stand for 1 minute. Stir over low heat until the gelatin is dissolved, about 10 minutes. Blend in the pumpkin and sugar substitute. Pour the mixture into a graham cracker crust and chill until firm.

Bavarian-Style Whipped Strawberry Pie

6 Servings

Exchange Values Per Serving
1 Serving = ⅙ Pie
1½ Fat
⅓ Fruit
1 Starch

216 Calories
(31% from Fat)
7.4 gm Total Fat
4.3 gm Saturated Fat
0 mg Cholesterol
154 mg Sodium
32.4 gm Carbohydrates
4.0 gm Dietary Fiber
4.9 gm Protein
115 mg Potassium

1 package (.3 ounce) sugar-free strawberry gelatin
1 cup boiling water
½ cup cold water
1 tablespoon lemon juice
1 container (8 ounces) fat-free whipping topping

1 cup chopped fresh strawberries
1 9-inch Graham Cracker Crust (p. 289)
   Strawberries for garnish

Dissolve the gelatin in boiling water in a bowl. Add the cold water and lemon juice. Chill until slightly thickened. Fold together the gelatin mix and the nondairy topping, and blend well. Fold in the strawberries. Pour the mixture into the pie shell and chill until firm, about 3 hours. Garnish with strawberries.

Apricot Bread Pudding

8 Servings

2¼ cups fat-free milk
1 carton (8 ounces) egg substitute
2 teaspoons vanilla extract
5 cups breadcrumbs
8 dried apricot halves, quartered

3 tablespoons dried currants
  Nonstick cooking spray
¼ teaspoon grated nutmeg
¼ teaspoon cinnamon
1 tablespoon sugar

Preheat oven to 325°. Beat together the milk, egg substitute, and vanilla in a mixing bowl. Combine the breadcrumbs, apricots, and currants in a large mixing bowl. Place the bread mixture into a large baking dish that has been coated with cooking spray. Pour the milk mixture over the bread mixture. Combine the nutmeg, cinnamon, and sugar in a cup and sprinkle over the top of the bread mixture. Bake for 35 to 45 minutes or until a fork inserted near the center comes out clean.

Exchange Values Per Serving
1 Serving = 3-Inch Square Slice
⅓ Fruit
½ Meat
⅓ Milk
1 Starch

154 Calories
(14% from Fat)
2.4 gm Total Fat
0.6 gm Saturated Fat
1.6 mg Cholesterol
223 mg Sodium
23.7 gm Carbohydrates
1.5 gm Dietary Fiber
9.0 gm Protein
321 mg Potassium

Chocolate Mousse Pudding

4 Servings

1½ cups fat-free milk, cold
1 package sugar-free instant chocolate pudding

1 cup nondairy fat-free whipped topping
  Mint leaf for garnish

Pour the cold milk into a blender. Add the pudding mix and blend on a low speed. When it begins to thicken, remove the mixer and use a spoon to fold in the whipped topping. Spoon into wine glasses and garnish with a dollop of whipped topping and a mint leaf.

Exchange Values Per Serving
1 Serving = ⅔ Cup
½ Fat
½ Milk
2 Starch

140 Calories
(14% from Fat)
2.2 gm Total Fat
2.1 gm Saturated Fat
1.7 mg Cholesterol
685 mg Sodium
23.9 gm Carbohydrates
1.0 gm Dietary Fiber
5.1 gm Protein
395 mg Potassium

Chocolate Espresso Trifle

12 Servings

Exchange Values Per Serving
1 Serving = ⅔ Cup
½ Fat
1½ Starch

211 Calories
(7% from Fat)
1.7 gm Total Fat
1.3 gm Saturated Fat
1.1 mg Cholesterol
518 mg Sodium
42.9 gm Carbohydrates
2.8 gm Dietary Fiber
9.1 gm Protein
203 mg Potassium

½	angel food cake	2	teaspoons instant espresso powder
½	chocolate angel food cake	1	container (8 ounces) fat-free whipped topping
¼	cup coffee-flavored liqueur		
2	packages sugar-free instant vanilla pudding mix	½	cup pure-fruit raspberry preserves
3	cups fat-free milk	1	pint raspberries

Cut each cake into 8 slices. Cut each slice into 32 triangles. Arrange on a baking dish and brush triangles with liqueur.

In a small bowl mix the pudding mix, milk, and espresso powder for 2 minutes. Gently fold in whipped topping.

Arrange cake triangles inside edge of 3-quart trifle bowl, standing upright to form tree shapes along the edges. Alternating, layer the remaining cake, pudding, raspberry preserves, and raspberries in bowl, ending with fruit. Cover and chill for at least 2 hours.

Light and Easy Poundcake

10 Servings

Exchange Values Per Serving
1 Serving = 1-Inch Slice with ¼ Cup Sherbet
2 Starch

166 Calories
(8% from Fat)
1.4 gm Total Fat
0.7 gm Saturated Fat
2.5 mg Cholesterol
128 mg Sodium
36.3 gm Carbohydrates
1.2 gm Dietary Fiber
2.4 gm Protein
142 mg Potassium

1	frozen reduced-fat pound cake (10¾ ounces)	5	fresh strawberries
2½	cups strawberry sherbet	2	kiwi fruit, sliced

Slice the frozen pound cake vertically into 5 slices, 1½ inches thick. Cut each slice in half diagonally. Top each slice with a ¼ cup scoop of sherbet, half of a strawberry, and 1 slice of kiwi fruit. Serve immediately.

Spicy Apple Cake

24 Servings

4	tablespoons sugar	¾	cup chopped nuts
1	teaspoon baking powder	3	egg whites
¼	teaspoon low-sodium baking soda	2	cups unsweetened apple butter
¾	cup whole wheat flour	2	cups finely chopped peeled apples
1½	cups all-purpose flour	1	teaspoon vanilla extract
1	teaspoon cinnamon	¼	cup low-fat margarine
¼	teaspoon grated nutmeg	¼	cup canola oil
⅛	teaspoon ground cloves		Nonstick cooking spray
½	cup dark raisins		

Preheat oven to 350°. In a medium bowl combine all dry ingredients. In a separate bowl whip the egg whites until soft peaks form. Add apple butter, apples, vanilla, margarine, and oil to dry mix. Fold in egg whites. Pour into a bundt pan that has been coated with cooking spray. Bake for 30 to 35 minutes or until a toothpick inserted in cake comes out clean. Let stand for 20 minutes before turning out onto a serving plate.

Exchange Values Per Serving
1 Serving = 1-Inch Slice
2⅔ Fat
½ Fruit
⅓ Meat
2⅔ Starch

320 Calories
(39% from Fat)
14.4 gm Total Fat
1.5 gm Saturated Fat
0 mg Cholesterol
162 mg Sodium
46.0 gm Carbohydrates
5.2 gm Dietary Fiber
4.3 gm Protein
231 mg Potassium

Cherry Supreme Cheesecake

8 Servings

1	package (8 ounces) fat-free cream cheese	2	cans (16 ounces each) tart cherries packed in water
16	packets artificial sweetener, divided	3	tablespoons cornstarch
1	teaspoon vanilla extract	¼	teaspoon almond extract
1	tablespoon fat-free milk	2	drops red food coloring
1	Graham Cracker Crust (p. 289)		

Combine the cream cheese, 8 packets artificial sweetener, vanilla, and milk in a food processor. Process until light and creamy. Pour into the pie shell and chill until firm.

Combine the cherries, cornstarch, and remaining sweetener in the top of a double boiler, and gently heat over the water until the mixture thickens. Remove from the heat and add the almond extract and red food coloring. Cool and spread over the cheese layer.

Exchange Values Per Serving
1 Serving = 1-Inch Slice
1⅓ Fat
⅓ Fruit
½ Meat
1½ Starch

217 Calories
(33% from Fat)
7.9 gm Total Fat
1.8 gm Saturated Fat
2.3 mg Cholesterol
331 mg Sodium
30.8 gm Carbohydrates
1.1 gm Dietary Fiber
5.9 gm Protein
132 mg Potassium

General Index

A

1, 500 Calorie Meal Plan, 50
2, 000 Calorie Meal Plan, 51
2, 500 Calorie Meal Plan, 52
ADA *see* American Diabetes
   Association
Alcoholic beverages
   advice concerning, 29–30
   caloric content *(list),* 30
   empty calories of, 18
American Diabetes Association
   diabetic diet of, 7, 10
   formulation of exchange lists, 13, 33
   statement on sucrose consumption,
     18–19
American Dietetic Association,
   formulation of exchange lists, 13, 33
Aspartame, about, 19–20

B

Beans
   dry, recommended servings, 17
   fiber in, 17
Best, Charles H., 24
Blood lipids *see* Lipid profile
Blood pressure, high *see* Hypertension
Blood sugar
   effects of carbohydrates on, 15–16
   high, 10, 24
   increase in after ingestion of
     glucose, 18
   lowered by exercise, 25
   raised by illnesses, 31
   testing, 26–27, 30
   values *(chart),* 27
Blood test, for cholesterol, 12
Blood vessels, failure due to
   hyperglycemia, 10
Bracelet, medical identification, 30, 31
Bread
   blood sugar and, 18
   recommended servings, 17
British measurement, 53
Brown sugar, 18, 19

C

Caloric intake, calculating ideal,
   12–13
Calorie-free, defined, 16
Calories, 11
   basal, 13
   required, 12
Carbohydrates
   calculating from nutrition labels, 15
   caloric requirement from, 14, 34
   counting, 14–16
   defined, 14
   impact on blood sugar, 15
   needed in diet, 12
Carbohydrates Exchange List, 46–47
Cereal, recommended servings from
   Food Pyramid, 17
Cheese, recommended servings, 17
Chicken, white meat, preferred over
   fatty meats, 9
Children, 7
Cholesterol
   blood
     high, 29
     lowering, 11
       with soluble fiber, 17
   described, 11
   lowered through exercise, 25
Cholesterol-free, defined, 16
Coma, diabetic, 32
Combination Foods Exchange List,
   48–49
Common cold, 31
Condiments List, 38
Corn syrup, 19
Cornflakes, glycemic index of, 16
Coronary artery disease, 10

D

Dairy products, high fat, 9
Dextrose, 19
Diabetes
   associated with coronary artery
     disease, 11

coma due to, 32
controlling, 24–25
diagnosis of, 23, 24
education classes, 24
how diet affects, 10
illness and, 31–32
incidence of lower during war, 9
increase in incidence of, 9
lowering complications of, 24
practical tips for living with, 23–32
statistics, 23, 24
supplies for, 30–31
traveling with, 30–31
type 1, 10, 23, 32
type 2, 10, 23, 32
Diabetes Education and Research
   Center, 21
Diabetes management team, 21
Diabetic diet
   designing, 10–11
   now recommended healthy eating, 7
Diarrhea, 31
Diet
   important to everyone's health,
     16–17
   see also Diabetic diet
Dietary Guidelines for Americans
   (USDA), 13, 17
   government's commitment, 16
Dietitian, 14
   nutritional assessment by, 33
   part of diabetes management team,
     21
Dining out, recommendations for, 29
Diseases, chronic, related to diet, 9
Drinks List, 38

E

Eggs, recommended servings, 17
England, diabetes incidence in, 9
Equal® *see* Aspartame
Eskimos, incidence of diabetes
   increased in, 9
Exchange lists

for meal planning, 13
  Combination Foods List, 48–49
  Condiments, 38
  Drinks, 38
  Fast Foods, 37
  Fat List, 35–36
  Free Foods List, 37
  Fruit List, 39
  Meat and Meat Substitutes List, 40–43
  Milk List, 43–44
  Other Carbohydrates List, 46–47
  Seasonings, 38
  Starch List, 44–46
  Sugar-Free or Low-Sugar Foods, 38
  Vegetable List, 47–48
Exchange Lists for Meal Planning, about, 33
Exchange values, are averages, 14
Exercise
  essential to good health, 9, 25–26
  type 2 diabetes can be controlled by, 10
External Insulin Pump, 32
Eyes, failure due to hyperglycemia, 10

F
Fast Foods Exchange List, 37
Fat-free, defined, 16
Fats
  composition of, 12
  monounsaturated, 12
  polyunsaturated, 11
  recommended daily intake of, 12, 34
  saturated, 11
  to be used sparingly in Food Pyramid, 17
Featherweight see Saccharine
Fever, 31
Fiber
  recommendations for, 18, 34
  two types of
    water-insoluble, 17–18
    water-soluble, 17
Fish
  preferred over fatty meats, 9
  recommended servings, 17
Food Exchange Lists for Meal Planning, 14
Food Guide Pyramid
  diagram, 17
  introduced by USDA, 16
  tool in managing blood sugar, 16
Foods
  "free," 13
  glycemic index of, 15
  labels see Nutrition labels
  major groups of, 13
  with the most carbohydrates, 14
  processed, avoiding, 11
"Free," defined, 16
"Free foods," 13

Free Foods Exchange List, 37
Fructosamine Test, 27
Fructose, 18, 19
Fruit, fiber in, 17
Fruit Exchange List, 39

G
General conversion table, 53
Germany, diabetes incidence in, 9
Glucagon, raises blood sugar, 28
Glucose, 19
  causes rapid rise in blood sugar, 18
Glycemic index
  comparison of values, 15–16
  defined, 15
Glycosylated Hemoglobin Test, 27
"Good source," defined, 16
Grains
  fiber in, 18
  whole, recommended servings, 17

H
Hard candy, 31
HDL (high density lipoprotein), 12, 25
Heart, failure due to hyperglycemia, 10
Heart attack, 11
Heart disease, 9
Herbs, substitute for salt, 11
"High," defined, 16
Honey, about, 19
Hyperglycemia, 10
Hyperlipidemia, 29
Hypertension, 10
  in some diabetic patients, 11
Hypoglycemia, 10, 32
  about, 28
  alcohol consumption and, 30
  risk of, 25

I
Immunizations, 30
Insulin, 12, 30, 31
  defects in secretion of, 10
  excess, 28
  external pump administration, 32
  hormone that facilitates blood-sugar metabolism, 23
  need for can be reduced by high fiber, 17
  therapy, 10
  warning to never skip, 32
Insulin infusion system, 30
Internet, diabetes resources on the, 21

K
Kidneys, failure due to hyperglycemia, 10

L
Labels, nutrition see Nutrition labels
LDL (low density lipoprotein), 12

Lemon juice, substitute for salt, 11
"Less," defined, 16
"Light," defined, 16
Lipid profile, 10
  blood test for cholesterol, 12
Liquid measurement conversion, 53
"Low-calorie," defined, 16
"Low-fat," defined, 16
"Low-saturated fat," defined, 16
"Low-sodium," defined, 16

M
Malnutrition, 29
Maltitol, a sugar alcohol, 20
Mannitol, a sugar alcohol, 20
Maple syrup, 19
Marshall Plan, 9
Meals
  guide to planning, 33–34
  timing of, 11
Meat, recommended servings, 17
Meat and Meat Substitute Exchange List, 40–43
Medical identification bracelet, 30, 31
Menstrual cramps, 31
Metabolism disorders, 10
Metric Conversions (table), 53
Milk, recommended servings, 17
Milk Exchange List, 43–44
Molasses, 19
Monounsaturated Fats List, 35
Myocardial infarction see Heart attack

N
Native Americans, incidence of diabetes in, 9, 23
Nausea, 31
Nerves, failure due to hyperglycemia, 10
Nurse-educator, 21, 27
Nutrasweet see Aspartame
Nutrition labels, 14, 34
  core terms defined, 16
  sample, 15
Nuts, recommended servings, 17

O
Oats, fiber in, 17
Obesity, 11, 13, 24, 29
Olive oil, recommended, 12
Orange juice, can prevent hypoglycemia, 28
Osler, Sir William, 23
Oven temperatures conversion, 53

P
Pasta, recommended servings, 17
Peanut oil, recommended, 12
Physician
  part of diabetes management team, 21
  should be endocrinologist, 24
Polyunsaturated Fats List, 36

Postprandial
defined, 14
testing of blood sugar, 26
Potatoes
blood sugar and, 18
glycemic index of, 15–16
Poultry, recommended servings, 17
Protein, needed in diet, 12, 34

R
"Reduced," defined, 16
Restaurants, dining in, 29
Rice, recommended servings, 17

S
Saccharine, 19
Salt
eliminating from the diet *(chart),* 11
substitutes for, 11
Saturated Fats List, 36
Seasoning List, 38
Smoking, 11
Sodium, restricting, 11
"Sodium-free," defined, 16
Sorbitol, a sugar alcohol, 20
Sore throat, 31
Sorghum, 19
Sprinkle® Sweet *see* Saccharine
Starch Exchange List, 44–46
Sucrose, known as table sugar, 18
Sugar
blood *see* Blood sugar

invert, 18
table
glycemic index of, 16
is sucrose, 18
Sugar alcohols, 20
Sugar beets, 18
Sugar cane, 18
"Sugar-free," defined, 16
Sugar-Free Foods List, 38
Sugars, 18
Sunburn, 31
Supplies, diabetic, 30–31
Sweet 'n Low® *see* Saccharine
Sweeteners
artificial, 19–20
two categories of
caloric, 18
noncaloric, 18
Syringes, 30
Syrups, about, 19

T
Triglycerides, 12, 25

U
Upper respiratory infections, 31
U.S. Department of Health and
Human Services, 16
U.S. Food and Drug Administration,
regulations governing nutrition
labels, 15
USDA

Food Guide Pyramid introduced
by, 16
regulations governing nutrition
labels, 15

V
Vegetables, recommended servings,
17
Vegetables Exchange List, 47–48
Vegetarians, 7
"Very low-sodium," defined, 16

W
Walking, recommended, 25
Weight
calculating ideal, 12–13
gain, 12
loss, 12, 13
Weight measurement conversion, 53
World War II, 9

X
Xylitol, a sugar alcohol, 20

Y
Yogurt, recommended servings, 17
Young, disease and, 9–10

Recipes Index

A
Ale-Poached Sea Bass with Pimiento
Sauce, 190
Angel Pasta with Crab, 207
APPETIZERS
Artichoke Spread, 84
Blue Cheese Avocado Dip, 80
Cheddar-Dijon Dip, 77
Cheese and Pears, 76
Cherry Tomato Appetizers, 86
Chicken Spread, 83
Christmas Night Miniature
Meatballs, 91
Colonial Orange-Spiced Walnuts, 75
Crab Pie Appetizer, 82
Dilly Dip, 77
Garlic and Parmesan Pecans, 75
Guacamole Dip, 78
Herb Dip with Asparagus, 81
Herb Meatballs, 91
Holiday Chopped Liver, 89
Hotty Totty Onion Dip, 79
Italian Carrot Antipasto, 86
Marinated Vegetables, 85
Munchy Crunchy Vegetable Dip, 79
Oriental Beef Kabobs, 89
Pasta Bites, 88
Piney Cheese Balls, 92

Quick Fajitas with Pico de Gallo, 90
Shrimp and Cheese Spread, 83
Shrimp Dip, 81
Spinach Vegetable Dip, 80
Stuffed Dill Mushrooms, 87
Stuffed Mushroom Caps, 88
Stuffed Apricots, 76
Stuffed Tomatoes, 87
Texas Bean Dip, 78
Vegetable Spread, 84
Your Own Crispy Crackers, 82
Zucchini Cheese Spread, 85
Apple Bread Dressing, 260
Apple Gelatin Dessert, 284
Apple-Cranberry Cobbler, 288
Apple-Orange Cider Salad, 132
Apple-Raisin Muffins, 147
Apple-Stuffed Squash with
Cinnamon, 243
Apples and Onions Side Dish, 240
Applesauce, 266
Apricot Bread Pudding, 291
Apricot Chicken, 171
Apricot and Chicken Pasta, 172
Apricot Cookies, 285
Apricot-Oat Bran Muffins, 148
Artichoke Spread, 84
An Apricot Drink, 60

ASPARAGUS
Asparagus and Basil, 231
Asparagus in a Chicken Blanket, 181
Fresh Asparagus Rice Pilaf, 231
Grilled Asparagus, 232
Herb Dip with Asparagus, 81
AVOCADO
Cucumber Avocado Bisque, 95
Guacamole Dip, 78
Spicy Cherry Tomatoes with
Avocado, 245
B
Baked Apples with Raisins, 277
Baked Beef Tenderloin with
Vegetables, 162
Baked Broccoli, 233
Baked Chicken and Rice, 172
Baked Flounder with Orange Sauce,
192
Baked Fluffy Potatoes, 224
Baked Fried Chicken, 173
Baked Grilled Cheese Sandwiches, 160
Baked Italian Onions, 241
Baked Potato Bread, 138
Baked Spicy Shrimp, 201
Baked Zucchini and Cheese, 245
Banana Bread, 140
Banana Muffins, 148

Banana-Grape Supreme, 274
Bavarian-Style Whipped Strawberry
    Pie, 290
BEANS AND PEAS
    Black-Eyed Peas and Wild Rice, 221
    Cajun Green Beans, 239
    French Green Bean and Rice
        Casserole, 240
    French Green Beans Amandine, 239
    Green Bean Salad, 120
    Lentil and Beef Soup, 109
    Mexican Black Bean and Rice, 221
    New Year's Black-Eyed Peas, 222
    Pea and Horseradish Sauce, 255
    Texas Bean Dip, 78
BEEF
    Beef and Barley Soup, 107
    Beef Bourguignon, 163
    Beef and Noodles, 162
    Beef Oriental, 165
    Beef Stew Base, 108
    Beef Tenderloin with Herbed
        Tomato Sauce, 167
    Chinese Green Pepper Steak, 164
    Fall Apple Pot Roast, 163
    Family Beef Stew, 109
    Herb Meatballs, 91
    Holiday Beef Steaks with Vegetable
        Sauté and Hot Mustard Sauce,
        161
    Lentil and Beef Soup, 109
    Old-Fashioned Beef, Macaroni, and
        Tomato Casserole, 213
    Oriental Beef Kabobs, 89
    Pepper Steak, 168
    Poached Beef Tenderloin, 166
    Quick Fajitas with Pico de Gallo, 90
    Round Steak in Wine Sauce, 165
    Spicy-Tangy Beef Soup, 108
    Steak and Roasted Vegetable Salad,
        126–127
    Stir-Fry Beef and Spinach with
        Noodles, 166–167
    Swiss Steak, 169
Beef and Barley Soup, 107
Beef Bourguignon, 163
Beef and Noodles, 162
Beef Oriental, 165
Beef Stew Base, 108
Beef Tenderloin with Herbed Tomato
    Sauce, 167
BEVERAGES
    An Apricot Drink, 60
    Blackberry Buzz, 61
    Breakfast Tomato Juice, 58
    Brunch Punch, 63
    Cantaloupe Refresher, 62
    A Carrot Cocktail, 69
    Chocolate Cafe Borgia, 73
    Chocolate Coffee Milkshake, 73
    Christmas Wassail, 72
    Citrus Punch, 63
    Cranberry Fizz Punch, 64
    Creamed Ice Tea, 55

Fall Apple Coffee, 57
Frosty Strawberry Delight, 67
A Fruit Shake, 68
Fruity Good-Morning Drink, 59
Fruity Punch, 65
Fruity Slush, 66
Hearty Tomato Saucy Drink, 70
Holiday Eggless Eggnog, 72
Hot Spiced Coffee, 56
Hot Spiced Tea, 56
Instant Breakfast Drink, 57
Lime-and-Raspberry Refresher, 66
Mint Tea, 60
Orange Frosty, 67
Orange Monster Drink, 59
A Peach of a Punch, 62
Southern Mint Juleps, 61
Spiced Low-Fat Buttermilk, 71
Spiced Russian Tea, 55
Strawberry Grog, 68
Strawberry Parfait Drink, 69
Tart and Bubbly Wake-Up Drink,
    58
Tea Punch, 64
Tomato Frappe, 70
Warmed Wintry Milk, 71
BISCUITS
    Breakfast Biscuits, 143
    Buttermilk Biscuits, 144
    Cranberry-Orange Biscuits, 145
    Whole Wheat and Yogurt Biscuits,
        145
Black Jack Muffins, 151
Black-Eyed Peas and Wild Rice, 221
Blackberry Buzz, 61
Blackberry Corn Muffins, 150
Blackberry and Zucchini Bread, 142
Blue Cheese Avocado Dip, 80
Blue Cheese Dressing, 258
Blueberry Crepe, 287
Blueberry Muffins, 149
Blueberry Slump, 281
Blueberry-Banana Muffins, 147
BREADS
    Apple-Raisin Muffins, 147
    Apricot-Oat Bran Muffins, 148
    Baked Grilled Cheese Sandwiches,
        160
    Baked Potato Bread, 138
    Banana Bread, 140
    Banana Muffins, 148
    Black Jack Muffins, 151
    Blackberry Corn Muffins, 150
    Blackberry and Zucchini Bread, 142
    Blueberry Muffins, 149
    Blueberry-Banana Muffins, 147
    Breakfast Biscuits, 143
    Buckwheat Buttermilk Pancakes,
        155
    Buckwheat and Yogurt Pancakes,
        155
    Buttermilk Biscuits, 144
    Carrot Cake Muffins, 149
    Cheesy Broccoli/Cauliflower

Bread, 138
Cinnamon French Toast, 157
Corn Bread Muffins, 158
Cornmeal Griddle Cakes, 156
Cranberry-Orange Biscuits, 145
Cranberry-Orange Muffins, 150
Dried Fruit and Buttermilk Drop
    Scones, 153
Golden Apple-Wheat Loaf, 140
Herb Bread, 137
Hot Apple Cinnamon Cereal, 143
Lemon Buns, 146–147
Lemon Zest Muffins, 146
Oat Bran Bread, 141
Oat Bran Muffins, 151
Oat Bran-Banana Muffins, 152
Oatmeal-Banana Muffins, 153
Old-Fashioned Corn Cakes, 156
Oven-Baked Orange and Vanilla
    French Toast, 157
Parmesan Pizza Crust, 270
Pepper Sweet Corn Bread, 159
Pumpkin-Apple Bran Muffins, 152
Pumpkin-Apple Bread, 142
Scottish Oat Cakes, 154
Scottish Oat-Bran Toast, 154
Southern Corn Bread, 158
Southern Corn Bread Stuffing, 159
Southern Pizza Crust, 268–269
Whole Wheat Bread, 139
Whole Wheat Carrot Bread, 139
Whole Wheat Pizza Crust, 269
Whole Wheat and Yogurt Biscuits,
    145
Yogurt Drop Biscuits, 144
Zucchini Bread, 141
Breakfast Biscuits, 143
Breakfast Tomato Juice, 58
BROCCOLI
    Baked Broccoli, 233
    Broccoli with Cream Sauce, 232
    Broccoli and Herbs, 233
    Broccoli and Mushroom Casserole,
        234
    Broccoli and Rice Casserole, 219
    Broccoli Turkey Casserole, 234
    Brown Rice Broccoli Casserole, 219
    Cauliflower with Broccoli Sauce,
        237
    Cheesy Broccoli/Cauliflower
        Bread, 138
    Cream of Broccoli Soup, 97
    Fresh Broccoli and Cauliflower
        Salad, 120
    Layered Turkey and Broccoli Pasta
        Salad, 126
Broiled Fish Steaks and Herbs, 191
Broiled Pepper Swordfish, 196
Broiled Scallops with Spinach, 204
Broiled Tomatoes, 244
Brown Rice Broccoli Casserole, 219
Brown Rice with Scallions, 220
Brunch Punch, 63
Brussels Sprouts with Chicken, 235

Buckwheat Buttermilk Pancakes, 155
Buckwheat and Yogurt Pancakes, 155
Buttermilk Biscuits, 144
Buttermilk Blue Cheese Dressing, 258
Buttermilk-Style Dressing, 257

C

CABBAGE
    Celery Cole Slaw, 121
    Creole Cabbage, 235
Cajun Green Beans, 239
Cajun Shrimp and Oyster Soup, 112
CAKE
    Cherry Supreme Cheesecake, 293
    Light and Easy Poundcake, 292
    Spicy Apple Cake, 293
Cantaloupe Refresher, 62
A Carrot Cocktail, 69
Carrot Cake Muffins, 149
Carrot and Ginger Soup, 96
CARROTS
    Carrot Cake Muffins, 149
    A Carrot Cocktail, 69
    Carrot and Ginger Soup, 96
    Cream of Carrot Soup, 97
    Golden Carrots, 236
    Sweet Carrots with Dill or Basil, 236
Catfish with Angel Hair Pasta, 200
Cauliflower with Broccoli Sauce, 237
Cauliflower Soup, 99
Celery Cole Slaw, 121
CHEESE
    Baked Grilled Cheese Sandwiches,
        160
    Baked Zucchini and Cheese, 245
    Blue Cheese Dressing, 258
    Buttermilk Blue Cheese Dressing,
        258
    Cheddar-Dijon Dip, 77
    Cheese and Pears, 76
    Cheesy Broccoli/Cauliflower
        Bread, 138
    Cheesy Whipped Potatoes, 224
    Cherry Supreme Cheesecake, 293
    Cottage Cheese Ranch Dressing,
        259
    Crispy Cheesy Apples, 275
    Monterey Jack Salsa, 250
    Mostaccioli al Forno, 214
    Old-Fashioned Macaroni and
        Cheese, 212
    Piney Cheese Balls, 92
    Ricotta Yogurt Dressing, 260
    Shrimp and Cheese Spread, 83
    Spicy Manicotti, 215
    Swiss Cheese Vegetable Bisque, 102
    Zucchini Cheese Spread, 85
    Zucchini Ricotta Casserole, 247
Cheese and Pears, 76
Cheesy Broccoli/Cauliflower Bread,
    138
Cheesy Scalloped Cucumbers, 238
Cheesy Scalloped Potatoes, 225
Cheesy Whipped Potatoes, 224

Cherry Supreme Cheesecake, 293
Cherry Tomato Appetizers, 86
CHICKEN
    Apricot Chicken, 171
    Apricot and Chicken Pasta, 172
    Asparagus in a Chicken Blanket, 181
    Baked Chicken and Rice, 172
    Baked Fried Chicken, 173
    Brussels Sprouts with Chicken, 235
    Chicken Breasts with Cranberry
        Chutney, 175
    Chicken a l'Orange, 174
    Chicken with Onion Marinade, 183
    Chicken Pasta Salad, 127
    Chicken Popovers, 175
    Chicken Rosemary, 174
    Chicken Spread, 83
    Chicken Tacos, 272
    Chicken Tarragon, 177
    Chicken Teriyaki, 176
    Chicken and Vegetable Soup, 105
    Chicken-Apple Dressing, 261
    Chutney Chicken Salad, 127
    Citrus Broiled Chicken, 177
    Gingered Lime Chicken, 178
    Gingered Parsnip and Chicken
        Soup, 106
    Herbed Marinated Chicken, 183
    Holiday Chopped Liver, 89
    Hot, Hot Gumbo Chicken, 113
    Kiwi Chicken, 180
    Lemon Pepper Chicken, 176
    Oven-Baked Chicken Livers, 184
    Poultry and Rice Pilaf, 179
    Sesame Chicken, 173
    Southern Chicken Fry, 180
    Stir-Fry Chicken, 179
    Stuffed Chicken Breasts, 182
    Vegetable and Chicken Outdoor
        Bake, 181
    Zesty Chicken Italiano, 182
Chicken Breasts with Cranberry
    Chutney, 175
Chicken a l'Orange, 174
Chicken with Onion Marinade, 183
Chicken Pasta Salad, 127
Chicken Popovers, 175
Chicken Rosemary, 174
Chicken Spread, 83
Chicken Tacos, 272
Chicken Tarragon, 177
Chicken Teriyaki, 176
Chicken and Vegetable Soup, 105
Chicken-Apple Dressing, 261
Children, dishes for, 267–275
Chinese Green Pepper Steak, 164
Chinese Rice Soup, 105
Chocolate and Banana Bars, 273
Chocolate Cafe Borgia, 73
Chocolate Coffee Milkshake, 73
Chocolate Espresso Trifle, 292
Chocolate Mousse Pudding, 291
Christmas Night Miniature
    Meatballs, 91

Christmas Wassail, 72
Chutney Chicken Salad, 127
Cinnamon French Toast, 157
Cinnamon-Raisin Spread, 264
Citrus Broiled Chicken, 177
Citrus Punch, 63
Clam Chowder, 114
Cold Weather Soup, 104
Colonial Orange-Spiced Walnuts, 75
COOKIES
    Apricot Cookies, 285
    Cranberry-Orange Bar Cookies,
        285
    Oat Bran Cookies, 286
    Peanut Butter Cookies, 286
    Rolled Sugar Cookies, 287
CORN
    Fresh Corn and Black-Eyed Pea
        Salad, 122
    Mexican Corn Soup, 104
Corn Bread Muffins, 158
Cornflake-Breaded Baked Fish, 189
Cornmeal Griddle Cakes, 156
Cottage Cheese Ranch Dressing, 259
COUSCOUS
    Couscous Salad, 123
    Fruited Couscous, 227
    Nutty Couscous Pilaf, 227
CRAB
    Angel Pasta with Crab, 207
    Crab Imperial, 206
    Crab Pie Appetizer, 82
    Italian Crab Cakes, 206
    Spicy Crab Soup, 111
Crab Imperial, 206
Crab Pie Appetizer, 82
Crackers, Your Own Crispy Crackers,
    82
Cranberry Chutney, 265
Cranberry Fizz Punch, 64
Cranberry and Pineapple Sherbet, 283
Cranberry Turkey Steaks, 188
Cranberry-Orange Bar Cookies, 285
Cranberry-Orange Biscuits, 145
Cranberry-Orange Muffins, 150
Cream of Broccoli Soup, 97
Cream of Carrot Soup, 97
Cream of Chicken and Wild Rice
    Soup, 106
Creamed Ice Tea, 55
Creamed Vegetables, 229
Creamy Cucumber Soup, 96
Creamy Rice Casserole with Chili
    Peppers, 220
Creamy Sherbet, 274
Creamy Squash Soup, 98
Creole Cabbage, 235
Crispy Cheesy Apples, 275
Crock-Pot Applesauce, 265
Crumbly Cauliflower, 237
Crumbly Peaches, 281
Cucumber Avocado Bisque, 95
Cucumber Sauce for Fish, Meats, or
    Vegetables, 253

CUCUMBERS
Cheesy Scalloped Cucumbers, 238
Cucumber Avocado Bisque, 95
Cucumber Sauce for Fish, Meats, or
  Vegetables, 253
Unsalted Dill Pickles, 247

D
DESSERTS
Apple Gelatin Dessert, 284
Apple-Cranberry Cobbler, 288
Apricot Bread Pudding, 291
Apricot Cookies, 285
Baked Apples with Raisins, 277
Banana-Grape Supreme, 274
Bavarian-Style Whipped Strawberry
  Pie, 290
Blueberry Crepe, 287
Blueberry Slump, 281
Cherry Supreme Cheesecake, 293
Chocolate and Banana Bars, 273
Chocolate Espresso Trifle, 292
Chocolate Mousse Pudding, 291
Cranberry and Pineapple Sherbet,
  283
Cranberry-Orange Bar Cookies, 285
Creamy Sherbet, 274
Crispy Cheesy Apples, 275
Crumbly Peaches, 281
Fluffy Fruit Flan, 279
Fruit and Yogurt Parfaits, 283
Graham Cracker Crust, 289
Ice Cream Peaches with
  Gingersnaps, 273
Light and Easy Poundcake, 292
Oat Bran Cookies, 286
Oat Bran Pie Crust, 289
Old-Fashioned Apple Crunch, 279
Orange Baked Apples and Pears,
  275
Peanut Butter Cookies, 286
Pear Cobbler, 288
Pears with Raspberry Sauce, 282
Pineapple and Orange Yogurt
  Freeze, 275
Pumpkin Pie in a Graham Cracker
  Crust, 290
Rolled Sugar Cookies, 287
Spicy Apple Cake, 293
Strawberry and Orange Pops, 282
Streusel Topping, 280
Winter Fruit Medley, 280
Yogurt Pudding, 284
Dijon Sauce, 254
Dijon Vinaigrette, 262
Dilly Dip, 77
DIPS
Blue Cheese Avocado Dip, 80
Cheddar-Dijon Dip, 77
Dilly Dip, 77
Guacamole Dip, 78
Herb Dip with Asparagus, 81
Hotty Totty Onion Dip, 79
Munchy Crunchy Vegetable Dip, 79

Shrimp Dip, 81
Spinach Vegetable Dip, 80
Texas Bean Dip, 78
Dried Fruit and Buttermilk Drop
  Scones, 153
Dried Fruit Chutney, 264

E
Eggplant Salad, 119
ENTRÉES
Ale-Poached Sea Bass with
  Pimiento Sauce, 190
Angel Pasta with Crab, 207
Apricot Chicken, 171
Apricot and Chicken Pasta, 172
Asparagus in a Chicken Blanket, 181
Baked Beef Tenderloin with
  Vegetables, 162
Baked Chicken and Rice, 172
Baked Flounder with Orange
  Sauce, 192
Baked Fried Chicken, 173
Baked Spicy Shrimp, 201
Beef Bourguignon, 163
Beef and Noodles, 162
Beef Oriental, 165
Beef Tenderloin with Herbed
  Tomato Sauce, 167
Broiled Fish Steaks and Herbs, 191
Broiled Pepper Swordfish, 196
Broiled Scallops with Spinach, 204
Catfish with Angel Hair Pasta, 200
Chicken Breasts with Cranberry
  Chutney, 175
Chicken a l'Orange, 174
Chicken with Onion Marinade, 183
Chicken Popovers, 175
Chicken Rosemary, 174
Chicken Tarragon, 177
Chicken Teriyaki, 176
Chinese Green Pepper Steak, 164
Citrus Broiled Chicken, 177
Cornflake-Breaded Baked Fish, 189
Crab Imperial, 206
Cranberry Turkey Steaks, 188
Fall Apple Pot Roast, 163
Fish Amandine, 189
Fish Bake, 192
Flounder and Vegetable Bake, 193
Gingered Lime Chicken, 178
Grilled Tuna with Citrus-Sage
  Marinade, 200
Ground Turkey Parmigiana, 186
Herbed Marinated Chicken, 183
Herbed Turkey, 185
Holiday Beef Steaks with Vegetable
  Sauté and Hot Mustard Sauce,
  161
Hot Tuna and Potato Bake, 198
Italian Crab Cakes, 206
Italian Turkey Fest, 188
Kiwi Chicken, 180
Leek and Mussel Poach, 208
Lemon Pepper Chicken, 176

Lemon Shrimp, 202–203
Lettuce-Baked Lobster Tails, 207
Mom's Meatloaf, 164
Old–Fashioned Beef, Macaroni, and
  Tomato Casserole, 213
Orange Roughy in Lemon Wine
  Sauce, 197
Oven-Baked Chicken Livers, 184
Pepper Steak, 168
Perfect Orange Scampi, 205
Pimiento Tuna in a Pepper Cup, 199
Poached Beef Tenderloin, 166
Poultry and Rice Pilaf, 179
Quick and Easy Zesty Fish, 190
Rock Shrimp and Oyster Maque
  Choux, 203
Round Steak in Wine Sauce, 165
Salmon Mousse, 194
Santa Rosa Shrimp, 201
Sausage and Spinach Casserole, 169
Savory Jumbo Shells, 214–215
Seafood Stuffed Eggplant, 205
Sesame Chicken, 173
Shrimp and Mushrooms, 204
Shrimp and Olive Pasta, 202
Skewered Seafood, 208
Southern Chicken Fry, 180
Spicy Salmon Cakes, 195
Spicy Turkey Jambalaya, 185
Stir-Fry Beef and Spinach with
  Noodles, 166–167
Stir-Fry Chicken, 179
Stuffed Chicken Breasts, 182
Stuffed Pork Roast with
  Mushrooms, 170
Swedish Meatballs, 168
Swiss Steak, 169
Thanksgiving Herbed Turkey,
  186–187
Trout Bake, 194
Trout with Pecan Sauce, 193
Tuna and Noodle Casserole, 198
Tuna Potato Casserole, 199
Turkey with Cranapple Sauce, 187
Turkey Frittata, 184
Veal Marsala, 171
Veal Provencale, 170
Vegetable and Chicken Outdoor
  Bake, 181
Very Orange Roughy, 197
Wakulla Grilled Grouper, 196
Ybor City Fillets, 191
Zesty Chicken Italiano, 182

F
Fall Apple Coffee, 57
Fall Apple Pot Roast, 163
Fall Harvest Chowder, 101
Fall Harvest Soup, 102
Family Beef Stew, 109
Family Style Chili, 110
FISH
Ale-Poached Sea Bass with
  Pimiento Sauce, 190

Baked Flounder with Orange
Sauce, 192
Broiled Fish Steaks and Herbs, 191
Broiled Pepper Swordfish, 196
Catfish with Angel Hair Pasta, 200
Cornflake-Breaded Baked Fish, 189
Fish Amandine, 189
Fish Bake, 192
Fish Soup, 111
Flounder and Vegetable Bake, 193
Grilled Tuna with Citrus-Sage
Marinade, 200
Hot Tuna and Potato Bake, 198
Orange Roughy in Lemon Wine
Sauce, 197
Pimiento Tuna in a Pepper Cup, 199
Potato and Salmon Salad, 129
Quick and Easy Zesty Fish, 190
Salmon Mousse, 194
Flounder and Vegetable Bake, 193
Fluffy Fruit Flan, 279
Fluffy Orange Yogurt Salad, 131
French Green Bean and Rice
Casserole, 240
Fresh Asparagus Rice Pilaf, 231
Fresh Broccoli and Cauliflower Salad,
120
Fresh Corn and Black-Eyed Pea Salad,
122
Frosty Strawberry Delight, 67
FRUIT
Apple Bread Dressing, 260
Apple Gelatin Dessert, 284
Apple-Orange Cider Salad, 132
Apple-Stuffed Squash with
Cinnamon, 243
Apples and Onions Side Dish, 240
Applesauce, 266
Apricot Bread Pudding, 291
Baked Apples with Raisins, 277
Banana-Grape Supreme, 274
Blueberry Crepe, 287
Blueberry Slump, 281
Cheese and Pears, 76
Chicken-Apple Dressing, 260
Cranberry Chutney, 265
Cranberry and Pineapple Sherbet,
283
Crispy Cheesy Apples, 275
Crock-Pot Applesauce, 265
Crumbly Peaches, 281
Dried Fruit Chutney, 264
Fluffy Fruit Flan, 279
Fluffy Orange Yogurt Salad, 131
Fruit and Nut Curried Salad, 133
Fruit and Yogurt Parfaits, 283
Fruited Couscous, 227
Gingered Fruit Compote, 134
Hearty Fruit Soup, 115
Ice Cream Peaches with
Gingersnaps, 273
Old-Fashioned Apple Crunch, 279
Orange Baked Apples and Pears, 275
Orange Pineapple Salad, 135

Orange Wild Rice with Currants
and Apples, 218
Orange-Cranberry Salad, 136
Peaches and Cream Salad, 134
Pear Cobbler, 288
Pear-Apple Butter, 263
Pears with Raspberry Sauce, 282
Pineapple and Orange Yogurt
Freeze, 275
Pineapple and Peach Soup, 116
Strawberry Gelatin Salad, 136
Strawberry and Orange Pops, 282
Stuffed Apricots, 76
Summer Strawberry and Burgundy
Soup, 116
Traditional Holiday Cranberry
Salad, 132
Tropical Fruit Salad, 133
Very Orange Salad, 135
Winter Fruit Medley, 280
Fruit Cubes and Fizz, 65
Fruit and Nut Curried Salad, 133
Fruit and Yogurt Parfaits, 283
A Fruit Shake, 68
Fruited Couscous, 227
Fruity Good-Morning Drink, 59
Fruity Punch, 65
Fruity Slush, 66
Fruity Sweet Potatoes, 226

G
Garlic and Parmesan Pecans, 75
Gingered Fruit Compote, 134
Gingered Lime Chicken, 178
Gingered Parsnip and Chicken Soup,
106
Golden Apple-Wheat Loaf, 140
Golden Carrots, 236
Golden Mediterranean Pilaf, 228
Graham Cracker Crust, 289
Greek Turkey Burger, 271
Green Bean Salad, 120
Green Onion Cream Sauce, 251
Grilled Asparagus, 232
Grilled Tuna with Citrus–Sage
Marinade, 200
Ground Turkey Parmigiana, 186
Guacamole Dip, 78

H
Ham with Mustard Garlic Apple-cue
Sauce, 253
Hearty Fruit Soup, 115
Hearty Potato Soup, 100
Hearty Tomato Saucy Drink, 70
Hearty Vegetable Soup, 101
Herb Bread, 137
Herb Dip with Asparagus, 81
Herb Meatballs, 91
Herbed Marinated Chicken, 183
Herbed Spice Dressing, 259
Herbed Tomato Soup, 93
Herbed Turkey, 185
Holiday Beef Steaks with Vegetable

Sauté and Hot Mustard Sauce, 161
Holiday Chopped Liver, 89
Holiday Eggless Eggnog, 72
Hot Apple Cinnamon Cereal, 143
Hot, Hot Gumbo Chicken, 113
Hot Spiced Coffee, 56
Hot Spiced Tea, 56
Hot Tuna and Potato Bake, 198
Hotty Totty Onion Dip, 79
House Salad with Dream Pepper
Dressing, 257

I
Ice Cream Peaches with Gingersnaps,
273
Instant Breakfast Drink, 57
Italian Carrot Antipasto, 86
Italian Crab Cakes, 206
Italian Meatball Soup, 110
Italian Turkey Fest, 188

K
Kiwi Chicken, 180

L
LASAGNA
Spinach Parmesan Lasagna, 212
Vegetable Lasagna I, 210
Vegetable Lasagna II, 210–211
Vegetarian Lasagna, 211
Layered Turkey and Broccoli Pasta
Salad, 126
Leek and Mussel Poach, 208
Lemon Artichoke Hearts and
Mushrooms, 230
Lemon Buns, 146–147
Lemon Butter, 263
Lemon Herbs, 262
Lemon Pepper Chicken, 176
Lemon Shrimp, 202–203
Lemon Zest Muffins, 146
Lemon-Dijon Mustard Sauce, 254
Lemon-Dill Crabmeat Salad on
Cucumber, 130
Lemon-Garlic Vinegar, 256
Lentil and Beef Soup, 109
Lettuce-Baked Lobster Tails, 207
Light and Easy Poundcake, 292
Lime-and-Raspberry Refresher, 66
Louisiana Creole Barbecue Sauce, 178

M
Macaroni Salad, 125
Manicotti with Eggplant-Tomato
Relish, 216
Manicotti with Ratatouille Sauce, 217
Maple Syrup, 266
Marinated Mushroom Salad, 119
Marinated Vegetables, 85
Mexican Black Bean and Rice, 221
Mexican Corn Soup, 104
Mexican Salsa, 249
Mint Tea, 60
Molded Cucumber Salad, 122

Mom's Meatloaf, 164
Monterey Jack Salsa, 250
Mostaccioli al Forno, 214
MUFFINS
    Apple-Raisin Muffins, 147
    Apricot-Oat Bran Muffins, 148
    Banana Muffins, 148
    Black Jack Muffins, 151
    Blackberry Corn Muffins, 150
    Blueberry Muffins, 149
    Blueberry-Banana Muffins, 147
    Carrot Cake Muffins, 149
    Corn Bread Muffins, 158
    Cranberry-Orange Muffins, 150
    Lemon Zest Muffins, 146
    Oat Bran Muffins, 151
    Oat Bran-Banana Muffins, 152
    Oatmeal-Banana Muffins, 153
    Pumpkin-Apple Bran Muffins, 152
Munchy Crunchy Vegetable Dip, 79
Mushroom Dressing, 261
Mushroom Soup, 98
MUSHROOMS
    Lemon Artichoke Hearts and
        Mushrooms, 230
    Marinated Mushroom Salad, 119
    Mushroom Dressing, 261
    Mushroom Soup, 98
    Orange Curried Rice and
        Mushrooms, 218
    Shrimp and Mushrooms, 204
    Stuffed Dill Mushrooms, 87
    Stuffed Mushroom Caps, 88
    Stuffed Pork Roast with
        Mushrooms, 170

N
Nacho Pizzas, 268
New Year's Black-Eyed Peas, 222
Nutty Couscous Pilaf, 227

O
Oat Bran Bread, 141
Oat Bran Cookies, 286
Oat Bran Muffins, 151
Oat Bran Pie Crust, 289
Oat Bran-Banana Muffins, 152
Oatmeal-Banana Muffins, 153
OATS
    Oat Bran Bread, 141
    Oat Bran Cookies, 286
    Oat Bran Muffins, 151
    Oat Bran Pie Crust, 289
    Oat Bran-Banana Muffins, 152
    Oatmeal-Banana Muffins, 153
    Oriental Oat Pilaf, 228
Old-Fashioned Apple Crunch, 279
Old-Fashioned Beef, Macaroni, and
    Tomato Casserole, 213
Old-Fashioned Corn Cakes, 156
Old-Fashioned Macaroni and Cheese,
    212
Old-Fashioned Potato Salad, 123

Orange Baked Apples and Pears, 275
Orange Curried Rice and
    Mushrooms, 218
Orange Frosty, 67
Orange Monster Drink, 59
Orange Pineapple Salad, 135
Orange Roughy in Lemon Wine
    Sauce, 197
Orange Wild Rice with Currants and
    Apples, 218
Orange Wilted-Spinach Salad with
    Pork, 117
Orange-Cranberry Salad, 136
Oriental Beef Kabobs, 89
Oriental Oat Pilaf, 228
Oven-Baked Chicken Livers, 184
Oven-Baked Orange and Vanilla
    French Toast, 157
Oyster Stew, 113

P
PANCAKES
    Buckwheat Buttermilk Pancakes,
        155
    Buckwheat and Yogurt Pancakes,
        155
    Cornmeal Griddle Cakes, 156
    Old-Fashioned Corn Cakes, 156
Parmesan Linguine with Garlic, 209
Parmesan Pizza Crust, 270
PASTA
    Angel Pasta with Crab, 207
    Apricot and Chicken Pasta, 172
    Catfish with Angel Hair Pasta, 200
    Layered Turkey and Broccoli Pasta
        Salad, 126
    Macaroni Salad, 125
    Manicotti with Eggplant-Tomato
        Relish, 216
    Manicotti with Ratatouille Sauce,
        217
    Mostaccioli al Forno, 214
    Old-Fashioned Beef, Macaroni,
        and Tomato Casserole, 213
    Old-Fashioned Macaroni and
        Cheese, 212
    Parmesan Linguine with Garlic, 209
    Pasta Bites, 88
    Pasta Primavera with Zucchini and
        Roasted Red Peppers, 209
    Pasta and Vegetable Salad, 124
    Red Pepper and Pasta Salad, 125
    Savory Jumbo Shells, 214–215
    Shrimp and Olive Pasta, 202
    Spicy Manicotti, 215
    Spinach Parmesan Lasagna, 212
    Tuna and Noodle Casserole, 198
    Turkey Ham Salad, 128
    Vegetable Lasagna I, 210
    Vegetable Lasagna II, 210–211
    Vegetable and Pasta Soup, 103
    Vegetarian Lasagna, 211
Pasta Bites, 88

Pasta Primavera with Zucchini and
    Roasted Red Peppers, 209
Pasta and Vegetable Salad, 124
Pea and Horseradish Sauce, 255
A Peach of a Punch, 62
Peaches and Cream Salad, 134
Peanut Butter Cookies, 286
Pear Cobbler, 288
Pear-Apple Butter, 263
Pears with Raspberry Sauce, 282
Pepper Steak, 168
Pepper Sweet Corn Bread, 159
Perfect Orange Scampi, 205
PIES
    Apple-Cranberry Cobbler, 288
    Bavarian-Style Whipped Strawberry
        Pie, 290
    Graham Cracker Crust, 289
    Oat Bran Pie Crust, 289
    Pear Cobbler, 288
    Pumpkin Pie in a Graham Cracker
        Crust, 290
PILAF
    Fresh Asparagus Rice Pilaf, 231
    Golden Mediterranean Pilaf, 228
    Nutty Couscous Pilaf, 227
    Oriental Oat Pilaf, 228
    Poultry and Rice Pilaf, 179
Pimiento Tuna in a Pepper Cup, 199
Pineapple and Orange Yogurt
    Freeze, 275
Pineapple and Peach Soup, 116
Piney Cheese Balls, 92
PIZZA
    Nacho Pizzas, 268
    Parmesan Pizza Crust, 270
    Southern Pizza Crust, 268–269
    Turkey Sausage Pizza, 267
    Whole Wheat Pizza Crust, 269
Poached Beef Tenderloin, 166
PORK
    Ham with Mustard Garlic Apple-
        cue Sauce, 253
    Orange Wilted-Spinach Salad with
        Pork, 117
    Stuffed Pork Roast with
        Mushrooms, 170
Potato and Leek Soup, 100
Potato and Salmon Salad, 129
POTATOES
    Baked Fluffy Potatoes, 224
    Baked Potato Bread, 138
    Cheesy Scalloped Potatoes, 225
    Cheesy Whipped Potatoes, 224
    Fruity Sweet Potatoes, 226
    Hearty Potato Soup, 100
    Hot Tuna and Potato Bake, 198
    Old-Fashioned Potato Salad, 123
    Potato and Leek Soup, 100
    Potato and Salmon Salad, 129
    Roasted New Potatoes with Herbs,
        225
    Skillet Apple Potato Salad, 124

Spicy Fries, 271
Spinach-Stuffed Baked Potatoes, 223
Stuffed Baked Potatoes, 223
Stuffed Spuds, 222
Sweet Potato Coins, 226
Tuna Potato Casserole, 199
Poultry and Rice Pilaf, 179
PUDDING
Apricot Bread Pudding, 291
Chocolate Mousse Pudding, 291
Pumpkin Pie in a Graham Cracker
Crust, 290
Pumpkin-Apple Bran Muffins, 152
Pumpkin-Apple Bread, 142

Q
Quick and Easy Zesty Fish, 190
Quick Fajitas with Pico de Gallo, 90
Quick French Onion Soup, 95

R
Red Pepper and Pasta Salad, 125
Red Raspberry Mint Vinegar, 256
RICE
Baked Chicken and Rice, 172
Black-Eyed Peas and Wild Rice, 221
Broccoli and Rice Casserole, 219
Brown Rice Broccoli Casserole, 219
Brown Rice with Scallions, 220
Chinese Rice Soup, 105
Creamy Rice Casserole with Chili
Peppers, 220
French Green Bean and Rice
Casserole, 240
Fresh Asparagus Rice Pilaf, 231
Mexican Black Bean and Rice, 221
Orange Curried Rice and
Mushrooms, 218
Orange Wild Rice with Currants
and Apples, 218
Poultry and Rice Pilaf, 179
Vegetable Rice Pie, 248
Ricotta Yogurt Dressing, 260
Roasted New Potatoes with Herbs,
225
Roasted Red Pepper Soup, 94
Roasted Vegetables, 230
Rock Shrimp and Oyster Maque
Choux, 203
Rolled Sugar Cookies, 287
Round Steak in Wine Sauce, 165

S
SALADS
Apple-Orange Cider Salad, 132
Celery Cole Slaw, 121
Chicken Pasta Salad, 127
Chutney Chicken Salad, 127
Couscous Salad, 123
Eggplant Salad, 119
Fluffy Orange Yogurt Salad, 131
Fresh Broccoli and Cauliflower
Salad, 120

Fresh Corn and Black-Eyed Pea
Salad, 122
Fruit and Nut Curried Salad, 133
Gingered Fruit Compote, 134
Green Bean Salad, 120
House Salad with Dream Pepper
Dressing, 257
Layered Turkey and Broccoli Pasta
Salad, 126
Lemon-Dill Crabmeat Salad on
Cucumber, 130
Macaroni Salad, 125
Marinated Mushroom Salad, 119
Molded Cucumber Salad, 122
Old-Fashioned Potato Salad, 123
Orange Pineapple Salad, 135
Orange Wilted-Spinach Salad with
Pork, 117
Orange-Cranberry Salad, 136
Pasta and Vegetable Salad, 124
Peaches and Cream Salad, 134
Potato and Salmon Salad, 129
Red Pepper and Pasta Salad, 125
Satellite Beach Salad, 130
Shrimp-Stuffed Tomato, 129
Skillet Apple Potato Salad, 124
Smoked Turkey Salad, 128
Spinach and Pomegranate Salad, 118
Spinach Salad, 118
Strawberry Gelatin Salad, 136
Steak and Roasted Vegetable Salad,
126–127
Tangy Tomato Aspic, 121
Traditional Holiday Cranberry
Salad, 132
Tropical Fruit Salad, 133
Tuna Salad, 131
Turkey Ham Salad, 128
Very Orange Salad, 135
Salmon Mousse, 194
SANDWICHES
Baked Grilled Cheese Sandwiches,
160
Sloppy Joe Pitas, 272
Santa Rosa Shrimp, 201
Satellite Beach Salad, 130
SAUCES AND DRESSINGS
Apple Bread Dressing, 260
Applesauce, 266
Blue Cheese Dressing, 258
Buttermilk Blue Cheese Dressing,
258
Buttermilk-Style Dressing, 257
Chicken-Apple Dressing, 261
Cinnamon-Raisin Spread, 264
Cottage Cheese Ranch Dressing, 259
Cranberry Chutney, 265
Crock-Pot Applesauce, 265
Cucumber Sauce for Fish, Meats, or
Vegetables, 253
Dijon Sauce, 254
Dijon Vinaigrette, 262
Dried Fruit Chutney, 264

Green Onion Cream Sauce, 251
Ham with Mustard Garlic Apple-
cue Sauce, 253
Herbed Spice Dressing, 259
House Salad with Dream Pepper
Dressing, 257
Lemon Butter, 263
Lemon Herbs, 262
Lemon-Dijon Mustard Sauce, 254
Lemon-Garlic Vinegar, 256
Louisiana Creole Barbecue Sauce,
178
Maple Syrup, 266
Mexican Salsa, 249
Monterey Jack Salsa, 250
Mushroom Dressing, 261
Pea and Horseradish Sauce, 255
Pear-Apple Butter, 263
Pears with Raspberry Sauce, 282
Red Raspberry Mint Vinegar, 256
Ricotta Yogurt Dressing, 260
Shrimp with Oriental Ginger Apple
Barbecue Sauce, 252
Simple Horseradish Sauce, 255
Steak Sauce, 251
Tartar Sauce, 250
Yogurt and Dill Seafood Sauce, 252
Sausage and Spinach Casserole, 169
Sautéed Cream Spinach, 242
Savory Jumbo Shells, 214-215
Savory Zucchini Soup, 99
Scottish Oat Cakes, 154
Scottish Oat-Bran Toast, 154
SEAFOOD
Ale-Poached Sea Bass with
Pimiento Sauce, 190
Angel Pasta with Crab, 207
Baked Flounder with Orange
Sauce, 192
Baked Spicy Shrimp, 201
Broiled Fish Steaks and Herbs, 191
Broiled Pepper Swordfish, 196
Broiled Scallops with Spinach, 204
Cajun Shrimp and Oyster Soup,
112
Catfish with Angel Hair Pasta, 200
Clam Chowder, 114
Cornflake-Breaded Baked Fish, 189
Crab Imperial, 206
Crab Pie Appetizer, 82
Fish Amandine, 189
Fish Bake, 192
Fish Soup, 111
Flounder and Vegetable Bake, 193
Grilled Tuna with Citrus-Sage
Marinade, 200
Hot Tuna and Potato Bake, 198
Italian Crab Cakes, 206
Leek and Mussel Poach, 208
Lemon Shrimp, 202–203
Lemon-Dill Crabmeat Salad on
Cucumber, 130
Lettuce-Baked Lobster Tails, 207

Orange Roughy in Lemon Wine Sauce, 197
Oyster Stew, 113
Perfect Orange Scampi, 205
Pimiento Tuna in a Pepper Cup, 199
Potato and Salmon Salad, 129
Quick and Easy Zesty Fish, 190
Rock Shrimp and Oyster Maque Choux, 203
Salmon Mousse, 194
Santa Rosa Shrimp, 201
Satellite Beach Salad, 130
Seafood Stuffed Eggplant, 205
Shrimp Dip, 81
Shrimp and Mushrooms, 204
Shrimp and Olive Pasta, 202
Shrimp-Stuffed Tomato, 129
Skewered Seafood, 208
Spicy Crab Soup, 111
Spicy Salmon Cakes, 195
Spinach-Stuffed Sole with Lemon-Mustard Sauce, 195
Trout Bake, 194
Trout with Pecan Sauce, 193
Tuna Chowder, 114
Tuna and Noodle Casserole, 198
Tuna Potato Casserole, 199
Tuna Salad, 131
Very Orange Roughy, 197
Wakulla Grilled Grouper, 196
Ybor City Fillets, 191
Seafood Stuffed Eggplant, 205
Sesame Chicken, 173
SHRIMP
Baked Spicy Shrimp, 201
Cajun Shrimp and Oyster Soup, 112
Rock Shrimp and Oyster Maque Choux, 203
Santa Rosa Shrimp, 201
Shrimp and Cheese Spread, 83
Shrimp Dip, 81
Shrimp and Mushrooms, 204
Shrimp and Olive Pasta, 202
Shrimp with Oriental Ginger Apple Barbecue Sauce, 252
Shrimp-Stuffed Tomato, 129
Shrimp and Cheese Spread, 83
Shrimp Dip, 81
Shrimp and Mushrooms, 204
Shrimp and Olive Pasta, 202
Shrimp with Oriental Ginger Apple Barbecue Sauce, 252
Shrimp-Stuffed Tomato, 129
Simple Horseradish Sauce, 255
Skewered Seafood, 208
Skillet Apple Potato Salad, 124
Sloppy Joe Pitas, 272
Smoked Turkey Salad, 128
SOUPS
Beef and Barley Soup, 107
Beef Stew Base, 108
Cajun Shrimp and Oyster Soup, 112
Carrot and Ginger Soup, 96

Cauliflower Soup, 99
Chicken and Vegetable Soup, 105
Chinese Rice Soup, 105
Clam Chowder, 114
Cold Weather Soup, 104
Cream of Broccoli Soup, 97
Cream of Carrot Soup, 97
Cream of Chicken and Wild Rice Soup, 106
Creamy Cucumber Soup, 96
Creamy Squash Soup, 98
Cucumber Avocado Bisque, 95
Fall Harvest Chowder, 101
Fall Harvest Soup, 102
Family Beef Stew, 109
Family Style Chili, 110
Fish Soup, 111
Gingered Parsnip and Chicken Soup, 106
Hearty Fruit Soup, 115
Hearty Potato Soup, 100
Hearty Vegetable Soup, 101
Herbed Tomato Soup, 93
Hot, Hot Gumbo Chicken, 113
Italian Meatball Soup, 110
Lentil and Beef Soup, 109
Mexican Corn Soup, 104
Mushroom Soup, 98
Oyster Stew, 113
Pineapple and Peach Soup, 116
Potato and Leek Soup, 100
Quick French Onion Soup, 95
Roasted Red Pepper Soup, 94
Savory Zucchini Soup, 99
Spicy Crab Soup, 111
Spicy-Tangy Beef Soup, 108
Spinach Florentine Soup, 94
Summer Strawberry and Burgundy Soup, 116
Swiss Cheese Vegetable Bisque, 102
Tofu Soup, 115
Tuna Chowder, 114
Turkey Chowder, 107
Vegetable and Pasta Soup, 103
Vegetable Soup, 103
Southern Chicken Fry, 180
Southern Corn Bread, 158
Southern Corn Bread Stuffing, 159
Southern Mint Juleps, 61
Southern Pizza Crust, 268–269
Spaghetti Squash and Vegetables, 244
Spiced Low-Fat Buttermilk, 71
Spiced Russian Tea, 55
Spicy Apple Cake, 293
Spicy Cherry Tomatoes with Avocado, 245
Spicy Crab Soup, 111
Spicy Fries, 271
Spicy Manicotti, 215
Spicy Salmon Cakes, 195
Spicy Turkey Jambalaya, 185
Spicy-Tangy Beef Soup, 108
SPINACH
Broiled Scallops with Spinach, 204

Orange Wilted-Spinach Salad with Pork, 117
Sausage and Spinach Casserole, 169
Sautéed Cream Spinach, 242
Spinach Casserole, 243
Spinach Florentine Soup, 94
Spinach Parmesan Lasagna, 212
Spinach and Pomegranate Salad, 118
Spinach Salad, 118
Spinach Vegetable Dip, 80
Spinach-Stuffed Baked Potatoes, 223
Spinach-Stuffed Sole with Lemon-Mustard Sauce, 195
Stir-Fry Beef and Spinach with Noodles, 166–167
SQUASH
Apple-Stuffed Squash with Cinnamon, 243
Baked Zucchini and Cheese, 245
Blackberry and Zucchini Bread, 142
Creamy Squash Soup, 99
Pasta Primavera with Zucchini and Roasted Red Peppers, 209
Savory Zucchini Soup, 99
Spaghetti Squash and Vegetables, 244
Stuffed Zucchini Shells, 246
Summer Squash Casserole, 243
Zucchini Bread, 141
Zucchini Casserole, 246
Zucchini Ricotta Casserole, 247
Strawberry Gelatin Salad, 136
Steak and Roasted Vegetable Salad, 126–127
Steak Sauce, 251
Steamed Vegetables, 229
Stir-Fry Beef and Spinach with Noodles, 166–167
Stir-Fry Chicken, 179
Strawberry Grog, 68
Strawberry and Orange Pops, 282
Strawberry Parfait Drink, 69
Streusel Topping, 280
Stuffed Baked Potatoes, 223
Stuffed Dill Mushrooms, 87
Stuffed Apricots, 76
Stuffed Chicken Breasts, 182
Stuffed Eggplant, 238
Stuffed Mushroom Caps, 88
Stuffed Peppers, 241
Stuffed Pork Roast with Mushrooms, 170
Stuffed Spuds, 222
Stuffed Tomatoes, 87
Stuffed Zucchini Shells, 246
STUFFING
Apple Bread Dressing, 260
Mushroom Dressing, 261
Southern Corn Bread Stuffing, 159
Summer Squash Casserole, 243
Summer Strawberry and Burgundy Soup, 116

Swedish Meatballs, 168
Sweet Carrots with Dill or Basil, 236
Sweet Potato Coins, 226
Swiss Cheese Vegetable Bisque, 102
Swiss Steak, 169

T
Tangy Tomato Aspic, 121
Tart and Bubbly Wake-Up Drink, 58
Tartar Sauce, 250
Tea Punch, 64
Texas Bean Dip, 78
Thanksgiving Herbed Turkey, 186–187
Tofu Soup, 115
Tomato Frappe, 70
TOMATOES
    Broiled Tomatoes, 244
    Cherry Tomato Appetizers, 86
    Hearty Tomato Saucy Drink, 70
    Herbed Tomato Soup, 93
    Manicotti with Eggplant-Tomato
        Relish, 216
    Manicotti with Ratatouille Sauce, 217
    Mexican Salsa, 249
    Old-Fashioned Beef, Macaroni, and
        Tomato Casserole, 213
    Shrimp-Stuffed Tomato, 129
    Spicy Cherry Tomatoes with
        Avocado, 245
    Stuffed Tomatoes, 87
    Tangy Tomato Aspic, 121
    Tomato Frappe, 70
Traditional Holiday Cranberry Salad,
    132
Tropical Fruit Salad, 133
Trout Bake, 194
Trout with Pecan Sauce, 193
Tuna Chowder, 114
Tuna and Noodle Casserole, 198
Tuna Potato Casserole, 199
Tuna Salad, 131
TURKEY
    Broccoli Turkey Casserole, 234
    Christmas Night Miniature
        Meatballs, 91
    Cranberry Turkey Steaks, 188
    Family Style Chili, 110
    Greek Turkey Burger, 271
    Ground Turkey Parmigiana, 186
    Herbed Turkey, 185
    Italian Meatball Soup, 110
    Italian Turkey Fest, 188
    Layered Turkey and Broccoli Pasta
        Salad, 126
    Manicotti with Eggplant-Tomato
        Relish, 216
    Mom's Meatloaf, 164
    Sausage and Spinach Casserole, 169
    Sloppy Joe Pitas, 272

Smoked Turkey Salad, 128
Spicy Turkey Jambalaya, 185
Stuffed Peppers, 241
Swedish Meatballs, 168
Thanksgiving Herbed Turkey,
    186–187
Turkey Burgers, 270
Turkey Chowder, 107
Turkey with Cranapple Sauce, 187
Turkey Frittata, 184
Turkey Ham Salad, 128
Turkey Sausage Pizza, 267
Turkey Burgers, 270
Turkey Chowder, 107
Turkey with Cranapple Sauce, 187
Turkey Frittata, 184
Turkey Ham Salad, 128
Turkey Sausage Pizza, 267

U
Unsalted Dill Pickles, 247

V
Veal Marsala, 171
Veal Provencale, 170
Vegetable and Chicken Outdoor
    Bake, 181
Vegetable Lasagna I, 210
Vegetable Lasagna II, 210–211
Vegetable and Pasta Soup, 103
Vegetable Rice Pie, 248
Vegetable Soup, 103
Vegetable Spread, 84
VEGETABLES
    Apple-Stuffed Squash with
        Cinnamon, 243
    Apples and Onions Side Dish, 240
    Asparagus and Basil, 231
    Baked Broccoli, 233
    Baked Italian Onions, 241
    Baked Zucchini and Cheese, 245
    Broccoli with Cream Sauce, 232
    Broccoli and Herbs, 233
    Broccoli and Mushroom Casserole,
        234
    Broccoli Turkey Casserole, 234
    Broiled Tomatoes, 244
    Brussels Sprouts with Chicken, 235
    Cajun Green Beans, 239
    Cauliflower with Broccoli Sauce, 237
    Cheesy Scalloped Cucumbers, 238
    Creamed Vegetables, 229
    Creole Cabbage, 235
    Crumbly Cauliflower, 237
    Flounder and Vegetable Bake, 193
    French Green Bean and Rice
        Casserole, 240
    French Green Beans Amandine, 239
    Fresh Asparagus Rice Pilaf, 231

Golden Carrots, 236
Grilled Asparagus, 232
Hearty Vegetable Soup, 101
Italian Carrot Antipasto, 86
Lemon Artichoke Hearts and
    Mushrooms, 230
Marinated Vegetables, 85
Roasted Vegetables, 230
Sautéed Cream Spinach, 242
Spaghetti Squash and Vegetables,
    244
Spicy Cherry Tomatoes with
    Avocado, 245
Spinach Casserole, 243
Steamed Vegetables, 229
Stuffed Eggplant, 238
Stuffed Peppers, 241
Stuffed Zucchini Shells, 246
Summer Squash Casserole, 243
Sweet Carrots with Dill or Basil,
    236
Unsalted Dill Pickles, 247
Vegetable and Chicken Outdoor
    Bake, 181
Vegetable and Pasta Soup, 103
Vegetable Rice Pie, 248
Vegetable Soup, 103
Zucchini Casserole, 246
Zucchini Ricotta Casserole, 247
see also Individual names of
    vegetables; Salads
Vegetarian Lasagna, 211
Very Orange Roughy, 197
Very Orange Salad, 135

W
Wakulla Grilled Grouper, 196
Warmed Wintry Milk, 71
Whole Wheat Bread, 139
Whole Wheat Carrot Bread, 139
Whole Wheat Pizza Crust, 269
Whole Wheat and Yogurt Biscuits,
    145
Winter Fruit Medley, 280

Y
Ybor City Fillets, 191
Yogurt and Dill Seafood Sauce, 252
Yogurt Drop Biscuits, 144
Yogurt Pudding, 284
Your Own Crispy Crackers, 82

Z
Zesty Chicken Italiano, 182
Zucchini Bread, 141
Zucchini Casserole, 246
Zucchini Cheese Spread, 85
Zucchini Ricotta Casserole, 247